21040

Latin
America
1977

Latin America 1977

Edited by Grace M. Ferrara

Writer: Christopher Hunt

Facts On File

119 West 57th Street, New York, N.Y. 10019

Latin America 1977

Library of Congress Cataloging in Publication Data
Main entry under title:
Latin America. 1972.
    New York, Facts on File, inc.
        v. 24 cm. annual. (A Facts on File publication)
    ISSN 0094-7458

    1. Latin America—Periodicals. I. Facts on File, inc., New York.
F1401.L325   918′.005   73-83047
                    rev   MARC-S

ISBN 0-87196-257-8

9 8 7 6 5 4 3 2 1
PRINTED IN
THE UNITED STATES OF AMERICA

Contents

Foreword

THIS IS THE SIXTH VOLUME of the FACTS ON FILE annual on Latin America. It records the history of Latin America and the Caribbean area during 1977.

The purpose of this series is to give researchers, students, educators, librarians and others a convenient, reliable, unbiased and inexpensive source of information on the many events that take place each year in this important part of the world. The 1977 volume, therefore, records the essential details of such events as the increased violence in Argentina, the renewal of limited relations between Cuba and the U.S. and the dispute over the future of the Panama Canal and the Canal Zone. But it also covers more than just the most important occurrences. It provides facts on economic developments, guerrilla operations, labor action, diplomatic relations, government corruption, political maneuverings, student activism, military affairs and many other events that make up the history of Latin America and the Caribbean area during 1977.

The material of the book consists largely of the Latin American record compiled by FACTS ON FILE in its weekly reports on world events. Such changes as were made in producing this book were largely for the purpose of eliminating needless repetition, supplying necessary amplification or correcting error. Yet some useful repetition was provided deliberately: for example, when two countries are involved in a single event, the report, or at least part of it, is often carried in the chapter for each of the two countries; this means more complete coverage of each country in the place the reader is most likely to look, makes it less likely that these items will be overlooked and reduces some of the need to consult the index and other chapters to locate a specific fact.

As in all FACTS ON FILE works, a conscientious effort was made to record all events without bias and to produce a reliable and useful reference tool.

Regional Developments

U.S. Pressure on Human Rights

During 1977 the U.S.' new Carter Administration applied pressure to end violations of human rights in Latin America as well as in the Soviet Union. This issue appeared to dominate the U.S.' public statements on dealings with Latin America.

U.S. cuts aid to 3 nations. U.S Secretary of State Cyrus R. Vance disclosed Feb. 24 that the Carter Administration planned to reduce foreign aid to Argentina and Uruguay because of concern about the human rights situation in those countries.

The disclosure was made in testimony before the Senate Appropriations Committee's subcommittee on foreign operations. Vance told the panel that relating the human rights issue to foreign assistance would be done on a country-by-country basis but was "a very difficult task." "In each case," he said, "we must balance a political concern for human rights against economic or security goals."

State Department officials gave some details of the planned aid reductions. A request to Congress for $32 million in military credits for Argentina in fiscal 1978 would be reduced to $15 million. A $48-million extension of credits for fiscal 1977 would remain unallocated. A $3-million request for military credits to Uruguay would be eliminated, and economic assistance would be cut to $25,000 from $220,000.

Congress had enacted legislation in 1976 opposing military aid for countries committing "gross violations" of human rights unless there were extraordinary circumstances warranting the aid. The Ford Administration generally had interpreted the restriction as counterproductive and had favored aid programs for continued U.S. influence in such countries.

Argentina, Uruguay reject U.S. aid— Reacting to Vance's testimony, the governments of Argentina and Uruguay announced March 1 that they would refuse U.S. aid linked to observance of human rights.

Argentine Defense Minister Gen. Jose Maria Klix said his government would not use the $15 million in military sales credits that the U.S. would offer for fiscal 1978. This would leave $700,000 in military training grants as Argentina's only assistance from the U.S.

Uruguayan Planning Minister Brig. Jose Cardozo said his government would reject "any type of economic aid from the U.S." Cardozo charged that the linking of U.S. assistance to respect for human rights "implies an inadmissible intrusion in the internal affairs of Uruguay . . . and total misinformation about Uruguayan reality."

The Argentine regime had made similar

3

charges Feb. 28. The foreign minister, Rear Adm. Cesar Guzzetti, issued a statement asserting that "no state, regardless of its ideology or power, can take upon itself the role of an international court of justice and interfere in the internal affairs of other countries." A "qualified navy spokesman" quoted by the Buenos Aires newspaper Clarin Feb. 28 said the U.S. aid reduction was "another example of certain chronic weaknesses in the U.S. which we have had to get used to."

The controlled Argentine press also protested the U.S. move. The Buenos Aires newspaper La Opinion Feb. 25 called the aid reduction a "hostile gesture" that was "politically motivated." Clarin called for "traditional internal solidarity" to combat the U.S. action, and the English-language Buenos Aires Herald called the U.S. move "scarcely cooperative, and irrational."

Venezuelan President Carlos Andres Perez appeared to praise the aid reductions without referring to them specifically. In an interview with the Mexican newspaper El Sol, published Feb. 27, Perez said President Carter's decision to "give primary importance to the observation of human rights is perhaps the best message the President of the U.S. could give Latin America."

U.S. submits rights reports. State Department reports on the general status of human rights for the nations receiving U.S. security assistance were released March 12.

The reports, submitted to Congress in compliance with the 1976 Foreign Military Assistance Act, were made public by the Senate Foreign Relations Committee's U.S. Subcommittee on Foreign Assistance. Congress had asserted its opposition to extending security assistance to governments that engaged in "a consistent pattern of gross violations of internationally recognized human rights," except in extraordinary circumstances.

Details of the U.S. State Department reports and reactions to them:

The report on Brazil drew immediate reaction, first a rejection of further U.S. military aid and then cancellation of Brazil's 25-year-old military aid treaty with the U.S.

The report on Brazil noted that "cases

of arbitrary arrest and detention have occurred" and that "fair hearings by impartial tribunals are not consistently available to political detainees." It pointed out that use of decree-laws had diluted legal safeguards against rights encroachments. Reports of arbitrary arrest and detention and torture of political prisoners also were noted.

On Argentina, the department reported that "the rights of life, liberty and security of persons are violated regularly by terrorists at both ends of the political spectrum." It said the right-wing terrorists were "operating with apparent immunity." (Argentina rejected the State Department report as unfounded, it was reported March 10.)

The long-standing democratic tradition in Uruguay had been "altered substantially," the department found, in the campaign against urban guerrillas in the late 1960s and early 1970s. Now, the report said, the armed forces dominated the government and cases of terrorism, subversion and crimes against the nation were handled by military courts.

Carter stresses human rights at OAS. In his first major address on U.S. relations with Latin America, President Carter April 14 defended his emphasis on human rights in formulating U.S. foreign policy.

Speaking to diplomats at the Washington headquarters of the Organization of American States (OAS), Carter pledged to support nations that respected individual liberties and to seek Senate ratification of the American Convention on Human Rights, which was negotiated by 10 nations in Costa Rica in 1969 but subsequently ratified by only Costa Rica and Colombia.

(The U.S. previously had been cool to the treaty, which contained 25 articles of individual liberties including the "right to life" from the "moment of conception." Carter Administration officials said the "right to life" and some other clauses of the treaty would not apply in the U.S.)

Carter also pledged to seek Senate ratification of a protocol attached to the 1967 Treaty of Tlatelolco, which banned atomic weapons in Latin America. (Carter signed the treaty May 26.)

If the U.S. Senate ratified the treaty, the U.S. would have to keep nuclear weapons out of its territories in the area, including Puerto Rico, the Virgin Islands, the Panama Canal Zone and the Guantanamo naval base in Cuba.

(The Pentagon had opposed signing of the protocol for fear it would be interpreted as outlawing the local transit of nuclear weapons, e.g. on a Navy ship that circled the continent or used Caribbean sea lanes, the Wall Street Journal reported April 15. The Carter Administration apparently had decided the protocol did not affect transit rights.)

Carter's promise to seek ratification of the two agreements brought the only spontaneous applause from his audience. Although the President received the customary standing ovation at the end of his address, his reception at the OAS was not overly enthusiastic, according to press reports. Five Latin American nations had rejected future U.S. military aid to protest Carter's emphasis on human rights, and other nations in the region were reported to be angry with the President over the rights issue.

Apart from his pledge on the two treaties and his stressing of human rights, Carter broke no new ground in U.S.-Latin American relations. Instead, he outlined some broad U.S. policy concerns in the region. "A single U.S. policy for Latin America and the Caribbean makes little sense," Carter told the assembled diplomats. "What we need is a wider and more flexible approach, worked out in consultation with you."

The President reaffirmed his commitment to negotiate a new Panama Canal treaty "in as timely a fashion as possible." The new pact should take account of "Panama's legitimate needs as a sovereign nation and our interests—and yours—in the efficient operation of a neutral canal," Carter told the diplomats.

In a brief reference to Cuba, the President said he was trying to determine whether relations with the government of Fidel Castro could be improved "on a measured and reciprocal basis." Most OAS member states had resumed full diplomatic relations with Havana.

Turning to economic issues, Carter said most Latin American economic problems "are also global in character and cannot be dealt with solely in regional terms." He pledged that his Administration would:

■ Take a "positive and open attitude toward the negotiation of agreements to stabilize commodity prices, including the establishment of a common funding arrangement for financing buffer stocks where they are a part of individual, negotiated agreements."

■ Actively pursue "multilateral trade negotiations with [Latin American] nations in Geneva," with an emphasis on minimizing trade restrictions, alleviating "the specific trade problems of developing countries" and providing "special and more favorable treatment where feasible and appropriate."

■ Improve programs to train Latin Americans in uses of U.S. science and technology.

■ Try to persuade Congress to "meet in full" the large U.S. financial pledges to "the Inter-American Development Bank and the other multilateral lending institutions which loan a high proportion of their capital to the relatively advanced developing countries of Latin America."

■ Direct "more of our bilateral economic assistance to poorer countries."

Latin American governments generally withheld comment on Carter's address, waiting to see what action followed the President's pledges, the Washington Post reported April 17. "On the whole, I'd say the reaction was positive," said an Argentine official quoted by the Post. However, the official voiced skepticism about Carter's promise to consult Latin American diplomats on major policy decisions. "[The Americans have] been saying they were going to consult us ever since Kennedy and the Alliance for Progress," he complained. "All through Kennedy, Johnson, Nixon and Ford—and they've never consulted us on anything."

Rights issue dominates OAS parley. The human rights issue dominated the seventh General Assembly of the Organization of American States (OAS), held June 14-22 on the Caribbean island of Grenada.

The rights issue deeply divided the OAS, many of whose members felt that human rights were internal matters that should not be allowed to overshadow the issues of trade and economic development, which normally dominated OAS meetings.

Following a long and acrimonious debate, the assembly approved three resolutions related to the observance of human rights. The most important of these was a strongly worded document that said, among other things, "there are no circumstances which justify torture, summary executions or prolonged detention without trial contrary to law."

The resolution, sponsored by the U.S., Venezuela, Costa Rica and many Caribbean nations, was passed June 22 by a vote of 14–0, with eight abstentions and three delegations absent. The abstaining countries were Argentina, Brazil, Colombia, Chile, El Salvador, Guatemala, Paraguay and Uruguay; the absent ones were Bolivia, Honduras and Nicaragua.

The resolution also:

■ Commended the OAS Inter-American Human Rights Commission "for its efforts to promote human rights" and provided for an increase in the commission's budget.

■ Urged all OAS member states to cooperate fully with the commission and not take reprisals against individual citizens who aided the panel.

■ Directed the commision to "organize, in cooperation with the member states, a program of consultation with governments and appropriate institutions and responsible organizations on the observance of rights in their countries."

■ Committed OAS nations to "the achievement of economic and social justice" without harm to "human dignity and freedom."

The other two resolutions apparently were designed to mollify countries that opposed the emphasis given to human rights at the assembly. The first, proposed by the Dominican Republic and approved June 21, condemned political terrorism and called for a study of acts of terrorism and extortion. The second, introduced by Colombia and passed June 22, called on advanced countries to increase economic cooperation with developing nations to help alleviate social tensions.

The human rights issue was raised at the first session of the assembly, immediately after the welcoming address by Grenada's prime minister, Sir Eric Gairy. As the host of the 1976 OAS assembly, it was Chile's privilege to respond to Gairy in the name of the other OAS members. However, a majority of OAS states decided to accord the privilege to Venezuela, which, in sharp contrast to Chile, was acknowledged to have a good record on human rights.

Venezuelan Foreign Minister Ramon

Escovar Salom delivered an improvised speech, saying "the international order can only be built on the principles of legality, which should not in any way compromise the rights of the human person." "It is not enough to support those principles here or to develop them in theory—they must be applied through practical means," Escovar said.

Escovar was followed by U.S. Secretary of State Cyrus Vance, who made the strongest appeal for human rights yet made by a member of the Carter Administration. Vance clearly tied U.S. economic aid to the observance of human rights, asserting that "gross violations of human rights" were a mockery of "cooperation in economic development."

Addressing the argument of military dictatorships that repression was necessary to combat left-wing subversion, Vance said: "The surest way to defeat terrorism is to promote justice in our societies—legal, social and economic justice. If terrorism and violence in the name of dissent cannot be condoned, neither can violence that is officially sanctioned."

Vance proposed an increase in the budget of the Inter-American Human Rights Commission and urged all OAS member states to grant the commission free access to their territories to investigate alleged rights violations. For the first time, the U.S. offered such access to the commission.

Vance emphasized one other issue at the assembly—reform of the OAS structure. First he called for a reduction of the U.S.' 66% share of the OAS budget, saying the percentage was unfair because Washington did not dominate the organization. Then he called for the merger of three OAS bodies (the Permanent Council, the Economic and Social Council and the Council for Education, Science and Culture), proposed that the OAS Secretariat be empowered to decide routine matters and suggested that "informal consultations . . . replace much of the standing bureaucracy."

Vance was in Grenada for 48 hours, during which he conferred privately with the foreign ministers of most OAS states, reportedly concentrating on the human rights issue. Without Vance's presence, newspapers reported, many of the foreign ministers would not have attended the assembly and endured the shortage of hotel rooms and other facilities on the tiny poverty-stricken island.

Representatives of military dictatorships denounced the emphasis on human rights in addresses to the assembly June 14 and 15. Chile's Foreign Minister, Vice Adm. Patricio Carvajal, asserted June 14 that the "real cause of supposed repression of human rights is not poverty or economic hardship but subversion and terrorism sponsored by the Soviet Union."

The Argentine foreign minister, Vice Adm. Oscar Montes, agreed with Carvajal June 14 and suggested that acts of terrorism were equivalent to abuse of human rights by governments. Brazil's foreign minister, Antonio Azeredo da Silveira, charged June 15 that the OAS was reviewing the human rights issue in a "strident, politicized and inquisitorial" manner.

These military regimes and the military-civilian dictatorship of Uruguay charged that the Inter-American Human Rights Commission "persists in attributing all violence to governments," disregarding the "dramatic aggression which our countries face," it was reported June 15. Commission chairman Andres Aguilar June 17 angrily denied that the commission was acting from political motivation. "The problem," he said, "lies in the fact that there is a constant violation of human rights on this continent."

The commission June 17 submitted to the assembly a report detailing continued rights violations in the Americas, accompanied by individual reports on rights abuse in Chile and Cuba. The assembly later rejected the report on Cuba on grounds that Cuba was not a member of the OAS.

Among other developments at the assembly:

—The U.S. and Panama each reported June 15 that substantial progress had been made in their negotiations for a new Panama Canal treaty.

—The assembly declined to consider the issue of Belize, the British colony over which Guatemala claimed sovereignty. Panama, Barbados, Grenada, Jamaica and Trinidad and Tobago issued a statement June 16 supporting independence for Belize. The Guatemalan government June 18 said it was prepared to go to war if Great Britain unilaterally made Belize independent.

—The assembly also failed to act on the issue of the Caribbean micro-states, such as Grenada, which had entered or were preparing to enter the OAS and might eventually forge a majority bloc, it was reported June 21. The U.S. and other nations supported creation of some form associate membership that would give the tiny countries the right to speak before the OAS but not to vote. Among prospective members of the organization were Dominica, St. Lucia and other Caribbean islands that were preparing for independence.

—Surinam (formerly Dutch Guiana) officially became the 25th member state of the OAS June 14.

—Grenadan security forces June 19 dispersed some 1,000 members of the Grenadan opposition who took advantage of the OAS delegates' presence to demonstrate in St. George's, the capital, against alleged repression by Gairy's government. Gairy kept order in Grenada with a 180-man force described in the foreign press as thugs and known in Grenada as "the Mongoose Gang."

U.S. seeks to cut OAS contribution—The U.S. touched off an acrimonious debate in the Organization of American States May 13 when its ambassador, Gale McGee, announced that President Carter wanted to cut U.S. financial contribution to the organization by 25%.

The U.S. currently contributed about two-thirds of the OAS's $60-million annual budget. Carter wanted to reduce this by about $10 million to 49%. McGee said the cut would help dispel the false impression that the U.S. dominated the inter-American organization.

The Panamanian and Peruvian delegates responded that the U.S. did dominate the OAS, not through its budget contribution but through its general economic power. The Panamanian representative, Nander Pitty Velazquez, warned that the budget cut would not be the last instance of U.S. pressure on the OAS.

Replying to Pitty, the U.S. delegation noted that Panama was behind in paying its share of the OAS budget. Pitty asserted that Panama "does not have the same capacity to pay as the U.S., which has been exploiting our principal resource, the Panama Canal."

World Bank to lend $349 million to human rights violators. U.S. Sen. James Abourezk (D, S.D.) told the U.S. Senate that the World Bank intended to lend $1.142 billion to nine Latin American nations in fiscal 1979. Three of these nations, scheduled to receive $349 million, had their military aid cut by the U.S. for human rights violations. Abourezk said that, according to a study made by the Center for International Policy, $110 million will go to Chile, one of the world's most "brutal dictatorships."

Abourezk went on to say:

'"Certainly the World Bank funds many praiseworthy projects including water supply and sewerage, agricultural development and other health and education projects. But unfortunately the full picture of World Bank activities is more complex, as the Center for International Policy study indicates. According to the preliminary 1979 World Bank loan list, included as the appendix to the study, the Bank intends to increase loans to four newly repressive governments twice as fast as to all others. These Governments—Chile, Uruguay, Argentina, and the Philippines—have all received major new loans since the onset of torture and repression and are tentatively scheduled to get $664 million in 1979, according to the World Bank document.

"The House Appropriations Committee has already said it will require submission of a list of fiscal year 1979 World Bank loans as a regular part of the administration's presentation. Although I am aware the World Bank is displeased at the disclosure of its confidential loan list, the real fault lies in that institution's excessive secretiveness."

A research study by the Center for International Policy included the following figures on World Bank loans to allegedly repressive Latin American countries:

Country	Amount (millions)	Standby projects
Argentina	$200	100
Brazil	640	310
Chile	110	
El Salvador	35	15
Guatemala	40	45
Haiti	23	
Nicaragua	22	25
Paraguay	33	25
Uruguay	39	

The study said that "World Bank loans to countries that have newly become repressive during the 1970's will rise more than twice as fast as to all other countries....

"Loans to the newly repressive countries—Argentina, Chile, the Philippines, and Uruguay, each of which have experienced military takeovers or martial law

since the early 1970's—will rise from an average total of $90 million a year in FY 1971–1973, when the countries were still democratic, to $664 million in the World Bank fiscal year 1979 ... (July 1, 1978–June 30, 1979). This sevenfold increase contrasts with an increase of three times in World Bank lending to all other countries over the same period."

Details of the World Bank's provisional FY 1979 program follow:

Chile will get $110 million, up from zero in the early 1970's. Chile received no World Bank loan commitments during the three years of the democratically elected government of the late President Salvador Allende because the international lending organization disapproved of his economic policies.[1]

Argentina will get $200 million (with another $100 million in possible standby projects). Under military rule since March 1976, the South American country got no World Bank loans during the previous five years (1972–1976) of lax military rule and democratically elected civilian government.

Uruguay will get $39 million, up from $11 million in the early 1970's (FY 1971–1973). Uruguay's congress was abolished in 1973 and repression intensified in November 1975. As in Chile and Argentina, the military has instituted World Bank-approved economic policies, and in FY 1976 the bank lent $52 million. ...

According to the study:

The following major World Bank recipients entered the 1970's with repressive governments already in place. They were also already applying World Bank-approved economic policies: ...

Brazil will get $640 million, up from $244 million in FY 1971–1973. The increase to Brazil will be roughly in line with (actually 14 per cent slower than) the increase to the rest of the world, although the bank lists another $310 million in possible standby operations for FY 1979. The World Bank frowned on the policies of the elected Goulart government in the early 1960's. Following the 1964 military coup, World Bank lending rose from zero to an average $73 million a year during the rest of the decade to reach $498 million in FY 1976. ...

The study continued:

The working paper gives these further details on loans to repressive regimes: ...

The Dominican Republic will get no loans in FY 1979 and received none in FY 1976. It received an average $7 million a year in FY 1971–1973.

El Salvador will get $35 million ($15 more

---

[1] The major West European governments and private banks continued aids and credits to Chile during the Allende period. Only the United States, the World Bank and the Inter-American Development Bank cut off loans to Chile. World Bank spokesmen call the pattern coincidental.

possible in standby), up from $14 million in FY 1971–1973 and roughly in line with the worldwide increase.

Guatemala will get $40 million in FY 1979, up from $13 million in FY 1971–1973, in line with the overall worldwide increase.

Haiti will get $23 million, up from $4 million average in FY 1971–1973, increasing twice as fast as the overall.

Nicaragua will get $22 million, up slightly from a $21 million average in FY 1971–1973 (while overall World Bank loans tripled).

Paraguay will get $33 million, a major jump from the $2 mililon a year average FY 1971–1973. ...

According to the study:

Officials of the World Bank claim that loans are made on the basis of a nation's objective "creditworthiness." In practice, this means that the bank has a marked preference for governments willing to implement tough austerity programs, to hold down labor unrest and to throw their countries wide open to foreign investments.

Ironically, in the name of stability and economic development, the World Bank has sacrificed human rights—the end purpose of economic development.

APPENDIX

World Bank FY 79 lending operations monthly report as of 3/31/77. (attached).

ABBREVIATIONS

EMENA—Europe, Middle East, North Africa.

E.A.C.—East African Community.

DFC—Development Finance Company.

FY—Fiscal year.

LAC—Latin American & Caribbean.

E.A. & P.—East Asia & Pacific.

IBRD—International Bank for Reconstruction and Development.

IDA—International Development Association.

U.S. contributions to international banks

—Congress Sept. 21 passed a bill authorizing $5.1 billion in new U.S. contributions to the World Bank and five other international lending institutions.

As the bill worked its way through Congress, President Carter and the House of Representatives had wrestled over a human rights provision. The House, when it first passed the bill, had included language directing U.S. delegates to the international banks to vote against loans to countries that consistently violated the human rights of their citizens.

Carter opposed the provision. His stand drew sharp criticism from a number of members of Congress, who charged that it was completely inconsistent with Carter's earlier professions of his commitment to the cause of human rights.

Carter responded that the U.S. could do more for human rights if its delegates to international banks were not bound by a strict rule: the freedom to vote either for or against a loan would give the U.S. a measure of leverage on other countries, which it would not have if its vote were foreordained.

The Senate went along with Carter's view, rejecting an amendment to incorporate a human rights curb similar to that in the House version of the bill. When the bill emerged from the House-Senate conference, it contained a relatively flexible provision dealing with rights. U.S. delegates to international banks were instructed to oppose loans to countries that consistently violated the rights of their citizens, but the President was authorized to waive those instructions if he determined that human rights "would be more effectively served by actions other than voting against" loans.

The House refused to accept the conference committee language. By a 230–153 vote, the House Sept. 16 voted down the conference committee version. The House then amended the conference report to require U.S. opposition to any loan to a country that violated human rights "unless such assistance is directed specifically to programs" to aid the poor.

The Senate Sept. 21 went along the House, clearing the bill with the new language by voice vote. As finally passed, the bill gave the Administration less flexibility than the President had sought.

Todman's Latin tour. Terrance Todman, U.S. assistant secretary of state for inter-American affairs, visited four South American countries May 8–17 in what was described in the press as a lightning "get-acquainted" tour.

Todman visited Colombia May 8–10, Venezuela May 10–12, Brazil May 12–14 and Bolivia May 14–17. An additional stop in Argentina, scheduled for May 11, was shelved when a Venezuelan commercial airline canceled the flight Todman was to have taken.

Todman was greeted warmly by Colombian President Alfonso Lopez Michelsen and Venezuelan President Carlos Andres Perez. However, he was shunned by Brazilian President Ernesto Geisel, at least partly because of comments he had made

The World Bank's Latin American & Caribbean Fiscal 1979 Regional Lending Program
(In millions of dollars)

Country and project	IBRD	IDA	Scheduled for approval	Probability in fiscal year/month
C. A. R.: DFC I—CABEI	40.0		January (NS)	1/1
Chile:				
Sites and Services I	20.0		October (NS)	1/1
Highway rehabilitation	30.0		January (NS)[2]	1/1
Power VII	60.0		NS	1/—
Total	110.0			
Costa Rica:				
Power VI	30.0		October (NS)	2/1
Sites and services	10.0		February (NS)	1/1
Total	40.0			
Ecuador:				
Rural electrification	25.0		August (NS)	2/1
Project preparation III	8.0		December (NS)	1/1
Ports III (Manta)[3]	10.0		May (NS)	1/1
Rural development II (from Fiscal Year 1978)[3]	20.0		NS[2]	3/1
Education III[3]	15.0		NS[2]	1/—
Total	78.0			
El Salvador:				
El Salvador: Power VIII	35.0		October (NS)	1/1
Guatemala:				
Sites and services	15.0		October (NS)	1/1
Agriculture credit[3]	25.0		February (NS)	2/1
Total	40.0			
Haiti:				
Education II[3]		8.0	April (NS)	2/1
Power II[3]		15.0	Jun (NS)	1/1
Total		23.0		
Honduras:				
Rural development[3]	25.0		May (NS)	2/1
Tourism[3]	18.0	10.0	May (NS)[2]	1/1
Total	43.0	10.0		
Mexico:				
Export oriented industry	75.0		January (NS)	2/1
Power XII	100.0		April (NS)	1/1
Livestock credit VI[3]	110.0		May (NS)	3/2
DFC III—Fonei[3]	75.0		May (NS)	1/1
Tropical agricultural development	40.0		May (June)	2/2
Vocational Training (from fiscal year 1978)	30.0		NS (June)	2/—
Total	430.0			
Nicaragua:				
Agriculture credit II[3]	10.0		December (June)	3/1
DFC[3]	12.0		December (NS)	3/1
Total	22.0			
Panama: Road maintenance[3]	8.0		April (NS)	2/2
Peru:				
Airports	20.0		September (NS)	2/1
Roads VII (maintenance)	30.0		October (NS)	1/1
Mining II	30.0		December (NS)	1/1
DFC II	40.0		January (NS)	1/1
Total	120.0			
Grand total	966.0	33.0		
Country programs department II:				
Argentina:				
Ports (from fiscal year 1976)	40.0		July (NS)[2]	2/1
Railways II	100.0		September (NS)[2]	2/—
Agricultural credit[3]	60.0		NS (November)	2/—
Total	200.0			
Bolivia:				
Urban development[3]	15.0		December (NS)	2/2
Agricultural credit II	20.0		June (NS)	2/1
Mining exploration fund[3]	5.0		June (Apr)	1/1
Agroindustry I	20.0		NS	1/—
Total	60.0			

The World Bank's Latin American & Caribbean Fiscal 1979 Regional Lending Program (cont'd.)

[In millions of dollars]

Country and project	IBRD	IDA	Scheduled for approval	Probability in fiscal year/month
Brazil:				
Steel (Mendes Junior)	100.0		October (February)[2]	1/1
Education IV	25.0		December (NS)	1/1
Water supply and sewer—N.E.	50.0		December (NS)[2]	2/1
DFC—Small enterprises I	30.0		December (NS)	2/1
Agricultural credit I—N.E.	100.0		January (NS)[2]	1/1
Lower Sao Francisco II	35.0		January (NS)	3/2
Rural development V—Pernambuco.	40.0		March (NS)	1/1
Minas Gerais Development II.	40.0		May (NS)	1/1
Railways V	100.0		June (NS)	1/1
Land settlement II—Matogrosso.	35.0		June (May)	1/1
Secondary and feeder roads II.	85.0		NS[2]	1/—
Total	640.0			
Colombia:				
Hydropower—San Carlos[3]	100.0		October (December)[3]	4,2
DFC VII	65.0		November (NS)	1/1
Agriculture extension	15.0		November (NS)	1/1
Tourism[3]	25.0		January (October)	1/1
Nickel Cerro Matoso[3]	30.0		April (November)[2]	3/1
Mesitas Hydro[3]	70.0		NS	1/—
Total	305.0			
Grenada: Tourism I		3.0	December (NS)	2/1
Guyana: Agriculture forestry[3]	14.0		February (April)[2]	2/1
Jamaica:				
Small scale fnt. development (OFC).	7.0		NS[2]	2/—
Urban development Kingston II.	10.0		NS[2]	2/—
Total	17.0			
Paraguay:				
Rural water supply[4]	6.0		December (NS)	1/1
Livestock V	20.0		April (NS)	2/1
Domestic airports[3]	7.0		May (NS)[2]	1/1
Total	33.0			

Country and project	IBRD	IDA	Scheduled for approval	Probability in fiscal year/month
Uruguay:				
Livestock VI	27.0		April (NS)	2/1
Vocational training and technology.[3]	12.0		May (NS)	2/1
Total	39.0			
Grand total	1,308.0	3.0		
Total regional lending program.	(61)2,274.0	(3) 36.0		
LAC—Fiscal year 1979 standby projects:				
Ecuador:				
DFC IV	30.0		March (NS)	2/1
Highways VI	20.0		May (NS)	1/1
Agriculture marketing and storage.	10.0		May (NS)	1/1
Guayaquil urban development I.	20.0		May (NS)[2]	1/1
El Salvador: Education IV	15.0		June (NS)	1/1
Guatemala:				
Education III	20.0		June (NS)	1/1
Port	25.0		June (NS)[2]	1/1
Mexico:				
Irrigation X	90.0		April (NS)	1/1
Rural development IV	100.0		May (NS)	1/1
W/S medium cities IV	70.0		May (NS)[2]	1/1
Airports II.	25.0		June (NS)	1/1
Nicaragua:				
Feeder roads.	10.0		April (NS)[2]	1/1
Power X.	15.0		June (NS)	1/1
Panama: Water supply ii and sewerage.	25.0		November (NS)[2]	3/1
Peru:				
Sites and services II.	30.0		April (NS)	1/1
Education II.	30.0		April (NS)	1/1
Argentina: Industrial credit II.	100.0		June (NS)	2/1
Bolivia: Highway maintenance.	15.0		February (NS)	2/1
Brazil:				
Salto de Divisa—Itapabi.	110.0		November (NS)[2]	1/1
Urban development.	75.0		June (NS)	1/1
DFC BNDE II.	125.0		June (NS)	1/1
Caribbean: Caribbean development bank II.	35.0		August (NS)	3/1
Paraguay: Highways VI.	25.0		June (NS)	2/1
Total standby projects.	(23) 1020.0			
Total fiscal year 1979 operations program.	(84) 3294.0	(3) 36.0		

about Brazil at a press conference in Caracas May 11.

The U.S. envoy told reporters that the Carter Administration "is not prepared to accept the policy of the governments of Richard Nixon and Gerald Ford, according to which Brazil is the leading country of Latin America, and it shows the way to the other nations of the continent." The comment apparently pleased Venezuelan leaders, who were wary of Brazil's economic and military power, but it irked the Brazilian Foreign Ministry, which replied drily that "each country has its weight in the community of nations, and Brazil is no exception. The U.S. is doubtless a leader not only in America but in the West. Perhaps that makes it easier for the U.S. to judge the importance of other nations."

Because of this exchange and recent U.S.-Brazilian conflicts over human rights and nuclear power plants, Todman's reception in Brasilia was chilly. The Brazilian government even hinted that Todman was lucky to get to see Foreign Minister Antonio Azeredo da Silveira, according to the Washington Post May 15. However, the U.S. envoy made a number of conciliatory statements during his visit and was praised by Brazilian officials after his departure.

Todman told reporters in Brasilia May 13 that Brazil's plan to purchase atomic energy facilities from West Germany, which the U.S. had opposed strongly, was an accomplished fact. "The U.S. considers Brazil and Germany to be sovereign nations that can sign any agreements they see fit," the U.S. envoy said.

Todman added that while the Carter Administration would give preferential treatment to foreign countries that respected human rights, the State Department gave Brazil higher marks than many other nations on this issue. Despite recent U.S.-Brazilian tensions, Todman said, Washington would maintain in principle the Ford Administration's "memorandum of understanding" giving Brazil special "consultant status" with the U.S.

Following Todman's departure for Bolivia, legislators of Brazil's ruling Arena party termed his visit a "complete success." Jose de Magalhaes Pinto, president of the Brazilian Senate, said that because of Todman's visit, Brazil and the U.S. henceforth would solve their problems "at proper levels and in due course, since contacts at the level of undersecretaries will be followed by contacts between ministers and later between presidents."

The human rights issue surfaced again in Bolivia, where representatives of U.S. nationals May 15 gave Todman a detailed report on alleged violations of civil liberties by the government of Gen. Hugo Banzer Suarez. The report charged that the government had arrested 120–150 persons for political reasons, denying them due process; had closed down all labor unions; had deported 58 journalists "for political and labor-union motives," and had taken over a number of radio stations, including one belonging to the Roman Catholic Church.

(The Bolivian government May 14 repeated its customary contention that charges of human rights abuse by the Banzer regime were invented by "an international press apparatus managed by elements of the extreme left." The same day, representatives of the Catholic, Lutheran and Methodist churches in Bolivia announced the creation of a Permanent Assembly on Human Rights to be headed by Luis Adolfo Siles Salinas, a former Bolivian president.)

Todman met with Banzer May 16. Their discussions were kept secret, but newspapers reported that the two leaders had conferred on Bolivia's search for an outlet to the Pacific Ocean and on Bolivia's imprisonment of 33 U.S. nationals on drug-related charges, among other topics.

U.S. Leaders Visit Region

Mrs. Rosalynn Carter and other U.S. representatives toured Latin America on official visits during 1977 to demonstrate the Carter Administration's desire to promote good relations with the area. The human rights issue came up repeatedly during these trips as the travelers discussed U.S. concerns with their Latin hosts.

Mrs. Carter on tour. Rosalynn Carter, wife of U.S. President Jimmy Carter, visited seven countries in the Caribbean and Latin America May 30–June 12 on a tour that combined goodwill gestures with substantive political and econome discussion.

Mrs. Carter visited Jamaica May 30–31, Costa Rica May 31–June 1, Ecuador June 1–3, Peru June 3–6, Brazil June 6–9, Colombia June 9–10 and Venezuela June 10–12. She was accompanied by Grace Vance, wife of U.S. Secretary of State Cyrus Vance, and by two of the Carter Administration's experts on Latin America—Terence Todman, assistant secretary of state for inter-American affairs, and Robert Pastor, senior staff member for inter-American affairs on the National Security Council.

Todman, Pastor and other U.S. officials had briefed Mrs. Carter extensively before the trip, and she had studied Spanish for several months. The Latin leaders who met Mrs. Carter reportedly were impressed with her preparation and convinced that she had full authority to speak—if not negotiate—for her husband.

Throughout the tour Mrs. Carter emphasized her husband's desire for closer ties to Latin American nations and his commitment to promoting the observance of human rights. Analysts said the President's support for democratic governments was evident in the selection of his wife's itinerary. Of the seven countries she visited, four—Jamaica, Costa Rica, Colombia and Venezuela—were democracies.

Before departing for Jamaica May 30, Mrs. Carter told reporters that she hoped to establish "personal" relationships with the leaders of her host countries. The President, seeing her off in Brunswick, Ga., said he was committed to treating Latin American countries "as individuals." "One of the problems of the past has been that we've looked on South America, Central America, the Caribbean, as parts of a homogeneous group of nations," the President declared. But in reality, he said, each country had "special individual problems and special opportunities in relation to us."

Among highlights of Mrs. Carter's tour:

Jamaica—Mrs. Carter was greeted in Kingston May 30 by Jamaican Prime Minister Michael Manley, with whom she conferred for more than seven hours during the next day and a half. Their discussions apparently centered on Jamaica's economic problems and on U.S. relations with Cuba, whose government was on very friendly terms with Manley's.

Mrs. Carter said May 31 that she had told Manley the U.S. was "making some gestures and exploring to see if Cuba wanted normalization with the U.S., but that we had some very difficult problems to face with Cuba before we do reach any kind of normalization."

Mrs. Carter revealed later that she and Manley had discussed ways in which the U.S. might help Jamaica obtain loans from banks and international lending agencies. Jamaica was in a state of economic crisis, having suffered a $350-million trade deficit in 1976 because of declines in tourism and the international price of bauxite.

Manley was eager to improve Jamaica's relations with the U.S. following several years of strained relations with former Secretary of State Henry Kissinger, who was suspicious of Manley's friendship with Cuban President Fidel Castro. Manley told Mrs. Carter he would sign the 1969 American Convention on Human Rights, which President Carter was promoting.

Costa Rica—Mrs. Carter was cheered at the San Jose airport May 31 when she briefly addressed the welcoming crowd in Spanish. She conferred later with President Daniel Oduber and Foreign Minister Gonzalo Facio, apparently concentrating on trade issues.

Mrs. Carter said the next day that while she understood Costa Rica's desire to increase its beef exports to the U.S., she had told Oduber that "Jimmy could not promise him anything that we could not deliver." She said Robert Strauss, the U.S. special trade negotiator, was reviewing the quota system set by the U.S. Congress on beef imports.

Facio said June 1, after Mrs. Carter's departure, that it had been "an extraordinary visit . . . she is a great lady, studious, capable and very modest. She has absolutely no arrogance." Oduber said June 5 that Mrs. Carter's visit had been "of great value for Costa Rica because now it will be easier to overcome problems such as those we have sometimes encountered with officials in Washington."

Oduber said Costa Rica "has been chosen by the Carter Administration as representative of Latin America in the defense of human rights." Costa Rican officials told Mrs. Carter they would bring up the human rights issue at the June meeting of the Organization of American States (OAS) in Grenada.

Ecuador—Quito was the only city on Mrs. Carter's tour where her visit was protested. An estimated 150–200 students demonstrated outside the Legislative Palace June 2, shouting "Rosalynn Carter, go home!" and throwing stones, bricks and at least two gasoline bombs at policemen and reporters. Mrs. Carter, who was inside the building conferring with members of Ecuador's military junta, apparently did not hear the disturbance. By the time she emerged from the palace the protesters had been dispersed or arrested.

Ecuador's leaders told Mrs. Carter of their concern over the military buildup in neighboring Peru and of their objections to President Carter's February veto of a proposed Israeli sale of Kfir fighter planes to Ecuador. (The U.S. could veto the sale because the planes had American-made engines.) Mrs. Carter replied that the veto was not directed against Ecuador but was part of her husband's "global policy" to reduce armaments.

Mrs. Carter also said that her husband was asking Congress to revoke 1974 legislation that denied preferential trade treatment to Ecuador because it belonged to the Organization of Petroleum Exporting Countries (OPEC).

(In Washington June 3, President Carter praised the Ecuadorean junta's program to return power to elected civilian officials.)

Peru—Mrs. Carter returned to the disarmament theme on her arrival in Lima June 3. She said there was a "need to control the growth of armaments throughout the world," and she reminded Peruvian leaders that they had not implemented an arms limitation agreement that Peru had signed with seven other Latin American countries in 1974.

Mrs. Carter conferred for several hours June 3 with President Francisco Morales Bermudez and his foreign minister, Jose de la Puente Radbill. Morales told her he would sign the American Convention on Human Rights, and de la Puente told her Peru was interested in signing an arms

control agreement with the other four members of the Andean Group.

Morales said June 4 that his talks with Mrs. Carter had been characterized by "great understanding," and that the Peruvian and American people were working "hand in hand" on the human rights issue. De la Puente praised Mrs. Carter June 5, saying "she has won us all over with her charm, her sweetness, her simplicity and the way she has treated us."

Reporters accompanying Mrs. Carter said she hit her stride in Peru, conducting her talks with Morales with little help from her aides and handling her press conferences confidently. After being tense and unsure of herself on the first days of her tour, Mrs. Carter relaxed in Lima, and her Peruvian hosts responded warmly, according to the New York Times June 6.

Brazil—The human rights issue dominated Mrs. Carter's visit to Brazil, which was highlighted by a short meeting she held with two American missionaries who claimed to have been "treated like animals" in a Brazilian jail.

The Brazilian government, which was angry at the U.S. for pushing the human rights issue and opposing Brazilian plans to build a nuclear power industry, gave Mrs. Carter a low-key welcome in Brasilia June 6. Foreign Minister Antonio Azeredo da Silveira said only that the government felt "pleasure and satisfaction" in receiving Mrs. Carter. Mrs. Carter extended her husband's greetings to the government and cited his "commitment to human rights, [his] recognition of the individuality and . . . the sovereignty of each of the countries of the hemisphere and [his] desire to press forward on the great economic issues which concern the developed and developing world."

Mrs. Carter met for more than an hour June 7 with President Ernesto Geisel. She said at a news conference later that she had stressed the U.S.' "deep, deep commitment to human rights" and that she and Geisel had discussed in general terms the "very hard question" of stopping the spread of nuclear weapons. Press reports said later that Geisel had refused Mrs. Carter's request that he sign the American Convention on Human Rights.

Mrs. Carter flew to Recife June 8 to

visit an old friend. There, in a gesture to dramatize U.S. concern for human rights, she met briefly with two American missionaries who said they had been stripped, beaten and humiliated by Brazilian police who arrested them May 15 and held them without charges for three days. The missionaries, Rev. Lawrence Rosebaugh and Thomas Capuano, worked with the poor in Recife.

Foreign Minister Azeredo da Silveira charged in an interview published in Brazil June 12 that the U.S. press had exaggerated the mistreatment of the two missionaries. Referring to the U.S. government, he said, "One cannot protect human rights in a cockeyed fashion, looking only to one side." He noted that American "police killed two demonstrators and injured 133 during a Puerto Rican demonstration in Chicago" recently.

Colombia—In talks with President Alfonso Lopez Michelsen in Bogota June 10, Mrs. Carter concentrated on the smuggling of narcotics from Colombia to the U.S. and on the imprisonment of 70 Americans in Colombia on drug charges.

Mrs. Carter said later that Lopez Michelsen had agreed that the drug traffic between Colombia and the U.S., worth an estimated $500 million a year, "is a very serious problem for both of our countries." She said President Carter would send two American drug experts to Colombia to discuss steps to halt the traffic.

Venezuela—Mrs. Carter met with President Carlos Andres Perez in Caracas June 12. They discussed the U.S. law denying Venezuela preferential trade treatment because it belonged to OPEC; the upcoming OAS meeting in Grenada, and Perez' planned visit to Washington in July.

Mrs. Carter later said she had thanked Perez for "Venezuela's being a reliable source of petroleum" during the Arab oil embargo in 1973–74, but had told him she could not "promise" that Congress would repeal the restrictive trade legislation. Perez told her Venezuela had signed and ratified the American Convention on Human Rights.

Perez called Mrs. Carter "an extraordinary woman." "I was surprised, very

pleasantly surprised, by her knowledge and her frankness," he said.

Andrew Young on tour. Andrew Young, the U.S. ambassador to the United Nations, visited 10 countries in the Caribbean region Aug. 5–17 to stress the Carter Administration's interest in good relations in the area.

Young visited Jamaica, Mexico, Costa Rica, Guyana, Surinam, Trinidad & Tobago, Venezuela, the Dominican Republic, Haiti and Barbados, conferring with their leaders and, in some cases, with members of the political opposition.

Throughout the tour Young emphasized the U.S.' desire to develop an "overall" policy toward the Caribbean after years of neglecting the region. He repeatedly expressed the Carter Administration's commitment to human rights and its willingness to help Caribbean nations economically within certain limits. He made it clear that the Administration was concerned less with a government's ideological stance than with its commitment to help its own people.

By all accounts Young's trip was a success. Caribbean leaders received him warmly, noting that he was an influential member of the Carter Administration who was genuinely concerned with the needs of the Third World, with which most of the poor Caribbean nations identified. Even those nations where Young's visit was tense—Mexico and Haiti—reportedly agreed with Young's plans for a regional partnership between the U.S. and the Caribbean states.

Among highlights of the trip:

Jamaica—Young, who had visited Jamaica 11 times before and said he considered himself "a Jamaican," was received warmly in Kingston Aug. 5. He met with Prime Minister Michael Manley Aug. 6 and 7 and assured him that the U.S. respected his efforts to forge political and economic policies representing a "third way" between capitalism and communism.

U.S. officials accompanying Young said Aug. 7 that they would put together an economic package increasing U.S. aid to Jamaica from the current $10 million to a projected $50 million to $60 million. The program, which required approval by the

U.S. Congress, would include a $12-million agreement covering surplus food sales; a $10-million commodity import loan that would allow Jamaica to purchase agricultural machinery and other badly needed equipment, and technical aid and development projects in agriculture and education.

Mexico—Young arrived in Mexico City Aug. 7 and conferred the next day with President Jose Lopez Portillo and Foreign Minister Santiago Roel. Their discussions apparently centered on President Carter's plan to resolve the problem of illegal Mexican immigration to the U.S.

Young called Carter's plan "one big step in the overall process of resolving the [illegal alien] problem," but he conceded that Mexico was not happy with it. Mexican officials wanted more trade concessions from the U.S. to help boost the Mexican economy, create more jobs and thereby relieve the pressure on Mexicans to emigrate. "Mexico will never be satisfied," Young noted, "until it exports commodities and goods to the United States and not people."

Despite tension in his talks with Mexican officials, Young described his Mexican visit as "very informative and very productive." He said he had covered "an amazing amount of material" in his talks with Lopez Portillo and Roel.

Costa Rica—Human rights dominated Young's discussions with Costa Rican leaders Aug. 8-9. At a press conference the second day, Young defended Carter's emphasis on the rights issue, asserting national boundaries and sovereignty were less important "when human need cries out." "Nobody thought [the U.S.] was denying sovereignty when we gave earthquake assistance," he said, "and in many respects human rights assistance is like earthquake assistance." Young reiterated U.S. support for Costa Rica's initiative to have the United Nations appoint a human rights commissioner, or ombudsman.

Guyana—Young arrived in Georgetown Aug. 9 and almost immediately eased the long-standing tension in relations between the U.S. and Guyanan governments. Young said Aug. 10 that the U.S. would increase its economic aid to Guyana, which had been cut sharply in the early 1970s when Prime Minister Forbes Burnham began to socialize his country's

economy. Relations between Washington and Georgetown had been strained since then, and the tension had increased in October 1976 when Guyana accused the U.S. Central Intelligence Agency of causing the crash of a Cuban airplane in which several Guyanans died.

Surinam—On his arrival in Paramaribo Aug. 10, Young praised Surinam as an example "for all the world" in its respect for human rights. The U.S. envoy said he was impressed because "all manner of people live in harmony" in the former Dutch colony.

At a press conference the next day Young commented extensively on the U.S.' improving relations with Cuba. The thaw between Washington and Havana was progressing "reasonably well," Young said, and the U.S. was encouraged by President Fidel Castro's support of the U.S.' and Panama's recently completed negotiations for a new Panama Canal treaty. Young said Cubans were "not supermen," and it was irrational for the U.S. to fear a Cuban presence in Africa or Cuba's position in the Western Hemisphere.

Trinidad & Tobago—Young took up the Cuban theme again at a press conference in Port of Spain Aug. 11, this time criticizing the Castro government's repression of internal dissent. "I don't know a great deal about Cuba," he said, "but from what I have read Cuba has its share of human rights problems." These would be weighed by the U.S. in formulating future policy toward Cuba, the American envoy said.

Young met with Trinidadian Prime Minister Eric Williams Aug. 11 and 12. Among other things they discussed providing U.S. technical help for the steel, petrochemical and other industries that Trinidad planned to develop with its new earnings from oil production.

Venezuela—After meeting with President Carlos Andres Perez Aug. 12, Young praised Venezuela's democratic system and asserted that the U.S. "doesn't give military aid to the dictatorships of Latin America." Perez in turn praised Young, saying he liked the U.S. envoy's outspokenness. "We in Latin America are developing a new diplomacy that avoids that style of half-truths and addresses problems directly," Perez said.

"We like Mr. Young's style and language very much, because we're doing the same thing."

Both leaders expressed satisfaction with the new Panama Canal accord announced by the U.S. and Panama two days earlier. Perez said the U.S. had shown a "great sense of justice and ethics" in the treaty negotiations, and Young said the accord exemplified the Carter Administration's "new approach to Latin America."

At a press conference Aug. 13 Young said the U.S. should develop "an approach to economic development for the entire Caribbean basin." This was a top-priority item, he asserted, even more important than reestablishing diplomatic relations with Cuba.

Dominican Republic—After arriving in Santo Domingo Aug. 13, Young met with leaders of three opposition groups—the Dominican Revolutionary Party, the Social Christian Revolutionary Party and the Popular Democratic Party. They all "exchanged impressions" on President Carter's "policy of human rights and non-intervention," Young later told newsmen.

Young met Aug. 14 with President Joaquin Balaguer, who told him the Dominican Republic had been hurt by U.S. tariffs on sugar imports. But Balaguer said he would sign the U.S.-sponsored American Convention on Human Rights, which prompted Young to call him a "leader of inspiration."

Young upset the Inter-American Press Association by telling reporters in Santo Domingo that he supported efforts by members of the U.N. Educational, Scientific and Cultural Organization to promote government controls on the press. Young said these controls were necessary because "the communications media are very powerful," the Dominican newspaper El Caribe reported. The Inter-American Press Association said Aug. 16 that Young's comments could only "encourage the authoritarian governments of the world to increase their restrictions on the press and deny their peoples the right to be fully and freely informed. This is the first step toward a totalitarian government."

Haiti—Haiti was the most difficult stop on Young's trip because it was the only country whose government he openly criticized. Before leaving on his Caribbean

tour, Young had told Haitian exiles in New York that he would press behind the scenes to get the Haitian government to show greater concern for human rights. However, Young thought that Haitian officials proved recalcitrant in their first talks with him Aug. 14, so he decided publicly to express his distaste for Haitian repression.

At a press conference in Port-au-Prince Aug. 15 Young referred to the "imprisonment of voices of dissent, the denying of access to families and the denial of the most fundamental due process" in Haiti. The American people, he said, no longer wanted to support regimes that violated human rights and favored the exploitation of the poor by the rich. In a clear warning to the Haitian government, Young said: "When people understand the way the winds are blowing and if they want to go with those winds, they trim their sails accordingly."

After the press conference a nervous Young met with President-for-Life Jean-Claude Duvalier, who reportedly told him that Haiti "believes in human rights."

(Press reports noted that abuse of human rights had decreased in Haiti since 1971, when Duvalier took office upon the death of his father, Francois [Papa Doc] Duvalier. Still, young Duvalier's government was a dictatorship that did not tolerate political dissent and that protected the interests of the island's wealthy minority—particularly the Duvalier family—at the expense of the extremely poor majority.)

Barbados—Young conferred with Barbadian officials after arriving in Bridgetown Aug. 16. Summing up his Caribbean tour before departing for the U.S. the next day, Young said he had found "a great appreciation of democracy" in the area, and had discerned training and ability that "far surpasses that of other continents."

"[The Caribbean is] a real growth area if we can overcome some of the petty rivalries, if economic and social integration can become more of a reality," Young said.

Asked what he thought of the spread of socialism in the Caribbean basin, the U.S. envoy said: "Anything that's going to feed hungry people, anything that aids rural development and anything that stabilizes population growth—the [U.S.] government can live with it, whatever it's called." "I don't even know what socialism is any more," he added.

Upon its return to the U.S. Young's team of political and economic experts began putting together a package of recommendations for the Carter Administration, including a recommendation of increased economic aid to the entire Caribbean region.

Vance visits South America. U.S. Secretary of State Cyrus Vance visited Argentina, Brazil and Venezuela Nov. 20–23 to confer with their leaders on human rights, atomic energy, petroleum prices and various other international issues.

Vance's tour was intended in part to make up for the postponement and subsequent rescheduling of President Carter's trip to Venezuela and Brazil, originally scheduled for late November. However, U.S. officials also stressed the importance of the matters Vance discussed with the South American leaders.

Vance arrived in Buenos Aires late Nov. 20. He met the next day with Foreign Minister Oscar Montes and the three members of Argentina's military junta—Lt. Gen. Jorge Videla, the president and army commander; Adm. Emilio Massera, the navy chief, and Lt. Gen. Orlando Agosti, the air force commander.

Vance and the Argentine leaders discused the human rights issue "at length," according to a State Department spokesman. One of Vance's aides asked the Argentine government for information on 7,500 persons who were listed as imprisoned or missing by human rights organizations in Argentina and the U.S. Vance and his assistants also met with local human rights activists, relatives of missing persons and representatives of Buenos Aires' Jewish community. Jews felt threatened by evidence of anti-Semitism in Argentina's security forces and by the imprisonment without trial of a prominent Jewish newspaper publisher.

The other major topic stressed by Vance in Argentina—atomic energy—produced the lone tangible success of his South American tour. The Argentine government agreed Nov. 21 to sign the Treaty of Tlatelolco, which banned atomic weapons in Latin America and the Caribbean.

The signing would facilitate the transfer of U.S. and Canadian technology to Argentina's atomic power industry, the most advanced in Latin America. Both Washington and Ottawa had banned such technology earlier in 1977 for countries that would not sign the Nuclear Nonproliferation Treaty or, in Latin America's case, the Tlatelolco pact. Among other things, Argentina needed U.S. and Canadian assistance in building a heavy water plant to extend its nuclear power program.

Atomic energy dominated Vance's discussions with Brazilian leaders in Brasilia Nov. 22, but the secretary failed to persuade Brazil to sign one of the nonproliferation treaties. A State Department spokesman described Vance's talks with President Ernesto Geisel and Foreign Minister Antonio Azeredo da Silveira as "frank, businesslike and friendly"—language normally used to indicate that no progress was made.

Since April 1976 the U.S. had held up export licenses for the shipment of uranium fuel to Brazil because Brazil would not sign a nonproliferation treaty and because it planned to build a plant that would produce plutonium, the main explosive in atomic weapons. The Carter Administration finally approved the licenses Nov. 16, a week before Vance's arrival in Brasilia, but this apparently did not make the Brazilians more accommodating.

(Brazil's hand had been strengthened by the recent support given to its atomic energy policy by Venezuelan President Carlos Andres Perez, according to the Latin America Political Report Nov. 25. Perez, who had extremely good relations with President Carter, visited Brazil Nov. 16–20.)

The U.S. had given up hope that it might stop construction of the Brazilian plutonium plant, and it now sought to persuade Brazil to make the plant a regional reprocessing factory for spent uranium fuel from atomic plants all over South America, according to the Washington Post Nov. 17. Vance apparently proposed this to Geisel in Brasilia, to no avail.

Vance stopped in Caracas for five hours Nov. 23 to talk with President Perez and his foreign minister, Simon Alberto Consalvi. Vance urged Perez to oppose a new price increase by the Organization of Petroleum Exporting Countries (OPEC), but Perez already had said in Brazil that OPEC would raise prices by 5%–8% at its meeting in Caracas Dec 20. Perez said Nov. 23 that "an oil price increase is justified because the industrial countries have raised the prices for what we (the OPEC countries) import."

"If there were international efforts to stabilize steel, machinery and tractor prices, I would be the leader of an effort to freeze petroleum prices," Perez declared. In any case, he said, Venezuela was not taking as "hard" a position on oil price increases as other OPEC nations.

Vance and Perez discussed human rights and other issues with more success. "We agreed on everything except oil prices," Vance noted before flying on to Washington.

Vance's visit to South America at a time of momentous developments in the Middle East emphasized the Carter Administration's interest in strong relations with Latin American countries, according to U.S. officials quoted in the Washington Post Nov. 24.

The trip also illustrated the Administration's country-by-country (rather than regional) approach to hemispheric relations.

There were different priorities in Washington's relations with each Latin American nation, as shown in the varying topics discussed by Vance in Brazil and Venezuela.

Finally, the Post said, the Administration was treating Latin American nations not as special American allies but as members of the Third World, with problems, aspirations and alliances that were increasingly bound with other underdeveloped nations in Africa, the Middle East and Asia.

Economic Developments

Regional economic growth reported. The gross domestic product of the Latin American and Caribbean region increased by 4.5%–5% in 1976, approximately doubling the 1975 increase of 2.4%, according to an IDB report issued May 30.

Latin America and Caribbean: Annual Variations in Gross Domestic Product, 1961–75[a]							
Country	1961–65	1966–70	1971	1972	1973	1974	1975
Argentina	4.5[b]	4.3	4.8	3.1	6.1	6.5	−1.9
Barbados	2.4	7.3	4.1	−2.3	2.3	−8.8	−3.1
Bolivia	3.9	6.3	3.8	5.1	6.9	6.7	6.8
Brazil	4.5	7.5	11.3	10.4	11.4	9.6	4.0
Chile	5.0	3.9	7.7	−0.1	−3.6	4.1	−12.9
Colombia	4.7	5.8	5.8	7.8	7.1	6.0	4.6
Costa Rica	4.6	7.4	6.8	8.2	7.7	5.4	3.4
Dominican Republic	3.1	7.7	10.6	12.4	12.1	7.5	5.1
Ecuador	5.3	5.7	5.8	5.7	18.3	13.6	5.3
El Salvador	6.9	4.5	4.6	5.7	4.3	6.0	4.3
Guatemala	5.3	5.8	5.6	7.3	6.8	6.4	2.1
Guyana	3.1	4.2	2.9	−3.5	−0.2	8.0	5.4
Haiti	0.7	1.0	6.5	1.0	5.9	4.3	3.5
Honduras	5.0	4.3	3.5	3.7	5.3	1.5	−0.1
Jamaica	4.7	6.2	1.8	8.2	−2.6	1.3	−2.3
Mexico	7.2	6.9	3.4	7.3	7.6	5.9	4.2
Nicaragua	10.1	4.0	4.8	3.6	4.2	13.4	1.8
Panama	8.2	7.7	8.7	6.3	6.5	2.6	1.7
Paraguay	4.8	4.2	4.4	5.1	7.8	8.3	5.0
Peru	6.7	4.4	5.1	5.8	6.2	6.9	3.5
Trinidad and Tobago	4.3	2.4	5.2	3.3	1.9	3.7	9.4
Uruguay	0.9	2.3	−1.0	−3.4	0.9	1.5	3.6
Venezuela	7.3	4.6	3.3	3.0	6.7	5.9	5.5
Latin America	**5.3**	**5.9**	**6.6**	**6.5**	**7.7**	**7.2**	**2.4**

[a]At constant prices with reference to the base year used by each country. For Latin America the figures were calculated by converting national values into United States dollars of 1973 purchasing power.

[b]All figures are percentages.
Source: Inter-American Development bank, Annual Report 1976. Based on official statistics of IDB member countries.

Most Latin American countries registered significant improvements over 1975 in production and prices, the report stated. The region's current account deficit fell to $13.5 billion in 1976 from the record $16.4 billion registered in 1975. The report attributed this favorable change to the general improvement in the world economic situation. [See accompanying table (p. 19), which does not show 1976 increases or decreases in gross domestic product]

Latin payments surplus grows. Latin American nations recorded a favorable balance of payments of $1.9 billion in 1976, surpassing the 1975 payments surplus of $600 million, according to figures compiled by the United Nations Economic Commission for Latin America and published in the Latin America Economic Report March 11.

Most nations recorded individual payments surpluses in 1976, although Venezuela had an $800-million deficit, due

Latin America's balance of payments 1975-76

(all figures in U.S. dollars)

Country	Exports		Imports		Trade balance		Payments balance	
	1975	1976	1975	1976	1975	1976	1975	1976
Argentina	3,000	3,700	3,533	2,830	−533	870	−962	650
Brazil	8,664	10,000	12,176	12,100	−3,512	−2,100	−897	1,100
Mexico	3,445	4,030	6,283	6,280	−2,838	−2,250	170	−350
Colombia	1,694	1,980	1,481	1,700	213	280	125	380
Chile	1,534	1,979	1,536	1,418	−2	561	−315	476
Peru	1,378	1,580	2,491	2,190	−1,113	−610	−532	−200
Costa Rica	488	570	627	680	−139	−110	−7	30
El Salvador	517	672	554	640	−37	32	28	70
Guatemala	650	750	717	850	−67	−90	108	150
Honduras	297	430	387	390	−81	40	54	60
Nicaragua	375	510	470	420	−95	90	33	30
Panama	329	260	803	680	−474	−420	−7	−7
Dominican Republic	894	540	773	775	121	−235	20	−50
Haiti	69	100	105	115	−36	−15	−10	10
Paraguay	176	190	215	200	−39	−10	30	40
Uruguay	385	650	496	510	−111	140	−63	90
Barbados	95	60	207	186	−112	−126	9	−5
Guyana	351	223	306	275	45	−50	49	−80
Jamaica	808	630	960	800	−152	−170	−69	−70
Total (non-oil exporting countries)	25,149	28,856	34,111	33,029	−8,962	−4,173	−2,236	2,234
Bolivia	437	460	470	550	−33	−90	−45	80
Ecuador	1,013	1,250	986	1,060	27	190	−79	110
Venezuela	8,899	9,400	5,330	6,710	3,569	2,690	2,504	−800
Trinidad & Tobago	1,704	2,386	1,368	2,050	336	336	456	200
Total (oil exporting countries)	12,053	13,496	8,154	10,370	3,899	3,126	2,836	−410
TOTAL	37,202	42,352	42,265	43,398	−5,069	−1,047	600	1,914

Source: Latin America Economic Report March 11. Data derived from U.N. Economic Commission for Latin America, based on official preliminary estimates from each country.

chiefly to a negative capital flow of $2.5 billion. A majority of Latin countries recorded individual trade deficits, although six—Argentina, Chile, El Salvador, Honduras, Nicaragua and Uruguay—moved from trade deficits in 1975 to surpluses in 1976. The Dominican Republic and Guyana moved from surpluses to deficits.

Brazil led the region in 1976 exports with $10 billion, followed by Venezuela with $9.4 billion and Mexico with $4 billion. Brazil also led in imports with $12.1 billion, followed by Venezuela with $6.7 billion and Mexico with $6.3 billion.

Kidnapping mars IDB meeting. The abduction of a Salvadoran official disrupted the 18th annual meeting of the board of governors of the Inter-American Development Bank (IDB), held in Guatemala City May 30–June 1.

El Salvador's ambassador to Guatemala, Col. Eduardo Casanova Sandoval, was kidnapped May 29 by members of the Guerrilla Army of the Poor, a small Guatemalan leftist group. Casanova was released unharmed June 1, after the IDB met his abductors' one demand—that a statement by the guerrillas be read aloud at the bank meeting.

The statement, read by an IDB official at the meeting's opening session, denounced the bank, Casanova and the military-dominated governments of El Salvador and Guatemala.

"The millions in credits from the [IDB]," the statement charged, "strengthen the exploiters of [the Latin American] people and support violence, repression and violation of human rights. As an instrument of international imperialism, the bank uses the mask of social welfare and foreign aid to disguise the domination of our countries by foreign countries."

Casanova, the statement asserted, was responsible for the murder of workers and peasants in El Salvador. The Salvadoran and Guatemalan governments consistently violated the human rights of their subjects, the statement added.

After the statement was read, Guatemalan President Gen. Kjell Laugerud entered the assembly hall under heavy armed guard and the meeting got under way.

IDB '76 annual loan report—IDB president Antonio Ortiz Mena submitted the bank's annual report, which noted that in 1976:

■ The IDB approved a record $1.528 billion in new loans, an increase of 11% over the 1975 record of $1.375 billion. In December 1976 the bank's net lending to Latin American countries since its founding in 1960 passed the $10-billion mark. [See table p. 22]

■ The IDB also provided a record $30.9 million in technical assistance to its member nations, mostly on a grant basis. This was 25% more than the 1975 record of $24.6 million.

■ Nine countries from outside the Americas joined the bank—Belgium, Denmark, West Germany, Israel, Japan, Spain, Switzerland, Great Britain and Yugoslavia. (Austria, France and the Netherlands joined on Jan. 10, 1977).

■ IDB members in the Americas increased the bank's resources by a total of $6.3 billion.

U.S. stresses human rights issue—The U.S. raised the human rights issue in the afternoon session May 30, coming into direct conflict with Ortiz Mena and most of the bank's Latin American member states. U.S. Treasury Secretary W. Michael Blumenthal said the Carter Administration would ask Congress for "substantial" new contributions to the IDB, but he warned that Congress wanted to make sure the money was "reaching the needy people of the developing world" and wanted to give priority in lending to countries that "respect and promote human rights."

Blumenthal said May 31 that the Carter Administration felt that "economic and human rights are closely linked." U.S. policy "is not directed against any country," Blumenthal declared, "but when we cast our vote in an international organization such as this bank, we will take into account whether the money is being used to benefit the people and whether there is respect for human rights."

The U.S. delegation to the IDB meeting tried to organize support for the human rights issue, according to press reports. However, most Latin American countries reportedly insisted that loans be judged strictly on economic grounds. The U.S. position was criticized June 1 by Ortiz

Mena and the representatives of Chile, Uruguay and Argentina. (The governments of each of these countries had been accused repeatedly of torturing political prisoners and generally violating human rights.)

"The United Nations is an adequate forum to discuss [human rights]," Ortiz Mena said at a press conference. "The only thing [the IDB] studies are the economic and social aspects [of loan policy]."

U.S. cuts Peru's copper from duty-free list. President Carter Feb. 28 signed an executive order that removed 115 items, including certain of Peru's copper exports from the U.S.' duty-free list, effective March 1.

The changes were required under the 1974 Trade Reform Act. The law provided for the withdrawal or suspension of special tariff preferences when a developing nation exceeded certain annual limits, that is, when the value of specific exports to the U.S. was more than $29.9 million or comprised more than 50% of total imports in that category. Another developing nation, however, might still be eligible to export that product to the U.S. on a duty-free basis.

Latin leaders set coffee fund. The leaders of five Latin American countries and Jamaica agreed Aug. 6 to create an international fund to regulate the coffee market and "assure reasonable price levels for producers and consumers, in the light of equitable . . . terms of exchange and the proper supply of the market."

A communique establishing the International Coffee Fund was issued by Prime Minister Michael Manley of Jamaica, Brig. Gen. Omar Torrijos of Panama and Presidents Carlos Andres Perez of Venezuela, Alfonso Lopez Michelsen of Colombia, Jose Lopez Portillo

Inter-American Development Bank Lending, 1973-76

(thousand U.S. dollars)

Country	1973	1974	1975	1976
Argentina	$ 12,454	$ 89,100	$ 201,000	$ 210,900
Barbados	—	9,100	9,700	6,600
Bolivia	46,528	46,200	54,100	40,200
Brazil	274,115	187,000	269,500	239,100
Chile	—	97,300	70,700	70,000
Colombia	105,900	—	75,800	109,000
Costa Rica	16,000	53,800	41,600	33,000
Dominican Republic	39,000	36,700	35,500	33,400
Ecuador	55,700	55,500	43,700	73,600
El Salvador	8,000	33,400	43,000	25,000
Guatemala	36,800	19,400	120,600	70,000
Haiti	22,200	—	41,100	5,000
Honduras	1,200	35,600	28,700	114,500
Jamaica	30,800	—	21,200	17,500
Mexico	113,467	186,400	167,300	183,200
Nicaragua	29,200	10,500	16,500	49,800
Panama	18,000	14,500	42,200	27,000
Paraguay	—	49,000	3,200	11,600
Peru	19,280	65,500	16,000	149,000
Trinidad and Tobago	2,400	5,300	—	—
Uruguay	3,100	21,400	35,400	36,400
Venezuela	43,100	—	—	—
Regional	6,800	95,000	38,200	23,000
TOTAL	**$884,044**	**$1,110,700**	**$1,375,000**	**$1,527,800**

Note: Of the $884 million in loans approved in 1973, a loan of $10.6 million for Venezuela was canceled and of the $1,111 million approved in 1974, one for $18.4 million to El Salvador was also canceled. A $1 million loan approved in 1975 for Peru replaced a similar amount voided in 1974. In addition, partial cancellations of $1,119,000 in loans approved in 1973 and $1,040,000 in loans approved in 1974 had been made as of Dec. 31, 1976.
Source: Inter-American Development Bank Annual Report, 1976

of Mexico and Daniel Oduber of Costa Rica. The six met in Colombia for two days, primarily to discuss the Panama Canal.

Venezuela would make an initial contribution of $100 million to the fund, according to the newspaper El Nacional of Caracas Aug. 7.

Coffee prices slump—Two major U.S. coffee roasters announced further reductions in their wholesale prices of ground coffee, which had been declining since mid-May.

General Foods Corp. Oct. 17 cut its wholesale price 10¢ a pound to $3.41. That was down $1.05 from the mid-April record level. Procter & Gamble's Folger Coffee division Oct. 14 had cut its wholesale prices 20¢ a pound to $3.18.

The slump in price, coupled with a decline in demand, meant that unsold supplies of green coffee beans had been piling up in warehouses in Brazil and Colombia, the world's chief coffee-exporting nations.

However, Brazil and Colombia adopted conflicting export strategies during the six-month price plunge in an effort to stabilize the market price.

Colombia chose an aggressive marketing policy, making extensive sales abroad at the lower prices. (By early November, green coffee beans were trading in New York as low as $1.50 a pound.) The Colombian government reasoned that a return to the record high prices set in April would only intensify the continuing drop in consumer demand. In the U.S., per capita coffee consumption had fallen 15% during 1977, largely because of the high cost of the beverage, according to Business Week Nov. 7.

Brazil took the opposite approach. The government decided to withhold its coffee crop from the world market in hopes of forcing the price back up to Brazil's official export level of $3.20 a pound. Ten other coffee-producing nations in Central and South America ratified Brazil's strategy Oct. 21. After a two-day meeting in El Salvador, representatives of that country, Guatemala, Honduras, Nicaragua, Panama, Costa Rica, the Dominican Republic, Ecuador, Venezuela and Mexico said they would stockpile their coffee until prices moved higher.

Brazil abandoned its boycott strategy in a surprise move announced Nov. 4 after secret negotiations with Colombia. The two nations agreed to coordinate their export policies in an effort to stabilize world price at about $2 a pound. Mexico, the Ivory Coast and El Salvador joined in action Nov. 9.

The chief reason behind Brazil's sudden turnaround was a fear of incurring a large trade deficit in 1977, according to Business Week. Government officials had concluded that unless earnings on coffee exports increased $500 million to $600 million, the country would not be able to balance its trade account by the end of the year, Business Week said.

Bauxite producers set base price. Ten members of the International Bauxite Association agreed Dec. 7 on a new minimum, or reference, price for base-grade bauxite sold in the North American market.

Base-grade bauxite was 45% aluminum oxide, from which aluminum was smelted.

The group, meeting in Jamaica, set the floor price at $24 a metric ton. (A metric ton equals 2,204.6 pounds.) That was slightly below the current price charged by Jamaica and Surinam, the chief suppliers to North America.

Agreement came after four years of discussion. Australia, a long-time holdout against the minimum-price policy, approved the new price. Also voting in favor of the minimum price were the Dominican Republic, Ghana, Guinea, Guyana, Haiti, Jamaica, Sierra Leone, Surinam and Yugoslavia. The IBA's eleventh member, Indonesia, did not attend.

3 nations discuss hydroelectric plans. Representatives of Brazil, Paraguay and Argentina met in Asuncion, Paraguay Sept. 22–23 to discuss three hydroelectric projects being planned on the Parana River.

The Parana begins in east central Brazil and flows to the southwest, moving along the Brazil-Paraguay and Paraguay-Argentina borders, entering Argentina and finally emptying into the River Plate just north of Buenos Aires.

Brazil and Paraguay jointly had begun building a massive dam and hydroelectric station on the Parana at Itaipu on their common border. Further downstream, Paraguay and Argentina planned to build two smaller stations at Corpus and Yacireta-Apipe on their common border.

Brazil and Argentina were at odds over the size and nature of the Itaipu project. Argentina wanted Itaipu to be as small as possible, for the larger it was, the less powerful it rendered Corpus and Yacireta-Apipe. Brazil, on the other hand, wanted a large Itaipu station to provide power for the burgeoning industries in southern Brazil. As the junior partner in each of the three Parana projects, Paraguay had a limited amount of influence in the dispute.

The Asuncion meeting was called to discuss only "technical" matters relating to the power projects, but Argentina managed to bring up its overall dispute with Brazil. The Argentine delegate spoke of "compatibilization," that is, the need for an agreement to insure that Itaipu did not make Corpus and Yacireta-Apipe impractical.

According to the Latin America Political Report Sept. 30, Argentina sought assurances from Brazil on two issues: the height of the Itaipu dam and the way in which the dam would be used.

The height involved both the level of the water in the reservoir above the dam and the level at which the water passed out through the turbines at the bottom. These levels placed constraints on the power potential of the Corpus project. If Brazil extracted the maximum amount of energy from Itaipu, the Political Report said, Corpus would not be viable.

As for the use of Itaipu, Brazilian technicians had said the most efficient method would be to run the turbines in bursts of four or five hours to provide more energy at times of peak demand, the Political Report said. Argentina wanted the water to flow through the turbines all day at a lower rate to prevent radical alterations of the lower course of the Parana.

The Asuncion meeting did not resolve the general dispute, but it was expected to lead to other tripartite meetings. The meeting itself was a small victory for Argentina, since Brazil previously had refused even to discuss Itaipu with Buenos Aires.

Armaments

Trends in Latin arms purchases change. U.S. State Department statistics for 1966–75 showed significant changes in the way Latin American countries had obtained their military equipment, according to the Latin America Political Report April 8.

The statistics, published by the State Department's Arms Control and Disarmament Agency, showed that Latin nations increasingly had acquired U.S. arms through direct commercial transactions (rather than aid), and increasingly had turned to countries other than the U.S. for their military supplies.

Arms Transfers of Major Suppliers to Latin America, 1966–75
(million dollars)

Recipient	Total	USA	USSR	France	UK	Others
Argentina	320	128	—	73	17	102
Bolivia	44	37	—	1	—	6
Brazil	531	243	—	145	47	96
Chile	246	81	—	12	106	47
Colombia	182	57	—	55	7	63
Cuba	312	—	310	—	—	2
Dom. Rep.	11	11	—	—	—	—
Ecuador	85	22	—	12	19	32
El Salvador	16	4	—	—	—	12
Guatemala	34	31	—	—	—	3
Honduras	16	10	—	—	—	6
Mexico	54	21	—	—	24	9
Nicaragua	11	10	—	—	—	1
Panama	14	8	—	—	3	3
Peru	493	67	84	73	56	213
Uruguay	47	36	—	—	—	11
Venezuela	326	97	—	130	46	53
Latin America*	**2,768**	**883**	**394**	**502**	**328**	**661**

*Totals include arms transfers to Latin American countries not listed in chart.

Source: U.S. Arms Control and Disarmament Agency, World Military Expenditures and Arms Transfers, 1966–75, cited in Latin America Political Report April 8.

The trend toward direct commercial transactions could make ineffective the Carter Administration's policy of reducing or denying military aid to Latin countries that abused human rights. Many of the direct purchases were financed by U.S. banks, which did not consider the human rights issue in their transactions.

Between 1960 and 1975, Argentina spent $52.9 million on military and police equipment bought directly from U.S. firms; Brazil spent $43.7 million, Colombia $18.6 million and Peru $17.6 million.

In 1976 the U.S. Congress voted to require advance notice of all commercial arms sales exceeding $7 million, but police equipment sales rarely went that high, according to the Latin America Political Report. Smith & Wesson, the largest producer and exporter of firearms and law-enforcement equipment in the U.S., had been particularly successful in selling arms to Latin America, the Report noted. The U.S. Defense Department occasionally helped promote deals between Latin American nations and U.S. arms manufacturers, according to the Report.

From the 1960s to 1975, U.S. share of the Latin arms market dropped to 14% from a high of 40%. France, Great Britain and the Soviet Union were among the countries to which Latin America was turning for its arms; Israel was an important supplier to Central America. In addition, some Latin countries—notably Argentina and Brazil—were developing their own arms industries with U.S., European and Canadian help.

U.S., Israel dispute arms sales. The U.S. was consulting Israel about published accounts that Israel had sold military equipment made with U.S.-supplied technology to several Latin American nations without Washington's permission, it was reported Jan. 8. The alleged deals were said to have been with countries to which the U.S. refused to sell arms.

One controversial transaction, involving the Israeli sale to Honduras of 12 Super-Mystere jets with American engines salvaged from other aircraft, had been settled to the satisfaction of the U.S., the State Department disclosed Jan. 17. A department spokesman said Secretary of State Henry A. Kissinger had discussed the matter with Israeli Ambassador

Simcha Dinitz Jan. 14 and the U.S. accepted Israel's "explanation. We consider the matter closed."

According to the spokesman, Dinitz had told Kissinger that the U.S. Congress had been informed of the details of the Honduran deal in conformity with U.S. arms-control legislation requiring such notification when third countries received U.S. military equipment. Dinitz assured Kissinger that Israel planned no further sales of the Super-Mysteres.

Chile and South Africa were among other nations on the U.S. arms ban list that had received American equipment via Israel.

The magazine Aviation Week & Space Technology had reported in December 1976 that Israel had sold Chile the Shafrir heat-seeking air-to-air missile, a weapon copied from the AIM 9D/6 made by Raytheon, a U.S. firm, it was reported Jan. 8.

A publication called The Military Balance identified Israel in its latest issue as a primary arms supplier to Bolivia, Ecuador, El Salvador, Mexico and Nicaragua, it was reported Jan. 15. The journal was an annual publication of the London-based International Institute for Strategic Studies.

U.S. delays police sales to Latins. The Carter Administration was holding up the sale of police weapons to four Latin American nations because the arms might be used to suppress human rights, spokesmen for the U.S. State Department said July 17.

About $1 million worth of sidearms and other weapons were being withheld from Argentina, Uruguay, El Salvador and Nicaragua while American human rights officials reviewed the U.S. aid program to Latin American police forces. Some sales to Guatemala also were being delayed.

The governments of all five countries had been accused by dissidents and independent observers of crushing political opposition and brutalizing demonstrators. The Carter Administration already had reduced military aid to Argentina and Uruguay, and it was holding up economic and military assistance to Nicaragua over the human rights issue. Argentina, Uruguay and El Salvador had rejected all U.S. military aid on grounds that the U.S. had no right to judge their record on civil liberties.

1977 Population Data

Region or country [1]	Population estimate mid-1977 (millions) [2]	Birth rate [3]	Death rate [3]	Rate of natural increase (annual, percent) [4]	Number of years to double population [5]	Population projection to 2000 (millions) [6]	Infant mortality rate [7]	Population under 15 yr (percent) [6]	Population over 64 yr (percent) [6]	Life expectancy at birth (years) [6]	Urban population (percent) [6]	Per capita national product (U.S. dollars) [6]
Latin America	336.0	36	9	2.7	26	608.0	78	42	4	62	59	1,030
Middle America	85.0	42	8	3.4	20	174.0	70	46	3	62	56	1,060
Costa Rica	2.1	29	5	2.4	29	3.6	38	44	4	68	41	910
El Salvador	4.3	40	8	3.1	22	8.6	58	46	3	58	39	450
Guatemala	6.4	43	12	3.1	22	12.2	80	45	2	53	34	650
Honduras	3.3	49	15	3.5	20	6.9	117	47	3	54	31	350
Mexico	64.4	42	7	3.5	20	134.6	66	46	3	63	62	1,190
Nicaragua	2.3	48	14	3.4	20	4.8	123	48	3	53	49	720
Panama	1.8	31	5	2.6	27	3.2	40	43	4	66	50	1,060
Caribbean	28.0	30	9	2.1	33	44.0	75	41	5	64	45	970
Bahamas	.2	20	5	1.4	50	.3	35	44	3	66	58	2,600
Barbados	.2	19	8	1.1	63	.3	38	34	9	69	44	1,260
Cuba	9.6	22	6	1.6	43	14.9	29	37	6	70	60	800
Dominican Republic	5.0	46	11	3.5	20	10.7	98	48	3	58	44	720
Grenada	.1	28	8	1.9	36	.5	32	(*)	(*)	63	15	370
Guadeloupe	.3	28	7	2.1	33		44	40	5	60	48	1,240
Haiti	5.3	36	16	2.3	30	7.9	150	42	4	50	20	180
Jamaica	2.1	30	7	2.3	30	2.8	26	46	6	68	37	1,290
Martinique	.4	22	7	1.6	43	.5	32	41	5	65	50	1,540
Netherlands Antilles	.2	20	5	1.5	46	.4	28	38	5	62	48	1,590
Puerto Rico	3.2	23	6	1.7	41	4.1	24	37	7	72	58	2,300
Trinidad and Tobago	1.0	24	6	1.8	38	1.3	34	40	4	66	12	1,900
Tropical South America	183.0	37	9	2.8	25	337.0	84	43	3	61	59	960
Bolivia	4.8	44	18	2.6	27	8.7	108	42	4	47	34	320
Brazil	112.0	37	9	2.8	25	205.0	82	42	3	61	59	1,010
Colombia	25.2	33	9	2.5	28	47.1	97	43	3	61	64	550
Ecuador	7.5	42	10	3.2	22	14.7	78	45	4	60	41	550
Guyana	.8	32	7	2.4	29	1.3	40	44	3	68	40	560
Paraguay	2.8	40	9	3.1	22	6.3	65	45	4	62	37	570
Peru	16.6	41	12	2.9	24	31.2	110	43	3	56	55	810
Surinam	.4	37	7	3.0	23	.9	30	50	4	66	50	1,180
Venezuela	12.7	37	6	3.1	22	23.2	49	45	3	65	74	2,220
Temperate South America	40.0	23	9	1.4	50	52.0	63	31	7	67	79	1,340
Argentina	26.1	23	9	1.3	53	32.9	59	29	8	68	80	1,590
Chile	11.0	24	8	1.6	43	15.8	77	36	5	63	76	760
Uruguay	2.8	21	10	1.1	63	3.4	45	28	9	70	81	1,330

[1] The data sheet lists U.N. members and geopolitical entities with a population larger than 200,000.

[2] Based on a population total from a very recent census or on the most recent official country or U.N. estimate; for almost all countries the estimate was for mid-1975. Each estimate was updated by the Population Reference Bureau to mid-1977 by applying the same rate of growth as indicated by population change during part or all of the period since 1970.

[3] Annual number of births or deaths per 1,000 population.

[4] Birth rate minus the death rate.

*Data are unavailable.

[6] Based on the rate of natural increase shown and assuming no change in the rate.

[7] Annual number of deaths to infants under 1-yr of age per 1,000 live births.

Population data sheets of various years should not be used as a time series. Because every attempt is made to use the most recent and most accurate information, data sources vary and radical changes in numbers and rates from year to year may reflect improved source material, revised data, or a later base year for computation, rather than yearly changes.

(El Salvador, however, continued to receive American military material that was approved before it formally rejected U.S. aid, it was reported July 25. Neither Salvadoran nor American officials in San Salvador were certain what the U.S. policy toward El Salvador was, according to the New York Times. The U.S. Embassy in the Salvadoran capital had not been informed beforehand of the Administration's decision to hold up police sales to El Salvador, the newspaper said.)

Other Developments

Peru-Chile border buildup detailed. Peru and Chile were building up defenses along their common border as tensions increased over Peruvian claims to northern Chilean territory and over the two nations' inability to agree on how to grant Bolivia an outlet to the sea, according to the Jan. 10 issue of Time magazine.

Peru had been moving tanks, troops and armored personnel carriers into military bases in its southern border provinces, Time reported. Chile had been mining the northern Atacama Desert, implanting tank traps and building fortifications to counter a possible invasion by Peru.

Peruvian leaders periodically had talked of regaining the Atacama, which was taken from Peru by Chile in the War of the Pacific in the late 19th Century. The desert had rich deposits of copper, silver and nitrates.

Peru recently had bought 36 Soviet Su-22 assault jets, adding to a stock of Soviet-made weaponry that included about 250 T-55 tanks and scores of SA-2 and SA-3 antiaircraft missiles, Time noted. Added to the French Mirage jets, British patrol boats and U.S. transport planes Lima had acquired since the late 1960s, the Soviet weapons made Peru the leading military power on South America's western coast, Time said.

Chile, which had more men under arms than Peru, was comparatively under-equipped because the U.S. and Great Britain had embargoed arms sales to the military government, Time said. The embargo included U.S.-made F-4 Phantom jets, which Chile eagerly sought and which

could easily handle Peru's Su-22s, the magazine reported.

Peruvian President Gen. Francisco Morales Bermudez denied Jan. 1 that Peru was preparing for hostilities with Chile. "If we have bought air force equipment from the Soviet Union," Morales said, "it is, in the first place, because it meets the technical conditions for national defense. The purchase does not imply a plan of aggression against any neighbor. The economic conditions we were offered [by the Soviet Union] were superior to other offers from three or four countries."

Guatemala severs Panama ties. The Guatemalan government announced May 19 that it had broken diplomatic relations with Panama to protest Panama's support of independence for Belize. Belize was the British colony in Central America over which Guatemala claimed sovereignty.

Panama's military strongman, Brig. Gen. Omar Torrijos, had infuriated Guatemalan leaders by declaring the previous weekend: "Yes, I have my hands in Belize, and I'm not going to take them out. . . . I'm going to help those people because they need it, I'm going to help George Price because he's a mystic who needs it, and I don't care if it makes Laugerud mad." Price was prime minister of Belize; Gen. Kjell Laugerud Garcia was president of Guatemala.

In an angry reply May 20, Laugerud called Torrijos "a man who doesn't know the meaning of honor" and a "pseudo-emulator" of Cuban President Fidel Castro and Ugandan President Idi Amin Dada. Laugerud warned Torrijos that if he "has his hands in Belize, he could get them burned."

Torrijos reiterated his support for an independent Belize May 20, on the first day of a visit to Panama by Price. Price said Guatemala's renunciation of ties with Panama was "an affront to the United Nations and to the countries of the Third World." (Both the U.N. General Assembly and the movement of nonaligned nations had passed resolutions in 1975 favoring Belizean independence.

Torrijos and others had argued that Belize's 150,000 inhabitants were not culturally, racially or historically related to Guatemala. The Belizean people, most of whom originally came from Jamaica,

Trinidad and Tobago and other Caribbean islands, spoke English.

Guatemala's ambassador to Mexico, Gen. Doroteo Monterroso Miranda, subsequently charged that Torrijos was supporting Belizean independence because he had invested more than $9 million in hotels and condominiums in the British colony, and he feared losing the investment under Guatemalan rule, it was reported May 24. Torrijos denied the charge and recommended that it be investigated by an international tribunal.

A Panamanian television station reported May 27 that Torrijos had asked Mexico, Venezuela, Costa Rica and Colombia to intercede to help resolve his difficulties with Guatemala. (At least two of those countries—Mexico and Venezuela—had come out strongly for Belizean independence in the past year, seriously weakening Latin American support for Guatemala's claim to Belize.)

Great Britain favored independence for Belize, but the colony did not want its freedom without a British commitment to defend it from attack by Guatemala. Price had given up trying to obtain an indefinite defense guarantee from London and was now aiming for a 10-year defense treaty, according to the Latin America Political Report May 20. Price reasoned that if Belize could survive the first 10 years of independence without attack from Guatemala, its diplomatic position in international forums would be established and its security thereafter assured, the Report said.

(Belize had announced in February that it would establish a defense force of regular and volunteer soldiers. British military officers would help set up the force, it was reported Feb. 13.)

Guatemala, meanwhile, opposed any unilateral action by Great Britain and asked for a continuation of talks between British and Guatemalan officials on the future of Belize. Laugerud had warned that Guatemala would "resort to arms" if Britain unilaterally made Belize independent, it was reported May 17.

In an earlier development, the Belize City Reporter had said Jan. 30 that Guatemalan nationals were crossing into Belize in droves. Border officials were capturing and deporting the illegal immigrants at a rate of 40 per day, the newspaper reported. It was unclear whether the migration was the result of hard times

in Peten, Guatemala's border province, or was an invasion sponsored by the Guatemalan government, the newspaper said.

Refugee situation in Latin America. Excerpts from the U.S. Committee for Refugees' "1977 World Refugee Survey Report" were inserted in the Congressional Record by Rep. Edward I. Koch (D, N.Y.) March 8. Among the comments on Latin America:

LATIN AMERICA

The search by refugees for asylum in Latin America has come to resemble a game of musical chairs.

As military coups have overthrown several governments in South America, opponents of these regimes have fled to neighboring countries. At first, when the leftist government of Salvador Allende ruled Chile, thousands of political refugees from Brazil and Bolivia came into the country. When a coup overthrew that elected government in September 1973, the right-wing military junta cracked down on these refugees.

Next, joined by thousands of Chileans, the refugee flow went to Peronist Argentina. Two years later, this regime too was overthrown by the military. The hunt for a fresh haven is now going on.

The unwillingness of many South American governments to accept many refugees is due to the fact that many of them are identified with the political left. Hence regimes fear that they will engage in leftist activities within the country of asylum or prove an embarrassment in relations with their home countries.

About 4000 of the refugees in Argentina—mostly Chilean but including many Bolivians and Uruguayans—have been resettled in 40 host states. Of the remainder, 2000 have received permanent work/residence permits in Argentina, 6000 are being supported by aid from UNHCR and voluntary organizations, and an additional 2000 are receiving no assistance.

Since a bloody guerrilla war between left and right wing terrorists has been going on in Argentina, inevitably some of the refugees have become targets. In June 1976, files were stolen from the offices of the leading voluntary agency—a Catholic group—engaged in refugee work in Buenos Aires. Two days later, 24 of those on the aid lists were kidnapped and tortured by rightist armed groups.

Understandably, UNHCR has made resettlement of the refugees stranded in Argentina a high priority.

Three thousand Chilean refugees have successfully transitted through Peru to resettlement in other countries. Only a very small percentage have been given permanent asylum there.

About 10,000 more Chileans have been

granted asylum in a wide variety of Latin American countries, particularly in Mexico.

Some controversy developed over whether the U.S. would take some of the refugees in, particularly given U.S. support for the anti-Allende coup. A number have been admitted, but congressional pressure sought to extend parole status. The Justice Department is considering admission of 200 refugees each from Argentina and Uruguay.

Health

Malaria upsurge in Latin America. A resurgence of malaria, particularly severe in parts of Central America, was reported Sept. 4 by the World Health Organization. Guatemala, Nicaragua, El Salvador and Honduras all reported significant increases in the disease.

There were 83,290 cases of malaria in El Salvador in 1976, compared with 66,691 in 1974. Honduras had 48,804 cases in 1976, compared with 7,503 in 1974. Of 142,000 malaria cases recorded in the Western Hemisphere in 1975, 40% were reported in Guatemala, Nicaragua and El Salvador.

There were currently an estimated 120 million cases of malaria around the world, Time magazine reported Sept. 12.

Experts attributed the comeback to the malaria-transmitting Anopheles mosquitoe, which had grown increasingly resistant to the pesticide DDT.

Argentina

Political Violence

Politically related murders, kidnappings, shootouts and bombings were reported in various parts of Argentina in 1977. The death toll for the year from such violence was at least 667, according to government and press reports.

Videla escapes bomb blast. President Gen. Jorge Videla narrowly escaped assassination Feb. 18 when a bomb exploded at Buenos Aires' municipal airport only seconds after the airplane in which he was traveling took off.

The bomb, detonated by remote control, had been placed in a culvert under the airport's runway. Videla's plane apparently missed the blast only because it took off at an unusually sharp angle. The aircraft landed at an air force base outside Buenos Aires for a thorough inspection and then continued on its course to Bahia Blanca, where Videla inspected offshore oil-drilling installations.

The explosion was the third unsuccessful attempt on Videla's life since March 1976. The previous attempts were credited to the Montoneros, the left-wing Peronist guerrillas, but responsibility for the airport blast was claimed by the Marxist People's Revolutionary Army (ERP).

The ERP's claim came as a surprise because the guerrilla group was presumed to have been crippled by the death or arrest of its top leaders. The Montoneros reportedly had carried out most guerrilla operations since the slaying of ERP chief Roberto Santucho in July 1976.

Guerrillas wound foreign minister. Left-wing terrorists May 7 shot and seriously wounded Vice Adm. Cesar Guzzetti, Argentina's foreign minister.

At least two members of the Montoneros guerrilla group slipped into a private clinic in Buenos Aires and attacked the foreign minister when he arrived for his weekly checkup. The insurgents beat Guzzetti and shot him in the head before escaping past his unsuspecting bodyguards.

Guzzetti was operated on immediately after the attack to remove the bullet lodged in his head. However, two bullet fragments remained in his head after the surgery, and the foreign minister was reported to be paralyzed on his right side. A medical report May 12 said he was recovering satisfactorily considering the gravity of his wound.

Envoy to Venezuela kidnapped. Hector Hidalgo Sola, Argentina's ambassador to Venezuela, was kidnapped July 18 as he left his home in Buenos Aires.

Hidalgo, on a visit to Argentina for his daughter's wedding, was seized by several armed men in civilian dress. His abductors were widely presumed to be security officers; some sources, cited by the Latin America Political Report July 27, said they were members of a naval flying squad that operated a torture center in the Argentine capital.

Several newspapers speculated that Hidalgo's kidnapping had been ordered by hard-line military officers who opposed President Jorge Videla's avowed plan to return Argentina slowly to democracy. Hidalgo, a member of the Radical Civic Union—the second largest political party in Argentina—was one of the few prominent politicians to collaborate openly with the military government. As ambassador to Venezuela, one of the handful of democracies in Latin America, he was instrumental in promoting Videla's image as a moderate who sought an accommodation with Argentina's civilian sectors.

Hidalgo had said in a recent newspaper interview, "There will be a democratic process [in Argentina] before many think there will be." "What is needed," he told the Financial Times (London), "is to find a civic-military meeting of minds that will give a stable democracy to the country." The Times, which published the interview July 22, said its own sources reported that President Videla wanted to hold municipal elections by mid-1978, to be followed, in stages, by provincial, congressional and presidential elections. Hidalgo was touted by many as a possible presidential candidate, the Times said.

The government denounced Hidalgo's kidnapping, and Videla was said to have ordered "all available resources" to be used in locating the ambassador. But on Aug. 1 Foreign Minister Oscar Montes said that the government had no "concrete" leads in the case.

Yofre's home bombed. A bomb exploded Aug. 22 in the home of Ricardo Yofre, deputy general secretary of the presidency. The house was damaged but no one was injured.

Guerrilla suspects & leftists slain. Government security officers killed hundreds of presumed leftists during 1977 in an effort to end guerrilla and terrorist attacks. The Montoneros, a left-wing Peronist group, were a major target of the anti-subversive crack-down.

The Montoneros lost scores of members in January, February and early March as security forces killed more than 250 persons officially described as guer-

rillas or suspected subversives. Some 150 alleged terrorists were reported killed from mid-January to mid-February, including Ana Maria Gonzalez, the Montonero schoolgirl held responsible for the murder of the federal police chief, Gen. Cesareo Cardozo, in June 1976. Gonzalez reportedly was shot by security officers Jan. 19 at a checkpoint in the Buenos Aires district of San Justo.

Four guerrilla suspects were killed in a shootout with security officers in Rosario Jan. 1. One of the victims was identified as Leonardo Bettanin, a former legislator who resigned from the Chamber of Deputies in 1974 to join the Montoneros.

Fourteen other guerrilla suspects were killed Jan. 4 in gun battles with authorities in Buenos Aires and Santa Fe.

A woman's bullet-riddled and mutilated body was found Jan. 3 in a vacation resort outside Buenos Aires. She was apparently killed by the Argentine Anti-Communist Alliance (AAA), the right-wing assassination squad.

Security forces Jan. 5 killed 10 alleged guerrillas whom they caught painting slogans on the walls of a Roman Catholic school near Buenos Aires. Authorities said one of the slogans referred to the Montoneros. Security forces in Rosario Jan. 5 reported killing Jose Ventura, a regional Montonero leader.

Eight Montoneros were killed Jan. 6 when 10 carloads of guerrillas attacked a military convoy transferring guerrilla prisoners from one jail to another in the La Plata area. Two of the victims were prisoners; one was Dardo Cabo, a top Montonero leader.

Horacio Novillo, editor of the Buenos Aires newspaper Prensa Libre, was found dead in his apartment in the capital Jan. 18. A fire had swept through the apartment but Novillo's body bore gunshot wounds and bruises. Prensa Libre recently had attacked the government's economic policies, and its publisher, Ricardo Bach Cano, had been arrested briefly at the end of 1976.

Miguel Rapoport, a political prisoner in La Plata, was summarily executed Feb. 5, according to the Spanish newspaper Diario 16 March 2. The London newsletter Latin America reported Feb. 11 that the Argentine government appeared to have embarked on a large-scale campaign to kill jailed militants. The water supplies in Cordoba and Buenos Aires reportedly had been contaminated by the decomposing bodies of executed political prisoners, which has been weighted and thrown into the cities' reservoirs by security officers.

The army announced June 4 that Julio Roque, a top leader of the Montoneros, had been killed in a shootout with soldiers May 29. The army said Roque was the only member of the Montoneros' four-man national command who had not fled the country.

Fourteen left-wing guerrillas were killed June 23–24 as Argentina's political violence continued. Nine of the victims were presumed members of the People's Revolutionary Army who died in a police raid on their hideout in Rosario.

Six more members of the Montoneros and one police inspector were killed July 21 when at least 10 of the leftist insurgents attacked a police station in Temperley, 12 miles south of Buenoes Aires.

The Montoneros received some encouragement July 23 from the Spanish Socialist Workers' Party (PSOE), the major opposition group in Spain. PSOE leader Felipe Gonzalez told Montoneros chief Mario Firmenich in Madrid that his party supported the Montoneros and other groups that were "fighting against the violent military dictatorship imposed by the junta headed by Gen. Jorge Videla."

Argentina's other guerrilla organization, the People's Revolutionary Army (ERP), announced in Rome July 20 that it would lay down its arms if the government agreed to respect human rights and the Argentine Constitution, to grant legal status to all political parties and the labor movement, and to enact an economic policy that would benefit all Argentines. The ERP, whose ranks had been decimated by security forces in the past year, announced that it had a new leader, Luis Mattini. He succeeded Mario Roberto Santucho, who was killed by Argentine police in July 1976.

Five presumed leftist guerrillas were killed outside Buenos Aires Aug. 6 when their car exploded in flames as they fled a roadblock under police fire. Three more suspected subversives were slain Aug. 16 in a police raid on a presumed guerrilla hideout in a suburb of the capital, according to the Associated Press.

Two more important Montoneros were among the guerrillas killed by the regime. Alberto Miguel Camps, chief of the Montoneros' southern command, was killed in a shootout with soldiers Sept. 7. Jose Luis Dios, propaganda director of the guerrillas' northern branch, was gunned down by troops Sept. 12.

(Camps was one of the three survivors of the 1972 Trelew massacre, in which guards at a naval prison in Chubut Province shot 19 jailed guerrillas, killing 16 of them. Camps had been released from prison in May 1973, in the general amnesty declared by former President Hector Campora.

Jews again under attack. Attacks against Argentine Jews and Jewish institutions resumed after a lull of several months. A bomb exploded Jan. 7 at a Jewish school in Buenos Aires, causing severe property damage but no casualties.

Another blast Jan. 7 severely damaged the home of Naum Kacowicz, owner of a Buenos Aires meatpacking plant, who had been kidnapped and ransomed by terrorists in 1973.

Unidentified persons stole $100,000 from the Israeli Bank of Cordoba Jan. 14. The explosion of two bombs that day destroyed a Cordoba movie theater that was showing "Victory at Entebbe," a film about the 1976 Israeli military operation that rescued 103 hostages being held by pro-Palestinian hijackers in Entebbe, Uganda.

Presumed Montoneros guerrillas fired on the home of a Chrysler Corp. executive in a suburb of Buenos Aires Oct. 13. The businessman was not there, but his guard and a neighbor were killed in the shooting.

Guerrillas were also reported to have murdered Francis Schwer, an official of the government oil company, in the capital Oct. 20. Three days later insurgents gunned down Ricardo Solar, an executive of the Lozadur crockery company, which had just dismissed more than half of its 1,300 workers in a salary dispute.

In a series of actions Oct. 26, guerrillas killed Rodolfo Matti, a retired air force officer who worked in the Buenos Aires city government; set off a bomb that wrecked the offices of Labor Minister Horacio Liendo; murdered Raul Castro Olivera, an aide in the Ministry of the Presidency, and assassinated Jose Martinez, board president of the Massalin y Celasco tobacco company. Martinez had been kidnapped sometime earlier; he was killed when police discovered the hideout where he was being held and tried to rescue him.

Finally, presumed guerrillas gunned down a naval officer and a federal policeman in a suburb of Buenos Aires Nov. 7.

The renewed attacks seemed designed to disprove the army's claim that it had put leftist guerrillas on the run. The military command in Tucaman Province said Sept. 28 that it had wiped out the column of the People's Revolutionary Army (ERP) that had been operating in the Tucuman mountains. Two days later the army chief of staff, Gen. Roberto Viola, announced that the ERP and the Montoneros no longer posed a "threat to national security."

Viola said 80% of the active leftist guerrillas had been killed or arrested since the March 1976 military coup. Of about 10,-000 guerrillas and collaborators operating at the time of the coup, only 1,200 remained alive and active, Viola said. Almost all of them were in the Buenos Aires metropolitan area, he claimed.

While Viola gave no figures on guerrilla casualties, it was estimated that 3,000 insurgents and suspected collaborators had been killed by security forces in the past year, according to the New York Times Oct. 2. Thousands more had been arrested and at least 1,000 persons had disappeared.

Auto executive assassinated—Andre Gasparoux, a top executive of the Argentine subsidiary of Puegeot S.A. of France, was killed by several gunmen as he drove to work in Buenos Aires Dec. 16. The assassins were presumed to be left-wing guerrillas.

Two bodyguards of an executive of Chrysler Corp. had been killed in a similar attack in a Buenos Aires suburb Dec. 2. The executive was not with them at the time.

Terrorist violence, economic problems vs. human rights issue. Former U.S. Ambassador to Argentina Robert C. Hill, in a speech before the Metropolitan Club in Washington summarized the problems facing Argentina's government and the efforts being made to solve them. In the following catalog of some events of 1973–77, which was printed in the Congressional Record July 1, Hill focused on the impact of terrorism, "the sustained, purposeful use of violence to secure political ends":

Among the variety of groups that emerged in the late 1960's, the largest and most destructive have been the Montoneros and the People's Revolutionary Army or ERP. Both are dominated by Marxist ideology.

During peak effectiveness in 1974–76, these two organizations ranked among the effectively trained, financed and most deadly proficient of their kind in the world.

Exact numbers are unknown, but a proportionate terrorist threat in the United States would number in the hundreds of thousands.

External aid in the form of training, financing and support came from Cuba and other communist sources.

Financing came primarily from bank robberies and kidnapping that netted tens of millions of dollars and monies from pro-Marxists abroad.

At peak efficiency in 1974–76 they executed mass attacks on military bases and arsenals killing scores of military and civilians.

Neither property nor life was secure from the onslaught. Victims included businessmen and civilians, both foreign and national; military/police officers; one former President and former Cabinet Ministers; politicians and labor leaders; two Chiefs of the Federal Police, one on his boat with his wife and another in his own bed at the hands of his teenage daughter's best friend. More recently, two attempts have been made on the life of President Videla, one inside the country's largest military garrison, and Foreign Minister Guzetti was brutally bludgeoned a few days before I left Buenos Aires.

Right-wing fanatics also contributed their share to the carnage, responding to the revolutionary left with a murderous campaign of their own.

The right-wing anti-communists operated with near impunity prior to the March 24 coup. Anyone identified with Marxist, liberal or leftist causes was considered fair game by the right.

As for the impact of terrorism on Argentine society beyond the thousands of lost lives and massive property damages, I would like to emphasize two points.

First, the tactics of the revolutionary left called for provoking a military takeover in the belief that repressive military rule would in turn ensure a popular uprising that the left could manipulate and lead into power. The ERP and the Montoneros were not solely responsible for bringing on the March 24th coup, but their violence was a contributing factor.

Second, part of the terrorists' approach to 'revolutionizing' society calls for destroying the legal, political, economic and social infrastructure that both reflects and protects the values of a society. By inhibiting the functioning and effectiveness of such institutional bulwarks as the court system, political parties, a free press, and free speech, and by making it impossible for a government to fulfill its fundamental task of guaranteeing life and property, terrorist violence tempts those exercising authority to resort to repression and brute force to maintain order. Here again, it can be argued that the terrorists succeeded in Argentina, aided as they were by the fact that the nation's institutional infrastructure was comparatively weak from the beginning and therefore vulnerable to the terrorists' challenge. It is not by accident, nor is it rhetorical excess when today Argentines in and out of government emphasize the task of restructuring domestic institutions.

Politically, the 1973-76 period once again exposed the ineptitude of civilian politics. As it turned out, the apparent emergence of a potentially productive national political consensus in 1973 was based on little more than common opposition to military government along with unfounded hopes that the civilians had finally learned their lesson. Instead, the traditional political patterns predominated. In a process that accelerated after Peron's demise in mid-1974, progressively deeper and wider rifts developed within the Peronist movement and between the Peronists and other political factions, and soon most were anticipating a military coup almost as though it was preordained.

National politics became a spectacle symbolized by the nefarious presence and mysterious influence of Social Welfare Minister Jose Lopez Rega. Cabinet positions rotated with revolving-door frequency; opposition leaders wrung their hands and issued dire public statements but seemed paralyzed; and Mrs. Peron gradually forfeited all but the smallest fraction of the public support she enjoyed upon taking office. In the end, the civilian politicans publicly defaulted their claim to leadership by refusing to constitutionally impeach an obviously incompetent chief of state. When the armed forces moved on March 24, 1976, the mourners were few and far between.

Economically, you are perhaps as familiar as anyone with the debacle wrought by the return to Peronist economics. Leaving aside the technical aspects of Peronist policies, it is sufficient to note that, as before 1950, the Peronists concentrated on the distribution rather than the production of wealth in a politically motivated effort to satisfy the demands of the dominant Peronist constituency—urban organized labor. Excessive and often capricious government controls; marked disincentives in the agricultural sector, Argentina's chief source of foreign exchange; and decreasing foreign investment due to terrorism and the rigidly nationalistic provisions of the 1973 foreign investment law were among the factors that combined to produce serious distortion in the domestic relative price structure; declining productivity in nearly all sectors; spiraling inflation; and a steadily worsening balance of payments crunch.

Moving to the post-March 1976 period, Argentina, of course, is once again ruled by armed forces. The three man junta consisting of President and Army Commander General Jorge R. Videla, Admiral Massera and Brigadier Agosti is publicly committed to restoring civilian government in Argentina, although probably not in the near future. The record of previous Argentine military governments is enough to make one dubious of success, but the Videla government has scored some notable successes to date and deserves political support and understanding at this crucial time in their history. Its energies and resources have been primarily directed at solving what were the two crucial problems on March 24, 1976—restoring a measure of economic health and controlling terrorist violence.

In the economic sphere, Argentina's remarkable recuperative powers and the capable hands of Economy Minister Jose Martinez de Hoz have produced noteworthy results. Hewing to a more free-market orientation with the emphasis upon production rather than distribution, Martinez de Hoz's policies have secured over a billion dollars in necessary foreign credits and loans, thereby avoiding debt default and advantageously restructuring the nation's debt profile; slowed, although not halted, domestic inflation; turned around a disastrous balance of payments situation; raised exchange reserves to an all time high; successfully encouraged the expansion of agricultural production; resolved most pending foreign investment disputes and established more liberal criteria for future investors; and initiated government withdrawal from a variety of enterprises taken over by previous administrations.

The battle has not been won by any means, and government officials say it may take three years before the effects of the present program can be appreciated. Two continuing soft spots that are worrisome include a disturbingly high fiscal deficit that continues to spur inflation, and the general social impact of the Martinez de Hoz approach. Labor has shouldered an inordinate share of the recovery burden to date, with wages having fallen well over 30 percent even by conservative estimates. Military government or not, organized labor is still a potent force in Argentina, and it is not clear how long labor will demur if some economic relief is not forthcoming.

As for controlling terrorist violence, the Videla government has enjoyed unquestioned success. Terrorists still bomb and kill sporadically, and it may be a long time until absolutely all terrorist activity is curbed. Nonetheless, the formidable revolutionary armies of two and three years ago are no more. With their leaders dead or outside the country; their membership rolls depleted by perhaps 85 percent; their arms factories and printing press largely destroyed, and police/military pressure relentless, the terrorists are on the run.

Unfortunately, however, this success has been purchased, in part, at the expense of human rights violations. The Junta and the security forces believe that they are engaged in a war to defend their society and way of life against Marxist subversion. They describe it as a "dirty war" in which tactics are determined by the exigencies of the battle rather than by the niceties of the law. As they view the situation, their national security, their survival as a nation, is at stake, and they are disposed to use whatever means prove necessary to win.

No one knows exactly the extent of the reprisals that have occurred, how many people have "disappeared" or been illegally detained, tortured and murdered. The State Department's report on human rights in Argentina submitted along with the executive's security assistance bill provides some information.

I have portrayed only in broadest outline the Argentina that I have known intimately over the past four years. However sketchy the portrait, I trust that it will stand as an adequate framework for some personal observations on U.S. relations with Argentina and current U.S. foreign policy.

Argentina is a nation in which the following present and potential U.S. interests are worthy of note:

It is the most advanced nuclear nation in Latin America.

Present U.S. economic interests in Argentina stand at US$1.4 billion in direct private investment and US$3 billion in loan exposure by our banks. We also run about a US$250 million annual trade surplus with Argentina.

As a potential food supplier for a hungry world, Argentina has few equals.

Some knowledgeable sources believe that Argentina's offshore oil reserves total in the tens of billions of barrels, a startling possibility despite the technical problems inherent in extraction.

Finally, we should not overlook Argentina's influence in Latin America. It will clearly not be to our advantage if Argentina and its Southern Cone neighbors who are also under human rights pressure decide to respond in concert by forming an anti-U.S. bloc.

Graiver-Montoneros Guerrilla Financing Scandal

Financiers invested guerrilla funds. A scandal broke in April when it was discovered that an Argentine financing group had invested about $17 million for the Montoneros, the left-wing Peronist guerrillas.

According to the newspaper La Nueva Provincia of Bahia Blanca, which reported the first details of the scandal April 11, government investigators had found that in 1974 the Montoneros had deposited the $17 million in Banco Comercial de la Plata, owned by Juan Graiver and managed by his son David.

The money, extorted by the guerrillas in various kidnappings, apparently was used by the Graivers to buy stores, industrial plants, real estate, part ownership of the newspaper La Opinion, and shares of a number of banks, including Century National Bank and American Bank & Trust Corp., both of New York, Banque pour l'Amerique du Sud of Belgium and Swiss-Israel Trade Bank of Switzerland. The Graivers reportedly paid the Montoneros monthly dividends ranging from $145,000 to $175,000.

The Graivers' financial empire began to fall apart after David Graiver was reported killed in the crash of a private airplane in Mexico in August 1976. Banco Comercial de la Plata subsequently failed, followed by American Bank & Trust Corp., Banque pour l'Amerique du Sud and Swiss-Israel Trade Bank.

(David Graiver's death remained something of a mystery, and there was speculation that he had not died but gone into hiding, according to press reports. The only human remains found after the crash of the plane, which carried three persons, were three hands and a torso, all charred beyond identification. However, David Graiver's wife, Lidia, identified the torso as her husband's and immediately had all the remains cremated.)

After newspapers reported the first details of the Graiver scandal, the Argentine government announced April 14 that Lidia Graiver, Juan Graiver, his son Isidoro and 12 other persons had been arrested for unspecified "economic crimes." The government added that "significant subversive activities implicating several of those [detained] are being investigated."

Other persons with direct or indirect connections to the Graivers were arrested or disappeared, according to press reports. The government's investigation reached beyond the business community to the press and officials of former governments.

Meanwhile, background information on the scandal was provided in the April 22 issue of the Latin America Political

Report. According to the Report, which quoted Argentine security sources, the military government had learned of Graiver's dealings with the Montoneros in mid-1976, when a captured guerrilla supplied the information under torture. The government brought pressure on Graiver to block the Montoneros' funds, but Graiver, who was then in New York, refused. Soon afterward, he was reported killed in the mysterious Mexican plane crash. However, before the crash he made arrangements for the guerrillas to recover control of their money, according to the Report.

The government's subsequent investigation of the Graiver case was half-hearted, the Report said, for at least two reasons. First, the Graiver family's clients included many prominent persons who were protected by the armed forces. La Opinion owner Jacobo Timerman, for instance, was protected by the army, and Peronist leaders Lorenzo Miguel and Victorio Calabro were protected by navy Adm. Emilio Massera. Secondly, President Jorge Videla and his army chief, Gen. Roberto Viola, made an arrangement under which the Graiver family would be left alone if it sold its shares in the mixed company established with the government to produce newsprint in Argentina. The shares were duly sold to a consortium made up of the newspapers Clarin, La Razon and La Nacion, the Report noted.

At this point, however, the case attracted the attention of the governor of Buenos Aires, retired Gen. Iberico Saint-Jean, a hard-line rightist who opposed the so-called "moderate" political line of Videla and Viola. (Saint-Jean was famous for having advocated the following government policy: "First we kill all the subversives; then we kill their collaborators; then . . . their sympathizers; then . . . those who remain indifferent; and finally, we kill those who are timid.")

At the end of March, Saint-Jean called together other hard-line generals, told them what he knew of the Graiver case and obtained their backing for a major investigation, the Report said. The first subject for questioning was La Opinion's Edgardo Sajon, who was kidnapped by security forces April 1 and later reported arrested. He resisted and was badly injured by his abductors, according to the report. His detention had been protested April 4 by ex-President Alejandro Lanusse, who had employed David Graiver as his undersecretary of social welfare during his presidency in 1971–73. The government assured Lanusse that Sajon's arrest had nothing to do with the Graiver case, but the newspaper La Nueva Provincia charged that both Lanusse and Sajon had been trying to stop the Graiver investigation.

Another former government official, Jose Ber Gelbard, had been implicated in the Graiver case but could not be arrested because he lived in the U.S., according to La Nueva Provincia April 11. It was Gelbard, as economy minister to the late President Juan Peron, who brought together David Graiver and the Montoneros in mid-1974, the newspaper reported. A third former official—Gustavo Caraballo, technical secretary to Peron's widow and successor, Isabel—was among those arrested for "economic crimes" April 14.

Jacobo Timerman, publisher of La Opinion, and Enrique Jara, his managing editor, also were arrested April 14. Enrique Raab, a former editor of La Opinion, was detained April 16. Jara was released April 23, but Timerman was held for trial for alleged economic crimes. He had denied that the Graivers were connected in any way with La Opinion, but sources at the newspaper later disclosed that the family held 55% ownership in the publication.

President Gen. Jorge Videla confirmed April 19 that the Graivers had handled money for the Montoneros and that formation of a military court to try the case was being studied. The army issued a report the same day claiming that the Montoneros had been "defeated" militarily and were now concentrating their efforts on infiltrating factories and other civilian sectors.

As the Graiver scandal broke, there was a wave of arrests, kidnappings and murders which might or might not have been connected with the scandal. Two newsmen and three leftist student leaders disappeared April 1, all presumably kidnapped by right-wing commandos. Hector Ferreiros, a reporter for the state news agency Telam, disappeared April 3 and was found shot to death April 5.

Robert J. Cox, editor of the English-language Buenos Aires Herald, was arrested for 24 hours April 22–23 for allegedly violating national security and subversion laws. After being released without bail,

Cox said he had been charged in connection with a report published by the Herald April 21 about a Montonero news conference in Rome. The guerrillas had announced that they were forming a new political party in Argentina.

The army announced May 4 that so far more than 100 persons had been arrested in the growing Graiver scandal, according to press reports. Among those detailed were Pedro Graiver, David's uncle, who was arrested April 23 as he tried to board a plane for Israel; Hugo Bagoada, former mayor of Cordoba, seized April 26; and Hector Timerman, vice president of the newspaper La Opinion, who was placed under "preventive detention" April 29.

The Central Bank froze the bank accounts of 30 persons connected with the Graiver case, it was reported April 26. Sixteen companies also had their accounts blocked, it was reported May 2. The Central Bank May 3 closed Graiver's Banco Comercial de la Plata and its 10 branches.

Orfila linked to scandal. Alejandro Orfila, secretary general of the Organization of American States (OAS), was linked to David Graiver by several newspapers. He denied that his association with the late financier was in any way illicit.

Rodolfo Schmidt, Orfila's former press secretary at the OAS, wrote in the Venezuelan newspaper El Nacional April 23 that Orfila had written a letter of recommendation for Graiver when Graiver opened his New York banking operations; had deposited funds in Graiver's banks, and had received a $300,000 loan from one of them. Schmidt also reported that Orfila had met with Argentine officials in Washington April 19 to discuss his dealings with Graiver.

Orfila, a former Argentine ambassador to the U.S., asserted April 25 that his association with Graiver had been entirely legal. He acknowledged receiving the loan, and said he had paid it back ahead of time. He also admitted attending the meeting in Washington April 19, but said the meeting was called to discuss human rights. It was he who had brought up the subject of Graiver at the meeting, Orfila said.

The newspaper La Prensa of Buenos Aires reported April 26 that Orfila had met with David Graiver, Jose Ber Gelbard and several other persons in the Dominican Republic in 1973 to discuss a joint financial venture with Robert Vesco, the fugitive U.S. financier. Orfila denied the story, but La Prensa stuck to it April 28. Gelbard confirmed April 29 that he had met with Orfila in Santo Domingo, but he said the meeting was called so Gelbard, then Argentina's economy minister, could offer Orfila the U.S. ambassadorship.

The OAS' Permanent Council gave Orfila a 23–0 vote of confidence April 27. The sole abstention was Venezuela, which was angry at Orfila for depositing Venezuelan funds at his personal bank, where less than the maximum interest rate was offered. The funds were for relief operations following the 1976 Guatemalan earthquake.

Gelbard and Klein die abroad. Two people involved in the Graiver case had died recently in foreign countries, the Miami Herald noted Oct. 16. Jose Gelbard, the former Argentine economy minister who allegedly introduced David Graiver to the Montoneros, died of a stroke in Washington Oct. 4. Jose Klein, a Chilean banking associate of David Graiver, died of a heart attack in Geneva Oct. 8.

Graivers, employes sentenced. Following an eight-month investigation and a secret trial, four members of the Graiver family and three of their employes were sentenced Dec. 9 by a military court in Buenos Aires.

The seven were found guilty of "illicit association" with the Montoneros guerrilla group, for which the Graiver family allegedly invested more than $17 million between 1974 and 1976.

The court handed down 15-year prison sentences to David Graiver's wife, Lidia; his brother, Isidoro, and their father, Juan. Juan's wife, Eva, received a four-year sentence, and three employes of the Graiver group were given terms ranging from four to seven and one-half years. An eighth defendant was acquitted.

The court declared that "the condemned have turned their backs on [Argentina], which is at war, and . . . knowingly aligned themselves in the ranks of the self-proclaimed 'Montoneros,' whom the nation, with a holocaust of men and materiel, is determined to annihilate, to save its traditions and way of life, which are based on freedom and human dignity."

The military communique on the court's decision did not describe the evidence on which the convictions were based. But military sources told the New York Times Dec. 10 that evidence had been obtained by questioning Jorge Rubenstein, a financial adviser to the Graivers, who died in the custody of security forces in La Plata.

Human Rights Controversy

U.S. charges violations. Argentina was charged with human rights violations in a State Department report released Jan. 1 by the U.S. House International Relations Committee and March 12 by the Senate Foreign Relations Committee's Subcommittee on Foreign Assistance.

Reports on rights violations had been a source of discord between the U.S. Congress and State Department in the past. Congress had sought the reports to determine whether to grant foreign aid, while the State Department had opposed them—at least if they were to be released publicly—on the grounds that they impeded good foreign relations without serving to improve the observance of human rights.

The reports had been requested by the House committee under the 1976 Foreign Military Assistance Act, which required State Department compliance. (In 1976, Secretary of State Henry A. Kissinger had refused to comply with an earlier law requiring such reports.

The State Department, in responding to the committee's request, had at first given the reports a classified status, barring public disclosure. The reports were declassified when the committee protested.

Although the State Department papers contained few charges that had not previously been reported, Rep. Donald M. Fraser (D, Minn.) said that they were "a lot better than I thought they'd be."

The State Department report on Argentina stated that Right-wing and left-wing terrorists had regularly violated the personal rights of life, liberty and security, the report said. Both the current military regime and the previous civilian government had "reportedly acquiesced in violations attributable to persons associated with the government." The right of habeas corpus had been suspended under the existing state of siege and "numerous persons" had been arrested under that and other laws. Argentine security forces reportedly had resorted to torture on occasion "to extract information from some prisoners, particularly suspected or proven terrorists."

The State Department said that the subject of human rights had been "raised repeatedly" in talks with Argentina in 1976. In the current fiscal year, U.S. security assistance came to $48.4 million in arms sales credits and less than $700,000 in grants for training. In urging that the support be continued, the department cited the need to demonstrate "our desire to cooperate militarily with a country which has 1,000 miles of coastline on the South Atlantic." The report also noted that the security assistance link could open the way to "improved communication with the Argentine military," which was characterized as the "dominant sector" in the nation.

U.S. cuts aid. U.S. Secretary of State Cyrus R. Vance disclosed Feb. 24 that the Carter Administration planned to reduce foreign aid to Argentina because of concern about the human rights situation there.

The disclosure was made in testimony before the Senate Appropriations Committee's subcommittee on foreign operations. Vance told the panel that relating the human rights issue to foreign assistance would be done on a country-by-country basis but was "a very difficult task." "In each case," he said, "we must balance a political concern for human rights against economic or security goals."

State Department officials gave some details of the planned aid reductions. A request to Congress for $32 million in military credits for Argentina in fiscal 1978 would be reduced to $15 million. A $48-million extension of credits for fiscal 1977 would remain unallocated.

Congress had enacted legislation in 1976 opposing military aid for countries committing "gross violations" of human rights unless there were extraordinary circumstances warranting the aid. The Ford Administration generally had interpreted the restriction as counterproductive and had favored aid programs for continued U.S. influence in such countries.

Argentina rejects U.S. aid—Reacting to Vance's testimony, the government of Argentina announced March 1 that it would refuse U.S. aid linked to observance of human rights.

Defense Minister Gen. Jose Maria Klix said his government would not use the $15 million in military sales credits that the U.S. would offer for fiscal 1978. This would leave $700,000 in military training grants as Argentina's only assistance from the U.S.

The foreign minister, Rear Adm. Cesar Guzzutti, had issued a statement Feb. 28. He asserted that "no state, regardless of its ideology or power, can take upon itself the role of an international court of justice and interfere in the internal affairs of other countries." A "qualified navy spokesman" quoted by the Buenos Aires newspaper Clarin Feb. 28 said the U.S. aid reduction was "another example of certain chronic weaknesses in the U.S. which we have had to get used to."

The controlled Argentine press also protested the U.S. move. The Buenos Aires newspaper La Opinion Feb. 25 called the aid reduction a "hostile gesture" that was "politically motivated." Clarin called for "traditional internal solidarity" to combat the U.S. action, and the English-language Buenos Aires Herald called the U.S. move "scarcely cooperative, and irrational."

Kennedy supports aid cut—U.S. Sen. Edward Kennedy (D, Mass.) charged Argentina with the "systematic violation of basic human rights" and said that it was time for "military disassociation" from Argentina. Kennedy's statement, as recorded in the Congressional Record June 15, said:

" The Argentine Commission for Human Rights has estimated that since the military coup of March 1976, 5,000 people have been killed and thousands arrested or abducted in Argentina. Last November an Amnesty International mission to Argentina compiled chapter and verse on such human rights violations, including deeply disturbing cases of official torture. I am convinced that the mission's conclusions were not exaggerated, when it stated that no one can rely on legal protection,' 'no one is safe from abduction and torture," and—

There is overwhelming evidence that many innocent citizens have been imprisoned without trial, have been tortured and have been killed. The actions taken against subversives have therefore been self-defeating; in order to restore security, an atmosphere of terror has been established; in order to counter illegal violence, legal safeguards have been removed and violent illegalities condoned.

"Just last month, the Assembly of Argentine Bishops protested "the fact that many prisoners have been subjected to tortures which are certainly unacceptable for any Christian, and which degrade not only those who suffer them but those who carry them out."

"The list of such unacceptable tortures . . . is almost endless. Amnesty International indicates that 'the para-police groups often operate in broad daylight and are never interfered with by the public authorities. They use vehicles of the same make and type as the police and military. In 1974 alone, there was strong evidence to show that these groups were responsible for over 300 murders. During 1975 and 1976 the activities of these groups increased; in the last quarter of 1976 reliable sources indicate that they were responsible for approximately 15 abductions a day.' . . .

"Nor is Argentine repression merely an "internal" matter. On the contrary, the Argentine security forces have increased their cooperation with the internal security forces of such countries as Uruguay, Paraguay and Chile in the persecution of political exiles. For example, more than a hundred Uruguayan exiles have "disappeared" in Buenos Aires, since the time when, 1 year ago, two prominent Uruguayan opposition leaders, Hector Gutierrez Ruiz and Zelmare Michelini, were assassinated in that same city. Of some, nothing more is known; others, however, are now found officially detained in Uruguay.

"A few months ago, a prominent conservative journalist of one of Uruguay's traditional parties, Enrique Rodriguez Larreta, visited the United States; his son, also a Uruguayan, disappeared in Buenos Aires on July 1, 1976. He had traveled to Argentia to take every legal recourse to find his son. On the night of July 13, when Mr. Rodriguez was visiting his daughter-in-law, a group of armed persons dressed as civilians forcibly entered the apartment, put sacks over his and his daughter-in-law's heads, and kidnapped them both. They were then taken to a private house, which held more than 100 prisoners—all of them Chileans, Uruguayans or Bolivians. At that place, all were brutally tortured and some murdered. Officials of the Uruguayan and the Argentine Army conducted these torture sessions. On July 26, they were taken by military truck to an army base in Buenos Aires, where they were transported in a Uruguayan military plane to Montevideo, where they are detained.

" In circumstances such as these, there is simply no justification for military training expenditures which include urban counterinsurgency and psychological warfare.

"It is no surprise that, in light of all these chilling reports, both the National Council of Churches and the U.S. Catholic Conference have expressed opposition to military support of the Videla regime.

"In the face of this record of systematic oppression, I believe there is no honorable alternative for the United States but to disassociate itself militarily from the Videla regime. To maintain a military relationship in these circumstances is to compromise our good name and standing, not only with the Argentine people but around the world.

"The United States should not compromise itself in this manner. Rather, it should seek potentially vaster sources of political and economic leverage—rallying countries both in the hemisphere and in the international lending institutions to require responsible behavior by the Videla regime in exchange for continued support.

" ... I welcome the reports of Secretary of State Vance's strong emphasis on human rights at the ministerial meeting of the Organization of American States in Granada, particularly his statement that—

If terrorism and violence in the name of dissent cannot be condoned, neither can violence that is officially sanctioned. Such action perverts the legal system that alone assures the survival of our tradition.

"It is precisely with these considerations in mind that I advocate termination of military assistance to Argentina, whose government figures persist in their official sanction of violence."

Sen. Church vs. military aid—U.S. Sen. Frank Church (D, Ida.) also declared his opposition to continued military aid to Argentina, singling out Argentina as one of the worst "torture chambers" in Latin America, rivaling Chile and Uruguay. Excerpts from his statement, as entered in the Congressional Record June 15:

" ... According to the State Department Report on Human Rights Practices, 'both the current and predecessor administrations [in Argentina] have evidently looked the other way with regard to violations attributable to persons associated with the government. Right-wing terrorism or counterterrorism has been carried out by vigilante squads operating with apparent impunity. Active duty and retired military and police personnel are reportedly members of such squads.'

"The individual victims of this repression who have come to my attention have been many. Earlier this year a witness of events in Argentina came to Washington to give extraordinary testimony about the present political situation in Argentina. Neither politician nor student of political affairs, the witness—a young Argentine scientist by the name of Dr. Cora Sadovsky—had no partisan ax to grind, no ideology to defend, no speeches to make. She came rather to talk in simple terms about basic human freedoms. She spoke calmly, as one might expect of a mind kept cool on a diet of mathematics, but her words were strong and disturbing.

"Dr. Sadovsky left Argentina in fear last year following the military coup d'etat. She now lives in exile in Venezuela. During her visit to America, she came to the Washington Office on Latin America to relate a shocking story of the deteriorating human rights situation in Argentina. According to Dr. Sadovsky, over 2,000 people have been victims of political murder since the coup in March 1976, and another 25,000 people have been jailed or are unaccounted for. Six hundred scientists have been banned from government work, which in the Argentine system is tantamount to complete expulsion from scientific research. Astonishingly, 26 of Dr. Sadovsky's personal friends—not acquaintances, but close friends—were murdered in the past year. Few had expressed any political views publicly, let alone joined political movements.

"This tragic story from Argentina lies closer to Washington than the thousands of miles between our countries would suggest, for in plain truth the military equipment used to suppress the citizens of Argentina comes directly from our military assistance programs. One elderly

Argentine scientist, who was educated in the United States and who—like so many of his countrymen—once looked upon us as a shining beacon for the free world, recently had a letter smuggled out of Argentina to Dr. Sadovsky in Venezuela. "The Americans are killing us," he wrote in anguish to her, referring to the weapons we have placed in the hands of the Argentine regime.

"Yesterday a young woman, Patricia Ann Erb, visited my office, accompanied by Mr. Delton Franz, Washington representative of the Mennonite Central Committee. She spoke movingly of the terrible torture she had personally experienced at the hands of the Armed Forces of Argentina. According to her testimony, she witnessed various forms of torture: beating with clubs, fists, kicking, immersing in water or fecal material almost to the drowning point, and applying electrical prongs to sensitive parts of the body. Rape of the prisoners was commonplace in the compound where she was kept.

"Ms. Erb is an American citizen from Pennsylvania. So, too, is Gwenda Lopez of Minnesota, who was arrested in 1976 for distributing political literature. She was interrogated and brutally tortured. Olga Talamante of California experienced comparable treatment and has returned to bear witness of the widespread repression in Argentina.

"And the terrible list goes on. The conclusion is clear: Torture has replaced the constitution and the law in Argentina as a means for providing order. "

A.I. human rights report. U.S. Rep. Robert Drinan (D, Mass.) had visited Argentina Nov. 6–15, 1976 as part of an official Amnesty International delegation investigating the human rights conditions in that country. Drinan summarized the delegation's findings in a statement recorded in the Congressional Record May 23. He said:

" · · · The delegates conducting the investigation for Amnesty International were Lord Avebury, a member of the British House of Lords and of the Human Rights Parliamentary Commission, Ms. Patricia Feeney of the International Secretariat of Amnesty International, and myself. Throughout our stay in Argentina, from November 5 to 16, the mission was subject to intense surveillance by the internal security forces. At least 20 plainclothes police followed us wherever we went, and they questioned and intimidated a number of people

whom we met. One young woman, without any suspicious political affiliations, disappeared immediately after meeting with me and was released 24 hours later, without explanation, by the police. Another woman was held by the police for 2 weeks following a discussion with one of the members of the Amnesty International delegation.

"As is common practice in Argentina, the families of the two women arrested after meeting with us were not informed of their detention. The Amnesty International report estimates that more than 15,000 individuals have disappeared or been abducted in Argentina in the past 2½ years. The situation has manifestly grown worse since the coup; we were able to determine that the Argentine Government receives an average of 10 requests for writs of habeas corpus per day. In August 1976, at the Ministry of the Interior, a register was opened in which the names of missing persons could be entered by their relatives. The daily limit for the receipt of such complaints was set by the government at 40. The maximum figure was attained routinely.

"The refusal of the Argentine Government to release a list of political prisoners constitutes a particularly outrageous and cruel violation of human rights. We met with many Argentine families whose relatives had been kidnaped, presumably with the complicity of the police or armed forces. These abductions typically take place in the middle of the night, and the abductors usually appeared to be off-duty police or military forces. The families of those so abducted—we met with more than 100 of them—are left completely in the dark as to the physical well-being and whereabouts of their relatives. Even among nations which are universally recognized as violators of human rights, the failure of the Argentine military junta to release the names of those arrested and imprisoned without charge or trial is a singularly outrageous action. Our report contains as one of its principal findings a recommendation that the government compile and release a list of those imprisoned for political reasons.

"Frequently, relatives and friends of suspected 'leftists' have also been kidnaped. A typical case which was described to us involved the family of a well-known political figure who had left Argentina and subsequently criticized the military regime from abroad. His wife and two children were abducted by men claiming to be the federal police. None of these individuals had any political associations whatsoever. His daughter, who was in poor health, was released from a federal prison after 10 days; the other two are still missing, more than 6 months after their abduction.

"Our mission was able to compile, for the first time, a comprehensive list of those disappearances which have occurred since the March 24, 1976, coup. This list includes all the cases which Amnesty International has been able to corroborate, and it omits the names of all those who have been released, found dead, or acknowledged to be held in official custody. A total of 480 individuals appear on this list of Argentines who have been abducted and whose whereabouts is not known.

"Based upon direct contacts with individuals in Argentina and testimony by people who have emigrated from that nation and Uruguay, our report was able to conclude that Argentine and Uruguayan internal security forces acted in concert to abduct from Argentina and transport to Uruguay at least 17 refugees. These people left Uruguay when a military dictatorship assumed power there. Direct testimony indicates that these refugees were abducted by agents of the Uruguayan security forces. The scale of these kidnapings inevitably implies the cooperation of at least some members of the Argentine armed forces and police. This action by the Argentine Government constitutes a direct breach of the Treaty on International Penal Law and the Convention on Extradition, to which it is a signatory.

"The military junta has suspended virtually all civil rights and individual liberties. As the report states in detail, the Argentine Government has prohibited all political activity, suspended parliament, imposed strict censorship, authorized arrest and indefinite detention without charge or trial, established military tribunals for all crimes pertaining to 'subversion,' permitted widespread torture of political prisoners, and engaged in abductions of its citizens. The report concludes:"

[M]erely on suspicion of subversion, a citizen may be abducted or arrested, held for a long period *incommunicado,* tortured and perhaps even put to death. He has no legal safeguards against these measures, and, if it happens that he is released, no hope of legal redress.

"During our discussions with officials of the Argentine Government, including the Under Secretary of Foreign Affairs, the Under Secretary of Justice, and an official at the Ministry of the Interior who is in charge of internal security, we received no assurances of any forthcoming reduction in the 'state of siege' measures abridging fundamental human rights. Thtey gave us no indication of a limit on the duration of the state of siege or of the military government which implements it. The draconian policies of the junta were ostensibly adopted to counteract left-wing terrorism. But government officials admit that left-wing violence has been greatly reduced; indeed, violence perpetrated by the security forces far exceeds that of the terrorists. In its efforts to combat left-wing terrorists, the government has itself established a far broader and more pervasive form of terrorism. As we state in our report:

The actions taken against terrorists have therefore been self-defeating: in order to restore security, an atmosphere of terror has been established; in order to counter illegal violence, legal safeguards have been removed and violent illegalities condoned.

"The extreme human rights violations of the Argentine military government bring into sharp focus the complex question of the proper United States and multilateral response to systematic abuses of this nature. Efforts such as that of Amnesty International to bring human rights violations to the attention of the world are certainly useful. As our report recommends, greater investigatory activity by the United Nations in the area of human rights is necessary. The decision of the Carter administration to drastically reduce military assistance to Argentina resulted, as we know, in the announcement by the Argentine Government that it no longer desired U.S. security assistance. In the light of similar pronouncements by other Latin American nations, including Brazil, Guatemala, and El Salvador, some have questioned the Carter administration's decisions. These questions ignore the central fact that U.S. law prohibits the provision of military assistance to any nation which engages in the systematic violation of the human rights of its citizens. This provision of the law, section 502(b) of the Foreign Assistance Act, is mandatory, not discretionary, in nature. It reflects not a tactical judgment, but a moral commitment. We must cease providing military equipment to nations such as Argentina not only in the hope that this will influence them to alter their human rights policies, but also because it is fundamentally wrong for the United States to arm a government which turns its arms against its citizens to deprive them of their fundamental rights.

"The question is, what more can we do? President Carter and Secretary Vance are to be commended for their forthright actions on the issue of human rights. The experiences of the Amnesty International delegates in Argentina and the report which we prepared bring home the essential point that the international debate on human rights involves the lives of thousands of people. The increasing violations of human rights in the Western Hemisphere and the demonstrated utility of the Helsinki Agreement in Europe suggest that the United States should take the lead in enforcing existing agreements among the nations of the Western Hemisphere pertaining to human rights. We should also endeavor, within the framework of the Organization of American States or in a separate international forum, to reach an intra-hemisphere agreement on the inviolability of certain basic human rights. Perhaps such an agreement could be accompanied, as is the Helsinki Final Act, by guarantees of increased economic co-operation, conditioned upon observance of human rights guarantees. Recent experience suggests that the United States is far more effective in appealing for the observance of fundamental human rights when we can speak in the context of multilateral agreements. This removes to some degree the stigma of the 'meddling outsider,' and provides us with a legal as well as a moral basis for our position.

"There are no easy solutions to the problem of systematic human rights violations such as those occurring in Argentina. By speaking out forcefully and consistently, we risk the temporary loss of influence in certain nations. But by failing to speak out, we risk the permanent betrayal of our most cherished principles. Our human rights policy must always concern itself with the question, 'What is most effective?' But we must not permit that concern to obscure the even more important question, 'What is right?'"

The concluding section of the November 1976 AI report was published in the Congressional Record June 15. It said:

In view of the current turmoil in Argentina, a report concerned with human rights must conclude by asking two basic questions. First, to what extent are human rights respected and defended by the government and to what extent are they violated? Secondly, to what extent are the violations explicable or necessary? On both of these questions, the assertions of the government are not supported by the facts available to Amnesty International.

After the coup in March 1976, General Videla stated that the military government had come to power 'not to trample on liberty but to consolidate it, not to twist justice but to impose it'. But legislation passed since the coup has progressively eroded the individual's liberty and numerous members of the security forces have trampled on that which remains. Justice has been perverted twice—by the imposition of laws which contravene the Constitution, and by the reluctance of the security forces to acknowledge any laws at all.

The state of martial law which is currently in force deprives all the citizens in Argentina of the most fundamental civil and political right, their constitutional guarantees. What it means in practice is that merely on suspicion of subversion, a citizen may be arrested or abducted, held for a long period incommunicado, tortured and perhaps even put to death. He has no legal safeguards against these measures, and, if it happens that he is released, no hope of legal redress.

Fundamental constitutional guarantees have been suspended since the coup, including the important Right of Option, which is now—unconstitutionally—at the discretion of the Executive Power. Military tribunals have been set up for all crimes pertaining to subversion; sweeping powers of arrest and detention have been conferred on the police. Furthermore, many of the decrees of the military junta free the police and the armed forces from any legal liability in the event of persons innocent of any subversive involvement or intention being detained, injured or killed.

The official suspension and unofficial neglect of fundamental legal rights has had alarming results. Since the coup, the number of political prisoners has increased—and more than three-quarters of these persons are detained at the disposal of the Executive Power: they have never been charged, have never been tried, and may be held indefinitely. Although, according to the Constitution, such prisoners are not supposed to be punished, they are held in punitive conditions. There is evidence that many have been maltreated during transfers and that the majority of them have been tortured as a matter of routine. Frequently, torture has been inflicted on people who have not been officially arrested but merely unofficially abducted. The number of abductions has increased since the coup. Friends and relatives find it all but impossible to ascertain the whereabouts of disappeared persons, though in many cases they eventually discover that the disappeared person is dead.

The neglect of human rights in Argentina is all the more alarming in that it has no foreseeable end. According to provisions in the Constitution, the State of Siege may be declared only for a specified period of time; but no limit has ever been fixed by the present or the previous government. The citizens of Argentina therefore face an indefinite period without constitutional guarantees; prisoners in preventive detention face indefinite incarceration. There is no limit to the duration of the military government, no limit to the period a prisoner may be held incommunicado and no limit to the time that may elapse before he is brought to trial.

The current legislation in Argentina, together with the latitude allowed to various security forces, has then quite definitely led to gross violations of basic human rights. According to the government, the draconian legislation has been necessary to 'restore full legal and social order'¹ and to implement the required program of 'national reorganization'². A government official explained to the Amnesty International delegation:

"Systematic subversion and terrorism have cost the lives of many police and military and have compromised the security of the Argentine people. These activities have been repudiated by all citizens. If anybody violates human rights in Argentina, murdering, torturing and bombing, it is undoubtedly the terrorists. These people use violence for its own sake or to create chaos and destruction. We understand that the state has a right to defend itself, using whatever force is necessary."

It is true that any impartial observer must condemn the outrages committed by left-wing extremist groups: they have detonated bombs in barracks and police stations, have kidnapped and assassinated members of the military and business executives. However, it does not seem to Amnesty International that terrorist violence may be held to justify the extreme, and extensive, measures taken since the coup by the government. Firstly, it is doubtful whether these measures are in fact entirely defensive, no more than what is necessary to contain guerrilla violence. The military itself admits that this violence has been greatly reduced*—yet abductions, torture and executions apparently committed by the security forces continue unabated. In 1976, left-wing extremists were allegedly responsible for some 400–500 deaths; the security forces and parapolice groups for over 1,000. Secondly, even if these measures were justifiable as a counter-response to extremist provocation, the undeniable fact would remain that they also strike at innocent citizens. Given the present legislation, no one can rely on legal protection, and in view of the practice of the security forces, no one is safe from abduction and torture. Amnesty International believes there is overwhelming evidence that many innocent citizens have been imprisoned without trial, have been tortured and have been killed. The actions taken against subversives have therefore been self-defeating: in order to restore security, an atmosphere of terror has been established; in order to counter illegal violence, legal safeguards have been removed and violent illegalities condoned.

---

*Speech of General Menendez in Famailla in the Province of Tucuman to celebrate the "Day of the Flag" (20 June 1976): "Subversion is generally in retreat and on the way to collapse."

Rights abuses & anti-Semitism charged.

Lawyers who represented the Argentine Commisssion for Human Rights told the United Nations Human Rights Commission in Geneva Feb. 21 that Argentine terrorism was "centralized in the hands of the military government." Argentines of all classes were victims of the terror, but the chief targets were Latin Americans who lived in exile in Argentina because of political persecution at home, the lawyers reported. They said that in the 11 months since Gen. Videla seized power, 2,300 persons had been killed, 10,000 had been jailed for political reasons and 20,000–30,000 persons had "disappeared," many of them certainly murdered.

Despite the lawyers' testimony, the U.N. Human Rights Commission voted not to pursue a formal investigation of human rights abuse in Argentina, it was reported March 4. Eastern European countries and Cuba, with which Argentina had maintained good relations, joined with Third World countries to vote down the proposed inquiry.

The Financial Times (London) reported March 3 that the Argentine government currently held 2,000–5,000 political prisoners, according to various estimates. The newspaper cited continuing reports of torture by security officers, with methods including beatings, rape, burning with lit cigarette ends and submersion in water.

The French magazine Le Nouvel Observateur charged Feb. 26 that the Argentine government was persecuting intellectuals in an effort to "kill everyone who thinks." In an article titled, "The Argentina of the Long Knives," the magazine said: "Men of science, students, union leaders and priests are victims of [this] repression which, in a country that has the fourth largest Jewish community in the world, can only be applied with a strong dose of anti-Semitism." The magazine cited several scientists who had been kidnapped or tortured, and it noted that the Argentine Mathematics Institute, "one of the most advanced in the world," had been closed on charges of being "a stronghold of subversion."

Foreign reports of Argentine rights abuse, coupled with moral and economic pressure from the U.S., appeared to put the military government on the defensive and to increase calls within Argentina for the release of political prisoners. Following the Carter Administration's decision in February to cut military aid to Argentina, more than 70 writs of habeas corpus were filed in Buenos Aires on behalf of persons who had disappeared and were presumed arrested, it was reported March 2. Argentines previously had not filed the writs in fear that they too might be arrested, according to press reports.

The government responded to the U.S pressure by rejecting all U.S. military aid, denying that Argentine human rights were being violated and even denying that there were any political prisoners in Argentina. President Videla asserted March 15 that he and his military colleagues were "fervent partisans of freedom" who would "restore constitutional guarantees . . . as soon as general conditions allow it."

In apparent response to foreign reports of widespread anti-Semitism in Argentina, the government March 3 closed down the publishing house Odal, the illegal successor to the banned pro-Nazi publisher Milicia. Among Odal's publications were the anti-Semitic tract "Protocols of the Elders of Zion" and the political testament of Adolf Hitler, "Mein Kampf."

Later in 1977, the English-language Buenos Aires Herald criticized four army generals for attending the June banquet of Cabildo, an anti-Semitic magazine whose most recent issue had been confiscated by the government for promoting "ethnic conflict." Herald columnist James Nielson wrote that any army officer "who swims in [Cabildo's] filthy rivulet of political and social thought has nothing to contribute to the construction of a genuinely democratic, tolerant, pluralist Argentina." In response, two of the generals challenged Nielson to a duel. He replied in his column July 6 that dueling by arms was illegal but that he would gladly meet the generals "with boxing gloves, Marquis of Queensberry rules." The fisticuffs never took place.

Although the confrontation between Nielson and the generals was comical, the government took the anti-Semitism debate seriously and worried about Argentina's image abroad, according to the New York Times July 7. No one called the regime anti-Semitic, but there was criticism of the regime's inability or unwillingness to end present harassment of Jews by rightist commandos and by security officers investigating left-wing subversive activities.

Jacobo Kovadloff, head of the Buenos Aires office of the American Jewish Committee, had emigrated from Argentina to the U.S. June 28 after he and his family received repeated anonymous threats with anti-Semitic overtones. The office was closed permanently July 8.

Kidnappings & arrests worry Jews. The disappearance and arrest of several Jews was worrying Argentina's large Jewish community, already disturbed by attacks on Jewish businesses and by the proliferation of anti-Semitic and Nazi literature in the major cities, according to press reports.

Jewish businessman Alejandro Deutsch, his wife and three daughters were kidnapped by armed men in Cordoba Aug. 27. The army revealed Sept. 6 that they had been arrested on suspicion of associating with leftist guerrillas. Two other Jews, Daniel and Monica Clujo, were kidnapped Sept. 11. Jewish leaders in Buenos Aires said between 30 and 50 Jews had disappeared in this fashion in 1977, according to the Miami Herald Sept. 13.

Jewish leaders also were concerned over the imprisonment without trial of Jacobo Timerman, former publisher of the prestigious newspaper La Opinion. The government announced Nov. 10 that Timerman had been stripped of his civil rights and of control over his private assets, and that he would be held in jail indefinitely.

Timerman was arrested in April because of his association with David Graiver, the Jewish financier who allegedly had invested money for Montoneros guerrillas between 1974 and 1976. A military tribunal had acquitted Timerman of involvement in subversive activities, but government sources later said he was being held for propagating "bad ideas" in La Opinion, according to the Washington Post Nov. 12.

Disappearances & deaths. Numerous disappearances, kidnappings and deaths continued to be reported in Argentina throughout 1977, and there were repeated accusations that security officers were frequently responsible.

The body of Aparicio Garcia Peralta, a Buenos Aires laborer who was kidnapped Jan. 9, was found floating in a river in the city Jan. 13. Garcia was presumed killed by right-wing commandos.

Beatriz and Enrique Prestes, children of the journalist Carlos Alberto Prestes, were kidnapped in Buenos Aires Jan. 11, hours after security officers had called at their home in search of their father. Ricardo Gilabert, a writer for the Buenos Aires newspaper La Opinion, had disappeared Jan. 9.

Diego Muniz Barreto, a former federal deputy who had belonged to the left-wing Peronist Youth, was kidnapped along with his secretary in Buenos Aires Feb. 16, according to the Buenos Aires Herald Feb. 25. Alicia Eguren, widow of the Peronist leader John William Cook, and Ernesto Margarinos, a member of the print workers' union, also were reported kidnapped Feb. 25.

Two magazine publishers were kidnapped March 1 and released unharmed March 7. Oscar Blotta, publisher of the satirical magazine The Western Mouse, and Mario Mactas, publisher of the erotic publication Emanuelle, were abducted after the government banned Emanuelle "to safeguard the people's moral health."

Six lawyers and a judicial employe, most of them Peronists, were abducted in Mar del Plata July 6–7. One of the Peronists, labor lawyer Norberto Centeno, was found beaten to death outside the resort city July 12. Two others were freed unharmed by their captors, and a third lawyer was rescued by police.

Lawyers probe disappearances—Eight attorneys in Buenos Aires April 11 asked the Supreme Court to investigate the disappearance of 425 persons who, the lawyers said, had been kidnapped by "armed groups acting under some official authority." The attorneys, who included Raul Alfonsin, a leader of the Radical Civic Union, represented 12 persons, including the wife of Oscar Smith, the labor union leader who had disappeared in February.

The lawyers asked for court orders requiring the police, the Justice Ministry and the Interior Ministry to turn over all information in their files concerning the 425 vanished persons. Habeas corpus petitions filed earlier on these persons' behalf had been returned by the police and the two ministries, which said the individuals were not and had never been in custody.

The government publicly denied holding any prisoners without charge, but officials privately admitted that there were many uncharged detainees, including persons whose connections to subversives were peripheral at worst, the Washington Post reported April 14.

(One well-known uncharged prisoner, former Sen. Hipolito Solari Yrigoyen, was sent into exile May 1. Solari, a leader of the Radical Civic Union, had been held in a Patagonian prison for eight months, and apparently was released at the behest of the Venezuelan government. Mario Abel Amaya, another Radical leader imprisoned with Solari, had died in jail after being denied medication he had claimed to need.)

A majority of Argentina's Roman Catholic bishops issued a document May 7 expressing "serious concern" over widespread reports of arbitrary arrests, torture, kidnappings, disappearances and assassinations in Argentina. The bishops condemned "Marxist subversion" but, in a departure from their usually unquestioning support of the military government, they asserted that "no theory of collective security, notwithstanding the importance of collective security, can be allowed to destroy the rights of persons."

Several journalists also disappeared and were presumed kidnapped. Ignacio Ikonikof, a prominent scientific writer, and his wife, Maria Bedoya, who edited a labor union magazine, disappeared June 25. Rafael Perrota, former owner of the newspaper El Cronista Comercial, and Lila Pastoriza de Jozami, an editor of the weekly Siete Dias and the daily Noticias, were reported kidnapped July 15. Juan Nazar, who published a newspaper in the town of Trenque Lauquen (Buenos Aires Province), was reported kidnapped July 21.

Lawyers filed writs of habeas corpus for these and others who had disappeared on the assumption that their clients had been seized by security forces. Judges then made inquiries with prison authorities or the police, almost invariably receiving negative replies. No further action was possible because the emergency laws invoked by the military government forbade judges to investigate the actions of security forces. Many persons who disappeared eventually turned up murdered, while others vanished without a trace.

Perez Esquivel held. The Permanent Assembly for Human Rights asked the government June 20 to explain why it had arrested the assembly's president, Adolfo Perez Esquivel. Perez had been detained April 4, apparently on charges of subversion. The assembly, composed of prominent Argentine religious leaders, politicians and intellectuals, pointed out that Perez had denounced "the violence perpetrated by terrorists of both the right and the left."

U.S. visitors see rights improvement. A number of U.S. government officials visited Argentina in August to examine the country's human rights situation. Those who commented on their findings said the situation appeared to have improved in recent months.

First came two officials of the Carter Administration, Patricia Derian and Terence Todman. Derian, the State Department's human rights coordinator, was in Buenos Aires Aug. 7-10 conferring with President Jorge Videla, officials of the Foreign Ministry and relatives of persons who had disappeared or had been abused by security forces. Todman, assistant secretary of state for inter-American affairs, visited the capital Aug. 13-16 and spoke with Videla, other officials and leaders of political parties and labor unions.

After meeting with Videla Aug. 15, Todman said the military government seemed to be "overcoming the abnormal conditions" that characterized the ousted Peronist regime. "Everyone I talked with believes there has been an important improvement in all areas," including human rights, Todman declared.

(Argentine authorities arrested more than 100 persons who demonstrated in front of the Government House as Todman arrived to meet Videla. The protesters, mostly women, demanded information on relatives who had disappeared recently and were believed arrested or kidnapped.)

The political leaders Todman saw included representatives of the two largest parties, the Peronists and the Radicals. They reportedly told the U.S. envoy they wanted the government to allow open political and union activity, but not necessarily immediate elections.

Eight members of the U.S. House of Representatives visited Buenos Aires Aug. 18-20 to assess local support for the new Panama Canal treaty and to examine the Argentine rights situation in the wake of Congress' decision to deny military aid to Argentina as of October 1978. The congressmen were treated cordially and given guided tours of Buenos Aires, in contrast with the treatment accorded one of their colleagues, Rep. Robert Drinan (D, Mass.), when he visited the city in 1976 as a member of an Amnesty International investigative team. Drinan was followed and some of his Argentine contacts were arrested and interrogated.

A member of the visiting congressional group, Rep. Gus Yatron (D, Pa.), Aug. 20 said the Argentine government was moving "toward a more stable and open society." Another visitor, Rep. Eligio De La Garza (D, Tex.), said: "I expected to see tanks in the street. I expected oppressed people without civil rights, but I have found something completely different. I wish each member of Congress could come here and see the truth."

Following the congressmen's departure, two U.S. senators arrived in Buenos Aires for a brief visit. One of them, Sen. Ernest Hollings (D, S.C.), declared that Argentina had a "free government" and that the Carter Administration had done "too much moralizing" on the human rights issue, it was reported Aug. 30. The senator accompanying Hollings was William Scott (R, Va.).

The cordial treatment given the U.S. visitors underlined Argentina's desire for a more benign international image following several years of reports of torture, illegal arrests and covert executions by the Peronist government and the military regime that replaced it. In a complementary move, the government pledged Aug. 26 to investigate fully the disappearance of several thousand persons since the armed forces took power in March 1976.

Disappearances increase. Despite the reports that the human rights situation in Argentina was improving, unexplained disappearances were increasing, according to press reports.

Persons who suddenly vanished were presumed to have been arrested by security forces or kidnapped by right-wing commandos that operated with virtual impunity. Many of those who disappeared later were found murdered, some of them horribly mutilated. Two mutilated bodies were found in Cordoba Aug. 26.

The most prominent person to disappear recently was Rodolfo Fernandez Pondal, who vanished from Buenos Aires Aug. 5. Fernandez Pondal was co-owner and deputy director of Ultima Clave, a prestigious political newsletter whose July 26 issue had denounced the kidnapping of the Argentine ambassador to Venezuela. The government told relatives of Fernandez Pondal that it would do its best to locate him.

Luis Gustavo Loiseau, a well-known cartoonist who used the pen name 'Caloi,' disappeared Aug. 8 along with his wife and an associate. They, too, were presumed kidnapped by right-wing commandos.

A number of kidnap victims were rescued by soldiers Aug. 3 from a Buenos Aires detention and torture house operated by extreme rightist military officers, according to the Latin America Political Report Aug. 26. The soldiers were looking for the son of Nehemias Resnizky, a prominent Jewish leader, who had been kidnapped July 28. Resnizky had appealed to a top aide of President Videla to save his son, and the aide had agreed as long as Resnizky did not publicize the abduction, the Political Report said. The house where young Resnizky and the others were found was decorated with Nazi insignia and portraits of Adolf Hitler, Benito Mussolini and Francisco Franco, according to the Political Report.

While most of those kidnapped were Jews, presumed leftists or presumed opponents of the government, some were security officers. An army lieutenant was kidnapped in Buenos Aires Aug. 20 and found dead the next day, a presumed victim of the left-wing Montoneros guerrilla group.

Two other prominent persons who had disappeared in Argentina were Alfredo Bravo, a union leader and human rights activist, and Oscar Serrat, a reporter for the Buenos Aires bureau of the Associated Press.

Bravo, secretary of the national teachers' union, vanished Sept. 8. After repeated inquiries by the Permanent Association for Human Rights—a Buenos Aires-based organization to which he belonged—the government admitted Sept. 20 that Bravo had been arrested and was being held "at the disposal of executive power." This meant that he was imprisoned at Videla's discretion, without access to the courts.

(Government sources estimated that 4,-000 persons were being held in Argentina under these circumstances, according to the Washington Post Sept. 22. Their names generally were not released, and thus their relatives had no idea where they were.)

Serrat was kidnapped on his way to work Nov. 10 and was released the next day. He said his abductors blindfolded him, took him to a place he thought was an army base, and questioned him about the internal operations of the Associated Press, the communiques it had received from guerrilla groups, and Serrat's relationship with Rodolfo Walsh, an Argentine newsman who was kidnapped in March and was widely presumed to have been murdered.

The French consulate in Buenos Aires disclosed Dec. 13 that a French nun had been kidnapped from her home in the capital Dec. 8 and another French nun had been abducted Dec. 10. Press reports speculated again that the abductors were security officers, but the French news agency Agence France-Presse said Dec. 17 that it had received a communique in which the Montoneros guerrilla group claimed responsibility for the kidnappings.

Pressure on Videla—The wives and mothers of many missing persons gathered in front of the Government House once a week to discuss their relatives' disappearances and to demand an audience with President Jorge Videla. About 350 women attended the Oct. 14 demonstration; police dispersed them and briefly detained 150 persons, including Argentine and foreign reporters who had attempted to interview some of the demonstrators.

It was unclear how much control Videla had over the soldiers and policemen who were presumed to have kidnapped and/or killed most of the missing persons. There was speculation in some press reports that the abductions were being ordered by extreme right-wing military officers to embarrass Videla, who was trying to project an image of moderation.

On a visit to Washington to sign the Panama Canal treaties, Videla had told the press Sept. 9 that right-wing terrorism in Argentine was an outgrowth of the government's "dirty war" against leftist guerrillas. "We understand but do not justify the spontaneous actions of groups that, perhaps with very good intentions, want to do what they think the government is not doing," Videla said. However, he added, such actions were "difficult to control from the highest strata" of the government.

Videla was reported to have told President Carter during his visit that he would do his best to wipe out right-wing terrorism in Argentina, according to the Financial Times (London) Sept. 12.

(Videla's government was under considerable U.S. pressure to improve its human rights record. Congress had barred military aid to Argentina as of 1978, and Carter personally had encouraged a leader of the Argentine Radical Party in his opposition to the government, according to the Latin America Political Report Sept. 2. The Radical leader, Hipolito Solari Yrigoyen, had told U.S. State Department officials in June that Videla was not in any sense a "moderate," the Political Report said. Solari told the American officials that when he was "kidnapped" in Argentina in 1976, he was held and tortured in an army barracks in Bahia Blanca. Army officers told him that they were members of the Argentine Anti-Communist Alliance, the right-wing assassination squad that had put a bomb in Solari's car in 1974, Solari said.)

Meanwhile, President Videla told foreign newsmen that his government soon would publish a list of persons who had been arrested since the armed forces seized power in March 1976, it was reported Dec. 10.

Videla said he could not give a list of persons who had disappeared, although he said they were not necessarily dead. He speculated that they might have vanished for a variety of reasons, including a desire for anonymity after they gave up subversive activities. The president conceded, however, that "some might have disappeared as a result of repression."

Videla said there were no political prisoners in Argentina, only about 4,000 "subversive criminals." He "denied absolutely" that there were concentration camps in Argentina, as had been reported in the European press.

Finally, the president claimed that his government's "struggle against subversive terror" was "reaching its end." He acknowledged that "excesses might have occurred" during the army's campaign against the left, but he said these had not been "authorized, condoned or encouraged" by his government.

The Videla government announced later that it would free 432 political prisoners in a holiday amnesty, it was reported Dec. 26. No prominent detainees were among them, however. The Interior Ministry said 3,607 prisoners were being held under the state of siege imposed in March 1976.

A U.S. research organization said there were actually 18,000 political prisoners in Argentina, however. The Washington-based Council on Hemispheric Affairs issued a report Dec. 22 saying Argentina was the "most flagrant violator" of human rights in Latin America.

Rights activists kidnapped—Between 15 and 25 human rights activists were kidnapped in Buenos Aires Dec. 8 by persons who were presumed to be plainclothed security officers, according to several press reports.

The mass abduction took place outside a church where the activists had been meeting to raise money to pay for a newspaper advertisement that would list some 800 persons who had disappeared recently in Argentina. Human rights organizations in Buenos Aires estimated that more than 2,000 persons had disappeared in 1977 and more than 20,000 in the last five years.

Those kidnapped outside the church included members of the human rights organizations and relatives of persons who had disappeared previously, according to the Buenos Aires Herald Dec. 10.

Vance visits Argentina. U.S. Secretary of State Cyrus Vance visited Argentina Nov. 20–21 to confer with Argentine leaders on the human rights issue and atomic energy.

Vance arrived in Buenos Aires late Nov. 20. He met the next day with Foreign Minister Oscar Montes and the three members of Argentina's military junta—Lt. Gen. Jorge Videla, the president and army commander; Adm. Emilio Massera, the navy chief, and Lt. Gen. Orlando Agosti, the air force commander.

Vance and the Argentine leaders discused the human rights issue "at length," according to a State Department spokesman. One of Vance's aides asked the Argentine government for information on 7,500 persons who were listed as imprisoned or missing by human rights organizations in Argentina and the U.S. Vance and his assistants also met with local human rights activists, relatives of missing persons and representatives of Buenos Aires' Jewish community. Jews felt threatened by evidence of anti-Semitism in Argentina's security forces and by the imprisonment without trial of a prominent Jewish newspaper publisher.

Arrest procedures & prison conditions. The following testimony by Dr. Maximo Victoria, a former member of the Argentine Atomic Energy Commission, was entered by U.S. Rep. Gerry E. Studds (D, Mass.) in the Congressional Record June 1:

I'm a physicist, doing research in physical metallurgy. I have worked for the Argentine Atomic Energy Commission (CNEA) since 1962. Since August 1973 I was a member (Director and then Vice-President) of the National Institute of Industrial Technology (INTI), on a leave of absence from the CNEA position.

After the military coup of the 24th of March 1976 I was asked to resign from my post at INTI, by the military authorities that had taken over that institution, when I returned to CNEA, I was asked to present myself at the Personnel Office. There I was told by the Personnel Manager, a Navy Captain, that I was under arrest. No reason was given to me for my detention.

At gunpoint I was taken back to the entrance hall of CNEA. I was then placed in a police car. About three blocks from the CNEA building the car went into a side road. I was then gagged, blindfolded and a hood was put over my head. Always at gunpoint, I was told to lie on the floor of the police car. I was then driven to what I suppose was the port of Buenos Aires, taken to a cabin in a navy boat, where I stayed for the next fourteen days, completely isolated. The whole procedure was very violent, being constantly beaten with fists and guns.

In the boat, I was constantly harassed by my guardians, who came to knock and

kick the cabin door at all times of the day, while shouting that I was next in line to be shoot or thrown into the sea. At no time I was allowed to see the faces of my custodians, since I had to face a wall each time the door was open or put a hood over my head when I had to go out of the cabin to use the toilet.

On April the 13th, I was given back my shoes, gagged and blindfolded once more and binded hands in my back, with one cord that tied my wrists and neck with self-adjusting knobs. With this procedure, I started to suffocate after a short period since even the smallest movement produced a tightening of the rope. I probably fainted. Sometime afterwards, I was told that I 'had survived for another day' and untied. The next day I went through the same procedure, but this time I was taken out of the cabin, placed in the floor of some sort of wagon and driven to another boat.

Here the treatment was even more rough, and I was not allowed to take off the hood and blindfold at any time. I was firmly chained to one of the bedposts in such a way that I had to remain rigidly in a seated position. I was interrogated a number of times by different persons, on my political and religious beliefs, and on my connections with several people many of them fellow scientists.

It was on this boat, on hearing the names of other prisoners being called, that I realized that other nine members of the CNEA were at the same place under detention. No food or water was given to us.

After one or two days, we were taken to Devoto Prison. I found out later from my family, that during this whole period we had been technically "kidnapped", since they couldn't obtain any information on my whereabouts or even if I was still alive, from the moment I was taken from the CNEA building on April 1st.

2. THE CONDITIONS AT DEVOTO PRISON

In Devoto we were all placed under arrest at the disposal of the Executive (PEN). In this condition a person can remain in jail for an indefinite period of time, even without any accusation being brought against him. Up to the military coup, an individual under PEN, had the constitutional right to leave the country into exile, but this right was 'suspended' by the military junta. In a number of cases I met in Devoto, people were placed under PEN after they had been discharged by normal judicial procedures.

Political prisoners are placed into Devoto in the 'high security ward'. This is a five floor building, totally occupied by political prisoners, from 100 to 120 people per floor. This means an average of five prisoners to a cell of about 2 by 3 meters, including a sector for the W.C. on the floor. They are not only very crowded quarters, but also very poor sanitary conditions. The food is extremely poor, with almost no proteins, meat, milk or cheese are seldom provided or hot at all. It was only in the last two months in Devoto that we were allowed to buy powder milk from the prison store.

Medical attention is almost nonexistent. When one is finally able to reach a prison physician, one is usually "checked" through the cell bars and given an aspirin. A number of fellow prisoners that had underwent torture still had ulcers from burns or electric shock. One of them had a deep wound in one foot as a result of a bullet. The resulting infection went on for months. The medical attention they received came mainly from three medical doctors who were imprisoned in the same floor.

The whole treatment of political prisoners is a violent and terrorizing one. We were subjected to constant body inspections or sent to solitary confinement on the least of excuses. These are isolation cells of 1 by 2 meters, where a mattress is provided at night and taken at six in the morning.

At one point, we were locked in our cells for 45 days, without any communication with the outside world. All visits, even from lawyers, were prohibited. No mail came in or went out. No reason was given for this procedure.

3. THE TRANSFER TO SIERRA CHICA PRISON

On the 6th of September about fifty political prisoners, Dr. Santiago Morazzo and myself among them, were taken from their cells at about 6:00 a.m., We were introduced into a large locutory, requisitioned and all our personal belongings taken out from us. We were transported to the military airport at Palomar, with a guard of four armored vehicles and a tank. At about nine o'clock. The beatings with both, sticks and guns started as we were introduced in a military transport plane, where we sat with our heads between our knees. About ten guards from the Federal Prison System continued to beat us, walk over our backs, while we were forced to shout "long live the military"! "long live, general Vilas", etc. After a 45 minute flight we arrived at an airport somewhere near Sierra Chica. The beating continued while we went down, the guards having been joined by army people with dogs and while we were transported to prison. Once in here, we were striped naked for a "medical check up" and forced through a double file of guards that beat with sticks.

The beating continued while we tried to pick up our personal belongings. One at the time and nude we were made to run the distance to the cell pavilion, about a hundred meters from the main building. The floor was covered with small sharp stones and it was probably here that two toes of my right foot were broken. We were waited at the pavilion by about fifteen· guards, and the beatings continued while we were taken to our cells. A few minutes afterwards, one by one, we were violently taken from our cells to the back of the pavilion and asked, among a shower of blows to pick our clothing, given an ice cold shower and brought back to our cells. It was about 5:00 p.m.

In the process, I had not only two broken toes, but also my front teeth beaten out and my back was covered with sores. Dr. Morazzo, whom I was to see somedays later had two broken ribs. The whole contingent were in

similar or worse conditions. No medical attention was provided. Two days afterwards we were asked to sign a paper saying that the wounds had been self inflicted or we would not be allowed visitors.

This sort of procedure during transfers of prisoners became standard, and I was a witness to reception of three other contingents.

4. CONDITIONS AT SIERRA CHICA PRISON

The conditions of political prisoners at Sierra Chica are even worse than at Devoto. We were initially placed in isolation, one prisoner to a cell. Because of the increasing number of prisoners, we were finally put two to a cell (I would calculated between 1000 y 1200 political prisoners are detained at Sierra Chica).

Prisoners are only allowed to go out of their cells into one of the prison yards only for half hour, three times a week. They are not allowed to lie down during the day and they can only sit in the metal frame of the beds. They are allowed to buy one newspaper, but books are prohibited. Sierra Chica is one of the oldest prisons in the country and the conditions of the buildings show their age. Every cell has leaks some of them have no running water.

The conditions I have described are not the exception but the rule, I have met entire families in prison that were detained because the agents of repression did not find someone whom they were looking for and instead took everyone in the house, after pillaging all belongings of value.

I have also witnessed the results of torture in those that survived it. In Sierra Chica at least two fellow prisoners were psychologically disturbed as a .result of torture. Another one had lost the use of one arm because of electrical shocks. No medical attention was given to them.

I was released on the 11th of October, 1976, from Sierra Chica. During the whole detention period I was not officially accused nor told the reasons for my detention. The same is true for the rest of the members of CNEA that were in prison with me.

Having been told that both, the security of my family and my own life were in danger. I left Argentina on October 11, 1976.

Extradition of Nazi ordered. The Argentine government announced July 4 that it had provisionally accepted a request from a West German court to extradite an Argentine resident to Hamburg to face charges of massacring Jews in World War II.

Eduard Roschmann, a former Nazi SS officer living in Argentina under the name Federico Wegener, was accused of being responsible for the extermination of 40,-000 Jews in Riga, Latvia, where he was in charge of the Jewish ghetto from 1941 to 1944.

The Argentine government normally did not accept extradition requests for former Nazis, but in this case there apparently was a reciprocal agreement under which the West German government would extradite Argentine leftist guerrillas living in West Germany, the Miami Herald reported July 22.

In any case, the extradition proceedings had only begun, and several steps would have to be completed before Roschmann could even be arrested in Argentina. The West German Embassy in Buenos Aires was unhappy over the slowness of the process, believing it gave Roschmann plenty of time to escape. No one in fact knew where he was.

A Paraguayan newspaper, ABC-Color, reported Aug. 11 that a man believed to be Roschmann had died of a heart attack in an Asuncion hospital. Interpol, the international police agency, confirmed that the dead man was Roschmann, ABC-Color reported Aug. 13.

Government & Politics

Regime sees 'dialogue' with civilians. The military government said several times in June that it would begin a "dialogue" with civilian political leaders to reach an agreement on how Argentina would be returned to constitutional democracy.

President Gen. Jorge Videla June 18 said the armed forces would give civilian leaders concrete proposals for the agreement. The next day, the weekly bulletin of the army commander said "democracy is the appropriate path" for Argentina to take in achieving "a mature, integrated and united society."

The proposed dialogue was denounced June 14 by the Buenos Aires newspaper La Prensa, which noted that Videla planned to consult political leaders without lifting the suspension of political parties. This was like trying "to make rabbit stew without the rabbit," the newspaper said.

The proposed dialogue also was discounted by the Latin America Political Report, which observed June 17 that while the government was predicting consultations with political leaders, the Interior Ministry was considering prosecuting

leaders of the Radical Civic Union who had signed a document calling for the restoration of democracy and the end of political repression.

The army currently was divided between "hard-line" and "moderate" officers, with Videla reported among the latter. In general terms, the hard-liners supported continued military rule and the economic predominance of the agrarian export sector; the moderates favored a gradual return to democracy and increased emphasis on the manufacturing industry, according to the Latin America Political Report June 3.

A hard-line officer, Gen. Acdel Vilas, was jailed for 30 days May 27–June 26 after newspapers published an open letter in which he said the casualties suffered by the army in its fight against leftist guerrillas "will not be the price of a new political compromise." Vilas, who had headed the army's successful anti-guerrilla drive in Tucuman Province, criticized the army command for retiring him when the drive ended. "Sometimes, when . . . risk and victory are rewarded like this, the beauty of obedience loses its meaning," Vilas wrote.

Radicals cleared of political charge. A federal judge in Buenos Aires July 2 dismissed charges against 50 members of the Radical Civic Union (UCR) for allegedly violating the 1976 law that suspended organized political activity.

The military government had filed the charges after the Radicals, including party president Ricardo Balbin, issued a document calling for an end to political repression and a return to democracy. But the judge ruled that the document was purely "polemical" and did not constitute a resumption of party activity.

The ruling barely interrupted the running feud between the armed forces and the Radicals, which cast considerable doubt on the government's avowed plan to restore democracy through a "dialogue" with Argentina's civilian leaders.

Taking direct aim at Balbin and his top party aides, the army recommended July 3 that all "civic organizations" replace their current leaders with members of "the next generation." The current leaders had "exhausted their cycles through long years in their functions," the army said. The election of new leaders, it asserted, would constitute "a valid reply to the process of national reorganization" proposed by President Lt. Gen. Jorge Videla.

The Radical party organ, Adelante, replied July 18 that political parties could not choose new leaders without meeting to do so, and political meetings, as the army well knew, were against the law.

The conflict was soon aggravated by the interior minister, Gen. Albano Harguindeguy, who said Argentines might as well forget about political parties for a while. The parties had "had their chance," Harguindeguy said, but had been "incapable of halting the country's march toward chaos." Replying July 24, Radical leader Raul Alfonsin noted that Argentina had been ruled mostly by military governments over the past 40 years, and he asserted that the armed forces bore "a share of the blame" along with the parties. Harguindeguy's statement, Alfonsin noted, clearly contradicted Videla's call for consultations between the armed forces and the political parties.

This forced Videla into the fray, but he did little to clarify matters. The president said Aug. 6 that his government would consult everyone except "subversives," "corrupt persons" and those who did not share "the objectives of the process [toward] a true democracy." He did not say who might be considered subversive or corrupt, or what the precise "objectives of the process" were.

Lanusse, former aides seized. Former President Alejandro Lanusse and three former members of his administration were arrested May 4 in connection with an investigation of an aluminum contract signed by Lanusse's government in 1971.

Detained along with Lanusse were his former defense minister, Gen. Jose Rafael Caceres Monie; his former air force commander, Brig. Carlos Alberto Rey, and his former navy chief, Adm. Pedro Alberto Gnavi.

The arrests were ordered by Federal Judge Eduardo Marquardt, who was investigating the 1971 contract for construction of the Puerto Madryn smelter of Aluminios Argentinos (Aluar). The contract, which included a five-year tax exemption and other controversial clauses, had been investigated without results by a congressional committee in 1975. It was unclear why the new probe had been undertaken.

Several newspapers linked the arrests to the growing scandal involving the Graiver financing group and the Montoneros guerrillas. Marquardt had asked authorities investigating the Graiver case to let him see any evidence they found linking the Graiver family to Aluar, the London Times reported May 5. Other sources noted that the group that built the aluminum smelter had been headed by Jose Ber Gelbard, the former Argentine economy minister who had been linked to the Graivers.

(Newspapers also noted that Lanusse was disliked by hard-line military officers who would not forgive him for allowing the Peronists to return to power in 1973. Lanusse had been arrested in 1976 for denouncing the arrests of several university professors.

Lanusse refused to testify before Judge Marquardt and asked that a military court be formed to try any corruption cases related to his administration, it was reported May 5. Lanusse's detained colleagues did testify for the judge, however. After his refusal Lanusse was transferred from the Buenos Aires civil jail to a military base outside the city. His home was raided by authorities looking for evidence in the Aluar case, according to United Press International May 5.

A federal appeals court in Buenos Aires June 13 revoked the preventive detention of Lanusse and his former aides. However, the appeals court said the investigation would continue.

President Gen. Jorge Videla had left Lanusse's case in the hands of the courts in defiance of hard-line generals who wanted assurances that Lanusse would stay in jail. The decision to release the former president helped to restore confidence in the independence of the Argentine federal judiciary, according to the New York Times June 22.

The Economy & Labor

Prices up 125% in '77. The cost of living in Argentina rose 125% in 1977, but the rise was well below the 1976 rate of 347.5%, according to a report Nov. 17.

The Videla regime had managed to reduce inflation by freezing wages and placing controls on price increases.

The policy pleased the financial sector, according to Inter Press Service Aug. 3, but it did little for the Argentine working class, which suffered from the continuing decline in real (inflation-adjusted) wages. Studies by an independent Argentine research institute indicated the purchasing power of real wages had fallen 57% over the past year, according to the Latin America Economic Report July 15.

Rents and the prices of bread, gasoline and public transportation had increased sharply between the beginning of March and the beginning of July despite a government-decreed "truce" on price rises. (The cost of beef, virtually a staple of the Argentine diet, had risen 128% in December and January, it was reported March 2.) Rents were up 95%, bread 23%, gasoline 88% and public transport 23%. The government lifted the "truce" July 7 and substituted regulations allowing private companies to raise prices by as much as 80% of state-decreed devaluations of the Argentine peso. (The peso was being devalued about 5% monthly, according to the Wall Street Journal July 8.) Larger increases required special government permission. In the first specially approved price rises, the government July 29 announced increases of 10% for gasoline, 50% for railway fares, 36% for buses and taxis and 20% for subways.

While the working classes were suffering, sectors of the middle classes were enjoying sharply increased purchasing power, according to the Latin America Economic Report July 22. Private construction activity was up 4% in the first quarter of 1977. Retail sales rose 17% in April and 4%-5% in May, and sales of consumer durables, such as cars and appliances, were up 113% in April.

The industrial sector continued to be depressed, with activity down 1.2% in the first quarter and 1.6% in the second. But there was a major boom in agriculture that eased the impact of the industrial decline with a 40% increase in tractor production in the first half of the year. Overall, the economy grew 1.2% in the first quarter and 1.5% in the second, after recording a negative growth rate in 1976.

These figures convinced the government its economic strategy was paying off, according to the Latin America Economic Report July 22. But the continuing decline in the purchasing power of the working classes was hurting major manufacturers,

the newsletter noted. In order to prevent organized expressions of discontent among the manufacturers, the government recently had dissolved their organizations—the General Economic Confederation, the General Commerce Federation, the General Industrial Federation and the Production Federation—and confiscated their assets.

Argentine wages had increased by only 153.9% in 1976, while prices rose by 347.5%, according to government figures reported by the London newsletter Latin America Jan. 14.

The real value of Argentine wages had fallen by 31% during the second half of 1976, according to the Latin America Economic Report Jan. 14. The 20% wage increase granted by the government Jan. 1, 1977 must be set against a cost of living increase of more than 55% in June–December 1976, offset only by a 12% wage increase declared Sept. 1, 1976, according to the Report.

Unions score government policies. Over 100 union leaders Jan. 6 called on the military government to change its economic policies or risk unleashing a "class struggle," Reuters reported. The labor leaders accused the regime of instituting the sort of free-enterprise system that led to starvation wages and massive unemployment. "Salaries which literally fail to feed a married couple with two children of school age are a generalized and dramatic phenomenon," the leaders charged.

Officials warned Jan. 7 that the regime would take over all labor unions in reprisal for criticism of its policies. The largest union, the 2.9-million-member Peronist General Labor Confederation, had been taken over after the March 1976 military coup, but some 30 independent unions, representing 50,000 workers, had continued to operate freely.

Subsequently, the opposition labor unions called off a national meeting they had scheduled for Jan. 12 to protest the government's economic policies. The government had warned unofficially that it would take sanctions against the unions if they met.

Workers protest labor law. Workers in greater Buenos Aires staged slowdowns and other protests in January, February and early March as the government began implementing Law 21,476, which regulated conditions of work in the state sector.

Under the law, disclosed Jan. 21, the workweek would be extended from 36 to 42 hours; thousands of workers would be laid off; trade union officials would cease to be paid for their union work and to participate in the management of their plants, and overtime pay and other benefits would be cut.

To minimize opposition, the government chose to implement the law gradually, beginning Feb. 1 with the three Buenos Aires power companies—Electric Services of Greater Buenos Aires (SEGBA), the Italo-Argentine Electricity Co. (CIAE) and Water and Energy (AYE). However, power workers began protesting the law before it was put into effect.

About 30,000 workers Jan. 24 began a work-to-rule slowdown, called "work of sadness." Two days later some 5,000 workers staged a march in Buenos Aires to protest the new law, and the government threatened reprisals against the protesters. When the new workweek was put into effect Feb. 1, power workers refused to work more than the previously normal 36 hours. The government threatened Feb. 3 to cut the workers' pay, and security officers raided the offices of the Light and Power Union in Mar del Plata, reportedly arresting 20 persons including several union leaders.

State railway workers began a slowdown of their own Feb. 5 as the government laid off 1,000 employes in the first step of a plan to lay off 10,000–20,000 railway workers. About 425 employes were laid off at the Agriculture Ministry, and there were reports that the government had begun implementing a plan to lay off 13,000 of the 48,000 workers at the state oil company, YPF.

Representatives of the Labor Ministry and the power workers reached an agreement to end the slowdown Feb. 11.

Ex-union official kidnapped—The power union settlement was marred by the kidnapping that same day of Oscar Smith, former secretary general of the Light & Power Union. Power workers throughout Buenos Aires struck for 14 hours Feb. 14 to protest the abduction.

Smith, a moderate Peronist, reportedly had been a key figure in the unofficial negotiations that settled the power workers' slowdown. In the talks, the Labor Ministry had agreed to continue negotiations on overtime pay and work timetables, to maintain the old timetable for caretakers and power-station workers, and to give a 16.5% increase in basic pay retroactive to Feb. 1, the London newsletter Latin America reported Feb. 25.

Smith was abducted as he drove his car in southern Buenos Aires. According to bystanders quoted in a local newspaper, the car was intercepted by civilians driving three Ford Falcons—the cars normally used by plainclothes policemen belonging to the Argentine Anti-Communist Alliance and other right-wing assassination squads. Most observers quoted in press reports felt that Smith had been seized by extreme rightists who wanted to scuttle any arrangement between moderate military leaders and the labor unions. Some observers suspected the navy, whose hard-line leaders were reported to be at odds with President Jorge Videla, army chief of staff Gen. Roberto Viola and other reputedly moderate officers, the newsletter Latin America reported Feb. 25.

The abduction caused fear and anger among the moderate labor leaders who had been cooperating with the Labor Ministry, according to the New York Times Feb. 21. Labor sources released a communique March 2 announcing that a 20-member secret steering committee had been formed to lead the labor movement. The railway, postal, banking, telephone and power unions were among those represented on the steering committee.

Workweek increased, government spending cut—The workweek was increased Feb. 25 for employes of the state telephone company ENTEL, and many employes were forced to work split shifts. Fifty ENTEL employes were fired for refusing to work the new hours, and another 8,000 were suspended for two days, according to reports March 4. Representatives of the telephone workers' union said a wage increase awarded along with the new hours was insufficient.

Meanwhile, the government had resolved to make drastic cuts in spending plans of all state industries to hold the 1977 budget deficit to 3% of the Gross Domestic Product (GDP). Argentina's GDP had decreased by 2.9% in 1976, chiefly because of a 4.7% decline in manufacturing and a 14.1% decrease in construction, according to the Associated Press Feb. 23.

The provisions of Law 21,476 reversed many of the gains made by workers in recent years, particularly under the Peronist governments of 1973-76. Real wages were reported to be at their lowest level in 30 years, having fallen by 60% in the past year.

Strikers demand pay increases. A series of strikes swept Argentina in October and early November as workers demanded more than double the wage increase allowed by the government.

The strike movement began in Cordoba Oct. 11 when about 5,000 workers at the Renault auto plant struck for higher pay. The government put down the stoppage Oct. 14 when it sent troops to surround the plant and dismissed an estimated 180 strikers from their jobs.

Another job action was reported Oct. 21 at the Lozadur ceramics company, where about 800 workers went on a slowdown to obtain wage increases. The company ended that movement by firing the 800 workers.

The strikes picked up Oct. 26 when railway workers walked out in the southern town of General Roca, cutting off rail service to Buenos Aires. In the next two days strikes were begun by railway workers on the Buenos Aires commuter line, the Buenos Aires subways and the line connecting the capital with northeastern Argentina. The strikers demanded wage increases of between 80% and 130%, well above the government's limit of 40%.

Intercity railway workers began returning to their jobs Nov. 2 after the government granted them pay increases averaging 34%. But subway workers and signalmen on other railways continued to strike, and bank workers began a stoppage of their own.

Troops occupied the subways Nov. 2 in a futile attempt to end the strike there. The next day a man was killed by soldiers who caught him discouraging railway workers from returning to their jobs. The subway and other railway strikes finally were suspended Nov. 4 when the government announced that it had begun sending telegrams of dismissal to striking workers.

Other strikes soon began, however. On Nov. 10 stoppages were reported at a Buenos Aires textile company employing 3,000 persons; among stevedores in the port of Buenos Aires; at the Argentine Credit Bank; at the Argentine Meat Corp. in Rosario, and among transport workers in Mendoza. All of the strikers demanded large wage increases.

The strikes were a clear response to the government's restrictive economic policies and to Argentina's inflation rate, which, at 125% for the first 10 months of 1977, was the highest in the world, according to a report Nov. 17.

Most of the strikers were state employes, who suffered more from inflation than private-sector workers. The government strictly enforced its 40% ceiling on wage increases, but private industrialists had found ways to get around it. As a result, wages in the private sector were considerably higher than in state companies, according to the Latin America Economic Report Nov. 11.

Because of chronic inflation, the real value of Argentine wages had fallen from a base of 100 in 1960 to 50 in September 1977, according to the Economic Report. In the state sector, real wages were reported to be about $50 a month for workers who joined the recent strike movement.

The government could do little for its workers, however, since most state companies were overstaffed and bankrupt, and the railways lost $700,000 a day. The government's long-term strategy was to force workers into the private sector, according to the London Times Nov. 10.

The continuing rise in the cost of living was provoking criticism of Economy Minister Jose Martinez de Hoz not only from workers but from members of the government, according to press reports. Martinez' policies had been opposed by Gen. Horacio Liendo, the labor minister, and by Adm. Emilio Massera, the navy commander and member of the military junta, according to the Miami Herald Nov. 6. Massera and other navy officers felt the economy minister had not done enough to curb inflation, increase the public's buying power and reduce the state's role in the economy.

The trade minister, Alberto Fraguio, had resigned to protest Martinez' policy of cutting tariff barriers to make Argentine industry internationally competitive, it was reported Oct. 21. Others who had denounced Martinez' trade policies included representatives of the engineering, textile and leather industries, which together accounted for more than 30% of

Argentina's exports, according to the Latin America Economic Report.

Record trade surplus. Argentina was having its biggest trade surplus in a decade, according to the Economc Report Dec. 2. Exports for the January–September period were worth $4.4 billion, while imports totaled $2.9 billion. The large surplus was due mainly to record exports from the 1976/77 wheat harvest.

Argentina had recorded a trade surplus of $883.6 million in 1976, following a $985-million deficit in 1975. The trade turn-around was accomplished without a significant rise in unemployment, which was holding at around 4%, the Journal of Commerce reported July 25.

Foreign investment law ineffective. Argentina's 1976 foreign investment law, designed to attract foreign investors by letting them send their profits home, had not borne fruit because the government had not decreed companion laws, regulations and resolutions to detail how the new philosophy would be carried out, the Wall Street Journal reported July 25. The Economy Ministry blamed the delays on "technical considerations."

IMF approves large loan. Expressing its support for Argentina's economic policies, the International Monetary Fund announced Sept. 19 that it would allow the Argentine government to purchase 159.5 million special drawing rights over the following 12 months. The authorization was equivalent to a credit line of $137 million.

In a similar development, the World Bank approved a $200-million loan to the Argentine national investment bank, it was reported Nov. 10. The loan was co-financed by Bank of America, Lloyds Bank International and other international lenders.

Foreign Affairs

Videla's visit to Peru protested. President Gen. Jorge Videla visited Lima March 3–6. The Peruvian government took extraordinary security precautions for him, lodging him in the presidential palace (not the Argentine Embassy) and rounding up Argentine exiles who presumably opposed Videla's government. Videla held extensive talks with Gen. Morales Bermudez, with whom he exchanged national decorations—the Peruvian Order of the Sun for Videla and the Argentine Order of the Liberator San Martin for Morales.

Videla's visit was protested by major Peruvian labor and political groups, which denounced the widespread abuse of human rights in Argentina. A document condemning Videla for allegedly persecuting labor leaders and instituting an economic "policy of hunger" was issued March 3 by the pro-Communist General Confederation of Peruvian Workers, the pro-government Workers' Union of the Peruvian Revolution, the Christian Democratic National Workers' Confederation, the right-wing Single Union of Education Workers, the Christian Labor Movement and the Peruvian Peasants Confederation, among other groups.

The National Federation of Peruvian Bar Associations issued a statement demanding respect for human rights in Argentina. The Revolutionary Socialist Party, headed by exiled army generals, condemned repression in Argentina, and the Roman Catholic National Office of Social Information (ONIS) denounced the Argentine government for allegedly imprisoning, torturing and murdering its opponents.

Despite the protests, both the Peruvian and Argentine governments expressed satisfaction with the results of Videla's visit. Peruvian Foreign Minister Jose de la Puente noted March 8 that the topics covered by the two presidents included a nuclear reactor deal and trade relations. Videla and his Peruvian counterpart, Gen. Francisco Morales Bermudez, signed an agreement to increase trade between Argentina and Peru and to promote Latin American economic integration. The two leaders, de la Puente said, had shown "a high degree of mutual respect."

Peruvian A-plant accord signed—Peru and Argentina signed an agreement March 5 under which a research nuclear reactor would be built in Peru using Argentine technology and equipment.

The nuclear project, reportedly budgeted at $50 million, involved not only the experimental reactor—a 10-megawatt unit capable of producing radio-isotopes for medical and industrial uses—but the training of Peruvian scientists in all peaceful uses of nuclear technology. The project exemplified Argentina's promotion of regional cooperation in the use of atomic energy.

(Argentina led Latin America in nuclear technology, with one 300-megawatt nuclear power station in operation and a 600-megawatt station under construction. Since the 1950s the Argentine Atomic Energy Commission had trained several hundred nuclear scientists and engineers, the most advanced group in Latin America. The U.S. and other countries worried that Argentina, which had large reserves of uranium ore, would use its technology to build atomic bombs.)

Argentina to sign nonproliferation treaty.
U.S. Secretary of State Cyrus Vance, on a tour of Latin America, noted that the Argentine government had agreed Nov. 21 to sign the Treaty of Tlatelolco, which banned atomic weapons in Latin America and the Caribbean.

The signing would facilitate the transfer of U.S. and Canadian technology to Argentina's atomic power industry. Washington and Ottawa had banned such technology earlier in 1977 for countries that would not sign the Nuclear Nonproliferation Treaty or, in Latin America's case, the Tlatelolco pact. Among other things, Argentina needed U.S. and Canadian assistance in building a heavy water plant to extend its nuclear power program.

East European fishing boats seized. The Argentine navy detained seven Soviet and two Bulgarian fishing vessels Sept. 21–Oct. 1 for allegedly fishing within Argentina's 200-mile jurisdictional limits in the South Atlantic.

Argentine cruisers seized four Soviet trawlers Sept. 21, another Soviet ship Sept. 28 and two Soviet and two Bulgarian vessels Oct. 1. An Argentine ship fired on the Bulgarian trawlers when they resisted capture; both vessels were damaged and a Bulgarian sailor was wounded. In addition, three Argentine petty officers trying to board a Bulgarian trawler drowned when their boarding vessel capsized in a storm.

The captured ships were towed into Puerto Madryn on the Argentine coast, where their crews were arrested and their catches confiscated. It was not known when they would be released or how much the ships' captains would be fined for allegedly violating Argentine fishing laws.

The Soviet Union protested the seizure of the first four boats Sept. 23, but Argentina replied that Moscow was well aware of Argentina's jurisdictional limits and its fishing rules. After the other three Soviet vessels were seized, the Soviet newspaper Izvestia denied Oct. 8 that any of the ships had violated Argentine waters. The newspaper charged that the Argentine navy had refused to give Moscow position fixes on the area where the vessels had been captured.

The Argentine attack on the Bulgarian vessels was reckless by international maritime standards, according to the London Times Nov. 4. It was extremely rare for a naval cruiser to fire on a defenseless fishing trawler, even if it ignored warning shots. However, the shelling was ordered by Argentina's naval commander, Adm. Emilio Massera, who allegedly said "the defense of [Argentina's] sovereignty is at stake."

Argentina was reported to have been overly sensitive to questions of territorial jurisdiction since April, when a British arbitration court settled a territorial quarrel between Argentina and Chile in Chile's favor. The dispute involved three small islands at the end of the Beagle Channel at the southern tip of South America, over which both countries claimed sovereignty. Since then, Chile had been claiming jurisdictional rights to a 200-mile zone in the Atlantic hitherto controlled by Argentina, the London Times noted.

One of the seven Soviet fishing vessels, the Soviet trawler *Nerey,* was allowed to sail home Nov. 9 after its cargo was confiscated.

Falkland negotiations to continue.
Representatives of Great Britain, Argentina and the Falkland (Malvinas) Islands met in New York for three days of talks on the islands' future, it was reported Dec. 18. The Falklands were a British territory over which Argentina claimed sovereignty. Argentine and Falklands representatives called the talks satisfactory and said they would resume in 1978.

Earthquake

Quake hits Argentina, toll nears 100. A strong earthquake Nov. 23 in Argentina's San Juan Province claimed 80 to 100 lives, injured 300 persons and left at least 10,000 homeless. The tremor was originally reported to measure 7 on the open-ended Richter scale but was recorded at 8.2 by Sweden's National Seismological Institute. The higher reading made it the strongest quake on record for the year.

The earthquake was centered 800 miles northwest of Buenos Aires in the Andean foothills near the town of Caucete, where 80% of the mostly adobe dwellings collapsed. Caucete was 18 miles east of San Juan City, the provincial capital, which was devastated by an earthquake in 1944 and subsequently rebuilt to resist seismic movement.

Six other agricultural communities in the area suffered extensive damage. The early-morning shock rattled buildings in Buenos Aires, causing many of the capital's eight million residents to panic and flee to the streets. Tremors registered in parts of several neighboring countries at localities up to 1,250 miles from the epicenter.

Bolivia

Human Rights Violations

U.S. envoy on tour. Terence Todman, U.S. assistant secretary of state for inter-American affairs, visited four South American countries May 8–17 in what was described in the press as a lightning "get-acquainted" tour.

U.S. missionaries in Bolivia May 14 gave Todman a detailed report on alleged violations of civil liberties by the government of Gen. Hugo Banzer Suarez. The report charged that the government had arrested 120–150 persons for political reasons, denying them due process; had closed down all labor unions; had deported 58 journalists "for political and labor-union motives," and had taken over a number of radio stations, including one belonging to the Roman Catholic Church.

The missionaries said in their report to Todman:

DEAR SIR: We who have read the State Department Report on Human Rights in Bolivia officially presented to the Congress and presumably prepared by the U.S. Consulate in Bolivia. As U.S. citizens (the majority of us with many years experience in Bolivia), we believe that the report as it stands gives a false impression of the human right situation in Bolivia. Many vague and misleading points need clarifying; other erroneous statements need correction; and finally, a number of significant facts need to be added, because they are simply omitted from the report. What follow is a topical commentary on the report, prepared in common by the group in the hope of offering to President Carter and the Congress a truer and more accurate picture of the situation of human rights in Bolivia.

(2.1.1) All union elections have been officially proscribed since the promulgation of the November, 1974, decrees, even in the least politicized unions where elections are carried out with full assurance of freedom and democracy.

(2.1.2) Despite this prohibition, the Government was not able to prevent the powerful Miners' Federation from holding democratic elections on local and national levels. However, as a result of the elimination of this Federation, it has not been possible since May of 1976 to hold any union elections whatever, whether they be labor or professional unions.

(2.1.3.) The Bolivian Workers' Central (C.O.B.), which is the central organization uniting the particular unions and federations, has been proscribed by the Government since August of 1971.

(2.1.4.) All federations have been shut down since November, 1974.

(2.1.5.) All the present union leaders (called coordinators), both on the national and regional level, have been named directly by the Government.

(2.1.6.) Those labor leaders who were democratically elected by the workers have been disauthorized by the Government.

(2.1.7.) All the officials of the Bolivian Workers' Central and the majority of the officials of the different national federations are actively persecuted and sought by the Government, or have already been exiled from the country.

(2.1.8.) The strikes which the report simply says "do occur", are carried out at great personal risk to the workers, who must suffer severe reprisals by the Government. As a result of the miners' strike in 1976, fifty-three union leaders were sent into exile to Chile.

where they remained confined in small and inhospitable villages in the South, and were subjected to strict police vigilance. As a result of both the miners' strike and the Manaco Shoe Factory strike in Cochabamba, also in 1976, a large number of workers were arrested, or threatened with exile and with being fired with loss of all their social benefits, in conformity with the November decrees.

(2.1.9.) At present there is not one labor union which functions. Workers prepresentation is exercised exclusively by the coordinators, in every case named directly by the Government through the Labor Ministry.

2.2. Economic situation of the Bolivian workers.—

(2.2.1.) Workers' salaries have been frozen since November 1972. But the cost of living has continued to rise, at moderate but constant rates. In 1976, the economy suffered a rate of 15% rate of inflation. The work "bonuses" granted by the Government have not been able to keep pace with this increase (cf. No. 3 below).

2.2.2.) The modest economic development which Bolivia is experiencing favors almost exclusively business sectors and the military and state bureaucracy, and not the workers or peasants.

(2.2.3.) Despite a 6.3% increase in the G.N.P. in 1976 a recent study published by the Catholic Church has shown that the real salaries of workers are 25% lower than six years ago. (cf. "Boletin de la Conferencia de Religiosos de Bolivia", No. 23).

2.3 Legal situation of the Country.—

(2.3.1.) The legislature has not been operative in Bolivia in the past ten years.

(2.3.2.) The Government of President Banzer formally recognizes the Constitution of 1967; nevertheless, in fact the Government has practically annulled the Constitution with its decree of 1972 stating that the provisions of the Constitution remain in effect only insofar as they are "not opposed to the present Government statute, to the dispositions of an institutional character and to the Decree-Laws which this Government adopts in the interests of the country."

(2.3.3.) Besides the latter decree, the Law of State Security is still in effect.

(2.3.4.) In Bolivia, the judiciary branch has traditionally been subordinated to the executive. At the prest time, this subordination of the judicial power is more strict and ironclad than ever before.

(2.3.5.) Since 1973, no "habeas corpus" has been heard by the courts.

(2.3.6.) Prior to that date, all the "habeas corpus" that were heard by the Banzer Government were declared null.

(2.3.7.) Not one political prisoner has been granted due process in the last two years.

(2.3.8.) The legal system suffers not only from the defect of "justice delayed" but also from the aberration of the presumption of guilt without trial. Furthermore, the Bolivian jail system includes many places of confinement for which there is no legal provision—illegal prisons where there are no visits by officials of the court, no legal controls, no checks against abuses of discipline,

and where prison life, punishments, torture, etc., are subject to the arbitrary determination of the director. Such is the case, for example, in the prisons for political prisoners in Chonchocoro, and Achocalla, outside of La Paza, as well as the "granjas," prisons for common criminals in Caranavi and Santa Cruz.

(2.3.9.) At present, the Bolivian Government sentences many political opponents to confinement, not only carcelary but territorial as well. Many political prisoners, once they are released from jail, still are obliged to present themselves to the security forces daily or weekly. The least suspicion is cause for their being arrested again.

(2.3.11.) In Bolivia, terrorism by leftist groups does not exist as a political tactic. With but few exceptions, persons are imprisoned or persecuted exclusively because of their opinions or because of non-violent political and labor activities.

2.4 Situation of political prisoners—

(2.4.1.) There are many prisoners who have been in jail for more than one year with no possibility of initiating a legal process; e.g. Nila Heredia, Antonio Peredo, Jorge Sologuren and Marcos Farfan.

(2.4.2.) The vast majority of political prisoners, after spending a lengthy period of time in jail with no trial, are expelled from the country. Those who avoid exile and succeed in staying in the country, are subjected to permanent vigilance by the security forces.

(2.4.3.) Although there are no accurate figures on the subject, it is estimated that since the Banzer Government took power, more than six thousand Bolivians have been exiled and can not return to Bolivia. They represent all the diverse social classes and walks of life: miners, professionals, university students, factory workers, professors and teachers, Indian peasants, political leaders, priests and nuns, etc.

(2.4.4.) The raiding of private homes without judicial permission or warrant is very common. In these raids, the agents usually cofiseate all personal documents and not infrequently steal whatever they find of value in the home, even from the poorest of families.

(2.4.5.) There are at present some 120 to 150 political prisoners.

2.5 Treatment of Political Prisoners—

(2.5.1.) It is common practice to hold prisoners in solitary confinement during the first few weeks of their detention.

(2.5.2.) Political prisoners of more importance are held totally incommunicale for months. At present there are twenty such prisoners. We can cite the names of Antonio Perede, Jose Fimentel, Ruben Eguino, Zenón Barrientos Mamani, Alejandre Rojas, Ivan Paz, Artemio Camargo, David Zapata, Ricardo Fernandez, Remberto Cardenas, Teodore Sarmiento.

(2.5.3.) There are also nine women prisoners being held in jail in *Viacha* in literally sub-human conditions. Some of them have been in prison for more than a year without legal process.

(2.5.4.) With regard to torture, we can affirm that it continues, only now in a much more subtle and systematic fashion. We submit the following proofs:

(2.5.4.1.) Bishop Alejandro Mestre, Catholic Auxiliary Bishop of Sucre and Executive Secretary of the Episcopal Conference, who for more than two years was the Bishops' official representative in visiting the prisoners, publicly affirmed the following: "Unfortunately I must admit that even at that time (1974 and 1975), and afterwards as well, there were deplorable cases of prisoners' being treated inhumanly. These can be found in the records of the Ministry of the Interior, undoubtedly, together with various letters of my own addressed to the Minister, protesting strongly against the excesses committed by some of the agents. . . . Recently there have been cases of inhuman treatment using ropes, whips, and beatings with truncheons, administered even to girls. I don't say this from mere hearsay, but I have been able to confirm it myself, at times seeing their bruises and wounds. Some prisoners were held manacled in their cells for some time. . . . I have repeatedly expressed verbally to the Minister my disagreement with the method followed in arrests, sometimes made on the basis of mere accusations (perhaps out of bad will or for personal ends), while due trial is delayed or omitted altogether." According to the newspaper which quoted this statement, "Bishop Mestre expressed the Catholic Church's concern, made known to the Minister of Interior, about political arrests made on the basis of intrigues or denunciations against innocent persons." ("Presencia", March 17, 1977).

(2.5.4.2.) Report of Father Robert Leibrecht, official representative of the Episcopal Conference from March, 1976, to December of the same year: "Some prisoners have signs of having been beaten or tortured; we saw their legs with wounds, their hands with no circulation, their bodies covered with bruises . . . (visit to the Panoptico jail, La Paz, June 16, 1976).

"We saw the signs (of beatings) on the bodies of five prisoners who had been tortured." (visit to the Department of Political Order, La Paz, June 17, 1976).

"There is a group (of prisoners) which has not received any visits for six months. The prisoners who have been in jail the longest time have had not a change of clothes for quite some time. The families of some of these prisoners did not know where they were because the Ministry of the Interior did not give them any information despite their pleas." (visit to D. O. P., La Paz, June 17, 1976).

"One group of ten prisoners has only one blanket among them. There are several who were beaten when taken prisoner. One has a fractured hand; another has broken ribs; and still another urgently needs a chest x-ray since he is in bad condition due to the beatings. They go to the bathroom in the open fields. No showers, no light, no running water. They have received no visit for two months, with the exception of one prisoner. Their families don't know where they are." (visit to the prison of Chonchocoro, June 17, 1976).

"There is a lack of blankets and mattresses. The five women prisoners urinate blood due to the cold. The men can go to the bathroom only twice a day; at 9:00 A.M. and at 8:00 P.M. The women have cans in their cells . . . There are four women who were badly tortured in Cochabamba and Oruro when they were taken prisoners. One of them was submitted to three interrogations at dawn, whipped and kicked in the stomach. Another was taken prisoner with her nine-month-old daughter, whom they used to torture her. Until our visit, they had no light, and they were given a light bulb the night before our visit. Their relatives don't know where they are there. This is the first visit they've had in six months." (visit to the prison of Viacha, June 18, 1976),

(2.5.4.3.) On the sixth day of May 1977, the priests of six parishes in the City of Cochabamba made a declaration publicly denouncing the torture of the student Faustino Tarrico in the police cells of the city prison. (Presencia, May 6, 1977).

(2.5.4.4.) There are many prisoners who remain totally incommunicado (even for the official Church and Red Cross representatives) precisely because visible on their bodies are the wounds from the torture they have received.

(2.5.4.5.) Some of the investigation group have heard tapes of trustworthy prisoners in which detailed information is given as to modern methods of torture, and in which they identify their torturers with their real and code names. Among the torturers still used by the Government are the notorious.

(2.5.4.6.) Also, some of us have personally helped to pay the medical expenses of prisoners who were badly tortured and then freed when their innocence was proved.

2.6 Serious violations of International Norms—

The Government of President Banzer has violated and continues to violate in a grave and systematic way established international norms with respect to Bolivian citizens who are forced to leave the country. Thousands of citizens have been expelled from Bolivia without any hope of returning. But, because most countries would object to receiving such persons as residents instead of tourists, the Bolivian Government has recourse to a stratagem calculated to fool the immigration officials of other countries. The passport of the expelled person contains nothing to indicate his condition of political deportee. He leaves Bolivia and enters another country officially as a tourist; nevertheless, he can not return to Bolivia, because the seal and signature in his passport are in red ink. This means that the security forces of Bolivia will no longer permit him to return to his country. Because of this fictitious tourist status, the person exiled must travel with return trip tickets, which of course he will never use.

2.7 Christmas Amnesty—

It is a tradition in Bolivia for the Government to dictate an amnesty on Christmas Eve. The Banzer Government could hardly deviate from this custom. However, not infrequently the amnesty has turned out to be a farce, for the following reasons:

(2.7.1.) Included in the list of those favored with amnesty are some prisoners who have been freed weeks or even months previously.

(2.7.2.) Some days before the amnesty, innocent peasants and workers are arrested, so that their release on Chirstmas Eve can swell the list of those freed.

(2.7.3.) In 1974, the Commission of Justice and Peace presented a report to the Bolivian Episcopal Conference proving that more than 50% of those released by amnesty were totally innocent and did not even have any political background.

(2.7.4.) Although the Government presents the Christmas amnesty as benefiting only political prisoners, it usually includes common criminals convicted of various crimes, again to swell the list.

2.8 Real faculties of the Bishops' representative who visits the prisoners—

According to the testimony of the priest who presently is the Bishops' representative to visit the jails, his mission is seriously limited by the following factors:

(2.8.1) He can not visit at all times all the places of detention (and never can he visit the cells in the Ministry of Interior itself).

(2.8.2) He can never speak to the more important political prisoners without agents of the Intelligence Service being present.

(2.8.3) There are some prisoners whom not even a priest has been allowed to visit for close to a year; e.g. Zenon Barrientos Mamani, Edmir Espinoza, Luis Stamponió ...

(2.8.4) Knowing that the priest who actually visits the prisoners would never cover up the truth and that he could formulate serious accusations against the Security Forces, the Ministry of the Interior has itself appointed a priest to visit the jails who enjoys the confidence of the Government. In this way there is no danger that this official Church representative will make a public declaration which is contrary to the Government's interests.

2.9 The reports of the Red Cross and of Amnesty International—

(2.9.1) The International Red Cross does not enjoy enough independence of the Government to allow it to visit all the political prisoners and to press for an improvement in the inhuman conditions in which most of them live. The Bolivian Red Cross, unfortunately, is excessively subordinated to the Government.

(2.9.3.) With reference to Amnesty International, it is most desriable that an official commission from Amnesty visit Bolivia to analyze the present situation of human rights. The last official visit of Amnesty to Bolivia was in 1974.

2.10. Freedom of the Press—

With regard to freedom of the press, it is sufficient to cite a few salient facts in order to put into perspective the present situation of oppression.

(2.10.1) There are fifty-eight Bolivian journalists who are presently living in exile. (We have the complete list.)

(2.10.2) Two journalists are presently prisoners in the Department of Political Order (D.O.P.) in La Paz, incommunicado for over two months: Ivan Paz and David Zapata.

(2.10.3) There are several radio stations under government interventions; e.g., the radios in the mining areas.

(2.10.4) The Church radio, Radio Fides was fined by the Government, and Radio Pio XII was destroyed by agents of the Government Intelligence Service in 1975. Radio Progreso was recently suspended for a week for opposing a government proposed exchange of territory with Chile to allow Bolivia an exit to the sea.

(2.10.5) Since June of 1976, no Bolivian or foreign journalist has been allowed to enter the mining centers to report on the situation there. This prohibition has been strictly enforced.

(2.10.6) By official communique of the High Command of the Armed Forces, October, 1976, the publication of all articles and commentaries critical of "state dignitaries" and members of the Armed Forces is forbidden.

(The Bolivian government May 14 repeated its customary contention that charges of human rights abuse by the Banzer regime were invented by "an international press apparatus managed by elements of the extreme left." The same day, representatives of the Catholic, Lutheran and Methodist churches in Bolivia announced the creation of a Permanent Assembly on Human Rights to be headed by Luis Adolfo Siles Salinas, a former Bolivian president.)

Todman met with Banzer May 16. Their discussions were kept secret, but newspapers reported that the two leaders had conferred on Bolivia's search for an outlet to the Pacific Ocean and on Bolivia's imprisonment of 33 U.S. nationals on drug-related charges, among other topics.

The Bolivian government currently had granted amnesty to 70 persons jailed in the country or living in exile, including two former Cabinet ministers, AP reported Jan. 1.

Politics

Banzer rejects presidential bid. President Hugo Banzer unexpectedly announced Dec. 1 that he would not run for the presidency in the 1978 general elections.

Banzer said that although military leaders wanted him to run, he felt that "six years of government are enough for a man to show what he can and should do, and they drain the health of any human being." (Banzer had ruled Bolivia since August 1971, when he seized power in a bloody military coup.)

Banzer said the elections would take place July 9, 1978. Bolivians would vote for a president and vice president who would serve four-year terms beginning Aug. 6, 1978. Voters also would elect a constituent assembly that would reform or replace the Constitution within 120 days and then become the national legislature.

Banzer's decision not to run surprised political observers and left Bolivian politics in a state of confusion. The armed forces were expected to put up a candidate for the presidency, and there was some speculation that he would be Gen. Juan Pereda Asbun, the former interior minister whom Banzer appointed air force commander Nov. 30. United Press International reported Dec. 22 that the navy had thrown its support to Pereda in the presidential race.

Banzer's election plan was denounced Dec. 26 by seven political organizations. "The government wants to hold elections without real opposition or real democracy, because otherwise it would be defeated across the board," the parties said in a joint communique. The signatories were the Revolutionary Nationalist Movement of the Left, the Revolutionary Party of the Nationalist Left, the Authentic Revolutionary Party, the Christian Democratic Party, the Socialist Party, the Movement of the Revolutionary Left and the Bolivian Communist Party.

The parties noted that the ban on labor unions would not be lifted for the elections, and that most prominent opponents of the military government would not be allowed to return from exile.

Anti-Banzer 'plot' foiled. The government said Dec. 9 that it had crushed a plot against President Banzer by "regressive elements opposed to the process of democratization."

Government officials gave different accounts of the alleged conspiracy, however, creating considerable confusion about the identities of the plotters and the existence of the conspiracy itself.

Interior Minister Guillermo Jimenez Gallo said Dec. 9 that the plotters were an army captain, three majors and a lieutenant colonel, all of whom had been placed under house arrest and were being interrogated. Army Commander Alfonso Villalpando, on the other hand, said the conspirators included politicians as well as army officers. Finally, military sources told the Associated Press Dec. 13 that no officers were implicated in the plot and none had been placed under house arrest.

The La Paz newspaper El Diario reported Dec. 9 that the leaders of the alleged conspiracy were Jorge Echazu, an army colonel, and Luis Mayser, the leader of a minority faction of the Bolivian Socialist Falange, a right-wing political party. Mayser told United Press International Dec. 9 that he had been arrested the previous day, interrogated for several hours at the Interior Ministry and then set free.

Partial amnesty set. The government announced Dec. 21 that it would grant amnesty to 284 political exiles as part of Bolivia's "process of democratization."

The amnesty did not, however, affect the country's most prominent exiles, who were excluded as "extremist elements." Among them were former President Hernan Siles Zuazo, former Vice President Juan Lechin Oquendo, former Cabinet minister Marcelo Quiroga Santa Cruz and many labor union leaders. Several of the union leaders were said to have re-entered Bolivia secretly according to the Associated Press Dec. 22.

Economic & Foreign Developments

Bolivia ... tin pact. Bolivia announced ... that it would ratify the fifth International Tin Agreement. The pact was designed to moderate price swings in the metal by means of a buffer stock that was used to withhold tin reserves when demand was slack and prices low and sell supplies when demand was strong and prices high.

The decision, announced in London at a meeting of the International Tin Council, saved the pact from collapse and helped halt a steep downward slide in tin prices on the London Metal Exchange.

Bolivia decided to ratify the accord after the council's producing and consuming nations agreed to semiannual reviews of the buffer stock's support-price ranges. Bolivia had contended that the price ranges were too low to stimulate investment in tin production. If the current world shortage of tin were to ease, Bolivia said, the price ranges must be increased.

The council had used export quotas and tin purchases to prop up prices when the market was weak during early 1976. Economic recovery soon caused the market to firm, particularly after it became apparent that world demand for tin was outstripping production. By December 1976, tin prices had soared 30%.

After Bolivia, the world's second-largest tin producer, threatened to withdraw from the price-control pact, speculators pushed the metal's price above the support ceiling. The council's buffer stock was depleted in an effort to halt the upward spiral.

Bolivian mining officials had said Jan. 19 that they would like to see the price of tin reach $5.00 a pound. They claimed their production costs were about $3.60 a pound, significantly higher than in the Southeast Asian countries, where most tin was dredged from riverbed sediment. Bolivian tin was mined from hard rock.

U.S. accord on drug prisoners. The U.S. and Bolivia had agreed in principle that Americans imprisoned in Bolivia on cocaine-smuggling charges could serve out their sentences in the U.S., it was reported Dec. 20.

Of the 32 Americans being held in Bolivia, however, only about six would be eligible for transfer when the treaty took effect. Three could leave sooner because they had been acquitted by a lower court (a higher court still had to approve their release), and another four would soon be eligible for parole. The rest had not yet been brought to trial.

U.S. oil executive convicted. Bob R. Dorsey, former chairman of Gulf Oil Corp. of the U.S., was convicted in absentia by a Bolivian court on charges stemming from the alleged bribing of Bolivian officials in the 1960s, it was reported Dec. 23.

Dorsey, who refused to go to Bolivia for trial or to answer the court's questions by mail, was sentenced to six years in prison. The term was later reduced to four years after the court-appointed defense attorney called the six-year sentence "illegal and excessive."

Brazil

Military Rule Strengthened, Opposition Continues Struggle

Political clashes between the ruling military regime and the opposition increased as Brazilian political forces gathered for the 1978 presidential election.

Geisel acts vs. opposition. President Ernesto Geisel suspended Congress April 1, two days after legislators of the opposition Brazilian Democratic Movement (MDB) blocked passage of a government bill to reform the judicial system.

The bill, an amendment to the Constitution, fell short of the required two-thirds majority without MDB support. The vote on it March 30 followed party lines, with 237 government (ARENA party) legislators voting in favor and 155 MDB members voting against.

The MDB leadership had charged that the bill dealt only with minor technical matters, failing to protect judges against summary removal by the executive branch and failing to restore the right of habeas corpus for political detainees. Alencar Furtado, opposition leader in the Chamber of Deputies, had said the MDB was obliged to block the bill "because the purpose of our party is to gain a return to democracy. The MDB refuses to be the regime's errand boy."

After closing Congress April 1, Geisel made a radio and television broadcast in which he accused MDB leaders of coercing members of their party into voting against the bill, thereby establishing a "dictatorship" in Congress. Geisel said he would reopen the legislature shortly, after he issued decrees enacting the judicial reform bill and "other reforms of a political nature [that are] indispensable for the country to continue to live in peace, without a crisis every year or two."

Jose Bonifacio, ARENA leader in the Chamber of Deputies, told government and opposition leaders in Congress April 2 that Geisel wanted them to stay in Brasilia during the suspension to help him draw up the reforms. Bonifacio said the changes under consideration included requiring only a simple majority vote to amend the Constitution and substituting an indirect ballot for the direct voting planned for the 1978 gubernatorial elections.

The MDB already had announced that it would not even discuss changing the balloting procedure in the 1978 elections. The MDB had defeated ARENA decisively in the direct elections for Congress in 1974, and it could be expected to win the state houses in Sao Paulo, Rio de Janeiro, Rio Grande do Sul, Minas Gerais, Bahia and Pernambuco if direct gubernatorial elections were held in 1978, according to the Mexican newspaper Excelsior March 4.

Geisel had arranged the 1974 elections and other liberal reforms since then, often over the opposition of hard-line military leaders. However, his regime had begun cracking down on the growing opposition as criticism of the government mounted in the MDB and in business circles. The crackdown was harshest in Porto Alegre (Rio Grande do Sul State), where two MDB members were dismissed from the city council in February and more than 20 members of the MDB's youth wing were arrested March 27-29.

MDB Sen. Marcos Freire had charged March 22 that the government violated human rights "in various aspects," particularly through Institutional Act No. 5, which gave the president dictatorial powers. The act "defies, ignores and rejects principles that are essential to social life" and "encourages arbitrary actions by lower-level leaders," Freire asserted.

Jose Papa Junior, chairman of the Sao Paulo chamber of commerce, had stunned the government Feb. 2 by asserting that "businessmen, contrary to what is said, desire freedom, democracy and direct elections." Papa, known as an ultra-conservative, reportedly had been emboldened by Industry and Commerce Minister Severo Gomes, who told a group of Rio Grande do Sul industrialists Jan. 21 that "a full democracy" was needed to overcome Brazil's economic problems. After repeating this assertion Feb. 2, Gomes was forced to resign Feb. 8.

Claudio Bardella, chairman of the influential Brazilian Association of Basic Industries, said Gomes' resignation "does not change the views of our sector," according to the Latin America Political Report Feb. 18. "I continue to think that the country needs a return to democracy and will say so whenever asked," Bardella asserted.

(Gomes was replaced Feb. 9 by Angelo Calmon de Sa, a former chairman of the Bank of Brazil who reportedly adhered to the economic ideas of Finance Minister Mario Henrique Simonsen. Gomes had opposed Simonsen's emphasis on exports, saying this harmed the domestic market.)

To appease the businessmen, the government said it would scrap an unpopular surtax on gasoline sales, reduce chaotically high interest rates, gradually dismantle the system of price controls and grant low-interest credits to small and medium-sized businesses, according to the Latin America Political Report March 25.

In another political protest, Gen. Rodrigo Octavio, a member of the Superior Military Tribunal, called Feb. 25 for a restoration of individual freedoms, of the powers of the judicial branch and of the independence of the three branches of government. Octavio said the Constitution should be reformed to democratize Brazil.

Military rule tightened—President Geisel April 14 decreed a series of political reforms that tightened military rule and made it virtually impossible for the MDB to gain power through elections. The decrees were issued under Institutional Act No. 5.

Geisel had decreed the judicial reform amendment April 13, along with two measures that had wide public appeal—an extension to 30 days of the annual paid vacation due to every worker, and the repeal of a rent law that allegedly discriminated against tenants.

Among the political reforms decreed April 14:

■ The gubernatorial elections scheduled for September 1978 were canceled. Henceforth, the 21 state governors would be chosen by electoral colleges composed of state legislators and city council members. (Under this system the MDB could expect to win only the Rio de Janeiro governorship, instead of the 15 state houses it had hoped to take in direct elections, according to most press reports.)

■ One-third of Brazil's 66 senators would be chosen by the state electoral colleges. The rest would continue to be elected directly, but under an altered vote-counting system that would help the ruling ARENA party more than the MDB. Each party would be allowed to run up to three candidates for each seat, and the party with the largest vote total would win the office. (Under the simple direct elections in force earlier, the MDB had been in a position to gain a majority in the Senate in 1978, according to the Washington Post April 15.)

■ The Chamber of Deputies would be apportioned on the basis of population, rather than registered voters. This would help ARENA, since illiterate voters were not allowed to cast ballots and ARENA was strongest in backward rural areas. In addition, no state would be allowed to have more than 50 representatives in the

Chamber, giving ARENA another advantage because it was weak in the most populous states.

■ No candidate would be allowed to discuss campaign issues on radio or television. This would help the government, since officials were still allowed to use the broadcast media to promote government programs.

■ The term of Brazil's president would be extended to six years from the current five, beginning with Geisel's successor, who would take office in 1979 after being chosen by a national electoral college that was controlled by ARENA.

■ Constitutional amendments would be passed by a simple majority of Congress, rather than the previous two-thirds majority. This would allow the government to pass any amendment with ease, since ARENA had the simple majority.

Geisel's reforms were denounced April 14 by one of the country's leading newspapers, Jornal do Brasil. The new decrees, Jornal do Brasil said, "have only one common denominator: the determination to remove the popular will from the process of choosing those who govern, to separate the power of the electors from those who are elected, to isolate the state from the nation, civilian society from the administrative apparatus."

The MDB had criticized the decrees a few days earlier when it learned the nature of the reforms. Marcos Freire, a leading MDB senator, had called Brazil "an oppressed and humiliated nation." "This is the hour for democratic resistance," Freire said. Alencar Furtado, opposition leader in the Chamber of Deputies, had said the MDB must not disband "just because it has been beaten down, surrounded and raped."

The new decrees represented an about-face for Geisel, who previously had promoted a mild political liberalization. Political observers agreed that Geisel had decided on the new measures largely on his own, rather than in response to pressure from hard-line military officers who had opposed his previous efforts to relax military rule.

Opposition leaders score government—Four leaders of the opposition Brazilian Democratic Movement (MDB) made a joint broadcast on radio and television June 27 to excoriate the military government and demand a return to constitutional democracy.

The government had approved the broadcast without ascertaining its content, according to the newspaper O Globo of Rio de Janeiro. When it found out early June 27 what the opposition leaders were going to say, the government made a late but futile attempt to block the broadcast, the newspaper reported.

MDB president Ulysses Guimaraes opened the program by denouncing "all kinds of dictatorships" and calling for a return to "democratic normality" in Brazil. Guimaraes had particularly harsh words for Institutional Act No. 5 and for federal censorship. Institutional Act No. 5, he said, was "the true enemy of the [military] revolution and the major cause of its failures." Censorship, Guimaraes added, "is a crime against the institutions, intelligence and culture of a country."

Alencar Furtado, MDB leader in the Chamber of Deputies, followed Guimaraes with a call for a constitutional convention, restoration of the right of habeas corpus and an end to "arbitrary arrests, unfair punishment and the disappearance of citizens." "The country cannot go on as it is," Furtado said. "It is time for us to come together. It is time for legality and liberation."

Franco Montoro, MDB leader in the Senate, spoke next and urged Brazil to follow the examples of Spain, Portugal and Greece, which had restored democracy after long periods of military rule.

Alceu Collares, who was a little-known MDB politician, denounced the accumulation of wealth in the hands of a few "while the majority suffers the consequences of the cost of development." Brazil's economic structure was "concentrated and elitist," Collares asserted. "It is unacceptable for the country to grow and the great Brazilian population to remain in need."

An estimated 25 million Brazilians watched or heard the broadcast, and a majority agreed with the MDB leaders, according to a poll published by the Rio newspaper Jornal do Brasil June 29.

The opposition broadcast followed a number of other protests against government policies.

The Brazilian Bar Association April 19 had denounced the judicial reforms decreed by Geisel. "Brazil is experic.̈ ing an obscurantist period of its constitutional history, characterized by a growing gulf between the actions of the government and the will of the people," the lawyers' group asserted.

Political reforms decreed by Geisel along with the judicial reforms had been criticized by ARENA. Sergio Cardoso de Almeida, an ARENA deputy from Sao Paulo, said May 4: "The political reforms were a government error and they can ruin ARENA." Claudio Lembo, the party's leader in Sao Paulo, said he would campaign for a return to democracy, it was reported April 29.

Finally, a group of 110 army and air force colonels began circulating a letter calling for a return to democracy. The document, first reported by the London Times May 26, called for the immediate formation of a freely elected constitutional convention; immediate amnesty for all political prisoners; repeal of the judicial reforms and restoration of the full rights of persons accused of crimes; abolition of Institutional Act No. 5 and all other dictatorial legislation, and formation of a provisional government chaired by the president of the Supreme Court and composed of representatives of the armed forces, the Brazilian Bar Association, the MDB and ARENA. The provisional government should "hand over power to those duly elected according to the rules laid down by the constitutional assembly," the colonels said.

The colonels, whom the government reportedly did not consider a serious threat, stood for military professionalism, according to the Latin America Political Report May 27. They said the armed forces had seized power in 1964 to "rescue" Brazil from "communism," but then had become "praetorian guards of the technocrats who were not part of the revolution ... but seized a power which was not theirs."

Furcado was dismissed by Geisel July 1 in response to the growing civilian criticism of the government. Furtado was deprived of his political rights for 10 years under Institutional Act No. 5.

No reason was given for the action, but it was assumed Furtado was being punished for having denounced the regime in the June broadcast. The ruling ARENA party charged late July 1 that Furtado had slandered the government and carried a "destructive message" to the Brazilian people.

Furtado said after learning of his dismissal that "to castrate one more opposi-

tion member politically is to return to terror, to try desperately to frighten into silence those who are fighting for the democratization of the country."

The MDB issued a statement denouncing Furtado's dismissal as "a brutality." However, the party was reported to be divided between members who felt this response was sufficient and others who wanted to disband the MDB as an ultimate protest against government repression. Paes de Andrade, a federal deputy belonging to the second group, said "there is no more room for institutional opposition. ... It is time for the party to decide on its own dissolution, leaving to the government the historical responsibility of installing a single party."

Political observers were surprised by Furtado's dismissal, and many attributed it to pressures on Geisel as the army prepared to select his successor. The leading candidates to replace Geisel in 1979 were the army minister, Gen. Sylvio da Frota, and the chief of the National Information (intelligence) Service, Gen. Joao Baptista de Figueiredo. In their efforts to secure as much military backing as possible, supporters of each candidate were adopting the most conservative stances on political issues, Inter Press Service reported July 3.

Military leaders had been infuriated by the June 27 broadcast, according to Inter Press Service. In what was interpreted as a clear warning to Geisel following the broadcast, Figueiredo told an interviewer, "And now, what is going to happen?" Geisel, long described as a moderate in Brazil's conservative military establishment, apparently responded to the pressure by dismissing Furtado, the most radical of the four opposition members who made the broadcast.

Guimaraes was acquitted by the Supreme Court Nov. 30 of charges brought against him in relation to the June television broadcast in which he strongly criticized the government.

The charges, which alleged that Guimaraes had broken Brazil's election laws, were unanimously rejected by the nine-member court.

MDB deputy fired—President Geisel June 14 dismissed MDB Deputy Marcos Tito and suspended his political rights for 10 years after members of ARENA found that Tito had delivered a speech in the Chamber of Deputies that he had plagiarized from an issue of the organ of the Brazilian Communist Party.

Presidential drive under way. Brazil's growing absorption with the presidential succession was heightened July 26 when a civilian leader of the ruling party announced his candidacy for the 1978 election.

Jose de Magalhaes Pinto, president of the Brazilian Senate, appeared to be challenging top military leaders who presumably wanted one of their own to succeed President Ernesto Geisel in 1979. There was some speculation that Magalhaes Pinto was a stalking-horse for one of the leading military candidates, but the senator insisted his candidacy was serious.

Brazilian presidents theoretically were chosen by an electoral college dominated by civilian members of the governing ARENA party. But in practice the electors accepted the recommendation of the army leadership. In the past three elections (in 1966, 1969 and 1974) the victorious candidate had been a four-star general.

The presidential campaign seemed to be in full gear despite Geisel's request that serious debate not begin until January 1978, ten months before the election. Magalhaes Pinto said he would abide by the president's request, but supporters of one leading military candidate, Gen. Joao Baptista de Figueiredo, appeared to ignore Geisel.

Humberto Barreto, head of the federal savings bank, told newsmen July 12 that he supported Figueiredo because of his "experience in government, his intelligence and his ability to debate political issues." The statement drew wide attention because Barreto was a close confidant of Geisel. However, certain sources said the president preferred neither Figueiredo nor the man widely touted to be his chief rival, Gen. Sylvio da Frota, according to the Latin America Political Report July 22. Geisel's first choice, the sources said, was the commander of the second military region, Gen. Dilermando Gomes Monteiro.

The press, meanwhile, concentrated its attention on Figueiredo, who headed the National Information (intelligence) Service. Brazilian newspapers and magazines were full of articles on the

general and his family, making them well-known overnight, it was reported July 26. Gen. Frota, the army minister, appeared to receive less publicity for reasons that were not clear.

Meanwhile, politicians who normally supported the armed forces were pressing for political reforms. Six state governors called on President Ernesto Geisel to allow a multiparty system, according to reports Aug. 22 and 27. Under the governors' scheme, the two existing parties—the ruling ARENA party and the opposition Brazilian Democratic Movement (MBD)—would be replaced by four parties representing right-wing, conservative, liberal and socialist political sentiments.

A survey of 49 former Cabinet ministers revealed virtually no support for continued military rule, the newspaper Jornal do Brasil reported Aug. 28. Seventeen of the ex-officials openly called for democratic reforms, the newspaper said. While the others either refused to speak or made vague statements, not one specifically favored the existing political system.

Sixty-three ARENA congressmen met with their party's Senate leader Aug. 31 and appealed for democratic reforms including the dissolution of ARENA and the MDB, according to the newspaper O Estado de Sao Paulo Sept. 2. The senator reportedly promised to take their suggestions to President Geisel.

Other ARENA legislators expressed their dissatisfaction with the system by endorsing the presidential candidacy of a fellow party member, Sen. Joao de Magalhaes Pinto. The candidacy had picked up vast public support, to the chagrin of the military leadership, which was determined to see an army general win the 1978 indirect election. A Gallup poll conducted in Rio and Sao Paulo showed that Magalhaes would easily defeat the leading military candidate if the president were elected by universal suffrage, it was reported Sept. 24.

That military candidate, according to most press reports, was Gen. Joao Baptista de Figueiredo, chief of the National Information (intelligence) Service. The Rio newspaper Tribuna da Imprensa reported Sept. 1 that Figueiredo would be promoted to four-star general to prepare the way for his election. His chief military rival for the presidency, Gen. Sylvio da

Frota, would be named ambassador to Portugal, the newspaper said.

Despite this apparent consensus on a military candidate, there was a debate in the armed forces over whether the next president should be a military man at all, according to the Sept. 9 Latin America Political Report. Officers of the third army division were seriously discussing a possible return to democracy and were divided on the issue, the Report said.

(Officers who called publicly for reform were punished, however. Retired Col. Ruy Castro was jailed Aug. 18–Sept. 2 for releasing a letter he had written to the army high command recommending a return to civilian rule.

Meanwhile, the lone civilian candidate for the presidency continued campaigning across Brazil. Sen. Jose de Magalhaes Pinto assured foreign reporters Sept. 30 that his candidacy was serious and that he sought to create "peace and understanding" among "all factions." He stressed that he had supported the 1964 coup and that the "aspirations" of the military "revolution" had included having "a civilian in the presidency."

Frota fired—President Ernesto Geisel intervened openly in the presidential campaign Oct. 12 by dismissing from his Cabinet a leading candidate, Army Minister Sylvio da Frota.

Geisel apparently acted to stem growing political divisions in the army and to consolidate the position of his own candidate, Gen. Joao Baptista de Figueiredo. Like Geisel, Figueiredo was perceived as a moderate even though he headed the repressive National Information (intelligence) Service. Gen. Frota represented the army's hard-line faction.

Geisel said publicly that he had removed Frota for "personal" reasons, but Frota said Geisel's motive was "purely political, with an objective that easily can be deduced." Frota issued a farewell letter Oct. 12 in which he lamented the "deformation and abandonment of the objectives of the [military] revolution" under Geisel. He criticized Geisel's administration for recognizing the Communist governments of China and Angola, and accused it of showing "criminal indifference to communist infiltration and leftist propaganda which are supported in the [Brazilian] daily press, in the universities and in the government itself."

Frota tried to rally support Oct. 12 by summoning top army commanders to meet him in Brasilia, but Geisel outmaneuvered him by having the generals met at the airport and driven to the inauguration of the new army minister, Gen. Fernando Belfort Bethlem.

The major reasons for Frota's downfall appeared to be his increasing undermining of Geisel and his considerable support within the army, according to press reports.

While the government proposed talks with the opposition party to insure peaceful congressional elections in 1978, Frota had been encouraging members of the ruling party to ask that the elections be canceled, according to the Latin America Political Report Oct. 14. The government had taken particular offense when an apparent spokesman for Frota, federal deputy Marcelino Linhares, charged that the administration was trying "to reduce the role of the army high command in deciding the presidential succession by stimulating opposition pressure on the system and disrupting the unity of the military hierarchy."

While Frota enjoyed the support of many members of the army high command, Figueiredo apparently did not. Figueiredo was not a four-star general—a virtual requirement for the Brazilian presidency since the 1964 military coup—and he was low in the pecking order for promotion, according to the Latin America Political Report Oct. 21. Nevertheless, Figueiredo was endorsed by all but three members of the Cabinet, according to the newspaper O Estado de Sao Paulo Sept. 21.

The Brazilian press generally portrayed the Frota controversy as one more reason to restore democracy to the country, according to the Political Report. Newspaper editorials said the crisis was precipitated by the military system of presidential rotation, not by opponents of the system. The liberal weekly Isto E said the government had become one of "absolutist presidentialism."

Opposition to Figueiredo within the army had been centered on Frota, but after his dismissal, the focus shifted to retired Gen. Euler Bentes Monteiro, according to the Latin America Political Report Dec. 2.

A magazine poll of 318 Brazilian business executives, reported Nov. 7, showed that 23% supported Gen. Bentes for the presidency, 19.5% backed the lone civilian candidate, Sen. Jose de Magalhaes Pinto, and 12.9% supported Gen. Figueiredo.

Geisel discloses his candidate—Geisel had told his closest advisers that he wanted Gen. Joao Baptista de Figueiredo to succeed him as president in 1979, according to O Estado de Sao Paulo and the Rio newspaper Jornal do Brasil Nov. 17.

The government did not specifically deny the newspaper reports.

President backs political reforms. President Ernesto Geisel announced Dec. 1 that he had approved a plan for political reforms that would abolish the "institutional acts" through which the military government had assumed dictatorial powers since 1964.

Geisel said, however, that the institutional acts must be replaced by constitutional "safeguards" to protect democracy and order. He did not say what these measures would be, but he said they would be discussed in the near future by representatives of the government and the single legal opposition party, the Brazilian Democratic Movement (MDB).

MDB chairman Ulysses Guimaraes sharply criticized Geisel's plan, it was reported Dec. 9. He charged that Brazil's entire Constitution was undemocratic, not just the institutional acts. He called for free and direct election to all political offices, freedom for political parties and freedom of the press, according to the Latin America Political report.

Other members of the MDB were upset over the government's timetable for the proposed reforms, it was reported Dec. 13. According to Sen. Petronio Portela, Geisel's chief go-between in contacts with the opposition, the reforms would not be submitted to Congress for debate until April 1978. Because the presidential and congressional campaigns would dominate politics between July and November, and Congress would recess in December, many MDB members feared that the reforms would not be enacted until a new president and Congress were seated in March 1979.

In any case, the opposition legislators noted, the 1978 elections would be held under the current restrictions that made it virtually impossible for the MDB to win

the presidency or control of Congress. The new Chamber of Deputies would function until 1982, and the new president would rule until 1985. At the very earliest, Brazil could have direct, democratic elections for president in 1984.

Geisel also had been criticized by O Estado de Sao Paulo, one of Brazil's most prestigious newspapers. After the president described Brazil's political system as "relative democracy," O Estado accused him of trying to "organize democracy by dogmatic indoctrination and authoritarian implementation, in effect by suppressing democracy," it was reported Nov. 4.

Press & Censorship

Censorship continues. The government continued press censorship, in part, at least, to limit reports of the growing movement for democratic reforms.

The Federal Police Department June 1 began receiving applications for 58 positions for "censorship technicians." Applicants would be required to pass exams on philosophy, history and Brazilian culture, among other subjects, and would have to pass physical tests including a 2,000-meter run to be finished in less than 12 minutes. Each censor be paid the equivalent of $466 per month.

More than 2,500 reporters signed a manifesto demanding freedom of expression in the press, radio and television. The document, released simultaneously in 10 state capitals June 8, charged that censorship "mutilates newspapers and magazines and has already destroyed various publications."

Author Renato Tapajos was arrested July 27 for having written a novel, titled *Em Camara Lenta (In Slow Motion),* on left-wing guerrilla activities in Brazil between 1964 and 1973. The Sao Paulo security chief, Col. Erasmo Dias, said of the book: "It's a good novel but it's more valuable to subversion than Mao Tse-tung's Little Red Book." The Sao Paulo journalists' union protested Tapajos' arrest as "one more act of violence against freedom of the press."

The newspaper Folha de Sao Paulo appeared without an editorial page Sept. 21 after its executive editor was replaced under apparent pressure from the government. The departing editor implied that the government would have closed down the paper unless it changed its editorial line, according to the Rio newspaper Jornal do Brasil.

A columnist for Folha da Tarde, Lourenco Diaferia, was arrested for allegedly insulting the army, it was reported Sept. 21. The charge apparently stemmed from an article in which Diaferia unfavorably compared a statue of the army patron to a policeman who had died rescuing a child from danger. Diaferia said he preferred "heroes of flesh and blood to heroes of stone."

The military government seized the news weekly Movimento after it carried extensive coverage of a campaign for a constituent assembly, it was reported Sept. 23. Radio and television stations were forbidden to cover the recent MDB convention—which also called for a constituent assembly—or to broadcast an address to students in Recife by two MDB senators, according to the same report.

Foreign publications to be censored. Justice Minister Armando Falcao announced May 28 that all books and magazines sent to Brazil from abroad would be examined by federal censors before they were distributed and sold in the country.

Censors would be assigned to post offices in major Brazilian cities to determine whether incoming publications "contain material contrary to public order" or "run counter to morality and good standards of behavior," Falcao said. Books and periodicals that failed the test could be confiscated.

The censorship directive, which technically violated the Brazilian Constitution, was widely criticized within Brazil. The directive was "one more document for fattening up international reports on human rights violations in Brazil," said O Estado de Sao Paulo, the nation's leading newspaper. "Brazil has become an island in all but the geographical sense," said Joaquim Bevilacqua, a congressman from the opposition Brazilian Democratic Movement.

Party broadcasts banned. President Geisel July 26 suspended a law that allowed the two political parties each to make two one-hour national broadcasts per year. The broadcast law was suspended under Institutional Act No. 5.

Catholic educator acquitted. Maria Nilde Mascellani, a Roman Catholic lay leader and authority on education, was acquitted by a military court of charges of spreading subversive propaganda and trying to "turn the people against the constitutional authorities," it was reported June 24.

Mascellani had been arrested early in 1974 for writing a study in which she asserted that the compulsory courses on "moral and civic education" taught in Brazil were based on Nazi ideas on education introduced to Brazil by the army's Superior War College. After her arrest Mascellani had been tortured for 70 days by the political police, according to the Latin America Political Report.

The court that acquitted Mascellani noted that while her study was subversive, it had not been published, and thus had not violated Brazil's national security law. The study had been seized by the political police as it was going to press.

Political Unrest

Students protest. Students in Sao Paulo, Rio de Janeiro and other cities demonstrated against government policies throughout May and into June.

The protests, the first widespread student disturbances in Brazil in nearly 10 years, were sparked by the arrest of four students and four workers in Sao Paulo May 1. The detainees were accused of distributing subversive pamphlets and belonging to the pro-Communist Workers' League, which the government characterized as a clandestine terrorist organization.

About 60,000 students at Rio's Pontifical Catholic University (PUC), the University of Sao Paulo, Sao Paulo State University, Sao Carlos University and Campinas State University went on strike May 3 to protest the arrests. The professors' association at PUC issued a statement of solidarity with the students. The strikers went back to classes the next day, but about 10,000 students from 80 schools throughout Rio de Janeiro State met at PUC and scheduled a massive student protest for May 10.

About 10,000 students demonstrated in Sao Paulo May 5, distributing pamphlets that demanded "an end to political torture, imprisonment and persecution, and a full amnesty for all political prisoners and exiles." As the students marched through the streets, residents of the city cheered them on and threw confetti from windows. Police controlled the demonstration with barricades and tear gas, but no arrests or serious violence were reported.

Student protests also were reported in other cities. In Belo Horizonte several hundred students went on strike May 5, and in Curitiba about 300 students demonstrated May 7 against the May 1 Sao Paulo arrests.

The government May 9 banned all "public concentrations" in an effort to head off the demonstration scheduled for the next day. However, between 3,000 and 4,000 students demonstrated May 10 at PUC in Rio, and some 500 students held a protest meeting at the federal university in Belo Horizonte. Authorities did not interfere with the Rio demonstration, but police helicopters flew low over the protesters so officers could photograph them.

As the demonstrations spread, leaders of the Roman Catholic Church came to the support of the students. Paulo Evaristo Cardinal Arns, archbishop of Sao Paulo, criticized the May Day arrests in a sermon May 8. The human rights commission of the Sao Paulo archdiocese issued a statement May 13 supporting "the recent popular demonstrations" and "encouraging all those who want respect for democratic freedom and the right of the people to participate in decision making regarding the country's future." Arns May 19 denied the Sao Paulo security chief's contention that the student protests were led by subversives and foreigners.

(Arns received an honorary doctorate May 22 from Notre Dame University in the U.S. President Carter, who also received an honorary degree, declared that Arns, in his "fight for human freedoms" in Brazil, represented "all that is best" in his country and his church.

Thousands of students demonstrated May 19 in Rio, Sao Paulo, Brasilia, Salvador, Porto Alegre and other cities in what student leaders called a "national day of struggle." Wire services reported that police dispersed demonstrators only in Sao Paulo, but the Latin America Political Report May 27 said there was violent police action in most of the cities. The worst incidents occurred in Salvador, where several journalists were beaten severely, according to the Report. Toward the end of the day the government ordered radio and television stations to stop reporting the events, the Report added.

The protests continued May 31 as more than 20,000 students went on strike at the University of Brasilia, denouncing the suspension of 19 students for their participation in recent demonstrations. Students were reported on strike in Belo Horizonte June 3 to protest the expulsion of 16 students for the same reason.

Police and soldiers occupied the university in Belo Horizonte June 4 after several hundred students sat in at the medical school. Authorities set up barricades along roads that led to the city, and they arrested about 800 students who demonstrated in the city's streets. Almost all of the students were released shortly after their arrest, but about 100 were indicted under the national security law.

About 50 student leaders were arrested in Brasilia June 6, shortly before the arrival of a visiting U.S. delegation headed by Rosalynn Carter, wife of U.S. President Jimmy Carter. Other student leaders gave the delegation a letter on the situation of students in Brazil, which Mrs. Carter promised to relay to her husband. The letter said in part that "what is happening at the University of Brasilia is not an isolated incident, but a symptom of the oppression that we as students have lived with nearly all our lives." The government denounced the student letter and closed the university for the three days of Mrs. Carter's visit.

About 2,000 policemen occupied the University of Brasilia June 7 after some 300 students tried to hold a meeting there. Students struck that day at at least eight universities in the states of Sao Paulo, Rio de Janeiro, Bahia and Rio Grande do Sul. The Federal University of Minas Gerais was closed by its dean to prevent student demonstrations there.

Among other developments reported June 15 as student protests entered their seventh week:

Police in Sao Paulo dispersed an estimated 2,000–4,000 students who gathered at a large square and shouted "We want freedom!" Dozens of students were arrested by the security officers, who used tear gas, fire hoses, billy clubs and attack dogs to quell the protest.

In Rio de Janeiro, police used tear gas to disperse a few hundred students who assembled in front of the legislative palace to demand the release of all political prisoners. At another demonstration in the city a student leader read a document charging that "the military government hunts, arrests and tortures all those who raise their voices against the situation of misery and oppression to which a large part of the Brazilian population is subjected."

Other, smaller demonstrations were reported in Campinas and Ribeirao Preto, in northern Sao Paulo State. In Porto Alegre, student leaders met to organize a "struggle" for the release of 1,500 alleged political prisoners.

Students at the University of Brasilia voted June 21 to continue their 22-day strike to denounce the arrest of student protesters and the expulsion from the university of 16 (or 19, depending on the press report) students who had led local demonstrations. The next day the university's rector declared the school closed until July 24.

Political protests continue. Protests against political repression continued in July, August and September as lawyers, scientists and students demanded respect for human rights and a return to democracy.

The Brazilian Bar Association, which had denounced the government in April, July 16 called for a return to "the state of law." At the end of a two-day meeting in Sao Paulo the association issued a document demanding observation of human rights, restoration of the right of habeas corpus and establishment of a constitutional convention to arrange Brazil's transition to democracy.

Another professional organization, the Brazilian Society for the Advancement of Science (SBPC), passed a resolution repudiating censorship and all violations of human rights, demanding a return to full democratic freedom and an amnesty for all intellectuals expelled from universities, and denouncing the use of public money in scientific projects that had not been examined and discussed by the scientific community, it was reported July 22. The resolution was adopted at the end of an SBPC meeting in Sao Paulo that the government had sought unsuccessfully to block. At the meeting's first session Mauricio Rocha e Silva, a well-known biologist, told the 4,000 participants that the SBPC henceforth would "represent not only academics but the people as a whole, with the participation of artists, writers, intellectuals, in fact, of all who dream of a better country, a country free from oppression and obscurantism."

Most of the 16,000 students at the University of Brasilia remained on strike July 25 despite the end of a month-long midyear recess. The students protested not only the government's repressive policies but the university administration's decision July 21 to expel 30 students involved in earlier demonstrations. (Another 34 students were suspended in the same action.)

About 100 students were arrested at the university July 25 as they tried to hold a demonstration in defiance of the 1500 soldiers and policemen who were occupying the campus. The government July 29 said 14 of the arrested students would be tried for alleged crimes against national security.

Some 450 students tried to stage a new demonstration at the university Aug. 3. When security officers prevented them from entering the campus, they held the protest in front of the federal Congress.

More than 100 prominent jurists and law professors added their voices to the protests Aug. 8 in an "Open Letter to Brazilians" read to an audience of 2000 persons at the University of Sao Paulo Law School. The document, read by Godofredo Telles, the law school's dean, said in part: "The juridical conscience of Brazil wants only one thing—the rule of law, now." The letter assured all Brazilians, "above all the young," that the signatories were "determined, as always, to fight for the defense of human rights, against the oppression of all dictatorships."

Several retired military officers unexpectedly joined the movement for political freedom, the New York Times reported Aug. 13. Gabriel Grun Moss, a former air force minister, wrote a letter to a Rio newspaper asking for a return to the rule of law. A few days later, Brazilian papers reported, three retired colonels sent letters to the army high command saying it was time for soldiers to return to the barracks. The letters were viewed as symptomatic of changing military thought, according to the Times.

Police in Rio de Janeiro reported Sept. 28 that they had arrested four students belonging to an extreme leftist organization. The group allegedly had infiltrated several Rio labor unions and urged workers to stage strikes and join in a "front against dictatorship, for socialism and for combatting the bourgeois demagoguery represented by the Brazilian political parties."

Students, who made the loudest protests, suffered the harshest treatment from the government. Police broke up demonstrations in Sao Paulo, Porto Alegre and Campinas Aug. 23, arresting more than 100 students and injuring a dozen more. Students in all three cities said they were beaten and kicked by security officers.

Several dozen students were arrested in Sao Paulo Sept. 18 after a rally to protest political repression. The rally was attended by more than 5,000 people including workers and Roman Catholic lay leaders. Maria Elena Gregorio, president of the human rights committee of the Sao Paulo archdiocese, was arrested along with the students.

Police prevented a national students' meeting in Sao Paulo Sept. 21. Two days later, when 1,000 students gathered to protest this at the city's Catholic university, police attacked them with truncheons and tear-gas canisters. About 500 students were detained for interrogation.

Archbishops score student arrests. Police raids on the Catholic university in Sao Paulo were denounced by Brazil's leading reformist archbishops, Paulo Evaristo Cardinal Arns of Sao Paulo and Helder Camara of Olinda and Recife.

Arns said Sept. 25 that policemen should be prosecuted for using violence in the raids, and that students arrested recently "will have the support of the people." Camara called Sept. 27 for an amnesty for arrested students and for a restoration of democracy in Brazil.

In an apparent attempt to justify the university raid, Sao Paulo's security chief

charged Sept. 27 that many student demonstrations had been instigated by the Communist Party. Col. Erasmo Dias displayed printed matter, signs and posters seized from the students and asserted that "some students" had "confessed" that the student movement was moving into "a real terrorist phase."

A military court in Sao Paulo acquitted 25 persons accused of belonging to the Communist Party, it was reported Oct. 28.

Human Rights Abuses & U.S. Relations

U.S. rights reports. U.S. State Department reports on the general status of human rights for the nations receiving U.S. security assistance were released March 12.

The reports, submitted to the U.S. Congress under the 1976 Foreign Military Assistance Act, were made public by the Senate Foreign Relations Committee's subcommittee on foreign assistance. Congress had asserted its opposition to extending security assistance to governments that engaged in "a consistent pattern of gross violations of internationally recognized human rights," except in extraordinary circumstances.

The report on Brazil noted that "cases of arbitrary arrest and detention have occurred" and that "fair hearings by impartial tribunals are not consistently available to political detainees." It pointed out that use of decree-laws had diluted legal safeguards against rights encroachments. Reports of arbitrary arrest and detention and torture of political prisoners also were noted.

Brazil rejects U.S. arms aid—Brazil, following the lead of Argentina and Uruguay, had rejected all U.S. military assistance because the Carter Administration had sought to link the aid to increased observance of human rights.

The Brazilian Foreign Ministry issued a statement March 5 refusing "any assistance of a military nature that depends, directly or indirectly, on previous inquiries by organs of foreign governments into matters that, by their nature, are the exclusive competence of the Brazilian government."

The statement charged that a report by the Carter Administration on Brazil's human rights situation contained "tendentious and unacceptable comments and judgments." The Administration had been required by law to submit the report to Congress in connection with a request for more than $55 million in military aid to Brazil. The study was not made public, but it was understood to deal with the treatment of political prisoners, pressures against the Roman Catholic Church, the situation of Brazilian Indians and the continuing activity of urban "death squads," according to the Financial Times (London) March 7.

The U.S. Embassy in Brasilia denied March 5 that it had interfered in Brazil's internal affairs, asserting: "Concern for human rights transcends national frontiers." The U.S. said it was bound to promote human rights by both the United Nations Charter and the Universal Declaration of Human Rights.

Brazil reiterated its rejection of U.S. military aid March 7, saying it would seek substitute assistance from other countries. The government did not disclose which countries it had in mind, but the newspaper O Estado de Sao Paulo said they probably included West Germany, France and Belgium.

Members of Brazil's opposition party joined the government in denouncing the U.S. despite their previous criticism of the government for violating human rights. Thales Ramalho, secretary general of the Brazilian Democratic Movement (MDB), said March 6 that he would offer President Ernesto Geisel the MDB's support "in this moment when the sovereignty of the country is at stake. We carry out opposition to the government, not to the nation."

The Brazilian government also announced March 11 that it was cancelling its military aid treaty with the U.S. in a further protest against the human rights report.

Under the military aid treaty, signed in 1952, the U.S. provided Brazil with credits and cash for the purchase of American military equipment; military schools in the two countries exchanged students, and the U.S. magazine Military Review published an edition in Portuguese.

Brazil's rejection of U.S. aid was regarded as largely symbolic, the New York Times reported March 12. Brazil's 196,000-man army, the largest in Latin America, had become less dependent on U.S. assistance in recent years as the country began building its own arms industry.

Torture reports continue. Reports of torture by Brazilian security officers continued to appear in the Brazilian and U.S. news media.

Brazilian newspapers published descriptions of the torture of political prisoners in Rio and Sao Paulo jails, it was reported Sept. 11. The prisoners were denied food and put in an electronic torture machine called the "refrigerator," according to the reports. After six days of such treatment, one prisoner said, he began beating his head against the wall.

A man who was freed Aug. 31 after four months' detention at Sao Paulo's Department of Public Order had a ruptured eardrum and pains in his spine and knees from beatings. After meeting with him, MDB congressman Joao Cunha denounced violence against prisoners.

Three weeks earlier, 18 political prisoners in Rio had held a hunger strike against torture. The prisoners were held on suspicion of belonging to the clandestine Movement for the Emancipation of the Proletariat, it was reported Aug. 18.

Five leaders of the Communist Party of Brazil, a Maoist group not connected with the orthodox Brazilian Communist Party, were sentenced to five years in prison for "attempting to reorganize a party banned in law," it was reported July 8. Seven others were convicted in absentia, and a few (the number was not disclosed) were acquitted. The defense lawyer charged during the trial that the defendants all had been tortured. The Maoists had been arrested in a police raid in December in which two of their comrades were shot dead. A third comrade arrested in the raid was later reported to have been "run over" (the government's code name for death under torture, according to the Latin America Political Report). The Maoist party had established an abortive guerrilla movement in the Amazonian state of Para, which was the subject of Renato Tapajos' novel.

Earlier, two French lawyers had reported Feb. 13 that Brazilian police were torturing common criminals and minors as well as political prisoners. Louis Joinet and Mario Stasi, who investigated the observance of human rights in Brazil on behalf of the International Commission of Catholic Jurists, said minors were being tortured at Sao Paulo's State Department of Criminal Investigation. Among the alleged torture victims were a young Communist and the son of an alleged drug dealer.

A local official who denounced human rights violations was removed from office Feb. 2 and stripped of his political rights for 10 years. Glenio Gomes Peres, a city councilman in Porto Alegre, was punished by President Geisel for comments he made Feb. 1 when he took office. Gomes Peres, an MDB member, had said among other things that in Porto Alegre "there are schools known as antiterrorist schools which are designed to train specialists in removing human fingernails, in causing people physical pain, in making a person pay with his blood, his life, for the right to think and to exercise his freedom."

A second city councilman in Porto Alegre, Marcos Klassman, was dismissed from office Feb. 16 and stripped of his political rights for 10 years after he criticized the government's rights record and its removal of Gomes Peres.

The federal censorship department ordered radio and television stations not to discuss Klassman's dismissal. When Klassman's party, the Brazilian Democratic Movement (MDB), took an ad in a Rio de Janeiro newspaper to protest the dismissal, two army generals publicly warned the party that the government would tolerate no criticism, it was reported Feb. 26.

The National Conference of Brazilian Bishops, the highest body of Brazil's Roman Catholic Church, charged that government repression had led to "permanent insecurity [among] the people," it was reported Feb. 26. The bishops denounced "arbitrary methods of repression without possibility of defense, compulsory internment, unexplained disappearances ... [and] acts of violence practiced with the facile valor of clandestine terrorism [with] frequent and almost total impunity."

Meanwhile, a military court in Sao Paulo rejected an appeal for a political prisoner to be examined by a private doctor for signs of torture, it was reported Feb. 16. The appeal was filed by

a lawyer on behalf of Aldo Silva Arantes, a suspected member of the Brazilian Communist Party who was arrested in December 1976. The court said the Sao Paulo military commander, Gen. Dilermando Gomes Monteiro, had reported that bruises on Silva's body were not the result of mistreatment in prison.

Political prisoners allege torture. O Estado de Sao Paulo printed a letter in its Oct. 26 edition in which 11 political prisoners charged that they had been tortured systematically by police and soldiers in Sao Paulo and Rio de Janeiro.

The prisoners, who were accused of belonging to a left-wing extremist organization, repeated their charges in several widely publicized court hearings, according to the Washington Post Nov. 10.

The letter contained the most detailed account of torture ever printed in the Brazilian press. The prisoners described various methods used by police and army torturers, including:

■ The "icebox," in which prisoners were put in "a refrigerated cement booth" and exposed to freezing temperatures over long periods of time, doused with cold water and subjected to "strident sounds of a high frequency" that induced "nausea, vomiting and even madness."

■ The "dragon," in which prisoners were strapped to a chair and subjected to electric shocks with wires connected to "a small instrument with a handcrank that increases the intensity of the current."

■ The "cross," in which a prisoner was pinned against a wall with his arms forced apart and his legs held together, and was kicked in the genitals.

■ Sexual abuse of both male and female prisoners.

The prisoners identified the Rio headquarters of the army's Department of Internal Order (DOI) as a major torture center. DOI offices were "veritable scientific laboratories of torture," the prisoners said.

The prisoners' allegations provoked a wave of public protest, according to the Washington Post. The national bar association called for a restoration of the right of habeas corpus, and the opposition Brazilian Democratic Movement called the torture of prisoners "a festival of bar-

barism and sadism, an authentic spectacle of bestiality."

President Geisel's press secretary, Col. Jose Maria de Toledo Camargo, described the prisoners' charges as "serious and impressive." He said the government would investigate the allegations thoroughly. Army officials, however, denied that any prisoner had received "inhumane treatment" in detention.

Meanwhile, more than 60 prisoners in Sao Paulo and Rio were on a hunger strike to protest the condition of female prisoners and alleged death threats against women in detention, the Post reported. Since the beginning of the strike two weeks earlier, some of the prisoners had been transferred to hospitals or released from preventive detention.

Policemen reported in death squad. A police officer assigned to investigate the Rio de Janeiro "death squad" announced Aug. 9 that seven policemen had been identified as members of the assassination gang.

Helber Murtinho said the death squad comprised three groups of policemen and hired assassins who were paid by shop and store owners to kill petty criminals. One of the groups already had been broken up and the other two would fall soon, Murtinho said.

The former police commissioner of Rio de Janeiro State, Silva Pereira de Andrade, was arrested Aug. 31 in connection with murders by the local death squad. He confessed to several crimes, according to press reports.

Other incidents involving the Rio death squad included the following:

■ Two bodies bearing signs of a "death squad" execution—multiple bullet wounds and evidence of torture—were found in Rio Sept. 4.

■ 12 persons were found murdered Oct. 18 in the district of Baixada do Fluminense, according to the Spanish news agency EFE Oct. 19.

The victims, mostly unskilled laborers, each had been shot at least 10 times in typical death-squad fashion.

In Sao Paulo, meanwhile, a court acquitted a top police official of participating in three death-squad murders in 1969.

Sergio Fleury, police director of criminal investigation, was widely believed to be the head of the Sao Paulo death squad, but nothing had been proved against him in several trials. In the latest trial, reported Oct. 14, the judge and the prosecutor received numerous telephoned death threats. Of the five prosecution witnesses, three failed to show up and the other two had only praise for Fleury, according to the Latin America Political Report.

Fleury faced three more trials on death-squad charges, the Report said.

The Rio death squad was blamed for the torture and murder of three persons whose corpses were found in the city's suburbs Nov. 14. The local newspaper Jornal da Tarde reported Nov. 17 that the Rio death squad was responsible for 95 killings in 1977. The victims, most of them minor criminals, usually were found shot to death next to isolated roads or floating in streams.

Only 20% of the murders had been solved and 15 persons arrested, the newspaper said. Seven of the detainees were military policemen.

Opposition congressman Jose Oliveira Costa charged that death squads were active in virtually all Brazilian states, it was reported Nov. 7. Costa said the national security was at stake and asked President Geisel to order an investigation of death squad crimes.

U.S. envoy on tour. Terence Todman, U.S. assistant secretary of state for inter-American affairs, visited four South American countries May 8–17 in what was described in the press as a lightning "get-acquainted" tour.

Todman visited Brazil May 12–14. He was shunned by Brazilian President Ernesto Geisel, presumably because of comments he had made about Brazil at a press conference in Caracas May 11.

The U.S. envoy told reporters that the Carter Administration "is not prepared to accept the policy of the governments of Richard Nixon and Gerald Ford, according to which Brazil is the leading country of Latin America, and it shows the way to the other nations of the continent." The comment apparently pleased Venezuelan leaders, who were wary of Brazil's economic and military power, but it irked the

Brazilian Foreign Ministry, which replied drily that "each country has its weight in the community of nations, and Brazil is no exception. The U.S. is doubtless a leader not only in America but in the West. Perhaps that makes it easier for the U.S. to judge the importance of other nations."

Because of this exchange and recent U.S.-Brazilian conflicts over human rights and nuclear power plants, Todman's reception in Brasilia was chilly. The Brazilian government even hinted that Todman was lucky to get to see Foreign Minister Antonio Azeredo da Silveira, according to the Washington Post May 15. However, the U.S. envoy made a number of conciliatory statements during his visit and was praised by Brazilian officials after his departure.

Todman told reporters in Brasilia May 13 that Brazil's plan to purchase atomic energy facilities from West Germany, which the U.S. had opposed strongly, was an accomplished fact. "The U.S. considers Brazil and Germany to be sovereign nations that can sign any agreements they see fit," the U.S. envoy said.

Todman added that while the Carter Administration would give preferential treatment to foreign countries that respected human rights, the State Department gave Brazil higher marks than many other nations on this issue. Despite recent U.S.-Brazilian tensions, Todman said, Washington would maintain in principle the Ford Administration's "memorandum of understanding" giving Brazil special "consultant status" with the U.S.

Following Todman's departure for Bolivia, legislators of Brazil's ruling Arena party termed his visit a "complete success." Jose de Magalhaes Pinto, president of the Brazilian Senate, said that because of Todman's visit, Brazil and the U.S. henceforth would solve their problems "at proper levels and in due course, since contacts at the level of undersecretaries will be followed by contacts between ministers and later between presidents."

Mrs. Carter in Brazil. Rosalynn Carter, wife of U.S. President Jimmy Carter, visited seven countries in the Caribbean and Latin America May 30–June 12 on a tour that combined goodwill gestures with substantive political and economc discussion.

Mrs. Carter visited Brazil June 6–9. Throughout the tour Mrs. Carter emphasized her husband's desire for closer ties to Latin American nations and his commitment to promoting the observance of human rights.

The Brazilian government, which was angry at the U.S. for pushing the human rights issue and opposing Brazilian plans to build a nuclear power industry, gave Mrs. Carter a low-key welcome in Brasilia June 6. Foreign Minister Antonio Azeredo da Silveira said only that the government felt "pleasure and satisfaction" in receiving Mrs. Carter. Mrs. Carter extended her husband's greetings to the government and cited his "commitment to human rights, [his] recognition of the individuality and . . . the sovereignty of each of the countries of the hemisphere and [his] desire to press forward on the great economic issues which concern the developed and developing world."

Mrs. Carter met for more than an hour June 7 with President Ernesto Geisel. She said at a news conference later that she had stressed the U.S.' "deep, deep commitment to human rights" and that she and Geisel had discussed in general terms the "very hard question" of stopping the spread of nuclear weapons. Press reports said later that Geisel had refused Mrs. Carter's request that he sign the American Convention on Human Rights.

Mrs. Carter flew to Recife June 8 to visit an old friend. There, in a gesture to dramatize U.S. concern for human rights, she met briefly with two American missionaries who said they had been stripped, beaten and humiliated by Brazilian police who arrested them May 15 and held them without charges for three days. The missionaries, Rev. Lawrence Rosebaugh and Thomas Capuano, worked with the poor in Recife.

Foreign Minister Azeredo da Silveira charged in an interview published in Brazil June 12 that the U.S. press had exaggerated the mistreatment of the two missionaries. Referring to the U.S. government, he said, "One cannot protect human rights in a cockeyed fashion, looking only to one side." He noted that American "police killed two demonstrators and injured 133 during a Puerto Rican demonstration in Chicago" recently.

As a result of the meeting with Mrs. Carter in June, Capuano was expelled from Brazil after state authorities denied his request for a permanent visa, it was reported July 27. A committee appointed by Pernambuco authorities Aug. 6 to look into Capuano's charges said Capuano and Rosebaugh had been beaten in a Recife prison but not by police. The culprits, the panel said, were "poor criminals" led by a prisoner who had been freed by the time the committee took testimony.

Capuano wrote in The New York Times Sept. 1 that police were conducting a reign of terror in the slums of Brazil's impoverished northeastern cities. He wrote that prisoners in Recife were subjected to a starvation diet, unsanitary conditions and arbitrary violence, including severe beatings.

Economy

Price controls & wage increase set. President Gen. Ernesto Geisel May 18 signed a series of anti-inflation measures that centralized the anti-inflation effort in the Finance Ministry and froze prices on 10 "critical products," including cigarettes. Price controls were imposed on public services such as water, electricity, gas, transportation and hospital care.

A 44.1% wage increase had been decreed effective May 1 to offset a 46.9% increase in the cost of living between May 1976 and April 1977. The trade union research department in Sao Paulo said the new minimum wage was still only half of what it would be if wages had maintained the purchasing power they had in 1959.

Steel firm gets massive foreign loan. A complex Eurocurrency loan worth $505 million was granted by 20 banks June 20 to Aco Minas Gerais S.A., a Brazilian steel company.

The loan, which was guaranteed by the Brazilian government, would allow work to begin on a $3.2-billion integrated steel complex near Ouro Branco in the Brazilian state of Minas Gerais. The plant would be able to produce about two million metric tons of steel a year when the first stage of construction was finished about 1983.

The loan was coordinated by Morgan Grenfell & Co. The other 19 banks involved in the arrangement included Chase

Manhattan Ltd., Libra Bank Ltd., Banque de Paris et des Pays Bas and Compagnie Luxembourgeoise de la Dresdner Bank AG.

Coffee exports curbed. The government May 20 announced a limit on its coffee exports in order to insure an adequate domestic supply. Starting in July, exporters would be required to provide the domestic market with one sack of green beans (132 pounds) for every two shipped out of the country.

As a part of the government's plan to reduce inflation, which had been running at a 45% annual rate in the previous 12 months, a freeze was imposed on prices paid by domestic roasters. The aim was to keep Brazil's retail price of coffee at about $2 a pound.

Coffee prices thereafter began to drop.

World coffee price issue—Two big U.S. coffee roasters announced further reductions in their wholesale prices of ground coffee, which had been declining since mid-May.

General Foods Corp. Oct. 17 cut its wholesale price 10¢ a pound to $3.41. That was down $1.05 from the mid-April record level. Procter & Gamble's Folger Coffee division Oct. 14 had cut its wholesale prices 20¢ a pound to $3.18.

The slump in price, coupled with a decline in demand, meant that unsold supplies of green coffee beans had been piling up in warehouses in Brazil and Colombia, the world's chief coffee-exporting nations.

However, Brazil and Colombia adopted conflicting export strategies during the six-month price plunge in an effort to stabilize the market price.

Colombia chose an aggressive marketing policy, making extensive sales abroad at the lower prices. (By early November, green coffee beans were trading in New York as low as $1.50 a pound.) The Colombian government reasoned that a return to the record high prices set in April would only intensify the continuing drop in consumer demand. In the U.S., per capita coffee consumption had fallen 15% during 1977, largely because of the high cost of the beverage, according to Business Week Nov. 7.

Brazil took the opposite approach. The government decided to withhold its coffee crop from the world market in hopes of forcing the price back up to Brazil's official export level of $3.20 a pound.

Ten other coffee-producing nations in Central and South America ratified Brazil's strategy Oct. 21. After a two-day meeting in El Salvador, representatives of that country, Guatemala, Honduras, Nicaragua, Panama, Costa Rica, the Dominican Republic, Ecuador, Venezuela and Mexico said they would stockpile their coffee until prices moved higher.

Brazil abandoned its boycott strategy in a surprise move announced Nov. 4 after secret negotiations with Colombia. The two nations agreed to coordinate their export policies in an effort to stabilize the world price at about $2 a pound. Mexico, the Ivory Coast and El Salvador joined in action Nov. 9.

The chief reason behind Brazil's sudden turnaround was a fear of incurring a large trade deficit in 1977, according to Business Week. Government officials had concluded that unless earnings on coffee exports increased $500 million to $600 million, the country would not be able to balance its trade account by the end of the year, Business Week said.

Iran trade pact signed. The governments of Brazil and Iran June 23 signed a five-year, $6.5-billion trade agreement that called for the exchange of Iranian petroleum for Brazilian agricultural and manufactured goods.

Brazil agreed to quadruple its Iranian oil purchases by 1978 and to buy 25% of its petroleum from Iran by 1979. In 1978 Brazil would purchase 160,000 barrels of Iranian oil per day, worth about $800 million. Brazil's oil requirements were currently valued at $4 billion a year.

Iran agreed to use at least 30% of its Brazilian oil payments to purchase Brazilian agricultural and manufactured goods, transporting them back to Iran in empty oil tankers. The agreement did not identify the Brazilian products, but they were expected to include soybeans, maize, sorghum, meat, rice, sugar and railway equipment, according to the Financial Times (London) June 27.

The agreement also called for joint agricultural ventures for soybean production in Brazil and vegetable-oil extraction facilities in Iran. A joint company would be established by the state-controlled Banco do Brasil, a Brazilian agricultural combine and some Iranian banks.

Brazil had reduced its oil consumption by 200,000 barrels per day in the first five months of 1977, the government announced June 24. The reduction was part of a government program designed to save the country $1 billion in 1977 and ease Brazil's balance of payments deficit.

The value of Brazil's oil imports had increased 38% in 1976, and was largely responsible for the $2.15-billion trade deficit recorded for the year, according to the Latin America Economic Report March 11. Government figures showed that Brazilian imports rose only 1.5% in 1976 while exports rose 16.8%. However, the rise in exports was roughly equivalent to the rise in the value of coffee exports, which earned the country $2.39 billion during the year, the Economic Report noted.

3 nations discuss hydroelectric plans. Representatives of Brazil, Paraguay and Argentina met in Asuncion, Paraguay Sept. 22–23 to discuss three hydroelectric projects being planned on the Parana River.

The Parana begins in east central Brazil and flows to the southwest, moving along the Brazil-Paraguay and Paraguay-Argentina borders, entering Argentina and finally emptying into the River Plate just north of Buenos Aires.

Brazil and Paraguay jointly had begun building a massive dam and hydroelectric station on the Parana at Itaipu on their common border. Further downstream, Paraguay and Argentina planned to build two smaller stations at Corpus and Yacireta-Apipe on their common border.

Brazil and Argentina were at odds over the size and nature of the Itaipu project. Argentina wanted Itaipu to be as small as possible, for the larger it was, the less powerful it rendered Corpus and Yacireta-Apipe. Brazil, on the other hand, wanted a large Itaipu station to provide power for the burgeoning industries in southern Brazil. As the junior partner in each of the three Parana projects, Paraguay had a limited amount of influence in the dispute.

The Asuncion meeting was called to discuss only "technical" matters relating to the power projects, but Argentina managed to bring up its overall dispute with Brazil. The Argentine delegate spoke of "compatibilization," that is, the need for an agreement to insure that Itaipu did not make Corpus and Yacireta-Apipe impractical.

According to the Latin America Political Report Sept. 30, Argentina sought assurances from Brazil on two issues: the height of the Itaipu dam and the way in which the dam would be used.

The height involved both the level of the water in the reservoir above the dam and the level at which the water passed out through the turbines at the bottom. These levels placed constraints on the power potential of the Corpus project. If Brazil extracted the maximum amount of energy from Itaipu, the Political Report said, Corpus would not be viable.

As for the use of Itaipu, Brazilian technicians had said the most efficient method would be to run the turbines in bursts of four or five hours to provide more energy at times of peak demand, the Political Report said. Argentina wanted the water to flow through the turbines all day at a lower rate to prevent radical alterations of the lower course of the Parana.

The Asuncion meeting did not resolve the general dispute, but it was expected to lead to other tripartite meetings. The meeting itself was a small victory for Argentina, since Brazil previously had refused even to discuss Itaipu with Buenos Aires.

Paraguay stands firm on electric grid frequency—In a major reverse for Brazil's hydroelectric power plans, Paraguay refused to change the frequency of its electric grid from 50 cycles to Brazil's 60 cycles. As a result, Brazil and Paraguay announced Nov. 11 that their joint power station at Itaipu on the Parana River would have half its generators at 50 cycles and half at 60 cycles.

Brazil had wanted Paraguay to change to 60 cycles because Brazil would be using most of Itaipu's power and because the change would have made it more difficult for Paraguay to pursue joint power projects with Argentina, which had a 50-cycle grid, according to the Latin America Economic Report Nov. 8.

Under the Itaipu treaty, Brazil and Paraguay were to share the station's power equally. Since Paraguay would be able to absorb only 5%–10% of its share of the power, and since it was prevented by the treaty from selling any of its surplus to Argentina, Brazil would have to install expensive converters to purchase Paraguay's surplus of 50-cycle electricity.

Other economic developments. Among other economic developments:

■ The Brazilian subsidiary of General Motors Corp. laid off 400 workers at the end of April, raising to 3,270 the number of workers laid off by the auto industry in 1977, it was reported May 6. The auto industry had dropped to zero growth following 20 years of rapid expansion, it had been reported March 25.

■ The Brazilian cruzeiro was devalued by 1.72% Dec. 6. These were the 12th and 13th "mini-devaluations" set by the Central Bank in 1977, bringing total devaluation during the year to 27.9%.

■ There had been an overall rise in the number of business failures in Brazil, according to the Latin America Economic Report June 3. The Lutfalla textiles firm and the Colorado television manufacturer were among companies that had failed recently. In Sao Paulo, the Economic Report noted, claims for unpaid bills against companies had risen by 110% in the first three months of 1977. The major cause of the problem was the growing indebtedness of Brazilian companies, the Report said.

Atomic Energy

U.S.-Brazil nuclear-reactor dispute. The U.S. and Brazil became involved in a dispute over a 1975 West German agreement to build eight nuclear plants for Brazil at a cost of $5 billion, a uranium enrichment plant, and a fuel-reprocessing plant.

U.S.-Brazilian talks on the controversy ended early March 2 after only one session.

The U.S. delegation, headed by Deputy Secretary of State Warren M. Christopher, left Brasilia before dawn, abruptly closing discussions that had begun the day before. The two countries issued only this communique:

"The two sides exchanged opinions on

nuclear matters and energy problems. Each side will now consider the expressed position of the other side. There will be further conversations on these matters."

According to press reports, Christopher had insisted that Brazil not establish the fuel-reprocessing and uranium-enrichment plants provided for in the 1975 agreement with West Germany. In return, Christopher said, the U.S. would provide Brazil with nuclear fuel or arrange to put the uranium-enrichment process under some kind of international control. The Brazilian negotiator, Foreign Minister Antonio Azeredo da Silveira, reportedly rejected Christopher's suggestions on grounds that they would make Brazil dependent on foreign sources for its energy needs. Azeredo also pointed out that the West German agreement already had been signed by both governments and approved by the Brazilian Congress.

The U.S. and several other countries believed that Brazil wanted a uranium-enrichment plant to make plutonium for medium-sized atomic bombs. While the Brazilian government insisted that it wanted only to satisfy the country's energy needs, military officers admitted privately that the agreement with West Germany was designed to raise Brazil to Argentina's level of nuclear development and to enable Brazil to build an atomic bomb, the London newsletter Latin America reported March 11. Although Brazil had agreed to international inspection and to safeguards beyond those required by the International Atomic Energy Agency, the U.S. remained convinced that they were unenforceable, according to The New York Times Feb. 7. Both Argentina and Brazil had refused to sign the Nuclear Non-proliferation Treaty.

West Germany honors Brazil agreement— Despite strong protests from the U.S., the West German government April 5 approved export licenses for blueprints of a pilot uranium-reprocessing plant and a demonstration uranium-enrichment plant to be built in Brazil.

West German Chancellor Helmut Schmidt had held up the export licenses since January, when Vice President Mondale visited Bonn and told him that President Carter had serious objections to the nuclear agreement with Brazil. U.S. Secretary of State Cyrus Vance visited Bonn March 31 to apply further U.S. pressure, but Schmidt reportedly was adamant, arguing that West Germany must honor its international agreements and that Brazil would use its nuclear technology for peaceful purposes.

(Despite Bonn's public determination, a U.S. State Department spokesman noted April 8 that West Germany's initial exports to Brazil would be limited to blueprints and other data, still leaving the U.S. time to convince Bonn and Brasilia to change their plans. West German officials noted that the actual construction of the enrichment and reprocessing plants would take years, and they said Bonn was willing to confer with the U.S. on possible additional controls in future contracts with other countries.)

The U.S. pressure evoked protests in both West Germany and Brazil. In West Germany, the weekly newspaper Die Zeit charged that the U.S. wanted to destroy the agreement between Bonn and Brasilia to secure the Brazilian contracts for the U.S. nuclear industry, it was reported April 9. Count Otto Lambsdorff, economic spokesman for the Free Democratic Party, said Bonn must honor the Brazilian agreement "to uphold the international credibility of the Federal Republic of Germany as well as to insure the future of German export technology." German labor unions estimated that as many as 200,000 jobs depended on the nuclear industry.

The U.S. pressure had brought U.S.-Brazilian relations to their lowest point in more than a decade, the New York Times reported March 28. Some ranking Brazilian officials believed U.S. pressure against the nuclear deal and in favor of greater observance of human rights in Brazil were part of a larger U.S. effort to prevent Brazil from becoming a major world power, according to the Times.

Brazilian Mines and Energy Minister Shigeaki Ueki said March 26 that Brazil would carry out its nuclear energy program "at all costs." Brazil planned to rely on nuclear and hydroelectric plants because it lacked domestic oil deposits and wanted to cut its purchases of high-priced foreign petroleum.

U.S. proposes ban on plutonium use. President Carter April 7 proposed that the U.S. "defer indefinitely" the use of plutonium as a fuel in commercial nuclear power plants.

Carter said that to make sure the U.S. did not need to use plutonium, he would propose an increase in the production of enriched uranium for nuclear power plant use. He also said he would propose legislation to allow the U.S. to guarantee supplies of uranium fuel to foreign countries so they would not have to rely on reprocessed plutonium either. (According to the Washington Post April 13, the U.S. was insisting that countries that purchased nuclear power plants from the U.S. waive their rights to the plutonium generated by burning U.S.-supplied uranium in those plants.

The Carter Administration was holding up approval of 28 export licenses involving the shipment of enriched uranium fuel to 13 countries, one of which was Brazil, according to a Washington Post report April 14.

Other Developments

Divorce legalized. The Brazilian Congress June 23 gave final approval to a constitutional amendment that allowed married couples to divorce "after three years of legal separation or five years of de facto separation."

The amendment replaced a constitutional clause saying marriage was "indissoluble." Brazilians previously had been able to obtain legal separations but not divorces. Seven million or more Brazilians, including Cabinet ministers and ambassadors, were thought to be living with second husbands or wives after having separated from their legal spouses, according to the Washington Post June 17.

The divorce amendment was approved despite a vigorous campaign against it by the Roman Catholic Church, which all but threatened excommunication of divorced couples and of legislators who voted for the amendment. More than 90% of Brazil's 110 million inhabitants were nominally Roman Catholic.

The divorce amendment narrowly had been defeated in Congress in 1976, when constitutional changes required a two-thirds majority vote. In April, however, President Gen. Ernesto Geisel issued a decree requiring only a simply majority to pass an amendment, although two congressional votes were required as before. The divorce measure passed 219–161 June 16, and 226–159 June 23.

Geisel, who had remained neutral during the debate on divorce, was expected to sign the amendment soon. Then Congress would have to pass bills regulating the terms of divorces before couples could take advantage of the amendment in court.

Rules adopted—Following a favorable vote in the Chamber of Deputies, the Senate Dec. 4 cleared a new law setting regulations under which Brazilians would be able to obtain divorces.

(Geisel signed the bill Dec. 26.)

Salvador mayor ousted. The mayor of Salvador (Bahia State), Jorge Hage, was removed by the state governor after Hage publicly detailed the city's serious economic and health problems, it was reported April 11. Hage also had alienated business and real-estate executives by trying to increase property taxes and cut tax delinquency. The local press had denounced him as "an irresponsible psychopath."

Chile

Regime Tightens Control

The military government imposed tighter political control over Chile during 1977 by outlawing the country's remaining four political parties. The four-year-old state of siege was to continue in effect indefinitely, President Augusto Pinochet Ugarte declared, and he indicated that even the elections promised for 1985 might be postponed.

Political parties banned. The government March 12 dissolved the four political parties that had not been banned after the 1973 military coup—the liberal Christian Democratic party, the conservative National party and two rightist groups.

President Gen. Augusto Pinochet had said March 11 that the parties, which officially had been "in recess," had to be eliminated "to keep them from returning Chile to chaos, misery and demagoguery." "I have always felt," Pinochet added, "that political parties are the most fertile ground for Marxist and Communist doctrine. [This doctrine] filters through everywhere but never shows its face; it penetrates within, to rot, destroy and annihilate."

Despite the inclusion of the three conservative parties, most observers felt the decree was aimed directly at the Christian Democrats, who had stepped up their criticism of the military regime in recent months.

Gen. Hernan Bejares, secretary general of the government, charged March 11 that the Christian Democrats were plotting to seize power. As evidence, Bejares gave newsmen copies of two documents drafted by the party's top leaders, Andres Zaldivar and Tomas Reyes. The documents, Bejares asserted, revealed a "subversive plan to bring about the fall of the government" in cooperation with the outlawed Communist party and "Marxist sectors in the outside world."

Zaldivar and Reyes heatedly denied Bejares' charges March 13, asserting that the documents expressed "democratic positions" and rejected cooperation with the Communists. The texts of the documents were printed by Santiago newspapers March 12. They called for a broad alliance with the left and moderate right to bring democracy back to Chile. The alliance would exclude right- and left-wing extremists and the Communist party, but it would take "a rational attitude" toward the "Communist problem," the documents said.

In an earlier move against the Christian Democrats, the government issued a decree Jan. 28 indefinitely closing the party's radio station, Radio Balmaceda. The government cited a decree law that forbade political parties to own radio stations, but Christian Democrats noted that this was the first time the law had been enforced in the three years since it was enacted. Radio Balmaceda had been criticizing the government over the recent spate of bankruptcies in private investment companies, which was threatening to disrupt Chile's financial structure.

The military government had closed Radio Balmaceda four times before, but never for longer than three weeks. The latest closing was for the duration of the state of siege, which had been imposed in September 1973 and was extended for another six months March 11.

Radio Balmaceda was one of the last independent radio stations in Chile. The last independent newsmagazine, Ercilla, fell under government control in mid-January when its managing editor, a Christian Democrat, walked out in a dispute with the magazine's new, pro-government owners, it was reported Feb. 3.

The former editor, Emilio Filippi, announced plans in February to open a new magazine. However, the government issued a decree March 11 forbidding the creation of new magazines or newspapers without express government permission.

Vatican scores Pinochet. The Vatican radio station charged Jan. 9 that a recent statement by President Augusto Pinochet Ugarte amounted to "political absurdity."

In one of its rare attacks on a head of state, the Vatican deplored Pinochet's recent definition of his military regime as a "totalitarian democracy" made necessary by the "menacing growth of a giant, that is, Marxism."

"Through the ages," the Vatican broadcast said, "the human mind has caressed mathematical absurdities such as squaring the circle and physico-mechanical absurdities such as perpetual motion. But the political absurdity of Gen. Pinochet does not seem very original. For some time we have observed the extreme prestige enjoyed by the concept of democracy—even the less democratic regimes try to adopt the label. What had not been tried until now was the leap of faith to the expression 'totalitarian democracy.' "

Pinochet defends rule. President Augusto Pinochet Ugarte marked his fourth anniversary in office Sept. 11 by vigorously defending his government and rejecting any possibility of political change in the near future.

In a televised address to the nation, Pinochet said the state of siege would be maintained until "we judge that the symptoms of normalization permit us to reduce or lift [it]." Since imposing it in 1973, the military regime had used the state of siege to ban unauthorized assemblies, censor the press, suspend the right of habeas corpus, dissolve all political parties and curb labor union rights.

Pinochet reaffirmed an earlier promise to hold elections in 1985, but only if "the profound reasons that required the [military coup] have been overcome." The government that emerged from these elections, he said, would be an "authoritarian democracy." In addition to executive, legislative and judicial branches, the government would have a "security power" through which the armed forces would "represent the permanent interests of the nation," he declared.

The president expressed particular pride in his economic program, which he called a "resounding success." He said inflation in 1977 would be less than 70%, compared with 400% in 1975. For the second year in a row, he added, Chile would pay nearly $1 billion of its foreign debt without seeking renegotiation from its creditors. He acknowledged that his fiscal austerity and laissez-faire policies had created a high level of unemployment, but he said Chile would not change its economic program under foreign pressure.

Pinochet obliquely blamed the U.S. for Chile's past problems, charging that the Alliance for Progress program of the 1960s had paved the way for "the penetration of demagogic Marxism" in Latin America. The U.S. loan and investment program, he said, had contributed to the breakdown of Latin American government structures and facilitated terrorism and Soviet "aggression." As a result, the armed forces of many Latin American countries had seized power to restore stability and justice, he asserted.

The U.S. frequently had criticized the human rights record of his government, but Pinochet said Washington was showing a "slow but progressive improvement in [its] attitude . . . toward the Chilean reality." Nevertheless, he repeated, Chile would not "modify the course it has planned" merely to "ingratiate itself with certain countries."

Pinochet had spoken with President Carter four days earlier when he visited Washington to attend the signing of the new Panama Canal treaties. He told American reporters Sept. 7 that he and his government "agree with President Carter about respect for human rights, and no one can doubt our good intentions." U.S. officials said Pinochet had "agreed in principle" to Carter's request that a United Nations team be allowed to enter Chile to investigate its human rights situation.

Violations of Human Rights

Hunger strikes protest disappearances. Twenty-four women and two men held a hunger strike at United Nations offices in Santiago June 14–23 to pressure the Chilean government to release information on 500 persons who allegedly had disappeared in Chile since the 1973 military coup.

The strike, at headquarters of the U.N.'s Economic Commission for Latin America (ECLA), ended after the government promised U.N. Secretary General Kurt Waldheim that it would supply the information and would not take reprisals against the hunger strikers. The strikers all claimed to be relatives of disappeared persons.

Smaller groups of Chilean exiles held sympathy hunger strikes in Paris and Mexico City June 14–23, and five Americans staged a sit-in and fast at ECLA's Washington office. These protests ended with the Santiago strike, but a new hunger strike was held June 23–27 by eight Chilean exiles at offices of the International Red Cross in Geneva.

Amnesty International had reported March 16 that at least 1,500 persons had disappeared in Chile since the armed forces seized power in 1973. The London-based organization said it had received the names of 1,000 persons from contacts in Chile and had compiled dossiers on 504 of them whose disappearances it had verified.

An Amnesty spokesman said most of the persons who had disappeared were still

alive and being held in concentration camps in remote areas of Chile.

In an Associated Press report released Jan. 1, the Chilean government had claimed to have had only one political prisoner, but legal sources close to the Roman Catholic Church said there were 541 persons known to be serving sentences for political offenses and 61 others awaiting court martial. A Red Cross official said there were 700–800 political prisoners in Chile, most of whom, he predicted, would be released if other countries agreed to let them immigrate.

Chilean official charged with torture. A high-ranking Chilean diplomatic aide who was visiting the U.S. as a guest of the State Department was asked by U.S. officials to cut his visit short after human rights organizations charged that he had tortured political prisoners in Chile.

Lt. Col. Jaime Lavin Farina, the third-ranking official of Chile's Foreign Ministry, had arrived in the U.S. Jan. 4 under the auspices of the International Visitors Program, a State Department-sponsored tour for potential leaders of foreign countries. Lavin was asked to leave Jan. 28 after Amnesty International, the National Council of Churches and other human rights groups charged that he was an officer of DINA, the Chilean secret police, and had tortured political detainees.

Rolando Miranda Pinto, a former Chilean air force colonel who lived in exile, said he had been tortured by Lavin after his arrest in Chile in September 1973 for opposing the military coup. Miranda asserted that Lavin had beaten him and subjected him to electroshock torture, it was reported Jan. 30.

The Chilean government Feb. 2 denied that Lavin was a torturer, asserting that Miranda was merely avenging his 1973 conviction for subversion by a military tribunal, of which Lavin had been a part.

(The Chilean government quietly withdrew the nomination of Mario Arnello to be its next ambassador to Canada after Chilean refugees in Canada protested that Arnello was connected with DINA, it was reported Feb. 26.)

Chilean refugee situation. U.S. Rep. Richard L. Ottinger (D, N.Y.) inserted a staff report on the Chilean refugee problem in the Congressional Record June 30. Among excerpts from the report:

. . . It has been over three-and-three-quarter years since the government of President Salvadore Allende was overthrown. Since that time, nearly 30,000 people have fled Chile. These Chileans, as well as many of their countrymen still inside of Chile, have faced, and continue to face, severe difficulties. Amnesty International reports that over 1,500 Chileans has disappeared since the September, 1973 coup; another 5,000 have been executed. In Argentina, during the past two-and-one-half years, between 3,000 and 30,000 persons have disappeared. Many of these people were Chileans. The Amnesty report concluded by observing:

" There are about 12,000 Latin American refugees in Argentina registered with the UNHCR/United Nations High Commission for Refugees/ and possibly as many as 100,000 in all (mainly unregistered). Many of these people are Chileans who fled from Chile after the coup there in September, 1973 and were caught up in a similar, if not worse wave of terror and repression in Argentina. Many 'have been intimidated, abducted, tortured, and even killed . . . Chilean refugees . . . are not only the target for the DINA/Chilean secret police/ but also for Argentine security forces and extreme right-wing groups such as the Argentinian Anticommunist Alliance (AAA)."

The threat of sudden separation from one's family, torture and even death is but a limited aspect of the refugee's life. In addition, Chileans face a myriad of day-to-day problems, perhaps the most pernicious being the necessity of moving from one country to another. The coup in Chile created a new band of migrants moving across Latin America. Receiving permission to live in Ecuador for six months, in Venezuela for three, families are never allowed to settle down. Such disruptions are particularly hard on the children of refugees. Special measures are needed if such uncertainty is to come to an end. . . .

. . . The Human Rights Commission of the Organization of American States reported in May, 1977 that while fewer persons are being arrested than in the past, the current military government continues to violate regularly the most basic human rights of its citizens.

. . . the United States Committee for Refugees reported that, at the beginning of 1977, there were approximately 10,000 Chileans in Argentina and approximately 10,000 in other Latin American countries.

. . . While some Chilean refugees may be Marxists, many more are not. Spokesmen for Amnesty International are willing to testify that the current military government has sought to quite a broad spectrum of democratic dissent, including that of non-Marxists as well as that of Marxists. The Chilean Refugee Bill (H.R. 5969, 7347, 7366) does allow consular officials to determine the degree to which the political views of a specific refugee might disqualify the applicant under current statutory restrictions.

. . . In June, 1975, the United States established a program to assist Chileans in Chile. In October, 1976, a similar program was begun to help Chileans in Argentina. Under the initial program, 400 heads of family (about 1600 people in all) have been allowed to enter the United States. In addition to these persons, 40 more heads of family have been accepted pending expansion of the numerical limitations by Congress.

While both programs represent first good steps, much more remains to be done. The International Committee for European Migration reported that, as of April 1, 1977, additional opportunities for 1,000 prisoners and their dependents now in Chile were needed in order to complete the prison release program. . . .

In creating new programs to help these people, or in extending the old programs, Congress must be particularly aware of the difficulties faced by hundreds of Chileans who applied for entrance to the United States under existing law. For example, there has been a dangerously long waiting period from the time of application to the time of entry. The first refugees under the 1975 program did not arrive in the United States until October, 1976; and the last families are only now arriving. Moreover, under the 1976 Argentine Parole Program, not one refugee has entered the United States as of May, 1977. This would not be unusual or noteworthy were it not for the fact that every day the application of a Chilean is delayed could cost that Chilean his or her life. This threat also often applies to whole families.

Under the current Parole Program, Chileans in Chile can apply only when they are actually under detention. Chileans are not eligible if they are under threat of arrest, or if they are picked up by the police, tortured, and released. Upon approaching the United States Embassy in Buenos Aires, those Chileans who did manage to flee to Argentina were told to register first with the Office of the United Nations High Commission for Refugees. However, that office has been broken into on no less than two occasions, with the files containing the identity and the whereabouts of Chilean refugees being stolen. Several individuals whose files were removed during these breakins soon disappeared. . . .

U.S. blocks loans to Chile. The U.S. State Department said June 28 that it would withhold two loans to Chile for 30 to 60 days "to see what changes might develop in the human rights situation" in the South American country.

The loans, worth $7 million and $2.6 million respectively, would have aided poor Chilean farmers. The decision to withhold them reportedly was made by

Deputy Secretary of State Warren M. Christopher following what was described in the press as an intense debate among officials of the Carter Administration.

One faction, led by Assistant Secretary of State Terence Todman and backed by officials of the Agency for International Development and the Defense Department, had argued in favor of the loans on the ground that the economic well-being of people was a "human right" as important as some political rights, the New York Times reported June 29.

The faction opposing the loans, which was led by Mark Schneider, a deputy coordinator for human rights, argued that the credits must be withheld to emphasize the U.S. commitment to defending human rights throughout the world.

In May, high Administration officials had met in Washington with leaders of Chile's outlawed opposition parties. Vice President Walter Mondale and President Carter's national security adviser, Zbigniew Brzezinski, conferred May 25 with Eduardo Frei Montalva, former president of Chile and leader of the Christian Democratic Party. Two days later, Christopher met with Clodomiro Almeyda, a former official in the leftist government of the late Chilean President Salvador Allende Gossens.

The Administration denied that it was supporting any opposition faction in Chile, noting that Frei and Almeyda had been political adversaries before Chile's military coup in 1973. "What's at work here is an attempt to reverse symbolisms," said an Administration official quoted by the New York Times May 30. Washington wanted to show the world that while it had once supported the Chilean junta, this support could no longer be taken for granted, the official said.

Chile rejects U.S. aid—The Chilean government June 28 rejected $27.5 million in U.S. aid to protest the Carter Administration's policy of linking economic assistance to the observance of human rights.

The aid rejected by Chile comprised $15 million for surplus wheat sales and $12.5 million for a variety of development loans and grants, including the farm credits withheld by the State Department.

Chile was the sixth Latin American nation to spurn U.S. aid in repudiation of President Carter's human rights policy.

Regime abolishes DINA. The government announced Aug. 12 that it had abolished the National Intelligence Directorate (DINA), the secret police that had been accused of arresting, torturing and murdering thousands of Chileans during the past four years of military rule.

An official decree, dated Aug. 6, said DINA would be replaced by a new organization, the National Intelligence Center (CNI). Its duties would be "to gather information at the national level that might be required for the adoption of measures to safeguard the internal security of the citizenry," the document said.

A government spokesman emphasized that the CNI would have none of DINA's police powers and would be directed by someone other than DINA's commander, Gen. Mario Contreras Tapia. It was unclear whether any of DINA's members would be transferred to the new intelligence agency.

Created shortly after the September 1973 military coup, DINA had been the government's most ruthless and effective instrument against political dissent. In four years its personnel had grown to an estimated 20,000 agents and paid informants, many of them taken from the intelligence agencies of the police and the three armed forces. Responsible solely to President Augusto Pinochet—and therefore beyond the control of the courts or apparently even the top military commanders—DINA was reported to have arrested citizens without charge, held them in torture centers and concentration camps, and sometimes executed them or simply made them vanish.

The government now said that DINA had "completed the delicate functions of national security for which it was created," and could therefore be dissolved. But several newspapers attributed the disbanding of the secret police to pressure from Western governments that were concerned over human rights, particularly the Carter Administration.

Todman visits, studies rights issue— The announcement of DINA's dissolution in fact came on the second day of a visit to Santiago by Terence Todman, U.S. assistant secretary of state for inter-American affairs. Todman, the first high official of the Carter Administration to visit Chile, had come to see if the human-rights situation was improving as the Chilean government claimed. He had been preceded Aug. 8 by Allard K. Lowenstein, a human-rights specialist on the U.S. delegation to the United Nations.

Todman met with Pinochet, other government officials and two prominent critics of military repression—ex-President Eduardo Frei, head of the outlawed Christian Democratic Party, and Raul Cardinal Silva Henriquez, primate of Chile's Roman Catholic Church.

American officials traveling with Todman felt the Chilean government had improved its human-rights record since January, according to the New York Times Aug. 12. Virtually all uncharged prisoners had been released, the Americans said, and there had been a sharp decline in reports of disappeared persons. In addition, Chilean officials reportedly had become less defensive about the human-rights issue, no longer attributing concern over human rights to a "Communist campaign" against Chile.

Nevertheless, eight Chileans were arrested Aug. 11 for attempting to see Todman and report to him on the alleged disappearance of 501 Chileans. The protesters were seized outside the Supreme Court building in Santiago where they were waiting for Todman to emerge from a meeting with the court's president, Jose Maria Eyzaguirre. They were released on bond three hours later, but one of them said they had been interrogated by a member of DINA. (Eyzaguirre had told President Pinochet only hours before Todman's arrival that DINA was hindering court investigations of the 501 alleged disappearances.)

Todman's visit followed somewhat contradictory statements on Chile by the U.S. State Department. The department had said July 11 that it was very pleased with a promise by Pinochet, announced two days earlier, to allow limited elections in Chile in 1984 or 1985. The department's satisfaction was reported widely in Chile. Then on Aug. 1 a State Department spokesman said the U.S. had not lost any of its concern over the Chilean junta's repressive tactics or its "failure to clear up questions about persons who have disappeared."

Disappearances remain unresolved.
Lawyers for relatives of persons who had disappeared in Chile since the military coup charged that the government was not fulfilling its promise to allow a thorough investigation of the disappearances, the Washington Post reported Sept. 5.

The attorneys said the courts were abandoning their investigations whenever they found evidence that the disappearances involved illegal arrests or kidnappings by the secret police.

In one case, the Post reported, the Santiago appeals court had ordered the release of a young Communist when it found that he had been arrested by members of DINA, the secret police agency that supposedly had been abolished in August. However, President Pinochet had ordered that the young man be kept in custody while a military court investigated the possibility that the "arbitrary arrest could have been carried out . . . by subversive [i.e., left-wing] elements." The appeals court handed over the case to the army and no more was heard of it.

Despite such incidents, there was evidence of some relaxation of the government's pervasive repression, according to numerous press reports. The press was being allowed to print some criticism of the government's political and economic policies, the Washington Post noted Sept. 15 And groups representing students, workers and former political parties were speaking out against the government "in terms which a year ago would have seemed unthinkable," according to the Latin America Political Report Sept. 16.

In late August, the Report said, 300 Christian Democratic students had sent a letter to President Pinochet denouncing his 1985 election plan as an attempt to "hide an authoritarian regime under a touched-up facade." The plan was later attacked by an organization of mostly Christian Democratic labor unions known as the "Group of Ten." The group declared that "if criticizing reality or making others see this reality means you are a Communist, then we are all Communists."

A recent Gallup poll showed that 65% of the Chilean population supported the military government and 71% favored its economic policies, the Washington Post reported Sept. 21. Pollsters admitted that "people are afraid to answer" survey questions because they feared reprisal from the government, but the poll director said he was confident that respondents had not lied when they said they supported the regime. Liars were weeded out by "check" questions, the poll director said.

■ Police in Santiago arrested 47 persons Nov. 17 at a rally of more than 100 pesons who demanded information from the government on relatives who had disappeared. The protest took place in front of a government building as the new U.S. ambassador to Chile, George W. Landau, arrived for an audience with Foreign Minister Patricio Carvajal.

Letelier murder probe implicates DINA. A year after Orlando Letelier, a former Cabinet minister and former Chilean ambassador to the U.S., was killed by a bomb in Washington, U.S. investigators believed that the murder had been ordered by the Chilean secret police.

Unnamed investigators told the Washington Post Sept. 7 that the Chilean Socialist leader most probably had been murdered by right-wing Cuban exiles hired by DINA. The wide-ranging investigation was now focusing on the Cuban exile community in the U.S., particularly in Florida and New Jersey.

Justice Department spokesmen would not tell the Post why they believed DINA was involved in the assassination. Syndicated columnists Jack Anderson and Les Whitten reported in the Post's Sept. 8 edition that the murder had been ordered by DINA commander Manuel Contreras Sepulveda, but a Justice Department official said this was "totally incorrect." However, the official said Contreras probably would have known about the plan to kill Letelier.

A federal grand jury in Washington that was still investigating Letelier's death had called at least 21 Cuban exiles to testify, according to the Miami Herald Sept. 10. At least 14 of the exiles were residents of Miami; others lived in New York and New Jersey, and one lived in Mexico. Most of the subpoenaed exiles belonged to the small Cuban Nationalist Movement or to Brigade 2506, the organization of veterans of the Bay of Pigs invasion.

Guillermo Novo, a member of the Cuban Nationalist Movement, had appeared before the grand jury at least twice. Novo denied before the grand jury that he had visited Chile in 1975 to see Orlando Bosch, a Cuban-born anti-Castro terrorist now in jail in Venezuela. The denial brought a perjury charge, and Novo promptly disappeared.

A close associate of Novo, Dionisio Suarez Esquivel, had been in jail since April for refusing to testify before the grand jury despite a grant of immunity.

Law enforcement sources told the Herald that at least one Chilean official, Hector Duran, a consul in Miami, had been called to testify before the grand jury, but Duran denied having seen the panel. Sources told the Herald that another, unidentified Chilean diplomat had been given a lie detector test, but they would not disclose the results of the test.

The Chilean government, meanwhile, steadfastly denied any connection with Letelier's murder. President Pinochet told U.S. reporters in Washington Sept. 7 that if his regime had wanted to kill Letelier, it would have done so while he was in jail in Chile in 1973–74.

Foreign pressure continues—Foreign pressure on the Chilean government to improve its human rights performance continued Aug. 31 as the Socialist International recommended that all socialist governments impose economic sanctions on Chile.

The European Economic Community added to the pressure Sept. 7 by announcing that it would close its Santiago office by the end of 1977. Roy Jenkins, president of the European Commission, said this was a move "to protest the violations of human rights in Chile."

Felipe Gonzalez, leader of the Spanish Socialist Workers' Party, visited Chile Aug. 28–31 to press the government to release imprisoned Chilean socialists. He met with two prominent socialist prisoners and with Chile's justice minister and the president of the Supreme Court. The prisoners were not released, but Gonzalez was favorably impressed nonetheless. "I saw everyone who wanted to talk with me without restriction or control," he said. "I found the situation [in Chile] is not as black and white as it is pictured abroad." He added that President Carter had an "historic opportunity" to help restore democracy to Chile.

U.N. rights resolution condemns Chile. The United Nations Human Rights Commission March 9 adopted a resolution condemning rights abuse by the Chilean government. The resolution, co-sponsored by the U.S., Cuba and six other countries, was based on a report by a U.N. panel, which said the Chilean government was continuing to torture detained persons as "a regular practice." Chileans were disappearing at a "considerably increased" rate, the report said, adding that "persons reported missing frequently turn up dead under suspicious circumstances."

The resolution was passed 26–1 with five abstentions. The lone negative vote was cast by Uruguay, which had been criticized by Brady Tyson March 8 for allegedly abusing human rights.

It was the first time the U.S. had co-sponsored a resolution condemning rights abuse in Chile. On previous resolutions the American delegation had abstained.

The U.N. General Assembly Dec. 16 passed a resolution "deploring" the abuse of human rights in Chile and expressing "particular concern and indignation" over "the continuing disappearance" of Chileans.

The resolution, based on an unfavorable report on Chile by the U.N. Human Rights Commission, passed by a vote of 96–14. The countries voting for it included the U.S., Western European nations and many communist and developing states. Those voting against it were Chile, 12 other Latin American countries and Lebanon.

Chilean delegate Sergio Diez Urzua denounced the resolution as a product of a "conspiracy of great powers." The Chilean Foreign Ministry had said Dec. 2 that although it had given its full cooperation to the U.N. Human Rights Commission, the commission had written a "scurrilous" report on Chile.

Despite the report, there was growing evidence that repression in Chile was becoming less severe, according to newspaper accounts. Of the 45 Chileans known to have been arrested in September, none had disappeared, and almost all had been charged and were being tried, according to the Latin America Political Report Nov. 11. And a military judge said that 15 soldiers had been tried and convicted of abusing civilians, according to the Washington Post the same day.

The judge, Gen. Enrique Morel, said investigations were being conducted into "abnormalities" committed by agents of DINA, the former secret police force, and of the National Information Center, the organization that replaced DINA in August. Morel recently had thrown out a long list of DINA charges, including one allegation that the Vicariate of Solidarity, a dependency of the Roman Catholic Church, was organizing "brigades" to overthrow the government.

Morel also had given only suspended sentences to two men convicted of possessing explosives, the Post noted. During their trial it was revealed that DINA had kidnapped a 16-year-old boy and forced him to accuse the defendants of abducting him.

Spokesmen for the Vicariate of Solidarity told the Post that reports of persons being picked up by security police and simply disappearing had practically ended. And those who were arrested were now being given the chance to defend themselves in military court, according to members of the Vicariate.

Still, the Vicariate and other human rights organizations in Chile were far from satisfied. "The church's position is that as long as there is not a clear set of laws and enforcement by civilian courts, citizens' rights are not really protected," a spokesman for the Vicariate said.

The Vicariate was among the victims of the less frequent yet continuing repression by the military government. Security forces raided a house used by the Vicariate Nov. 16. No arrests or confiscations were made, but the government charged that the house had been used for "political" meetings.

■ Three Chilean women who had traveled to United Nations headquarters in New York to publicize the arrest and alleged torture of relatives were denied reentry to Chile Nov. 23. They were detained at the Santiago airport and put on a plane to Argentina, from where they returned to New York. The Chilean government later agreed to readmit the women, but only if they signed a statement promising not to engage in "political" activities. The women rejected the offer and its implication that their activities on behalf of Chilean prisoners were political, it was reported Nov. 28.

Economic Developments

Economic recovery measures. The military government May 1 enacted a series of economic measures designed to increase purchasing power and "speed up Chile's socioeconomic recovery."

The measures included:

■ A 4% wage increase for public employes (including members of the armed forces and police) and for private employes earning the minimum wage.

■ A professional allowance for public employes and an equivalent allowance for doctors working in the public sector.

■ A special "responsibility allowance," worth 40% of starting salary, for special government consultants with particularly sensitive or unstable jobs, and for top members of the judiciary.

■ A $14-million fund for universities to make supplementary payments to full-time staff.

■ A $20-million appropriation for housing, to help revive the stagnant construction industry.

■ Reductions in income, property and import taxes and a reduction in legal reserves requirements.

The measures would be of most benefit to professionals at the top of the wage scale, according to the Latin America Political Report May 6. New increases in the prices of flour, bread, rice, tea, coffee, train fares, diesel fuel and liquid gas wiped out the 4% wage increase for poorer Chileans, it was reported May 9.

Doctors, judges and other professionals had protested government policies in recent months, helping to spur the new economic measures. The Chilean Medical Association noted that 12.5% of the country's physicians had moved abroad in 1976, according to the New York Times May 3. Of those who remained, only 6% were in private practice, and doctors with less than three years' experience earned an average of about $220 per month. "Under these conditions," a leading doctor said, "they cannot even hope to pay their rent."

The government, however, was confident that the economy was recovering, the Times reported. Officials noted that their strict measures had produced a trade surplus and had raised Chile's credit rating sufficiently to attract a growing amount of foreign bank loans.

The government also pointed to the continuing decrease in the rates of inflation and unemployment. The National Statistics Institute announced April 5 that inflation in the first quarter of 1977 had been 18.9%, only half the 38.8% rate of the first quarter of 1976. Unemployment in Greater Santiago had fallen to 14% in the last quarter of 1976 from a high of 19% in the last quarter of 1975, it was reported Feb. 11.

Critics of the military government and some foreign publications accepted the government's figures but said that they had been achieved at a high cost to Chileans in general and the poor in particular. The living standards of most Chileans had dropped as sharply as inflation had, the New York Times noted May 3. The poorest Chileans suffered widespread malnutrition, the newspaper added.

Chilean agricultural production had dropped in nearly every commodity, and industrial production was still below the level at which it stood when the armed forces seized power in 1973, according to Marcus Raskin of the Washington-based Institute for Policy Studies. The government's unemployment figure was deceptive because about 5% of the work force was employed in "impressed labor," Raskin added in a letter published by the New York Times June 5.

(More than 200,000 persons—over half the total number of unemployed throughout Chile—were employed in the government's Minimum Employment Program [PEM], working for municipal authorities sweeping roads, cleaning up public parks and performing similar duties for half the minimum wage, according to the Latin America Economic Report March 18. More than 22% of PEM's employes formerly had worked in the construction industry, the sector hardest hit by the Chilean recession.)

Foreign investment laws. The government had decreed that private investment companies must recall all their loans within 30 days in order to register formally with the central banking authority, according to the Latin America Report Jan. 7.

The decree, a move to regulate the chaotic capital market, followed the collapse of several investment firms since early December 1976. The bankruptcy of one company, Manuel Rodriguez, had caused a panic among investors in other companies, who began withdrawing their funds from those firms. (The government acknowledged Feb. 18 that it was holding 14 prisoners in connection with the scandal surrounding the collapse. The detainees included the president and vice president of Banco Osorno, which was taken over by the government at the beginning of 1977 and was being investigated thoroughly.

Another new law decreed March 18, would, according to a Central Bank official, make Chile "the best place in Latin America to invest."

The new law replaced Decree-law 600, which followed guidelines set by the Andean Group. Chile had left the Andean Group in 1976, claiming its restrictions on foreign investment were hampering Chile's economic recovery.

Officials said the new law would cut bureaucratic procedures in the investing process and give foreign investors all the advantages of Chilean companies. Under the new regulations:

■ All restrictions on repatriation of profits were lifted.

■ Foreign firms could choose to be taxed at the same rate as local companies (currently 48.5%), or at a higher rate of 49.5% which would be fixed for 10 years.

■ Import-export regulations in force at the time of investment would remain unchanged for foreign investors regardless of modifications subsequently introduced for local companies.

■ Foreign investors could liquidate their Chilean assets after three years and take home their original capital, including money, equipment and technology.

■ Many investments of less than $5 million could be authorized by the executive secretary of Chile's foreign investment committee with the approval of the Chilean president. Larger investments must be reviewed by the entire committee, which comprised five Cabinet-level officials.

Rights issue & debit problem. Because of alleged violations of human rights by the military government, Chile's creditor nations had refused to renegotiate its foreign debt, forcing Chile to triple its

debt-service payments to $1 billion a year through 1980, it was reported May 3. These payments were equal to 10% of the nation's annual gross national product.

Chile received $594.5 million in foreign credits in 1976, according to government statistics reported March 18. The government received $308.5 million of the total. The principal sources of the credits were the International Monetary Fund ($140 million), the World Bank ($99 million) and the Inter-American Development Bank ($69.5 million).

Anaconda Co., a subsidiary of Atlantic Richfield Co. of the U.S., announced March 31 that it had settled the claims it had filed against Overseas Private Investment Corp. (OPIC) in connection with the nationalization of Anaconda's Chilean copper operations in 1971. Anaconda said that OPIC, a U.S. government agency, would pay Anaconda $47.5 million in cash and guarantee $47.6 million of Chilean government notes issued to Anaconda in 1974. Anaconda would assign $27.5 million of the notes to OPIC as the insurer's share of the settlement.

Chilean government revalues peso. The Chilean government March 4 had revalued the peso, the national currency, upward to 17.77 pesos to the U.S. dollar from 19.75 pesos to the dollar. The move was designed to aid Chilean industry by reducing the cost of imported machinery and materials, thus lessening inflationary pressures, according to the Latin America Economic Report March 11.

Southern oil find reported. The state oil company said it had found petroleum deposits in the Strait of Magellan off Chile's southern coast, it was reported Jan. 6.

Three of the five exploration wells drilled in the strait since September 1976 had struck oil, the company said. Commercial production was expected to begin in about two years, according to the report.

Chile refuses to join copper cutback. Three major copper-producing countries—Zaire, Zambia and Peru—agreed Dec. 7 to reduce their production despite the refusal of Chile, the world's leading copper exporter, to join the cutback.

The four nations and Indonesia, which composed the Intergovernment Council of Copper Exporting Countries (CIPEC), had met in Jakarta to discuss ways to support sagging copper prices. Although CIPEC was regarded as one of the strongest producer cartels in existence, the meeting ended in a stalemate because of Chile's refusal to cut production. Chile contended that world demand would soon increase and cause prices to rise.

In 1975 CIPEC had tried and failed to support copper prices by reducing its copper output, which accounted for 40% of the total world production. CIPEC blamed the failure on Chile's refusal to comply fully with the cutback decision.

U.S. firm buys Chilean copper mine. Exxon Mineral International, a subsidiary of Exxon Corp. of the U.S., had bought a major Chilean copper mine for $107 million, it was reported Dec. 28. The purchase of the La Disputada mine at Los Bronces, 40 miles north of Santiago, represented the largest private American investment in Chile since the military coup of September 1973.

U.S. Involvement in Allende Coup

CIA, U.S. firms opposed Allende in '64. A former U.S. ambassador to Chile charged Jan. 11 that there had been a "massive undertaking" by the Central Intelligence Agency and several U.S. corporations to prevent Salvador Allende from winning Chile's 1964 presidential election.

Edward M. Korry, the U.S. envoy to Santiago in 1967-71, told the Senate Foreign Relations Committee that the anti-Allende effort was just one example of extensive collaboration between the White House and multinational corporations, begun under the Kennedy Administration, to bribe foreign officials and finance political parties friendly to the U.S.

The Senate committee was holding hearings on the nomination of Cyrus R. Vance to be the next U.S. secretary of state. Korry testified that Vance, as a former secretary of the Army and deputy secretary of defense, had "played a not unimportant role" in helping forge the links between the White House and the companies.

Korry had charged earlier, in a television interview broadcast Jan. 9 in the CBS program "Sixty Minutes," that the integration of U.S. businessmen with covert U.S. intelligence operations had been started in 1963 by President John F. Kennedy and his brother, Attorney General Robert F. Kennedy. Korry said he had told this to the Senate Select Committee on Intelligence in 1976, but his testimony was being "bottled up" by the committee's former chairman, Sen. Frank Church (D, Ida.).

"My knowledge would embarrass and compromise highly placed individuals," Korry explained. Vice President-elect Walter Mondale, he said, "knows that I received letters from Vice President Hubert Humphrey, his political mentor, urging the U.S. to oppose Allende in 1968."

Korry also told "Sixty Minutes" that Allende and his aides had accepted bribes from multinational corporations in return for assurances that the companies would not be nationalized after Allende's election in 1970. Korry said Allende's campaign director had asked him for a $1-million contribution, which he had refused to give.

In December 1976 Korry had given the New York Times State Department documents showing that Anaconda Co. and other U.S. firms had offered to funnel money through the State Department to an opponent of Allende in the 1970 election.

U.S. disavows aide's apology on coup. The U.S. government disavowed an apology made March 8 by Brady Tyson, a member of the U.S. delegation to the United Nations Human Rights Commission in Geneva, for the part played by Americans in provoking the 1973 military coup against the late Chilean President Salvador Allende.

Tyson made the apology during a discussion of a report prepared by a U.N. panel on human rights abuse in Chile. "Our delegation," Tyson said, "would be less than candid and untrue to ourselves and our people if we did not express our profoundest regrets for the role some government officials, agencies and private groups played in the subversion of the previous democratically elected Chilean government that was overthrown by the coup of September 11, 1973.

"We recognize fully that the expression of regrets, however profound, cannot contribute significantly to the reduction of suffering and terror that the people of Chile have experienced in the last two years."

Tyson did not identify the U.S. groups and officials that allegedly had subverted Allende's government, but he said these persons and their policies had been rejected by the American people in the November 1976 elections.

The U.S. State Department and the White House immediately disavowed Tyson's statement. A spokesman for President Carter said Carter had "not been consulted" about the apology. A State Department spokesman said Tyson's statement was "a personal one that was not approved in advance and is not an expression of the Administration's views."

The State Department summoned Tyson home March 9 for "instruction in diplomatic procedures." A spokesman noted that Tyson, a Methodist minister and former college professor, was new to diplomacy and apparently did not understand "the ground rules." Before leaving Geneva March 9, Tyson apologized for speaking without "clearance" but said he believed his "personal statement" to be "in the spirit of the Carter government foreign policy as I understand it."

Carter said at a press conference March 9 that although he was concerned about the human rights situation in Chile, a report in 1975 by a U.S. Senate committee had not found "any evidence that the U.S. was involved in the overthrow of the Allende government in Chile." The U.S. apparently had given financial aid to "political elements that may have contributed to the change of government" in Chile, Carter admitted, but he said there had not been "any proof of illegalities there."

Press reports noted that Carter had gone considerably further than this during his presidential campaign. In his televised foreign policy debate with then-President Ford in October 1976, Carter had said the

Republican Administration "overthrew an elected government and helped establish a dictatorship" in Chile.

The Soviet newspaper Izvestia March 9 noted the contradictions in Carter's statements, asserting that former President Richard Nixon's support for the Chilean military coup "was well known to world public opinion." In Geneva, meanwhile, U.N. delegations said U.S. credibility had been damaged by the Tyson affair. The Chilean delegation accused Tyson of interfering in internal Chilean affairs.

Dispute over CIA funds charge. The former Chilean President, Eduardo Frei said March 4 that he had received a letter from President Carter apologizing for U.S. press reports that Frei had received money from the Central Intelligence Agency. According to Frei, Carter said in his letter that he could not prevent the press from printing "unfounded accusations," and that he hoped "malicious stories will not cast a shadow on our traditional friendship."

Frei heatedly had denied the press reports, which appeared Feb. 19. In a public reply Feb. 21, he called the reports "part of a very well-orchestrated campaign to discredit my administration, the Christian Democratic party and myself." Frei said the Christian Democrats mistakenly had been identified as the recipients of money that the CIA and U.S. corporations gave to opponents of Salvador Allende in 1964.

These payments had been revealed earlier by Edward M. Korry, former U.S. ambassador to Chile. Frei said he had received a letter from Korry expressing regret that the Christian Democrats' name had been "soiled." According to Frei, Korry called Frei's administration (1964-70) "the most decent, progressive, and humane administration as well as the least corrupt of all I have known" in Chile.

Foreign Relations

Peru-Chile border buildup detailed. Peru and Chile were building up defenses along their common border as tensions increased over Peruvian claims to northern Chilean territory and over the two nations' inability to agree on how to grant Bolivia an outlet to the sea, according to the Jan. 10 issue of Time magazine.

Peru had been moving tanks, troops and armored personnel carriers into military bases in its southern border provinces, Time reported. Chile had been mining the northern Atacama Desert, implanting tank traps and building fortifications to counter a possible invasion by Peru.

Peruvian leaders periodically had talked of regaining the Atacama, which was taken from Peru by Chile in the War of the Pacific in the late 19th Century. The desert had rich deposits of copper, silver and nitrates.

Chile, which had more men under arms than Peru, was comparatively underequipped because the U.S. and Great Britain had embargoed arms sales to the military government, Time said. The embargo included U.S.-made F-4 Phantom jets, which Chile eagerly sought and which could easily handle Peru's Su-22s, the magazine reported.

Meanwhile, Chilean President Augusto Pinochet Ugarte Jan. 5 began a 10-day trip to four southern provinces and the Antarctic. The main purpose of the trip, according to the London Times Jan. 6, was to reassert Chilean claims to about half of the Antarctic. Much of the same territory was claimed by Great Britain.

Chile, East Germany trade prisoners. The Chilean government June 18 exchanged its most prominent political prisoner for 11 prisoners held in East Germany.

Jorge Montes, a former Communist senator jailed in Chile in 1974, was flown to Frankfurt while the East German prisoners were sent to West Germany. U.S. sources cited by the Washington Post June 20 said two of the East German prisoners had worked for U.S. intelligence. They had been sentenced to life imprisonment by the Communist regime, while the other nine prisoners had received jail terms of seven to nine years.

Chile claimed Montes was its last political prisoner, but critics of the military government asserted that opponents of the regime were still being ar-

rested without charge or were simply "disappearing," i.e. being murdered by the Chilean secret police, it was reported June 19.

Other Developments

Corvalan pension restored. The military junta had restored the government pension of former Sen. Luis Corvalan, sending the Communist leader the $340 he was due for December 1976, the Santiago newspaper La Cronica reported Jan. 5.

Corvalan had been freed from a Chilean jail in December 1976 in exchange for Vladimir Bukovsky, the Soviet dissident. Corvalan currently was living in Moscow. La Cronica described the junta's gesture as "a new demonstration of tolerance. Now Corvalan can use Chilean funds for anti-national action organized by the Russian government."

Chilean jets hijacked. Five Chileans—four men and a woman—hijacked a domestic Ladeco Airlines flight en route from Arica to Santiago July 5 and ordered the plane carrying 55 other persons to fly to Lima, Peru. There the hijackers released their hostages and demanded to be flown to Paris. After five hours of negotiations, the hijackers agreed to accept political asylum in Cuba.

On June 21 an employe of the Ministry of Public Works seized a Lan-Chile Boeing 727 with 78 persons aboard and forced it to fly over the Andes to Mendoza, Argentina. The hijacker had initially demanded a larger plane to fly him to Algeria but was persuaded to surrender. There were no reported injuries in either incident.

Bombs explode in Santiago. Four bombs were detonated by unknown persons in Santiago Oct. 4. The government charged the next day that the saboteurs were "subversive elements" who wanted to dispel Chile's "image of tranquility."

At least 10 more bombs exploded in the city the night of Oct. 14–15. One device injured five students, three of them seriously. This time the government made no comment and asked the press not to report the blasts, according to the Latin America Political Report Nov. 11.

Another bomb exploded in Santiago Nov. 5, killing two of its presumed manufacturers, the Political Report said.

Regime punishes strike leaders. On orders from President Augusto Pinochet, seven labor leaders had been confined in remote mountain villages as punishment for leading strikes and other labor actions considered disruptive, it was reported Dec. 4. The detained men, who represented independent unions in the copper, shipping, construction and metal sectors, had orchestrated demands for higher wages, more jobs and a restoration of union rights. The largest recent labor action was a strike at the huge El Teniente copper mine Nov. 2.

Colombia

Labor & Student Unrest

Workers and students demonstrated repeatedly in Colombia throughout 1977 as the cost of living soared and politicians began campaigning for the 1978 elections.

Observers attributed most of the unrest to discontent over prices, which rose 26.2% since January, for a total rise of 43.5% in 12 months, it was reported July 4.

Disturbances mount. The growing worker unrest accelerated in February. Army troops occupied the state oil refinery at Barrancabermeja to forestall a strike by several thousand workers, it was reported Feb. 4. Workers, students and other persons demonstrated in Bogota and 11 other cities Feb. 17–18 after the government authorized price increases for milk, bread, salt and other staples, and for bus and railroad fares.

Taxi drivers struck in Bogota Feb. 21 to demand fare hikes to compensate for an 18% increase in the cost of gasoline; six of the strike leaders were sentenced to 30 days in jail, it was reported March 3.

About 5,000 teachers struck for higher wages in Antioquia Department March 3. In Popayan (Cauca Dept.), army troops were sent into the streets to prevent popular demonstrations against inflation that were scheduled for the next day.

More than 100,000 workers marched in Bogota March 4 to protest the high cost of living. The workers, who included teachers, dockworkers and laborers in the oil and steel industries, threatened to strike if the government did not authorize new pay increases.

Refinery workers at Barrancabermeja again voted to strike March 5, provoking another army occupation and the arrest of union leaders. The workers finally agreed March 9 to accept arbitration, which President Alfonso Lopez Michelsen had been pressing on them for several weeks.

Workers at 29 public hospitals struck March 8, paralyzing the institutions. Most of Colombia's public hospitals were on the verge of bankruptcy and their workers had not received raises in two years, according to press reports. The government immediately announced that it had budgeted $10 million to attend to the hospitals' needs.

More than 100,000 state employes struck in Bogota and other cities March 10, paralyzing more than 40 government dependencies, including courts, clinics, schools and customs offices. There were riots in Buga (Valle del Cauca Dept.) and Bucaramanga (Santander Dept.). In Buga, eight students were wounded when they and other rioters attacked an army detachment.

The labor situation began to relax

March 11 when telecommunications workers agreed to a settlement that averted an imminent strike. Port workers also reached a settlement, agreeing to a 19%–22% wage increase, and steelworkers reached a last-minute settlement as well, it was reported March 18. However, teachers continued their protests, over a new law that allegedly made teachers in public schools liable to dismissal for political reasons.

National University closed. The National University in Bogota was closed for two weeks April 27, following repeated student disturbances and the occupation of the campus by authorities.

The university was shut down immediately after a student riot in which three cars were burned. The students were protesting a decision by the mayor of Bogota to place the campus under permanent police occupation.

The mayor, Bernardo Gaitan Mahecha, had announced his decision April 23 despite opposition from the university's academic council and Colombia's education minister, Rafael Rivas Posada. More than 15,000 students and teachers at the university went on strike April 25 to protest the decision.

Police and soldiers had occupied the campus April 20, following two days of student riots in which at least seven cars were burned. One student had been wounded during an army raid on the university April 18. Troops claimed to have found 69 Molotov cocktails in the raid.

In earlier unrest, police had clashed with thousands of students March 30 in separate disturbances at the National University, at Narino University and at Santander Industrial University. The students were protesting police and army raids on all three campuses. Many arrests were reported.

Army units had invaded the National University March 24 to break up a student meeting on a number of university problems, including a decision to close student dormitories because authorities deemed them centers of "subversive plotting." Students threw stones at the soldiers, who struck back with billy clubs.

Disturbances continued at the National University March 25 as students stoned a car belonging to the Bulgarian Embassy and two belonging to Colombian officials. The next day students rioted at Atlantic University in Barranquilla, forcing the postponement of elections for the university's board of directors.

Strikes & violence. The Colombian army occupied the town of Florencia (Caqueta Dept.) July 19 to end a week-long general strike protesting the high cost of living and the shortage of electricity. However, protests continued there the next day on the 167th anniversary of Colombian independence.

About 5,000 primary school teachers struck in Antioquia Dept. July 26 to demand back pay and wage increases. Another 5,000 teachers joined the indefinite strike the next day, leaving 300,000 children without instructors.

Workers at the state oil refinery in Barrancabermeja held staggered strikes July 26 to protest alleged violations of their collective contract.

Some 1,000 workers at cement plants struck July 26 for a 50% wage increase (their employers were offering 25%). They were joined the next day by another 2,000 workers, paralyzing the cement-making industry and threatening to shut down construction projects around the country.

Protests began to accelerate in August and early September as teachers, cement workers and oil laborers struck in a continuing effort for economic and other demands.

The government was forced to suspend cement exports as cement workers indefinitely extended their two-week-old strike, it was reported Aug. 12. The stoppage forced a halt to most construction projects, according to press reports.

Primary and secondary school teachers went on strike across the country Aug. 22 as their union, the Colombian Educators' Federation (Fecode), demanded wage raises, the reinstatement of fired teachers, abrogation of the 29-year-old state of siege, repeal of a "repressive" new education statute which allegedly made teachers in public schools liable to dismissal for political reasons and the reopening of the closed state universities, particularly the National University in Bogota.

At least half of Fecode's 160,000 members observed the strike, leaving an estimated one million children without teachers, according to the Associated Press. Nearly all teachers struck in Barranquilla and Medellin. Few teachers struck in Bogota, although most teachers there said they supported Fecode and its demands. Like the cement workers' strike, the Fecode stoppage was indefinite, and it extended into the September general strike.

More than 5,000 employes of the state petroleum company, Ecopetrol, struck Aug. 25 as their union demanded pay increases, reinstatement of workers fired for union organizing, reinstatement of the oil union's legal status and abrogation of the state of siege. The government put Colombia's oil installations, including the Barrancabermeja refinery, under military control, and troops began arresting union leaders. The strike continued, however, and by Aug. 30 an acute gasoline shortage was reported.

Soldiers and oil workers clashed Aug. 26 in the town of Tibu, near Colombia's eastern oilfields. A curfew was imposed there and liquor sales were banned.

As the cement workers, teachers and oil laborers continued their strikes, and as the national labor federations began planning for a September general strike, the government increased the repressive measures allowed under the state of siege.

A law was decreed Aug. 26 allowing the detention for 30 to 180 days of anyone who "organized, led, promoted or encouraged" strikes. The law also enabled employers to fire striking workers. After the law was decreed, police began breaking into the homes of leaders of the oil workers in attempts to find and arrest them.

Edilberto Cabrera, president of the oil workers' federation, was reported under arrest Aug. 26. He charged from prison Sept. 7 that he and a fellow union leader, Florentino Martinez, had been beaten and kicked by their jailers in Barrancabermeja.

President Lopez began negotiating with the UTC and the CTC near the end of August in an attempt to head off the general strike. But these talks broke down Sept. 1 over Lopez' refusal to consider the 50% wage increase and to negotiate also with the leftist unions, the CSTC and the CGT.

Following this failure, the government made another unsuccessful attempt to intimidate potential strikers—it had police in the cities arrest persons who could not produce identification papers on request. About 400 persons were reported arrested this way in Bogota Sept. 3.

Soldiers joined riot police in patrolling Bogota as of Sept. 8, and outdoor public meetings were banned. But neither this nor a final warning by Lopez Sept. 12 deterred the strikers from shutting down the major cities Sept. 14.

14 die in strike violence—At least 14 persons were killed in a violent general strike Sept. 14 and continued disturbances the next day.

The strike was called by the four largest labor federations, which demanded a 50% wage increase and other concessions from the government. Although barely one-fifth of Colombia's workers were unionized, enough joined the stoppage to paralyze Bogota and several other cities.

The government mounted a massive operation against the strike, which it termed illegal and subversive. The army was mobilized, radio and television coverage of the strike was banned, strikers were arrested and employers were authorized to fire all workers who joined the stoppage. At least 4,000 persons were arrested Sept. 14–15, mostly in Bogota, where prisioners were herded into a bull ring and a soccer stadium.

Police and soldiers fought running battles with rioters and looters, notably in the slums of Bogota. Rioters stoned passing cars, burned parked vehicles and spread nails in the city streets to hinder state-organized emergency transportation. Total damages in the disturbances were estimated at $1.5 million-$2 million.

Reports of deaths and injuries varied. The government said 14 persons were killed Sept. 14–15, while the Mexican newspaper Excelsior put the number at 20. The Miami Herald said 120 persons were injured but Excelsior raised that figure to 500.

Excelsior reported at least six deaths in Bogota the day of the strike. The newspaper said two persons were killed by police while trying to set fire to a police car; two were shot to death while looting a store; a student was killed by a stray bullet, and a state-employed driver was crushed to death when demonstrators overturned his truck.

Bogota was put under an 8 p.m.-5 a.m.

curfew that was not lifted until calm returned to the city Sept. 16. There also was a curfew in Barrancabermeja, the Pacific port where oil workers had been on strike for three weeks and where numerous clashes between strikers and police were reported Sept. 14–15. Other cities crippled by the general strike and related unrest included Cali, Barranquilla and Medellin.

President Alfonso Lopez Michelsen went on radio and television Sept. 14 and again Sept. 15 to denounce the strikers and call for public repudiation of their action. He blamed the strike deaths on political "extremists" who allegedly had resorted to violence when the strike itself "failed totally."

Lopez flatly rejected the strikers' wage demands and said wage policy should be determined by the National Council of Salaries. This body consisted of representatives of the government, private companies and two of the striking labor federations—the Colombian Workers' Union (UTC), a conservative coalition, and the Colombian Workers' Confederation (CTC), affiliated with Lopez' Liberal Party. It excluded the other two striking federations, the Communist-controlled Syndical Confederation of Colombian Workers (CSTC) and the independent leftist General Workers' Confederation (CGT).

Although the four labor federations did not try to extend the strike beyond Sept. 14, they warned Lopez Sept. 19 that there would be another stoppage if he did not grant their demands. A UTC spokesman said the labor alliance was demanding the rehiring of all workers fired as a result of the Sept. 14 strike; the release of all labor leaders and workers arrested for participating in the stoppage; the admission of the CSTC and the CGT to the National Council on Salaries; government consideration of an increase in all wages and not just the minimum wage; retraction of allegedly anti-labor legislation, and effective government action to freeze the prices of essential articles.

The demands were somewhat toned down from the original strike demands, which included the 50% across-the-board wage increase. That increase had been demanded to compensate for the rise in the cost of living, estimated at 30% for the first eight months of 1977. The minimum

wage, about $59 per month, while official statistics showed a subsistence wage was closer to $100 per month.

The teachers' strike, which had begun in August, ended Oct. 6 when the government agreed to review teachers' salaries, reinstate teachers who had been fired for striking and issue a new statute to govern the teaching profession. The strike at the Finance Ministry, begun Oct. 18, was ended by a similar agreement Nov. 4. But the oil workers' stoppage, begun late in August, continued with no apparent hope of an early resolution.

The oil strike occasioned numerous terrorist attacks, at least some of them attributed to left-wing guerrillas. Oil and gas pipelines were bombed throughout Colombia, and Barrancabermeja was under almost constant military occupation. The state oil company, Ecopetrol, claimed that during the strike there had been 30 acts of sabotage causing total losses of $4.2 million, it was reported Nov. 11. The legal status of the oil workers' union had been suspended until January 1978, about 50 union leaders had been arrested and 217 workers had been dismissed, according to the Latin America Political Report.

Meanwhile, the four labor federations that had organized the Sept. 14 general strike continued to put pressure on the government. The unions led peaceful demonstrations throughout Colombia Nov. 18 to support demands for a 50% across-the-board wage increase, abrogation of the state of siege, reinstatement of all workers fired for striking and dismissal of Labor Minister Oscar Montoya Montoya. The government mounted a massive security operation to discourage rioting during the demonstrations. Entire sections of Bogota were occupied by the army.

The government flatly rejected the unions' demands, repeatedly charging that the strikes had political—not economic—goals. The government had decreed a 38% increase in the minimum wage Oct. 13, and it reportedly offered 20% raises to workers earning higher pay. This was rejected by the unions, which noted that the 20% increase would not even make up for recent inflation.

(The National Association of Financial Institutions reported Nov. 14 that prices had risen more than 23% in the first six months of 1977. The government claimed that inflation for the year would not exceed 30%, but the International Monetary Fund put the figure at 40%, according to a report Nov. 9.)

The government's economic policies were attacked not only by the labor unions but by representatives of management. Fabio Echeverri Correa, president of the National Association of Industrialists, charged Sept. 30 that government programs had helped to "accentuate injustice, inequality and the concentration of wealth." He noted that agricultural production had dropped in the last two years—with the exception of coffee—and exports had stagnated since 1974.

Universities closed. Following clashes between local students and policemen, the government closed the University of Cauca in Popayan Dec. 13 and the National University of Cordoba the next day.

The previous week the government had shut down Tolima University in Ibague, the University of the Atlantic in Barranquilla and the law school of the National University in Bogota. (The National University had reopened Oct. 17 after being closed for six months to prevent student disturbances).

Terrorism & Political Violence

Attacks by guerrillas, kidnappings by common criminals and alleged executions by army "death squads" continued to plague Colombia throughout 1977.

Political violence unabated as election drive starts. Josue Cavanzo, a Communist peasant leader and town councilman in Cimitarra (Santander Dept.), was murdered by presumed political opponents early in January, it was reported Jan. 12. Cavanzo had been arrested briefly in 1976 on charges of belonging to the Colombian Revolutionary Armed Forces (FARC), the pro-Moscow guerrilla group.

Rafael Bayona Jimenez, leader of the steelworkers in Boyaca Dept., was murdered Feb. 13. His death and Cavanzo's increased fears that right-wing terrorists

were operating in Colombia, according to the London newsletter Latin America March 18. A Communist congressman, Humberto Criales de la Rosa, had drawn up a list of left-wing activists whom he claimed had been killed by an army death squad since September 1975, Latin America reported. The list included several peasant leaders.

Adela Perez, a councilwoman in the hamlet of Yacopi (Cundinamarca Dept.), charged Feb. 22 that the army was torturing and executing local peasants whom it suspected of collaborating with rural guerrillas. Naming several alleged victims of summary execution, she said: "Persecution in the countryside is growing daily; no one can be sure of what will happen. There is no justice, and in Yacopi there is no law." National Defense Minister Gen. Abraham Varon Valencia Feb. 23 said he had ordered a thorough investigation of Perez' charges.

The army's tactics did not appear to be hampering guerrilla operations, although 23 guerrillas were reported arrested after a shootout with police near Puente Nacional (Santander Dept.) Jan. 28. FARC members raided the northwestern town of San Vicente del Congo Jan. 29, killing a policeman.

About 50 guerrillas raided La Macarena (Meta Dept.) Feb. 14, killing a policeman, robbing an agrarian bank and several stores and kidnapping an American botanist whom the FARC accused of working for the Central Intelligence Agency. The botanist, Richard C. Starr, was a member of the Peace Corps, which denied that he had any connection with the CIA. (Authorities said Feb. 24 that the bodies of two of Starr's kidnappers had been found in the mountains outside La Macarena.)

The FARC also kidnapped a wealthy rancher, Fernando Restrepo, demanding a $300,000 ransom, it was reported March 13. Unidentified kidnappers March 13 seized Giuseppe Mondini, manager of the Bogota branch of the French and Italian Bank for South America. A ransom demand of $5 million was reported later.

The growing violence was blamed on President Lopez Michelsen by politicians who were gearing up for the 1978 elections. The major political battle looming was between ex-President Carlos Lleras Restrepo and former Foreign Minister

Julio Cesar Turbay Ayala, who sought the presidential nomination of Lopez' Liberal Party. The two candidates, who led separate Liberal factions, agreed March 21 to let the February 1978 congressional elections serve as an unofficial presidential primary. The leader of the Liberal faction that did best on the congressional vote would be the presidential nominee.

Guerrillas continue attacks & kidnappings—Left-wing guerrillas staged more attacks in Bogota and in rural areas of Colombia. Three political leaders in the town of Cimitarra (Santander Department) were shot to death March 29, presumably by members of the pro-Moscow FARC. The Colombian army claimed March 29 that the FARC had executed five army informers in three isolated localities along the border between Santander and Boyaca departments.

Members of the pro-Cuban National Liberation Army (ELN) kidnapped the son of a wealthy department-store executive in Bogota April 6. The youth was the tenth person kidnapped by guerrillas or common criminals in Colombia in recent months. Virgilio Molina Vidales, a wealthy rancher in Cimitarra, was reported kidnapped May 2 by guerrillas of the FARC, who reportedly demanded a $3 million ransom.

Unidentified guerrillas attacked an army patrol in Taraza (Antioquia Department) April 24, killing two soldiers, wounding 15 and stealing arms and equipment from the victims. Thousands of troops were sent in pursuit of the insurgents April 25.

Members of the FARC were reported April 27 to have executed two farmers in Bolivar (Cauca Department) for refusing to cooperate in insurgent activities.

In other unrest, unidentified persons set off six incendiary bombs before dawn May 2 at banks, factories and office buildings in Bogota. The bombings followed the withdrawal of large contingents of soldiers and policemen who had patrolled the city May 1 to prevent violence during massive May Day demonstrations. The marches, which protested the soaring cost of living, were peaceful except for some stone-throwing by a Maoist group and a shootout among members of the opposition National Popular Alliance (ANAPO). Six persons were reported wounded in the gun battle.

Gunmen July 1 attacked the home of Gen. Alvaro Mejia Soto, air force chief of staff. He escaped, but one of his military guards was killed. Five days later assassins gunned down the chief of civil aeronautics, Col. Osiris Maldonado, as he drove to work in the capital.

Credit for both attacks was claimed by the ELN, but credit for the assault on Mejia's home also was claimed by the People's Liberation Army, a Maoist group.

Police July 14 announced they had raided the ELN's chief hideout in Bogota, arresting 15 guerrillas. But the Defense Ministry July 25 reported other ELN members had occupied and sacked the hamlet of Torama in Santander Department, their rural base of operations.

Soldiers hunting guerrillas in various rural regions were killing peasants whom they suspected of aiding the insurgents, according to leftist politicians in Bogota. Gilberto Vieyra, general secretary of the Colombian Communist Party, charged July 5 that since the inauguration of President Alfonso Lopez Michelsen in 1974, soldiers had "executed" more than 500 leftists in rural areas, particularly in Santander.

The victims, Vieyra said, had ties to the National Opposition Union (UNO), a coalition to which the Communists and several other leftist parties belonged. The guerrillas the victims were alleged to have aided belonged to the Colombian Revolutionary Armed Forces (FARC), which had close ties to the Communists.

Another member of UNO, Sen. Humberto Criales, July 25 said soldiers in Antioquia Department had killed 36 peasants in the previous four days on charges of aiding or belonging to the FARC. Criales released a list naming 33 of the alleged victims.

In the cities, meanwhile, there was a rash of assaults and kidnappings that were attributed variously to urban guerrillas and to common criminals. Thirteen persons were reported being held by kidnappers July 8; a Bogota businessman had been abducted that day after his captors raped his two daughters.

There also were more bombings—six in Bogota July 20 and three in Popayan July 29–30—and student disturbances. The government closed Pereira Technical University July 21 and Medellin National

University July 27 after alleged riots on each of the campuses. A total of eight universities were suspended indefinitely.

Members of the M-19 guerrilla band kidnapped former Agriculture Minister Hugo Ferreira Neira in Bogota Aug. 19. Ferreira, a member of President Lopez' Liberal Party, was chairman of the board of Indupalma, a company that made vegetable oil. Indupalma's workers had been on strike for two days to protest the firing of 90 fellow workers who had tried to organize a union. M-19 said it would kill Ferreira unless Indupalma raised its wages and reinstated the fired workers. Indupalma complied. Ferreira was freed by the guerrillas Sept. 16.

The army occupied the town of Cimitarra (Santander Department) Aug. 30 following the murders of six members of the Liberal and Conservative parties during the previous two weeks. The killings were blamed on the FARC which frequently attacked Cimitarra to kill political leaders and steal supplies for guerrilla operations.

FARC was also presumed responsible for the kidnapping of three wealthy ranchers in Caqueta Department, reported by police Aug. 30.

FARC took a series of actions to support the oil workers' strike. On Sept. 3 it burned down the home of an Ecopetrol executive in Puerto Wilches. Two days later FARC blew up a section of the oil pipeline from Barrancabermeja to Medellin, and the following day it blew up some pipeline between Barrancabermeja and Bogota.

Several members of the ELN seized a radio station in the city of Bucaramanga Oct. 19 and broadcast a harangue against government economic policies. Members of the EPL killed two policemen in Bogota Oct. 26.

The government said Nov. 1 that guerrillas increasingly were leaving their rural bases of operation and concentrating on attacks in the cities. However, the insurgents continued to occupy rural towns briefly to steal supplies and lecture the residents on revolutionary politics. Members of the FARC seized the northern towns of El Para (Nov. 5) and Sabanagrande (Dec. 7). FARC members threw grenades at a police convoy in Guare (Huila Department) Dec. 1, killing eight officers and injuring another six. In an earlier ambush, FARC guerrillas had

wounded seven soldiers outside Yacopi (Cundinamarca Dept.) Oct. 22.

The kidnappings increased significantly toward the end of the year, causing the government to mount a special campaign to arrest abductors. Ninety-five persons were arrested Dec. 18–19 on suspicion of kidnapping, but only 15 were charged. Three more abductions were reported Dec. 21, raising the number of kidnappings in 1977 to 89. Twenty-five victims were still in the hands of their captors.

Most of the kidnap victims were wealthy ranchers and business executives. Many were ransomed by their families, but some were killed when their relatives refused to pay for their release. Rancher Jorge Torres was murdered for this reason Nov. 10, and businessman Alberto Pardo Leon was killed Dec. 22. Another wealthy executive, Carlos Abusaid, was shot to death when he resisted an attempted kidnapping in Bogota Nov. 3.

Abusaid's assailants and the kidnappers of other Colombians were known to be left-wing guerrillas, but it was suspected that many of the abductions were the work of common criminals.

Politics

Presidential race under way. The campaign for the June 1978 presidential election officially began as several small parties chose their candidates.

Sen. Jaime Piedrahita Cardona, a member of the National Popular Alliance (Anapo), was nominated July 16 by the Front for the Unity of the People, a coalition of Anapo's socialist wing and several small leftist groups.

Another Anapo member, Rep. Julio Cesar Pernia, was nominated Aug. 7 by the National Opposition Union, which comprised a larger sector of Anapo and several other leftist groups including the Colombian Communist Party.

Yet another leftist group, the recently formed Socialist Bloc, disclosed Aug. 10 that its presidential candidate would be Socorro Ramirez, secretary of the Colombian Educators' Federation (Fecode).

Another new party, the United Patriotic Front, launched the candidacy of Gen. Alvaro Valencia Tovar, once Colombia's army commander and more recently a newspaper columnist, it was reported Sept. 16.

All the candidates denounced the government of President Alfonso Lopez Michelsen, most frequently for administrative corruption. Pernia and Ramirez also charged that Lopez had sharply increased political repression since his inaugural in 1974. Pernia said the president had condoned torture and summary executions by security officers, while Ramirez denounced government actions against striking labor unions. Ramirez said she had lost her job as a teacher for participating in a recent teachers' strike.

The Conservative party candidate, Belisario Betancur, who apparently had the support of both Conservative factions, was chosen at the end of 1977. The Liberals planned to choose theirs after the February 1978 congressional elections. The Liberals, however, were deeply divided, with two leading candidates and two others as well.

The major Liberal candidates were former President Carlos Lleras Restrepo, 69, and former Foreign Minister Julio Cesar Turbay Ayala, 61. The other Liberals in the race were Hernando Agudelo Villa and Carlos Holmes Trujillo. They all assured President Lopez (himself a Liberal) Aug. 17 that they would abide by the results of the February 1978 congressional elections; that is, the candidate whose supporters won the most congressional seats would become the Liberal presidential nominee and would be supported by his rivals.

Like the leftist candidates and Gen. Valencia Tovar, Lleras was campaigning hard on the corruption issue. But they were not the only ones to denounce the government on the issue. The president of the Colombian Episcopal Conference (national council of bishops), Msgr. Jose de Jesus Pimiento, criticized the administration Aug. 9 for corruption as well as for the rising levels of inflation, crime and civil unrest.

Corruption fought. Corruption in Bogota was tackled by the city's mayor, Bernardo Gaitan Mahecha, it was reported July 8. Gaitan had fired more than 100 local government officials for offenses ranging from embezzlement to insulting the public, and he was investigating another 800 bureaucrats, according to the Latin America Political Report.

The General Accounting Office had announced at the beginning of June that the House of Representatives was riddled with corruption, the Political Report noted. The office condemned irregularities in the budget and dubious contracts, and it began an investigation of a mysterious fire that destroyed the records of the congressional procurements department in 1976. Many arrests were promised.

Other Developments

World coffee price issue. The Colombian coffee industry suffered when two major U.S. coffee roasters announced further reductions in their wholesale prices of ground coffee, which had been declining since mid-May.

General Foods Corp. Oct. 17 cut its wholesale price 10¢ a pound to $3.41. That was down $1.05 from the mid-April record level. Procter & Gamble's Folger Coffee division Oct. 14 had cut its wholesale prices 20¢ a pound to $3.18.

However, Brazil and Colombia adopted conflicting export strategies during the six-month price plunge in an effort to stabilize the market price.

The slump in price, coupled with a decline in demand, meant that unsold supplies of green coffee had been piling up in warehouses in Brazil and Colombia, the world's chief coffee-exporting nations.

Colombia chose an aggressive marketing policy, making extensive sales abroad at the lower prices. (By early November, green coffee beans were trading in New York as low as $1.50 a pound.) The Colombian government reasoned that a return to the record high prices set in April would only intensify the continuing drop in consumer demand. In the U.S., per capita coffee consumption had fallen 15% during 1977, largely because of the high cost of the beverage, according to Business Week Nov. 7.

Brazil took the opposite approach. The government decided to withhold its coffee crop from the world market in hopes of forcing the price back up to Brazil's official export level of $3.20 a pound.

Ten other coffee-producing nations in Central and South America ratified Brazil's strategy Oct. 21. After a two-day meeting in El Salvador, representatives of that country, Guatemala, Honduras, Nicaragua, Panama, Costa Rica, the Dominican Republic, Ecuador, Venezuela and Mexico said they would stockpile their coffee until prices moved higher.

Brazil abandoned its boycott strategy in a surprise move announced Nov. 4 after secret negotiations with Colombia. The two nations agreed to coordinate their export policies in an effort to stabilize the world price at about $2 a pound. Mexico, the Ivory Coast and El Salvador joined in action Nov. 9.

The chief reason behind Brazil's sudden turnaround was a fear of incurring a large trade deficit in 1977, according to Business Week. Government officials had concluded that unless earnings on coffee exports increased $500 million to $600 million, the country would not be able to balance its trade account by the end of the year, Business Week said.

Mrs. Carter on tour. Rosalynn Carter, wife of U.S. President Jimmy Carter, visited seven countries in the Caribbean and Latin America May 30 June 12 on a tour that combined goodwill gestures with substantive political and economc discussion.

Mrs. Carter visited Colombia June 9-10. During her talks with President Alfonso Lopez Michelsen in Bogota June 10, Mrs. Carter concentrated on the smuggling of narcotics from Colombia to the U.S. and on the imprisonment of 70 Americans in Colombia on drug charges.

Mrs. Carter said later that Lopez Michelsen had agreed that the drug traffic between Colombia and the U.S., worth an estimated $500 million a year, "is a very serious problem for both of our countries." She said President Carter would send two American drug experts to Colombia to discuss steps to halt the traffic.

Murder of unfaithful wives barred. The Supreme Court March 23 struck down an article of the penal code that allowed a man to kill his wife if he found she had committed adultery.

The article, in force for 40 years, excused the husband on grounds that he had killed "in defense of his love." The Supreme Court upheld a lower court judge who voided the article on the ground it constituted "a death sentence" for unfaithful wives.

Cuba

Campaign to Improve
U.S.-Cuban Relations

During 1977, with a new American president in office in Washington, there was an increase in pressure for a resumption of normal relations between Cuba and the U.S. This pressure, despite some vocal opposition (in the U.S., at least), resulted in several steps toward "normalization." Several U.S. legislators paid visits to Havana. The U.S. eased its bans on tourist travel to Cuba. The two countries negotiated fishing accords. And finally the two governments set up "interest" offices in each other's capitals.

Renewed ties proposed. The U.S. made a number of qualified public overtures to Cuba in January-March, culminating in President Carter's announcement March 9 that he would end restrictions on travel to the island.

In an informal setting Feb. 12—a news conference of sorts while the President strolled around his home town of Plains, Ga.—Carter had pinpointed human rights as the key to improved relations between Cuba and the U.S. He expressed hope that recent conciliatory talk by Castro "can be followed up by mutual efforts to alleviate tensions and reduce animosities."

Carter did not identify his "indirect sources" of information, but President Jose Lopez Portillo of Mexico mentioned the subject of Cuban-U.S. relations at the conclusion of a two-day visit with Carter Feb. 15. Meeting with newsmen in Washington, Lopez Portillo said with regard to normalizing diplomacy between the U.S. and Cuba, "If the United States or Cuba require our good offices, we would be only too happy to make any effort in that regard, but I don't think it will be necessary because there seems to be goodwill on both sides."

Carter said Feb. 16 that he would "very much like to see the Cubans remove their soldiers from Angola and let the Angolan natives make their own decisions about their government ... [That] would be a step toward full normalization of [U.S.] relations with Angola. The same thing applies ultimately to the restoration of normal relationships with Cuba.

"If I can be convinced that Cuba wants to remove their aggravating influence in this hemisphere, will not participate in violence in nations across the oceans, will recommit the former relationships which existed in Cuba toward human rights, then I would be willing to move toward normalizing relationships with Cuba," Carter declared.

In reply, President Fidel Castro told American visitors to Cuba that he was very interested in improving relations with the U.S., particularly in resuming trade. However, Castro reacted angrily to the Carter Administration's attempts to link improved relations and greater observance of human rights in Cuba.

U.S. Secretary of State Cyrus Vance said in mid-January that Washington would consider the release of Cuban political prisoners as "one indication that Cuba is seriously interested in starting a dialogue with the U.S." Vance made the statement during his confirmation hearings before the Senate Foreign Relations Committee. The committee released the testimony Jan. 27.

Vance said Feb. 3 that the U.S. hoped to hold direct talks with Cuba on a possible renewal of the 1973 U.S.-Cuban antihijacking pact, which was scheduled to expire April 15 and which Castro had vowed not to renew. At those talks, Vance said, it would be "constructive" if the two nations discussed their other major differences.

In an interview broadcast on the CBS Evening News program Feb. 9, Castro said he thought it was possible for Cuba and the U.S. to establish normal relations. He said that if Carter wished, "I will with pleasure talk with him." Castro called Carter a "man of morals," adding, "I think that a man like Carter may abide by a policy of international principles, not the Marxist principles nor the capitalist principles, but rather the principles accepted universally among the people."

A spokesman for Carter said Feb. 19 that the President considered Castro's remarks "interesting and positive."

Vance met Feb. 25 with seven Cuban exile leaders who claimed to represent the views of many of the more than 600,000 Cubans who emigrated to the U.S. after Castro took power in 1959. The seven, including former Cuban President Carlos Prio and several leaders of the abortive 1961 Bay of Pigs invasion, said they were unalterably opposed to U.S. negotiations with the Castro government.

Castro met Feb. 26 and 27 with Benjamin C. Bradlee, executive editor of the Washington Post. In an account of the talks, published by the Post March 6, Bradlee said Castro admired Carter but was "appalled" by his remarks linking improved U.S. relations to greater respect for human rights in Cuba.

"If one message came ringing loud and clear through conversations with Castro," Bradlee reported, "it was this: Don't talk to Fidel Castro about human rights; he

truly believes he has nothing to learn from the U.S. on this particular subject."

"What does Cuba have to learn about human rights, [Castro] asks, from the country that mounted an invasion of Cuba and has relentlessly tried to assassinate Cuba's leader for 20 years?" Bradlee wrote. "These attempts are no longer speculative, but fully documented by the Senate's Church Committee, [Castro] notes."

As other reasons for discounting U.S. concern over human rights, Castro cited U.S. military involvement in Vietnam, U.S. racial discrimination, American "businessmen [who] regularly bribe public officials of other countries," the Watergate scandal, and U.S. support for "every totalitarian regime in Latin America," Bradlee reported.

Castro also expressed dismay at Vance's willingness to meet Cuban exile leaders, who, Castro said, were "known by Cubans to personify everything that was corrupt in pre-Castro Cuba or involved in the Bay of Pigs invasion," Bradlee wrote. (However, Bradlee noted, news of Vance's meeting with the exiles was censored in Cuba.)

Asked what single thing the U.S. could do to open a new era in Cuban-American relations, Castro recommended that Washington end its trade embargo of the island. Such a move would create goodwill toward the U.S. in Europe and the Third World and would allow Cuba to purchase badly needed products ranging from tomato seeds to spare auto parts, Castro said.

Cuban Foreign Trade Minister Marcelo Fernandez said March 4 that Cuba was eager to buy a wide variety of American goods from foodstuffs and fertilizers to heavy industrial equipment. In return Cuba could sell the U.S. sugar, rum, cigars and raw materials including chrome, copper and nickel.

Vance proposed March 4 that Havana and Washington discuss a broad range of issues without preconditions. Meanwhile, persons close to President Carter made apparently contradictory statements on the U.S. trade embargo. Vice President Walter Mondale said March 4 he thought the U.S. was "far short" of a decision to lift the embargo. Charles Kirbo, a close friend and adviser to the President, predicted that Cuba and the U.S. would develop normal trade relations by the end of 1977, according to a published report March 5.

Finally, the State Department approved Castro's suggestion that U.S. athletic teams go to Cuba for friendly competition. A team of college basketball players from South Dakota was authorized to go to Cuba at the end of March or beginning of April, the Washington Post reported March 5. And authorization was given March 8 for professional baseball to send a team to Cuba.

Castro specifically had invited the New York Yankees, defending champions of the American League, but baseball commissioner Bowie Kuhn said March 8 that he would send only an all-star team composed of players from both the American and National Leagues. Kuhn said there might not be enough time to assemble such a team before the U.S. baseball season officially opened in early April.

Rep. Jonathan B. Bingham (D, N.Y.) also reported on the subject Feb. 15 after returning from a visit to Cuba and more than eight hours of talks with Castro. Bingham said that Cuba would not begin full negotiations with the U.S. until Washington lifted its ban on exports of food and medicine to the island. Cubans considered the ban "a knife at their throat," Bingham said. While Castro insisted that the U.S. embargo on trade with Cuba was barring negotiations on normalizing relations, Bingham reported, "There are several subjects that can and should be discussed without any preconditions immediately."

He said Castro had indicated his willingness to hold discussions with the Carter Administration on such subjects as a 200-mile fishing limit, cultural and sports exchanges and joint efforts to curb spread of a sugar cane blight.

Bingham had gone to Cuba Feb. 10 in his role as chairman of the subcommittee on economic policy and trade of the House International Relations Committee.

Bingham also reported that Cuban officials had told him the number of Cuban troops in Angola had been reduced by one-half since the preceding spring. He said that Castro and others had informed him, however, that Cuba would keep troops in Angola for some time and leave only when requested by the Neto government or possibly the Organization of African Unity.

U.S. officials disclosed March 28 that State Department and Cuban representatives had held several secret meetings in the U.S. between November 1974 and November 1975 to discuss bilateral issues and the normalization of relations. The talks, begun at the initiative of then-Secretary of State Henry Kissinger, apparently broke down because of Cuba's military intervention in the Angolan civil war.

In a further development, during an ABC-TV interview with Barbara Walters June 9, Castro said he was "honestly and seriously interested in improving relations" with the U.S., but he doubted that full diplomatic ties could be established soon. "Maybe in Carter's second term, between 1980 and 1984," he said. He described the President as "an idealistic man with certain ethical principles that have their roots in his religious convictions. He is a well-prepared man, . . . an intelligent man, and also . . . a man who trusts himself."

U.S. basketball team, officials visit. A team of basketball players from two South Dakota universities visited Cuba April 4–8, accompanied by a 90-member delegation that included three members of the U.S. Congress—Sens. George McGovern and James Abourezk, both Democrats of South Dakota, and Rep. Les Aspin (D, Wis.). [See p. 181B1]

The basketball team, representing the University of South Dakota and South Dakota State University, toured the island and lost two games to a taller and stronger Cuban national team. A third game was canceled to give the weary American players a rest.

The U.S. legislators, meanwhile, met with Cuban officials to discuss ways of improving relations between Havana and Washington. McGovern, Abourezk and Aspin met April 7–8 with Gen. Raul Castro, Cuba's defense minister, who was overseeing the Cuban government while his brother, President Fidel Castro, was on a month-long tour in Africa and the Soviet Union. McGovern and Aspin remained in Cuba after the South Dakota basketball team left. They met April 9 with Fidel Castro, who had returned from Moscow earlier that day.

Raul Castro April 8 said the basketball

team's visit was an important step in restoring normal relations between Havana and Washington. Addressing American reporters during a break in his talks with McGovern, Abourezk and Aspin, Castro compared U.S.-Cuban relations to a bridge in wartime. "I think it was you who blew it up, but I won't say it," Castro said. "The war has ended and now we are reconstructing the bridge brick by brick—90 miles from Key West to Varadero. It takes a long time. At the end of the bridge we can shake hands, without winners or losers."

McGovern said after the talks that Raul Castro had demanded cancellation of the U.S. trade embargo against Cuba as a precondition for negotiations on other bilateral issues, such as reparations for the $1.8 billion worth of U.S. assets nationalized by Cuba after the 1959 revolution. McGovern said he agreed with Castro. "The embargo has never made any sense from the standpoint of U.S.-Cuban relations," he asserted. "[The U.S.] can trade with Peking, we can trade with Moscow. I don't see why not with Havana."

McGovern said Castro also had complained about overflights by the American SR-71 reconnaissance plane. According to Castro, the overflights began in September 1974 and were repeated on 16 later occasions, the last flight occurring Jan. 11. Castro said Cuba had protested privately to the U.S. three or four times but had received no response. Castro noted, however, that no overflights had occurred since the inauguration of President Carter.

Aspin said Castro had repeated his brother's earlier denial that Cuban troops had participated in the recent invasion of Zaire from Angola. Castro also told the U.S. legislators that Cuba was reducing its military force in Angola but was sending more "civilian technicians" there.

McGovern and Aspin met with Fidel Castro April 9 at Santa Maria del Mar, on the Caribbean coast outside Havana. Castro told reporters that day that the U.S. was torn between "the idealism of President Carter and the realism of the country." He said he would like to follow U.S.-Cuban developments a little longer before meeting with Carter.

Castro expressed satisfaction with the basketball team's visit and the recent lifting of U.S. restrictions on travel to Cuba, but he said full normalization of U.S.-Cuban relations would "take time."

U.S. tourists would be received in Cuba "with respect and friendship," Castro said, although "we don't have many hotels." "In these years of revolution," he explained, "no one has tried to create feelings of hostility toward the North American people. We have criticized the government. We have criticized the system. Instilling hatred is easy. What is hard is developing political conscience and culture."

McGovern said April 11, after returning to Washington, that Fidel Castro had insisted on the repeal of the U.S. trade embargo as a condition for the renewal of the 1973 anti-hijacking agreement between the U.S. and Cuba, which would expire April 15 on Cuba's initiative. Castro said, however, that he would enforce the agreement even after the lapse of the formal pact. He also indicated that even a partial lifting of the embargo could open the way for negotiations on other bilateral issues, McGovern said.

McGovern said he had given Castro a message from President Carter assuring Castro that the U.S. wanted to work for a normalization of U.S.-Cuban relations and expressing appreciation of Cuba's cooperation in recent fishing negotiations with the U.S. In response, McGovern said, Castro had called Carter "an idealist, a religious man and a good man."

McGovern said he would press Carter to repeal the trade embargo. (McGovern already had proposed a partial lifting of the embargo, to permit trade in food and medicines, as an amendment to the State Department authorization bill that was being considered by the Senate Foreign Relations Committee.)

The South Dakota senator said he would also work to expand U.S. athletic and cultural exchanges with Cuba, and to set up an exchange program for Cuban and American college students. Cuba had agreed to send its basketball team to play college teams in the U.S., and to host exhibition baseball games between a Cuban team and an all-star team from the U.S. major leagues, McGovern said. U.S. baseball commissioner Bowie Kuhn said the exhibition could be arranged for the fall of 1977 or spring of 1978.

Sen. Church's visit—A further step in the effort to promote U.S.-Cuban amity was a visit by U.S. Sen. Frank Church (D, Ida.) to Cuba Aug. 8–11.

Church arrived in Havana Aug. 8 on a U.S. Air Force plane, the first to land in Cuba in 16 years. He said he hoped his visit would help "heal the wounds" between the U.S. and Cuba, a phrase he used often during his visit. Castro replied at one point that there were "wounds" but no "cancer" in U.S.-Cuban relations.

U.S. officials said Aug. 8 Church's visit to Cuba was of "enormous importance" to Carter. The senator met with the President before departing for Havana, and he also conferred with Carter's national security adviser, Zbigniew Brzezinski.

Church spent most of Aug. 9 and 10 with Castro, but they did not get down to substantive talks until late in the second day. Then they discussed a wide range of problems, including Cuba's economic straits, its military presence in Africa, U.S. detente with the Soviet Union, the Panama Canal, the U.S. trade embargo against Cuba and 'the fate of seven American citizens jailed in Cuba for allegedly carrying out subversive activities sponsored by the Central Intelligence Agency.

Castro and Church reportedly made progress on the last issue, which Carter considered a key obstacle to good relations between the U.S. and Cuba. A member of Church's party said Castro had agreed to "review the seven [prisoners] on a case-by-case basis," the New York Times reported Aug. 12. Castro, Church and their aides declined to give more details of the two leaders' talks.

At a press conference before his return to the U.S. Aug. 11, Church thanked Castro for giving him "three days of his time" and said he believed they had become personal friends. Castro in turn praised Church as an "important, courageous politician" who was "capable, serious and intellectual . . . a man you can talk to."

Church later told reporters: "I found [Castro's] views to be reasonable, objective and surprisingly moderate. Most surprising of all, he did not display bitterness toward the U.S. . . . If any man had a reason to be embittered it might have been him."

Church said that during their talks Castro had never requested a specific concession from the U.S. The Cuban leader "clearly hopes that relations will continue to improve and [he] looks forward to the end of the embargo," Church said. "But he said he understands the complexities of American politics, and he sees it more difficult for President Carter to make a decision than for him to do so."

Church said Castro had conceded that the new U.S.-Panamanian agreement on the Panama Canal, which some American conservatives considered a "giveaway" to Panama, would increase pressure on Carter not to make any deal with Cuba that appeared to grant Cuban demands.

U.S. tourism & currency restrictions eased. The U.S. Treasury Department May 13 announced it would allow travel agents to arrange group tours to Cuba. Heretofore, only individuals had been allowed to travel to the island, with exceptions made for certain government-sponsored groups.

In an earlier development, an Arlington Va. travel agent who recently took 20 colleagues on a tour of Cuba, said the island was ready to accept U.S. tourists, the Washington Post reported Feb. 8. Alex Lopez said 50 new hotels were under construction in Cuba. The island had a goal of 300,000 tourists by 1980, he said. The U.S. travel agents visited vacation sites, hospitals, factories and government ministries on their tour.

Also the Carter Administration March 25 eased currency restrictions on American visitors to Cuba. Under a new Treasury Department regulation, U.S. citizens who obtained visas to visit Cuba could spend U.S. dollars there and could buy up to $100 worth of Cuban pesos for personal use every six months. A visitor buying goods in Cuba was required to bring them back to the U.S. in his personal luggage.

The MTS Daphne, the first U.S. cruise ship to sail to Cuba in 16 years, left New Orleans May 15 for Havana. The eight-deck liner was filled to capacity with more than 300 tourists and jazz musicians Dizzy Gillespie and Earl (Fatha) Hines. The departure was protested by several hundred Cuban exiles including President Castro's sister, Juanita.

Mackey International Airlines, a small

Miami-based company, canceled its plans to operate regular flights to Cuba after a bomb exploded in its Fort Lauderdale offices early May 25. Anti-Castro Cuban exiles claimed credit for the blast, which caused property damage but no casualties.

American citizens from Puerto Rico and the U.S. mainland were among 87 volunteers of the 10th "Venceremos Brigade" who arrived in Cuba April 8 to help with sugar harvesting and construction work until mid-May. Some 200 American volunteers were reported in Cuba by April 11. They planned to build a monument to Cuban soldiers killed in Angola, according to the London Times.

Fishing accords signed. American and Cuban delegates signed fishing agreements April 27 following three days of talks in Havana. The first pact set provisional boundaries for fishing zones between the two countries, and the second covered terms under which Cuban fishermen would be allowed to fish for certain species in surplus supply within the U.S. zone. Cuban ships would also be able to call at U.S. ports to obtain supplies and equipment and to undergo repairs.

U.S. and Cuban delegates had met in New York March 24–29 for the first round of negotiations on an agreement to regulate fishing in waters between the two countries. The talks, described by the State Department as "the first formal, face-to-face negotiations" between the U.S. and Cuba in 16 years, were occasioned by the recent establishment by both countries of 200-mile fishing zones. Since Cuba was only 90 miles from the Florida coast, an accord was needed to define each country's area of jurisdiction.

A seven-man State Department delegation came to Havana April 24 for the fishing talks. The group was headed by Terence Todman, assistant secretary of state for inter-American affairs, who was the first high-ranking U.S. diplomat to visit Cuba since 1961. Todman and four other members of the delegation returned to the U.S. April 28. The two other delegates remained in Cuba until May 2 to interview some of the 27 U.S. citizens held in Cuban jails.

Republicans oppose renewed ties. Leaders of the U.S. Republican Party criticized

the Carter Administration's moves toward renewed relations with Cuba, asserting the Cuban government had not yet made sufficient concessions to the U.S.

Sen. Jesse Helms (R, N.C.) told the U.S. Senate May 11 that he opposed a resumption of trade or diplomatic relations with Cuba. Among Helms' remarks, according to his statement as printed in the Congressional Record:

" When President John F. Kennedy imposed the trade embargo on Cuba in 1962, he said:

The present Government of Cuba is incompatible with the principles and objectives of the Inter-American system; and in the light of the subversive offensive of Sino-Soviet Communism with which the Government of Cuba is publicly aligned, (The OAS) urged the member states to take those steps that they may consider appropriate for their individual and collective self-defense.

"One's first temptation is to say that nothing has changed. But the situation has changed—it has changed for the worse. Since President Kennedy's proclamation, the vast majority of South America—at least 80 percent, if one measures by land area or by GNP—has been deeply smitten by Castro-inspired and assisted Communist revolution, and has had to go through the agony of revolution and chaos before order has been restored. One need only mention Brazil, Chile, Uruguay, and Argentina to see the extent of the rejection of Castro's doctrines.

"Now that the tide has turned—as the result of tremendous sacrifice by those nations afflicted by communism—Castro has switched operations to Africa and has imposed Communist minority rule on Angola and Mozambique.

"As far as the United States itself is concerned, there are, today, more Soviet reconnaissance bombers in Cuba than there were at the time of the Cuban missile crisis.

" Mr. President, only 3 weeks ago, Soviet reconnaissance bombers flew within 60 miles of the U.S. coast, flying over several American warships, including the carrier, U.S.S. *Saratoga*. This is a direct violation of the Soviet-United States agreement on nonharassment. The Soviet bombers stayed until they were chased away by two U.S. F-4 Phantom jet fighters which scrambled from Seymour Johnson Air Force Base in my own State of North Carolina.

"It is ironic that this provocative act occurred only days before the signing of the 200-mile fishing agreement with Cuba.

"The Foreign Relations Committee proposal has been limited to sales of food and medicine, as though Cuba were seeking purely humanitarian purchases. The fact is that both food and medicines are strategic items in time of conflict. The fact that Castro has 3,000 wounded troops in Angola right now in need of medicine speaks for itself. And even if an agreement were reached with Cuba not to reexport medicines, there is no way to guarantee that the American supplies would not merely replace what was being sent to Angola to aid the Communist military effort there.

"Moreover, we must not forget that Castro is still holding 27 known American prisoners, 8 of whom are designated to this day as political prisoners. At least 10,000 Cubans and probably as many as 40,000 Cubans are being held in prison camps and so-called reeducation camps. And nearly 800 Cuban-Americans with dual citizenship who are seeking to emigrate to the United States are being held in Cuba against their wills."

Helms had asked the State Department to provide him with whatever information it had on political prisoners in Cuba. The following are excerpts from a letter written by Assistant Secretary of State Douglas J. Bennett Jr. and inserted by Helms in the Congressional Record May 11:

Cuba is presently holding eight Americans in prison on political charges. These people are serving 20 to 30 year prison sentences handed down in the 1960's:

Frank Emmick of Ohio;
Everett D. Jackson of Illinois;
Lawrence Lunt of Massachusetts;
Claudio Rodriguez Morales of Puerto Rico;
John Tur of Florida;
Rafael Del Pino of Cuba;
Antonio Garcia Crews of Cuba; and
Carmen Ruiz of Cuba.

19 other Americans are serving jail terms in Cuba on criminal charges.

The Department has no precise information on the number of Cuban citizens held on political charges. Cuba has consistently refused to permit inspection of its jails by the OAS Human Rights Commission or other international bodies. Based on information developed by private US groups, and on the public statements of Cuban officials, we estimate that there may be as many as 10-15,000 persons under detention in Cuba for political reasons. A large portion of this number are probably held in maximum security-type institutions. We know that several prominent early opponents to Castro, such as Hubert Matos, are still in prison serving sentences of up to 20 years.

Helms went on to say, "It is highly sig-nificant that the State Department admitted that Castro refused to permit any international organizations into Cuba to inspect the conditions of its prison camps and jails. A few days after I received this letter, however, the State Department itself was allowed to send two of its Foreign Service officers to meet with the U.S. citizens. No word has been released on the results of these meetings, nor has any impartial international body yet been allowed to study the conditions of prisoners in general." He continued:

"The case of Hubert Matos, mentioned in the State Department's letter, is a typical example of the way Castro treats his opponents. Matos was once a ranking commander in Castro's rebel Army who became a military commander of Camaguey province in January, 1959, immediately following Castro's takeover of Cuba.

"Ten months later, Matos resigned protesting increased Communist domination of the Castro regime. He was actually arrested on the ironic charge of 'slandering the revolution by referring to it as 'Communist,' a charge later changed to treason. Sentenced to 20 years, Matos has been in various political prisons since October 1959. He has been held incommunicado for the past 6 years. Members of his family in Cuba, including his father who is now over 90 years old, have repeatedly tried to visit Matos during this period, but without success. Chile has offered to release several top Communists in exchange for Matos' freedom, but Castro still refuses.

"Yet, Mr. President, this is the regime that today we would begin to recognize."

Senate Minority Leader Howard Baker (R, Tenn) said June 3 that Cuban military involvement in Africa made this "the worst time in history" for Washington to seek diplomatic relations with Havana, it was reported June 5. "I can't believe for one minute that Cuban troops are in Ethiopia, or other parts of Africa, as an extension of Cuban foreign policy," Baker said. "They're there as surrogates for Russia, and this is exactly the wrong time for the United States to get cozy with Cuba."

Former President Gerald Ford expressed a similar view in a talk with newsmen in Houston, it was reported June 5. "I think it would be a mistake to resume diplomatic relations with Cuba as long as Cuba has 15,000 to 20,000 troops in

Angola," Ford declared. Washington and Havana could renew ties "under certain conditions," he said, but not while Cuba was "expanding its military operations . . . doing the things they're doing to promote communism."

Most Americans for renewal of ties. A study by a Washington-based research group showed that most Americans wanted renewed relations with Cuba but under terms that heavily favored the U.S., it was reported Aug. 8. The study, made by Potomac Associates and based partly on a Gallup poll conducted in mid-April, said 59% of those polled favored establishing normal relations with the Castro government, although 51% saw Cuba as a threat to U.S. security. The poll found 52% opposed to a partial lifting of the trade embargo before normal relations were established, and 59% opposed to paying Cuba reparations for damages caused by the embargo or the Bay of Pigs invasion. In addition, those polled wanted Cuba to pull its troops out of Africa (46% to 35%) and to release American political prisoners from its jails (62% to 23%).

U.S., Cuba exchange 'interest' offices. The U.S. and Cuban governments Sept. 1 established "interest sections" in each other's capitals.

The 10-man offices would occupy their governments' former embassy buildings and function as virtual embassies despite the absence of normal diplomatic relations between the two countries. The Cuban office in Washington officially would be part of the Czechoslovakian Embassy to the U.S., and the American office in Havana would be part of the Swiss Embassy there.

Establishment of the offices brought the U.S. and Cuba one step closer to full diplomatic ties, which were broken by Washington in January 1961. But officials of both countries said normal relations could not be expected soon. Both sides wanted to negotiate a number of bilateral issues first, and the Carter Administration wanted to downplay Cuban relations while it sought Senate ratification of the new Panama Canal treaties.

U.S. and Cuban officials hailed their steady rapprochement at a ceremony

opening the Cuban office in Washington Sept. 1. Philip C. Habib, U.S. undersecretary of state for political affairs, said creation of the interest offices was "a beginning, not an end. It is not a big step, but it is a significant one just the same." The new offices would allow the U.S. and Cuba to "speak to each other directly," although "the dialogue won't always be an easy one," Habib said. The "ultimate goal" of President Carter's policy toward Cuba was "full friendship," he declared.

The head of the Cuban interest office, Ramon Sanchez Parodi, said his government was prepared "to analyze deeply and with a constructive spirit . . . those matters that the U.S. government considers as issues of the existing conflicts between our two countries."

Sanchez Parodi said his government could not renew relations with Washington until the U.S. lifted its trade embargo against Cuba. He also said the U.S. must clamp down on "the aggressive actions" carried out by Cuban exiles "against Cuba from U.S. territory." He noted that the initiative for opening the interest offices had come from the U.S., but he added, "Cuba has always been open to establishing normal relations between our two countries."

The U.S. office in Havana was headed by Lyle Franklin Lane, 51, a career foreign service officer who would hold the rank of counselor in Cuba. Lane had served previously in Costa Rica, Ecuador, Guatemala and Peru, most recently as deputy chief of the U.S. Embassy in Lima. The chief U.S. consular official in Havana would be Thomas L. Holladay, 31, who had been working in the State Department's Office of the Coordinator of Cuban Affairs.

Neither interest section immediately occupied its embassy building because each site was being repaired after 16 years of neglect. The Cuban government was charging the U.S. about $250,000 to renovate the American Embassy in Havana, while the U.S. was charging Cuba four times that amount to fix up its properties in Washington, the Washington Post reported Aug. 16. President Fidel Castro said this showed that the Cuban people were very honest and American wages were too high, but the Post noted that the U.S. was importing much of the equipment and supplies for its Havana embassy, thereby reducing the cost of Cuban work on the renovation.

The Carter Administration had said that while the agreement represented "an improvement" in U.S.-Cuban affairs, it was not "tantamount to diplomatic relations." Jody Powell, President Carter's press secretary, said the establishment of interest sections could be seen "as a step—primarily a procedural step—that will make it less difficult to have discussions that hopefully can resolve the substantial differences that still exist" between Havana and Washington.

U.S. Trade Curbs Under Attack

A major aspect of the campaign to promote "normal" U.S.-Cuban relations was the effort to end—or at least modify—the U.S. curbs on trade with Cuba. Only minor actions toward this goal were taken during 1977.

U.S. panel votes to ease trade curbs. The U.S. Senate Foreign Relations Committee May 10 approved an amendment that would allow Cuba to buy medicine, food and agricultural supplies from the U.S.

The amendment, to a pending State Department authorization bill, was a diluted version of a measure proposed by Sen. George McGovern (D, S.D.) with the apparent blessing of President Carter. McGovern had suggested a complete lifting of the embargo on U.S.-Cuban trade in agricultural products and medicine.

A majority of the committee had opposed McGovern's original proposal, arguing that it would give away vital U.S. bargaining power in future negotiations with Cuba. The State Department had shared this objection, although it did not say so until after the compromise amendment was passed by a 10–6 vote.

The following day, on the initiative of committee member Jacob K. Javits (R, N.Y.), the panel voted to give President Carter authority to halt shipments to Cuba at any time.

Passage of the May 10 amendment was greeted with little enthusiasm in Cuba,

whose leaders had demanded a complete lifting of the U.S. trade embargo as a prerequisite for further negotiations on outstanding U.S.-Cuban disputes. President Fidel Castro said May 11, "The partial abolition of the economic blockade against Cuba is inadequate and does not resolve [our] problem with the U.S. government."

Nevertheless, observers saw the amendment as one more step toward normal relations between Havana and Washington. Cuba was eager to buy U.S. medicine and food, although it was desperately short of foreign exchange with which to make the purchases.

The Senate June 16 approved the State Department authorization after Sen. Robert J. Dole (R, Kan.) provoked debate with an amendment saying that Cuba should not be recognized and that the U.S. trade embargo against the country should not be even partially lifted unless Cuba withdrew its troops from Africa, paid $1.8 billion in compensation to U.S. companies for confiscated property and met several other conditions.

An attempt to table, and so kill, the Dole amendment failed, 39–53. However, the Senate then adopted, 54–37, a compromise amendment offered by Byrd. Byrd's amendment simply said that U.S. negotiators with Cuba should not disregard Cuban activities in Africa and that the negotiations should proceed on a reciprocal basis.

Minnesota businessmen visit island. Fifty-two U.S. businessmen from Minnesota visited Cuba April 18–22 for talks with Cuban officials in anticipation of a relaxation of the U.S. economic blockade. Cuban officials spoke frankly about the island's serious economic problems, and held out the prospect of substantial but not massive U.S.-Cuban trade once the embargo was lifted. President Castro met with all 52 Minnesotans April 20, and then conferred with 16 of them the next day. The 16 represented food and financial concerns.

Castro said Cuba was interested in exporting nickel, iron ore and other items to the U.S., and in buying industrial machinery and other American products. He went out of his way to praise President Carter, according to press reports, citing the "political courage" of Carter's recent energy message.

The businessmen's trip was sponsored by the Greater Minneapolis Chamber of Commerce and arranged with the help of Minnesota's Democratic senior senator, Hubert Humphrey. Castro sent boxes of cigars to Humphrey, Vice President Walter Mondale and Sen. McGovern. The Minnesota businessmen delivered them during a stopover in Washington on their return trip to Minneapolis.

Rep. John B. Anderson (R, Ill.) entered into the Congressional Record May 19, an article that appeared in the Sanborn Sentinel, a weekly newspaper, describing the impressions of one Minnesota delegation member, Russell Schwandt, president of the Minnesota Agri-Growth Council and a leader in the Minnesota agricultural community. Excerpts follow:

We have what they need, said Schwandt. They're short of dairy products and meat. and that's because they're so short of feed grains and proteins. They need wheat, corn, soybeans and soybean products, meat products—processed turkey hams and so forth and dairy products, especially butter and powdered milk. Not only that but we're so much closer than their present suppliers— Argentina, Russia, or whoever they're buying from—that by buying from us they could save fifty cents a hundred weight on freight. . . . Being the first trade delegation from the United States puts us in a good position as far as the Cubans are concerned. With 52 Minnesota businessmen making the trip, national press coverage, its a natural time for Carter to move for an end to the embargo. The embargo doesn't make sense any longer. if it ever did. We do business with Russia and Red China right now, why not with Cuba? . . .

Schwandt went on to say that the Cubans "currently buy 300,000 tons of corn and 100,000 tons of beans from other sources—it could just as well be from us. They want to trade tobacco, rum, seafood —a real growth industry for Cuba, it increased over 10 times to 50 million pounds exported last year from 5 million in 1950." He continued:

. . . They also export nickel and sugar, although with sugar prices as depressed as they are in this country, there is probably little that we can do with them in that area. But it doesn't make sense to not trade with them when you see American cars driving the streets of Havana—cars built by subsidiaries of American companies in Argentina. Those cars could just as well have been built in Detroit.

USDA weighs Cuba's potential as a farm market. A U.S. Department of Agriculture assessment of the U.S.' possibilities of selling farm products to Cuba was published May 16. Written by Roger Neetz of the department, it appeared in the department's publication Foreign Agriculture. The article said:

Once the seventh largest U.S. farm market—as well as a top U.S. supplier of sugar, tobacco, and fruit—Cuba could again become a major importer of U.S. farm products should relations between the two countries be normalized and Cuba's foreign debt situation improve.

Current analyses indicate that under such circumstances the United States might gain at least a third of Cuba's farm imports. (In 1976, Cuba's food [1] imports stood at $760 million out of total imports of $3.5 billion, for a 150 percent increase over such imports in 1972.) And a U.S. share of at least two-thirds of this trade is possible considering the commodity composition of Cuba's imports— wheat, rice, corn, flour lard, canned milk, cotton, and vegetable oil.

All of these products rank as important exports for the United States and can be delivered to Cuba at highly competitive prices. However, Cuba, since the breakoff in trade relations with the United States in 1959, has developed strong trade ties with other nations, including Canada, Argentina, and other Western nations in addition to the USSR and Eastern Europe. Cuba also has a $4.6-billion debt with the USSR, which might hinder trade with Western countries. and a more than $1-billion hard-currrency debt with Western countries, which poses even greater potential problems.

Nonetheless, Cuba holds potential as an importer of a number of U.S. farm products. Among them:

Wheat. Cuban wheat and flour imports are expected to hold at current levels of about 900,000 metric tons a year. Canada now has the largest share of this market, which could complicate U.S. re-entry, but the United States would be competitive given its freight advantage and ability to offer the same quality wheat as Canada.

Rice. These imports total 250,000-300,000 tons annually, helping keep Cuban per capita rice consumption the highest in Latin America. The Chinese and Soviets have been supplying much of this rice in recent years, but U.S. long-grain varieties have been preferred in the past.

Coarse grains. These imports, which consist mainly of corn, have reached an annual level of more than 300,000 tons, with the bulk of them coming from Argentina. The U.S.

---

[1] Cotton, vegetable oils, and other raw materials also account for a sizable portion of Cuban trade, but are not broken out from total trade.

freight advantage should make U.S. corn highly competitive in this market.

Pulses. As a onetime major supplier of pulses to Cuba, the United States is believed capable of selling 20,000–80,000 tons there today.

Vegetable oils. These imports, estimated at about 65,000 tons, annually, now consist mainly of USSR sunflower oil. They could be replaced by U.S. vegetable oils.

Cotton. The United States is believed capable of obtaining a sizable share of this market, which is estimated at 100,000 bales annually.

Other products. U.S. exports to Cuba of lard, cured pork, cheese, butter, and processed milk averaged about $14.2 million a year in 1955–59—a trade that has been taken over by Canada and other suppliers. In addition to the possibility of resuming sales of these products, there exists in Cuba a new market for breeding cattle, poultry breeding stock, and hatching eggs.

Historically, there is a strong precedent for U.S. farm trade with Cuba. Prior to the partial and full embargoes on trade with Cuba in 1959 and 1962, the two countries counted one another as key trading partners. Until 1959, the United States was Cuba's largest trading partner, accounting for about 65 percent of the country's total trade turnover.

Agriculture's share in this trade—on both the import and export sides—was significant. In the 1950's Cuba ranked as the largest Latin American market for U.S. farm products and the seventh largest market worldwide, while the United States was Cuba's top farm market. During 1955–59, the United States supplied 68 percent of Cuban farm imports, and took 69 percent of Cuba's agricultural exports, which were dominated by sugar, tobacco, and fruit for an average dollar value of $405 million annually.

Cuban imports of U.S. agricultural products during that same period averaged $131 million annually.

Following the United States 1959 partial embargo on trade with Cuba, Cuba and the USSR concluded the 1960 Bilateral Trade and Payments Agreement, redirecting trade to Communist countries. By the end of 1962, Eastern Europe and the USSR comprised 83 percent of Cuba's trade with Communist countries totaled $4.6 billion, or 71 percent of the country's total trade.

Trade with Western countries—Japan, Spain, West Germany, and Canada—has made slow but observable gains since 1961, although the product exchange remains principally sugar for machinery, manufactured goods, and agricultural products from both Communist and market economies.

Since late 1975, there have also been some modifications in the U.S. embargo to permit foreign companies owned or controlled by U.S. firms to trade with Cuba in nonstrategic foreign-made products. Export licenses issued by the U.S. Treasury Department for $334 million of nonstrategic products were approved between October 1975 and June 1976—$233 million of which was foreign grains sold by subsidiaries of U.S. firms.

Almost as dramatic as Cuba's trade shift has been the rapid growth in its total trade. Between 1959 and 1975, the country's total trade turnover grew from $1.9 billion to $7.2 billion, dipping in 1976 to an estimated $6.5 billion.

This trade expansion gives a new dimension to normalization of commercial ties, especially since much of the growth has occurred in imports of farm products. Rice imports, for instance, rose 43 percent between 1957 and 1975 to 275,000 tons; wheat imports soared more than fourfold to 405,000 tons; wheat flour imports gained by almost fourfold to 350,000 tons; corn imports shot from negligible quantities in 1957 and 160,000 tons in 1968 to 330,000 in 1975; and raw cotton imports rose more than threefold to 30,000 tons.

Cuba's main interest in the U.S. farm market, of course, would be to resume sugar shipments, which in the 1950's earned about $335 million a year in the United States alone. However, current political concern over Cuban sugar imports without equivalent concessions precludes any immediate imports. Also Cuba's interest in the U.S. market may not be strong right now given the low world price for sugar and Cuba's agreement to supply some 3.5 million tons this year to the USSR at a fixed price equivalent to around 66 U.S. cents per kilogram—more than double the current price.

That agreement with the USSR has been both a boon and a burden to Cuban trade during the last few years of widely fluctuating world prices for sugar. As world prices for sugar began to move upward during the early 1970's, the pact became increasingly onerous, since world prices were above those offered by the USSR. Cuba consequently began diversifying trade away from the USSR to countries like Japan and Spain, where it could earn much-needed hard currency. But following sugar's steep price decline of 1975–76, the agreement once again became a plus factor, and Cuba responded by relying more heavily on the Soviet market.

Cuba has, in fact, agreed to supply 1 million tons more to the USSR this year over the 2.5 million reportedly sold in 1976. Because of this, the Government has announced that no additional sugar will be sold until July 1977, and after that supplies also could be tight.

With a population of nearly 10 million and an average per capita income of $820, Cuba needs agricultural trade. Whether some of this will shift to the United States—with the attendant advantage to Cuba of earning hard currencies—depends on Cuba's willingness to comply with provisions of Title IV of the 1974 U.S. Trade Act. This would include entry into a bilateral trade agreement and assurances on free emigration, both subject to Congressional approval. Without such agreement, most-favored-nation tariff status, as well as Eximbank (Export-Import Bank of Washington) and Commodity Credit Corporation credits, would continue to be denied Cuba.

CURRENT U.S. TARIFF SCHEDULE FOR SELECTED PRODUCTS

Commodity	Column 1, MFN tariff	Column 2, non-MFN tariff
Sugar	1.987 cents per pound.	1.987 cents per pound.
Cigars	95 cents per pound plus 5 percent ad valorem.	$4.50 per pound plus 25 percent ad valorem.
Rum	$1.75 per gallon.	$5 per gallon.

There is also a debate about Cuba's tariff preferences that existed at the time of the U.S. embargo and currently remain in a suspended status. One point of view is that the Trade Act supersedes these rights, and Cuba would be subject to the higher Column 2 U.S. tariff rate. This would not, however, affect sugar sales, since U.S. tariff rates are currently the same for all countries (except for those developing countries receiving tariff preferences under the Generalized System of Preferences). And since the expiration of the Sugar Act, the United States has imported sugar from any source—except Cuba, Rhodesia, and North Korea—under a nonrestrictive annual global quota set at 7 million short tons.

President Carter recently announced a sugar support program and rejected restrictions suggested by the International Trade Commission. Cuba could become price competitive in the U.S. market under a lifting of the embargo since tariff rates are the same for all countries excluding GSP nations.

For other commodities, a lifting of the embargo would not give Cuba any additional advantages because the Column 2 tariff would prevail. Cigars, a premium export item for Cuba in the pre-embargo period, would face strong competition from other suppliers in the U.S. market.

Another important factor is Cuba's enlarged debt. Estimates indicate a debt with the USSR of $4.6 billion, which has been deferred until 1986. Payment in hard currency is not required. However, Cuba's capacity to import from the West could be affected by the need to divert a portion of its export capacity to the Soviet Union in order to effect repayment to the Soviets.

Credit lines of $3 billion reportedly have also been extended by several Western countries but have not been used extensively. Currently, Argentina, Spain, the United Kingdom, France, and Canada are the principal sources of credits.

Finally, there is the question of U.S. national claims to $1.8 billion worth of property in Cuba, expropriated after the 1959 revolution—as well as Cuban claims to $60 million in assets frozen in the United States.

Dole vs. ending curbs. U.S. Sen. Robert J. Dole (R, Kan.) said June 10 that there was "little practical" reason for the U.S. to resume normal trade ties with Cuba at this point. Dole's statement, as printed in the Congressional Record, included these remarks:

"Several business groups have recently visited Cuba, and some have come back expressing optimism about potential Cuban markets for American products. Of course, the resumption of exports to Cuba would require the lifting of the 1962 U.S. trade embargo against Cuba. A few of my colleagues in the Senate have already suggested that the embargo be partially lifted to permit the sale of food and pharmaceutical items—presumably as an indication of "Good faith" on the part of the United States.

"In fact, however, the prospects for significant trade with Cuba in the event that the embargo is lifted are not optimistic. . . .

"To those American businessmen who contemplate major new markets just 90 miles from our shores, I will pass on some rather sobering trade·prospects formulated by the U.S. Department of Commerce. Cuba, because it has essentially a one-crop economy, has a very limited hard currency capability for purchasing products abroad. Commerce Department figures suggest that the maximum hard currency import capability of the Cuban Government over the next 2 to 3 years will amount to no more than roughly $800 million to $1 billion. The Department anticipates that, under the very best of conditions, brought about by a complete lifting of the U.S. embargo, Cuba could afford to import no more than $300 million worth of U.S. products at the most. In relation to our annual trade level of about $100 billion, the Cuban market prospects are relatively insignificant.

"It is my understanding that there has been little interest expressed by Cuban officials in future purchases of U.S. wheat. At present, Cuba has been importing about 750,000 tons of Canadian wheat and flour annually on its Soviet account, and there is no reason to believe that they would abandon that source and turn to the United States for grain supplies.

"At present, about 60 percent of Cuban trade is with other Communist countries, and Cuba currently owes the Soviet Union about $5 billion. This is in addition to a Cuban hard currency debt to non-Communist countries estimated at $1.3 billion by the Central Intelligence Agency. It is clear the Cuban economy is hard-pressed, and I would have to say that the Castro regime would make a poor trading partner at this time."

U.S. ends foreign-ships blacklist. The U.S. quietly ended its 14-year old practice of "blacklisting" foreign ships that called at Cuban ports. Under the policy, such vessels were forbidden to haul U.S. government-generated cargo (such as foreign aid or agricultural commodities) or to refuel in U.S. ports. The policy change was decided by the National Security Council June 10 but not announced by the Maritime Administration until Sept. 7.

Castro on U.S. relations & trade. Addressing a crowd of some one million persons in Havana's Revolution Square Sept. 22, Fidel Castro asserted that U.S.-Cuban relations could not improve substantially until the U.S. lifted its trade embargo against the island. He also demanded that the U.S. remove its naval base from Guantanamo Bay in eastern Cuba, a base Castro often had called "a dagger in Cuba's heart."

Castro said he was willing to discuss the $1.8-billion worth of claims by U.S. businesses that Cuba had nationalized since 1959. But he said the U.S. first must compensate Cuba for damages caused by the 16-year trade embargo and by the Bay of Pigs invasion and other U.S. "aggressions."

Castro sent Foreign Trade Minister Marcelo Fernandez Font to Washington Oct. 3 to discuss U.S.-Cuban trade once relations were normalized. Fernandez told a conference of U.S. businessmen that the compensation demanded by Castro was higher than the $1.8 billion claimed from Cuba by the U.S.

Fernandez said that once the trade embargo was lifted, U.S. exports to Cuba might reach $350 million in the first year of "normal trade" and pass the billion-dollar mark within three or four years. But he said this volume could be reached only if the U.S. fully opened its markets to Cuba by restoring Cuba's most-favored-nation trading status and by giving the island special tariff preferences.

U.S. officials were less sanguine about the early possibilities for U.S. exports to Cuba. They noted that certain restrictions were imposed by the 1974 Trade Act and that Cuba was quite short of hard currency reserves.

Fernandez said Cuba was interested in buying American foodstuffs, animal feeds, drugs, fertilizers, ferrous and non-ferrous metals and machinery, and other industrial equipment including entire plants. In exchange, Cuba wanted to sell the U.S. sugar, tobacco, shellfish and nickel.

Other U.S.-Cuban Developments

CIA linked to '71 swine fever. With at least tacit approval from the U.S. Central Intelligence Agency, operatives linked to anti-Castro terrorists had introduced the African swine fever virus into Cuba in 1971, the New York newspaper Newsday reported Jan. 9.

Six weeks after the virus was introduced, a Cuban outbreak of the fever forced the slaughter of 500,000 pigs to prevent a nationwide animal epidemic. The previously unexplained outbreak—the only one ever to occur in the Western Hemisphere—was called the "most alarming event" of 1971 by the United Nations' Food and Agriculture Organization.

African swine fever was a highly contagious and usually lethal disease that infected only pigs and, unlike swine flu, could not be transmitted to humans.

A U.S. intelligence source told Newsday that early in 1971 he was given a sealed, unmarked container at Ft. Gulick in the Panama Canal Zone, a U.S. Army base where the CIA operated a paramilitary training center for career personnel and mercenaries. The source said he was instructed to turn over the container to an anti-Castro group. He gave it to someone in the Canal Zone who took it by boat to a fishing trawler off the Panamanian coast. The source said he was not told until after the Cuban outbreak that the container held swine fever virus.

A CIA-trained Cuban exile who was involved in the operation told Newsday that he was on the trawler when the virus was put aboard. He said the container was carried to Navassa Island, a tiny, deserted U.S. property between Jamaica and Haiti. From there it was taken to Cuba in late March 1971, where it was given to other operatives on the southern coast near the U.S. Navy base at Guantanamo Bay.

Cuban officials said the first sick pigs in Cuba were found in Havana about May 6. A non-Soviet bloc agricultural technician then in Cuba said the disease easily could have gone undetected for months, Newsday reported. Newsday's sources said they had no direct knowledge of whether the virus from Ft. Gulick was responsible for the outbreak in Havana, 500 miles northwest of Guantanamo.

Neither the intelligence source nor the source on the trawler could confirm that the operation was approved by the CIA. Another intelligence source in Miami said: "In a case like this, [the CIA always would have] plausible deniability." A CIA spokesman, asked by Newsday to comment, said: "We don't comment on information from unnamed and, at best, obscure sources."

Cuban officials said the island's entire pork production was halted until the disease was confined to Havana Province and eradicated by slaughtering the infected pigs and burning their remains.

Cuba frees U.S. citizens. The Cuban government announced June 3 that it would free 10 American prisoners immediately and review the cases of the other 20 U.S. citizens jailed on the island.

The 10 favored prisoners, all aged 20–30 and held by Cuba on drug charges, were flown to Mexico June 12 on to the U.S. the next day. U.S. consular officials in Mexico City said the former prisoners appeared to be in good health.

A State Department spokesman June 3 asked Cuba to show "compassionate consideration" for the 20 American prisoners that stayed behind, some of whom were elderly persons held for years on political grounds. Cuba held seven Americans for "crimes against the state," according to the Miami Herald June 8.

President Fidel Castro said Aug. 11 he would allow more than 80 U.S. citizens to leave Cuba with their families. The Americans always had been free to go but had refused to leave without their Cuban-born wives and children.

Castro made the announcement at the end of a four-day visit to Cuba by U.S. Sen. Frank Church (D, Ida.). Church said

the Cuban leader's action was "a very important, humane gesture of goodwill" that was certain to please President Carter.

Castro also agreed to free the crews of two U.S.-registered boats that had been seized recently in Cuban waters. Church had told him that the wife of one of the crew members was dying of cancer. Another crew member was reported to be a nephew of Charles G. (Bebe) Rebozo, a close friend of former President Richard Nixon. His boat reportedly was carrying a large cargo of marijuana when it was seized.

The first fifty-five U.S. and Cuban citizens were flown from Havana in a U.S. Air Force plane to the Homestead base near Miami Sept. 22. It was unclear how many of them were U.S. citizens and how many were Cubans. The New York Times counted 29 Americans and 26 Cuban relatives; Reuters said it was 31 Americans and 24 Cubans, and the Miami Herald gave two conflicting counts—31 Americans and 24 Cubans in its lead news article, and 16 Americans and 39 Cubans in a news analysis essay.

The emigrants were greeted by Joseph Aragon, a special assistant to President Carter on issues concerning Hispanic Americans. Aragon read a message from Carter calling the release of the emigrants "the first in what we hope will be a series of similar humanitarian actions on the part of the government of Cuba."

Carter's message also expressed hope that "in the near future we shall begin to see the bringing together of other families, both Cuban and Americans, who have been separated over long periods of time, which can only be measured in terms of anguish."

The U.S. State Department estimated that there were 55 more American citizens in Cuba with about 200 close Cuban relatives. About half of the Americans wished to be repatriated, a department spokesman said. They would be departing for the U.S. as soon as their papers were processed.

U.S. prisoner to be freed—The U.S. State Department said Dec. 13 that Cuba would release a 63-year-old American prisoner it had held for 14 years.

The prisoner, Frank Emmick, was a former businessman who had been jailed in 1963 on charges of heading operations of the U.S. Central Intelligence Agency

(CIA) in Cuba. Emmick denied the charges, but admitted to having smuggled a letter out of Cuba in 1972 or 1973 to Richard Helms, then director of the CIA, the Washington Post reported Dec. 7.

U.S. Reps. Frederick W. Richmond (D, N.Y.) and Richard Nolan (D, Minn.) had urged President Castro to release Emmick during their visit to Cuba earlier in December. They reminded Castro that Emmick had suffered two heart attacks in prison and recommended his release as a "humanitarian" gesture.

U.S. informing on Cuban exiles—The U.S. State Department Aug. 3 said the U.S. was giving Cuba information on terrorist acts being planned against the island by Cuban exiles in Miami and elsewhere. An assistant U.S. attorney in Miami said Aug. 15 that a planned raid on Cuba by exiles based in Miami had been foiled earlier in the summer when federal and Florida State agents informed the Cuban government of the plot, seized three armed boats to have been used in the raid and arrested one boat's owner. He was Pedro Gil, a member of Brigade 2506, the Miami-based organization of veterans of the 1961 Bay of Pigs invasion.

Exiles in Miami Aug. 31 said they would continue "all kinds of actions to fight against the Communist tyranny" in Cuba. The threat was made by Brigade 2506.

'Exporting Revolution,' Activities in Africa

Castro's troops in Africa. Sen. Jake Garn (R, Utah) told the U.S. Senate May 20 that the Castro regime was "systematically destabilizing governments all over the world."

He want on to report on the activities of Cuban soldiers in Africa:

"Angola: Despite promises by Castro that Cuban troops would be removed from Angola, there are still more than 12,000 Cuban soldiers in that country. It is true that that represents a reduction from a year ago, but the 3,000 regulars which have been brought home have been replaced by 3,000 civilian advisers and technicians. That hardly represents a commitment to reduce Cuban presence. The Cuban troops are fighting directly against the Unita guerrillas in southern Angola, and are reported to be in action against Cabindan rebels in the North. In addition to training the Angolan Army, the Cubans train the troops of terrorist organizations for raids into Southwest Africa. There are indications that the Cubans trained and supplied the invaders in Zaire's Shaba province.

"Congo People's Republic: Cubans first came to this country on their way to Angola, in support of the Agostinho Neto forces. While there they assisted in the transshipment of Soviet material being sent to Angola. Three hundred of them remain.

"Guinea, Guinea-Bissau, Equatorial Guinea: Guinea was the site of the first Cubans sent to Africa. They came in support of the rebels against the Portuguese in neighboring Guinea-Bissau. More than 100 remain in Guinea-Bissau as advisers and instructors, 300 are still in Guinea, training Sekou Toure's army, and guarding his person—against other Guineans, I suppose. Equatorial Guinea, a former Spainsh colony, also has its allotment of 3,000 to 4,000 Cuban troops.

"Mozambique: The 500 Cubans in Mozambique are training the army of that country, and also the guerrillas terrorizing Rhodesia from bases within Mozambique.

"Tanzania: There have been persistent reports that Cubans are also training the black Rhodesian guerrillas operating out of Tanzania.

"Somalia: The presence of Cubans in Somalia is certain; their most likely task is the training of guerrillas for operations against the Ethiopian Government. Apparently the regular Somalian Army is trained by Soviet regulars.

"Ethiopia: Reports are starting to appear that there are Cuban troops in Ethiopia. As Ethiopia's ties to the West weaken, and are replaced by cooperation with the Soviet Union, the Soviets will use Cubans to orchestrate the switch, rather than doing it directly.

"Unconfirmed reports continue that Cubans are in Libya, bolstering the Qaddafi regime—and protecting his person from other Libyans—and that they are training and assisting the Polisario guerrillas fighting in the western Sahara and in Mauritania.

⁚ Whether these last reports are accurate or not, Mr. President, we do not have a picture of a peace-loving, unambitious member of the family of nations. It is inconceivable to me that we could consider the reestablishment of relations with this harsh, repressive, autocratic regime, which is systematically destabilizing governments all over the world. I urge the Senate to resist the Madison Avenue rehabilitation of Castro, and to see him as he is."

Castro tours Africa. Cuban President Fidel Castro visited eight Arab and black African nations March 1–April 2, conferring with their leaders and with Cuban soldiers and civilians who were stationed in some of the countries.

Castro's itinerary, often improvised on short notice, was: Algeria March 1; Libya March 1–10; South Yemen March 10–12; Somalia March 12–14; Ethiopia March 14–16; Tanzania March 17–21; Mozambique March 21–23; Angola March 23–31, and Algeria again March 31–April 2. After leaving Algeria, Castro paid an unscheduled visit to East Germany April 2–4 and then flew on to Moscow to meet with Soviet leaders.

Castro conferred with Algerian President Houari Boumedienne during a brief stopover in Algiers March 1, after which he flew to Tripoli. During his 10-day stay in Libya, Castro toured the country and conferred extensively with the head of government, Col. Muammer el-Qaddafi. The two leaders signed an agreement March 10 to increase economic, commercial, scientific and cultural exchanges between Cuba and Libya.

The two governments were secretive about Castro's talks with Qaddafi, but newspapers reported that the two leaders had discussed the civil war in Ethiopia, among other topics. In their final communique March 10, Castro and Qaddafi denounced "imperialist maneuvers against the Ethiopian revolution," presumably referring to Sudanese support for opponents of Ethiopia's military government.

Castro began an unscheduled visit in Ethiopia March 14, after two-day stops in South Yemen and Somalia. Despite official secrecy about Castro's talks with these countries' leaders—South Yemen's President Salem Ali Rubaye, Somalia's President Mohamed Siad Barre and

Ethiopia's Lt. Col. Mengistu Haile Mariam—Western diplomats and newspapers reported that the principal topic of discussion was Ethiopia's conflict with Somalia over the future of the French Territory of the Afars and Issas (Djibouti), which was scheduled to become independent in June.

Castro reportedly urged Ethiopia, Somalia and South Yemen—all of which had leftist governments—to form an alliance that would keep Djibouti independent and serve as a "common anti-imperialist front." This plan, endorsed by the Soviet Union, was opposed by the U.S., Egypt, Sudan and Saudi Arabia, which were using offers of economic aid to try to entice Somalia out of the Soviet sphere of influence. Castro's chief obstacle in promoting the alliance was Somalia's claim to sovereignty over Djibouti and a part of eastern Ethiopia. The Ethiopian government, which used Djibouti as its major port, wanted the territory to be independent.

Lt. Col. Mengistu supported the proposed alliance, according to the Cuban newspaper Granma March 15. (Mengistu also asked Castro to give his government military support against Eritrean and other rebels, but Castro made no commitment, according to diplomatic sources quoted by the Washington Post March 17.)

Castro left Ethiopia March 16, but he did not arrive at his next scheduled destination—Dar es Salaam, Tanzania—until the next day. Newspapers speculated that he had returned to Somalia or South Yemen to continue pressing his alliance plan.

In Tanzania, Castro addressed other African issues. He said March 20 that Cuba could not afford to give more aid to Tanzania because of its economic and military commitments to the Angolan government. At a press conference in Dar es Salaam March 21, Castro denied that Cuban soldiers had been involved in the recent invasion of Zaire, and he said Cuban troops would not be sent to aid black nationalist guerrillas in Rhodesia or Namibia (South-West Africa). "We believe the struggle for independence is primarily a task which belongs to the people concerned themselves," Castro said. "Independence is not bought from abroad."

The Cuban leader made an unscheduled

visit to Mozambique March 21, where he conferred with President Samora Machel. Castro continued to Angola March 23 for a nine-day visit that was considered the highlight of his African tour.

Castro declared March 24 that Cuba would "not place any limit on its cooperation" with Angola and would give the Luanda government "all the aid it needs." At a rally March 28, Castro pledged continued military support for Angola despite U.S. opposition. "The day will come when Angola has sufficient military units, tanks, cannon, airplanes and soldiers to confront all imperialist aggression," he said. "How many years, how many [Cuban] soldiers will stay in Angola? We don't have to discuss that with Yankee imperialists."

Following Castro's departure from Angola, the Luanda government April 2 issued a joint communique in which Castro and Angolan President Agostinho Neto pledged to "support with all the means at hand, the just struggle for the liberation of the peoples of South Africa, Zimbabwe (Rhodesia) and Namibia."

(Three southern African nationalist leaders were in Angola during Castro's visit, but it was not known whether they met with him. Joshua Nkomo of the Rhodesian Patriotic Front, Sam Nujoma of the South-West Africa People's Organization and Oliver Tambo of the African National Congress had flown to Luanda March 29 from Lusaka, Zambia, where they had conferred with Soviet President Nikolai Podgorny, who was on an African tour of his own.

Castro ended his African tour in Algeria. On arriving in Algiers March 31, he said: "Just like Christopher Columbus, I have discovered a continent in struggle. I have been able to evaluate the possibilities of a long and protracted liberation struggle, which can only be victorious."

Castro flew April 2 to East Germany, which was believed to be one of the Communist nations most deeply involved in African politics, providing military and economic support for black liberation movements and left-leaning black governments, according to Reuters. Castro conferred with East German leaders, presumably about his tour.

The Cuban leader arrived in Moscow April 4, where he was hugged at the airport by Soviet Communist Party leader Leonid Brezhnev, Premier Alexei

Kosygin, and President Podgorny, who had returned from Africa only the day before. The presence of the top Soviet leaders at the airport and the warmth of their greeting signaled the great importance they gave Castro's visit, according to press reports. Castro conferred with the Soviet leaders in Moscow April 5-6.

Cuban-Angolan war role. A report was published Jan. 31 by Robert Moss, a former editor with The Economist, on Cuba's involvement in the Angolan war. Moss said Cuban soldiers had been operating in Angola several months before Nov. 5, 1975, the date on which the Cubans officially said they had decided to intervene. Moss was responding to an official account by Cuba of its role in Angola, written by the Colombian author Gabriel Garcia Marquez.

According to Moss, Cuban Deputy Foreign Minister Carlos Rafael Rodriguez had revealed in a December 1975 speech that there were 230 Cuban military instructors with the MPLA as of the spring of 1975. In August 1975, MPLA Defense Minister Iko Carreira visited Moscow to ask for Soviet troops. Moscow had turned down the request, fearing a confrontation with the U.S., but had suggested Carreira request help from Cuba. The Soviets had given Cuba assurances of direct Soviet intervention if the U.S. blockaded Cuba or sent troops to Angola, Moss reported.

More Cuban military instructors arrived in Luanda Aug. 16, 1975, and shipments of military equipment and troops were reported in September and October. By Nov. 11, 1975, Angola's independence day, there were 4,000 Cuban troops in the country, 2,500 of them in Luanda, Moss said.

Angolan rebellion suppressed. Angolan government troops, backed by Cuban forces, May 27 suppressed a rebellion by supporters of two purged government officials. Rebels demanding the reinstatement of Nito Alves, former interior minister, and Jose Van Dunem, a former army political commissar, had briefly captured the national radio station that morning and the international airport in

Luanda, the Angolan capital. The two men had been expelled from the ruling Popular Movement for the Liberation of Angola (MPLA) May 21, reportedly because of their hard-line pro-Soviet stance and their opposition to establishing diplomatic relations with Western countries.

The short-lived uprising had posed a serious threat to the government of the Popular Movement for the Liberation of Angola (MPLA), according to a report June 20 in the New York Times.

The report said Cuban troops had played an important part in putting down the coup despite Neto's denials of Cuban participation. A group of rebels had seized the Luanda radio station in the early morning, and another group had freed Nito Alves and Jose Van Dunem, two former MPLA officials, several hours later. (Alves had been purged from the MPLA Central Committee because of his close ties with the U.S.S.R. According to reports cited by the Times, Alves was opposed to the Cuban presence in Angola.)

In addition to facing internal dissent, the ruling party was engaged in a struggle against several anti-MPLA guerrilla groups. The National Front for the Liberation of Angola (FNLA) had issued a communique claiming "resounding victories" over Cuban and Angolan forces, according to a report May 31 in the Financial Times (London). The communique said that FNLA forces controlled the northern third of the country, and that Cuban-backed MPLA forces held only the large cities. A spokesman for the Front for the Liberation of the Enclave of Cabinda (FLEC) May 4 said the rebels have driven back a Cuban-led offensive in the oil-rich province. The spokesman said FLEC held two-thirds of Cabinda.

Dole on Cuban troops in Angola. U.S. Sen. Robert J. Dole (R, Kan.) expressed his concern in a statement in the Senate June 10 at the continued presence of Cuban troops in Angola. Dole said that his concern was essentially confirmed by Castro's remarks during several interviews in which Castro disclosed that he had stopped withdrawing Cuban troops from Angola in April despite his June 1976 promise that the 20,000 Cuban troops would be withdrawn from Angola at the rate of 200 a week. The State Department currently estimated that between 10,000

and 15,000 of those troops had never been withdrawn from Angola.

Dole continued:

"In an April interview with the French magazine Afrique-Asie, Castro candidly suggested that 'The possibilities of a fundamental revolution are very substantial on the African Continent,' and stated that 'As far as southern Africa is concerned, I do not believe that peaceful and diplomatic solutions will persuade the racists and their allies to give up their regime.' It is clear that Castro envsions a bloodbath throughout Africa and intends to lend encouragement in that direction."

Excerpts from the Afrique-Asie interview as inserted by Dole in the Congressional Record June 10:

CASTRO. Any aggression against Angola will be energetically repulsed. Any attack against Angola will be regarded by us as an attack directed against Cuba. Let there be no mistake about it: Fighting side by side with the Angolan people, we will defend Angola with all means at our disposal. . . .

I want to make this very clear (he said in forceful voice). Everybody shall know that we will never negotiate our solidarity with Angola with the U.S. This is not a negotiable matter. Would it not be absurd if we, for example, were to discuss the withdrawal of U.S. troops from Europe, Iran, South Korea, the Philippines, Japan and Saudi Arabia? No, it is really absurd that the U.S. make such conditions. Our position is clear and without ambiguities. . . .

Young in Africa, Cuban activities cited. Andrew Young, U.S. representative to the U.N., visited Africa as an ambassador from the new Carter Administration Feb. 3–10. The visit was marked by a series of policy observations that seemed to be at variance with Administration positions.

Young stopped off in London before and after his African trip for discussions on the Rhodesian situation. He met both times with Ivor Richard, British chairman of the Geneva talks on Rhodesia. On his first visit to London Feb. 2, the discussions were joined by British Foreign Secretary Anthony Crosland.

The first of Young's controversial policy observations concerned Angola. It was made in a television interview days before his trip, on Jan. 25. Young had remarked that the presence of Cuban troops there brought "a certain stability and order" to Angola.

At a State Department news conference April 11, Young defended his remark. He said that Cuban forces were helping to defend the Gulf Oil Co. installations in the Angolan province of Cabinda against two anti-government guerrilla groups. In this instance, he said, the Cubans were helping to keep the oil flowing to the West, which was vital to Angola's economy.

Of the 10,000 or so Cubans reported to be in Angola, Young said: "We don't known how many are troops and how many are" agriculturalists, physicians and technicians helping to fill the vacuum left by the flight of several hundred thousand Portuguese from Angola just before it became independent.

"I'm not defending what the Russians and the Cubans did in Angola," he said. "But once they are there, it seems to me that there needs to be a realistic assessment of what their role is."

Secretary of State Cyrus Vance, at a news conference Jan. 31, said the presence of any outside forces in Angola was "not helpful to a peaceful solution." The matter was one "that should be settled by the Africans themselves," Vance said.

The official State Department position, released Feb. 2 by spokesman Frederick Brown, was that "neither Ambassador Young nor the secretary condones the presence of Cuban troops in Angola."

Young also irked U.S. officials May 26, when he suggested in London that the presence of Cuban military advisers in Ethiopia "might not be a bad thing" if they could halt the killings there. Only the day before, the State Department had expressed official concern about the Cubans' reported presence in Ethiopia. Moreover, Vice President Walter Mondale, speaking shortly after Young made his remarks, reiterated that the U.S. would view the sending of Cuban troops to Ethiopia as "very serious" and a "destabilizing factor."

One important official whose support for Young appeared unshaken by the latest controversy was President Carter. At a news conference May 26, Carter said he knew of "no instance when Andy Young has violated" Administration policy. In an interview published in the June 6 U.S. News and World Report, Carter said there had been no disagreement between himself and Young "on the thrust of our policy or statements on Africa."

Cuban military advisers reported in Ethiopia. The U.S. State Department said May 25 that it had received reports of the arrival of 50 Cuban military advisers in Addis Ababa and warned Cuba that intervention in Ethiopia "could impede the improvement of [Cuban] relations" with the U.S.

A State Department spokesman said the U.S. had no confirmation of reports that 400–500 Cuban troops would be dispatched to Ethiopia in the future, but added that the U.S. "will be watching closely" any Cuban activity in Africa.

In an ABC-TV interview broadcast in the U.S. May 24, Cuban President Fidel Castro had denied there were Cuban military advisers in Ethiopia, saying all Cuban nationals in the country were "accredited as diplomatic personnel." He did not rule out sending military instructors if requested to do so by the Ethiopian government.

U.S. Rep. Ronald Dellums (D, Calif.) said June 1 that Cuba would increase its personnel in Ethiopia by 311 doctors and medical technicians. Dellums, who had met with Castro in Havana May 28, said the Cuban leader had assured him that the Cubans now in Ethiopia were not military instructors but "diplomatic personnel." Dellums said he was convinced that "Cuba will send no troops to Ethiopia." He briefed President Carter June 3 on his meeting with Castro.

Increased Cuban involvement seen—The U.S. State Department estimated Nov. 14 that there were 400 Cuban officers and soldiers assisting Ethiopian forces in the Ogaden region. A spokesman said the increase in Cuban aid meant that there were at least 550 Cubans providing military and civilian assistance to Ethiopia, up from 50 in May.

A State Department estimate Nov. 4 had put the total of Soviet and Cuban military advisers at 250, of which 150 were estimated to be Cubans. Cuba the next day had denied stationing troops, in reply to previous charges by Somali President Mohamed Siad Barre that there were 15,000 Cuban troops in Ogaden. (The State Department reported Dec. 16 an estimated 500 Soviets and 800 Cubans helping Ethiopian troops.)

Somalia expels Soviets, Cubans. In a surprise move, Somalia Nov. 13 ordered all Soviet advisers to leave the country, terminated the 1974 Soviet-Somali friendship and cooperation treaty and broke diplomatic relations with Cuba. The Somali action was the abrupt climax of a steadily worsening diplomatic crisis resulting from the U.S.S.R.'s pro-Ethiopia stance in the Horn of Africa conflict.

The announcement came after an emergency session of the central committee of Somalia's ruling Socialist Revolutionary Party. Soviet advisers, said to number at least 1,500, were given a week to leave, while Cuban personnel were given 48 hours. The announcement indirectly accused the U.S.S.R. and Cuba of having "brazenly interfered in the struggle of the peoples fighting for their liberation from the Ethiopian government," a reference to the Somali-backed guerrillas in the Ogaden region of Ethiopia.

The U.S. Nov. 14 expressed satisfaction over the Somali move. The State Department said Somalia was in "a far better position to pursue a truly nonaligned foreign policy" as a result, and it ruled out any U.S. moves to fill the Soviet vacancy. A U.S. spokesman blamed the troubles in the Horn of Africa on the increased Soviet and Cuban military involvement, adding that "African problems should be solved by Africans themselves."

Castro reaffirms Africa role. President Fidel Castro asserted Dec. 5 that Cuba's military presence in Africa was not negotiable and had nothing to do with Cuba's relations with the U.S.

Speaking with reporters after meeting with two U.S. congressmen in Havana, Castro rejected the Carter Administration's persistent calls for a gradual Cuban pullout from Africa. "It has nothing to do with Carter, it has nothing to do with the U.S.," he said. "If it becomes an issue, it's going to be an impediment."

The American congressmen—Reps. Frederick W. Richmond (D, N.Y.) and Richard Nolan (D, Minn.)—had given Castro a message from President Carter urging Cuba to "get out of Angola." The message came a few days after Andrew Young, the U.S. ambassador to the United Nations, implied in a speech that Cuba was aiding African governments that kept power by "killing off the opposition."

Young continued his criticism of Havana Dec. 6, charging that the Soviet Union and Cuba were "contributing to the escalation of death and destruction in Africa." Young said the two communist nations should "assist Africans in the task of nation-building" instead.

Castro reaffirmed his position Dec. 24 after receiving a letter from 40 U.S. senators urging him to cut back Cuba's military involvement in Africa. Speaking to the closing session of the National Assembly in Havana, Castro accused the Carter Administration of conducting a "policy of blackmail" against Cuba.

Castro said Cuba would "never trade our ties with the Third World for a smile from the U.S., for the smallest concession on their part." He acknowledged that trade relations with the U.S. would benefit Cuba, but he said they would not be "decisive." "Our relations with the Soviet Union and the socialist camp are decisive, and the U.S. will never be able to replace those relations," he declared.

Other Foreign Developments

Comecon to build nuclear plant. Comecon, the Communist bloc's economic association, would build the first atomic power station in Cuba, the Soviet news agency Tass reported Jan. 6.

Under an agreement signed in Moscow in April 1976, the first stage of the plant would have "an output capacity of 440 megawatts." Cuban President Fidel Castro had said the plant eventually would have twice that capacity.

Cuban exile leader slain. Juan Jose Peruyero, 46, a leader of Miami's anti-Castro Cuban exiles, was shot to death Jan. 7 by unidentified assailants. Police described the killing as a "political assassination." Peruyero was a former president of the Bay of Pigs Invasion Brigade Veteran Association.

Peruyero was the seventh Cuban exile leader to die in the last three years. During the same period, about 100 bombs were exploded in the Miami area and a number of reporters, both Cuban and American, had received death threats.

Canada deports alleged spies. Canada Jan. 10 ordered the expulsion of five Cubans, including three members of the Cuban Consulate in Montreal, on charges of recruiting and training intelligence agents to be sent to Rhodesia.

According to an official in the External Affairs Department, the three consular staff members had been ordered "withdrawn" and the Department of Immigration had issued deportation orders against two more Cubans living in Canada on nonimmigrant status. "On the basis of investigations," the official said, "it was determined that there was an intelligence operation being conducted in Canada involving the Cuban nationals in contravention of their status in Canada."

The Canadian government refused further comment on the case, but a report in the Jan. 10 Gazette, a Montreal newspaper, cited details first reported by the Sunday Mail of Salisbury, Rhodesia. According to the report, the existence of the Montreal operation was revealed by a U.S. citizen, David Bufkin, who said he had been recruited and trained by the Cubans. He was also reported to have spied on the Cubans for the U.S. Central Intelligence Agency. The Salisbury newspaper quoted Bufkin as saying he had been recruited in Mexico, trained in Montreal and sent to Rhodesia for "undercover activity," but had reported his mission to Rhodesian authorities upon his arrival in Salisbury.

The Cuban government Jan. 12 admitted using its Montreal consulate as a base for recruiting agents but denied "any actions . . . that would interfere with normal relations between Canada and Cuba." The Cuban Foreign Ministry in Havana said it had recruited informants to operate against the National Front for the Liberation of Angola (FNLA), not against the Rhodesian government as had been suspected. Cuba accused the FNLA of attacking Cuban diplomats and said it was a "normal right" to gather intelligence on the group. The Canadian Department of External Affairs refused to comment on the Cuban statement, saying it had been issued to journalists and thus was not an official intergovernmental communication.

Four Cubans who had been ordered expelled from Canada in connection with the case left for Havana Jan. 12. They were: Montreal Consul General Jesus Rodriguez Verdes, Vice Consul Rene Valenzuela Acebal, consular employe Raul Hernandez Cuesta and Hector Arazoza Rodriguez, a lecturer at McGill University in Montreal. Fernando E. Rivero Milan, third secretary at the Cuban Embassy in Ottawa, was in Cuba on leave and was informed he would not be permitted to return to Canada.

Canadian Solicitor General Francis Fox said Jan. 16 that the Cuban consulate in Montreal had been under surveillance for months before the four Cuban nationals were ordered to leave the country Jan. 10.

In a radio interview, Fox said the Royal Canadian Mounted Police (RCMP) had been aware of illegal Cuban activities prior to the disclosure by a U.S. mercenary of Cuban espionage recruiting and training in Canada. Fox added that the U.S. Central Intelligence Agency, for whom the mercenary, David Bufkin, claimed to be working, had denied employing the alleged double agent. Fox said the CIA and the RCMP had an "understanding . . . that there would be no CIA operatives operating in Canada without our permission." He added, "We were definitely not advised that he [Bufkin] was a CIA operative."

Domestic Developments

Castro on political prisoners. Cuban President Fidel Castro discussed political prisoners in a TV interview broadcast in the U.S. June 9.

Under questioning from ABC-TV correspondent Barbara Walters, Castro admitted that Cuba held "maybe 2,000 or 3,000" political prisoners, having once held "more than 15,000 prisoners" when "the activity of the United States was more intensive against Cuba." It appeared to be the first time Castro had estimated the number of political prisoners in Cuba since a 1967 interview in which he put the figure at 20,000.

(The U.S. State Department estimated there were currently between 10,000 and 15,000 political prisoners in Cuba, it was reported June 9.)

Exile commandos freed. The government freed two Cuban-born anti-Communists who had been jailed in the 1960s for infiltrating the island from exile to carry out subversive activities, it was reported Aug. 2.

Manuel Humberto Reyes, who re-entered Cuba before the 1961 Bay of Pigs invasion, had been held for 15 years. Carlos Ibarra Vasquez had been arrested in 1969 when he tried to organize a resistance group in eastern Cuba.

Upon their release both men went to Venezuela, where Ibarra held citizenship through his Venezuelan father. They told reporters in Caracas that they had been held in tiny, one-man cells and had been forbidden to speak for more than three years, but that they had never been tortured.

The two prisoners were freed following appeals to President Castro from officials of the U.S., Venezuela and Panama, according to Cuban exile sources in Miami.

and participated in government work projects. But if the prisoners continued to oppose the government, they were beaten, denied adequate nourishment and put in solitary confinement in dark, unsanitary cells. Some prisoners had been killed by guards, and others were held after their prison term had ended, Amnesty International said.

Amnesty said the majority of political prisoners in Cuba had opted for rehabilitation, but some, like former guerrilla commander Huber Matos, had maintained their opposition to the government and suffered the consequences.

Amnesty added that prison conditions in Cuba had improved in the last few years. The government had "closed the worst . . . penal institutions and there are indications of great progress in [prison] conditions, with the exception of the Boniato jail in Santiago." Prison guards at Boniato had killed some prisoners, Amnesty reported.

Amnesty group cites prison abuse. Amnesty International reported Sept. 17 that there were about 5,000 political prisoners in Cuba and that some of them were subjected to beatings and others forms of mistreatment.

Amnesty International said Cuban political prisoners were treated well if they agreed to be "rehabilitated," that is, if they accepted political indoctrination

National Assembly meets. The National Assembly, Cuba's new legislature, met for its first working session July 12-14. The 479-member congress convened to discuss and approve a number of proposed laws that would bring existing statutes into line with the recent reorganization of Cuba's administration. It was the first working session of a Cuban legislature since the 1959 revolution.

Ecuador

Government & Politics

New Cabinet sworn in. President Carlos Andres Perez swore in a new Cabinet Jan. 7, one day after all ministers had resigned to allow him to reorganize his administration.

Perez had created seven new ministries Jan. 4 in a move to increase efficiency. The portfolios were: environment and renewable natural resources, urban development, information and tourism, youth, transport and communications, energy and mines, and secretary of the presidency. Perez abolished the old ministries of communications, mines and hydrocarbons, and public works.

The new Cabinet:

Interior—Octavio Lepage; foreign affairs—Ramon Escovar Salom; finance—Hector Hurtado; defense—Gen. Francisco Alvarez Torres; environment and renewable natural resources—Arnoldo Jose Gabaldon; development—Luis Alvarez Dominguez; urban development—Roberto Padilla Fernandez; education—Carlos Rafael Silva; health—Antonio Parra Leon; agriculture and livestock—Carmelo Contreras; labor—Jose Manzo Gonzalez; transport and communications—Jesus Vivas Casanova; justice—Juan Martin Echeverria; energy and mines—Valentin Hernandez Acosta; information and tourism—Diego Arria; youth—Pedro Paris Montesinos; secretary of the presidency—Jose Luis Salcedo Bastardo; chief of Cordiplan (planning)—Lorenzo Azpurua Marturet; international economic affairs—Manuel Perez Guerrero; president of the Investment Fund—Constantino Quero Morales; basic industries—Carmelo Lauria Lesseur; governor of the Federal District—Manuel Mantilla.

Civilian rule delayed. The military government announced April 5 that the transfer of power to a civilian president, scheduled for January 1978, would be postponed for nine months.

Former President Galo Plaza, head of the transition program, attributed the delay to difficulties in drawing up a new electoral register. Because the register could not be completed until November, Plaza said, the referendum on a new constitution would be put off until March 1978, the presidential election until the following August and the transfer of power until September.

The delay was denounced by numerous political parties, including the Liberals, Conservatives and Velasquistas. Political observers generally agreed that the government was buying time to find a way of preventing populist leader Asaad Bucaram from winning the presidential election, according to the Latin America Political Report April 22.

The armed forces had seized power in 1972 to prevent a presidential election that Bucaram had been favored to win. Since then, the former Guayaquil mayor seemed to have grown in popularity, according to the Latin America Political Report. Recent estimates suggested he could win 40% of the next presidential vote, while no other candidate could command more than 25%.

The government had hoped Bucaram's

candidacy would be barred by one of the two commissions assigned to draw up rival constitutions for the upcoming referendum—one a completely new charter and the other a revision of the 1945 Constitution. However, the first commission rejected a clause prohibiting the election of a president whose parents were not Ecuadorean (Bucaram's were Lebanese). The second commission approved but later rejected a clause barring a president who, having held dual citizenship, had not rejected the non-Ecuadorean citizenship between the ages of 18 and 25 (Bucaram still held dual citizenship in Ecuador and Lebanon).

Many political leaders shared the government's dislike for Bucaram; leftists considered him neo-fascist and rightists thought him demagogic, according to the Latin America Political Report. Former President Jose Maria Velasco Ibarra, who lived in exile but remained powerful in Ecuadorean politics, told a newspaper March 3: "Bucaram does not constitute an element of national coordination. He does not have an Ecuadorean soul. He is basically Arab."

Bucaram asserted March 4 that his presidential candidacy had been "launched by the people," and he challenged Velasco to return to Ecuador and run against him. Velasco said March 25 that he would return only if Ecuadoreans revolted against the military junta and demanded the convening of a constituent assembly to prepare a new national charter.

Velasco's partisans, the Velasquistas, Feb. 11 had joined several other right-wing parties in rejecting the junta's transition program. The program, they charged, "will only lead us to chaos and foster the military's remaining in power due to apparent necessity." Although the Velasquistas boycotted the commissions drawing up the new constitutions, the commissions approved a clause sought by the Velasquistas, allowing former presidents to run in the 1978 election.

Bucaram formally launched his candidacy July 18. Abdon Calderon Munoz, leader of the Alfarista Radical Front (an offshoot of the Liberal Party), was reported to be running Aug. 26.

A third candidate, Jaime Acosta Velasco, was generally acknowledged to be running although he had not announced his candidacy, according to the Latin America Political Report Aug. 26. Acosta was the nephew of ex-President Jose Maria Velasco Ibarra. Velasco had said from his exile in Argentina that he had abandoned his National Velasquista Party in favor of Ecuadorean Democratic Action, a new right-wing organization formed to support his nephew's candidacy.

In other political developments:

—The Ecuadorean Communist Party and five other leftist groups formed a coalition called the Leftist Broad Front, it was reported Aug. 26. The alliance could count on support from the three national labor federations, according to the Latin America Political Report.

—Soldiers in Quito broke up a meeting of politicians and military officers Aug. 31, arresting about 40 persons. The government claimed that the meeting had been called to "create a supposed civic command and proclaim a rebellion." The army raid was denounced Sept. 1 by several politicians including leaders of the Conservative Party, the Democratic Left and the National Poncista Party. The last group consisted of supporters of former President Camilo Ponce.

Constitutional referendum set. The government announced Sept. 13 that the referendum on a new Ecuadorean constitution would be held Jan. 15, 1978.

The referendum would allow Ecuadoreans to choose between two constitutions prepared by a government commission. Both would pave the way for democratic elections and a return to civilian rule later in 1978, according to government pledges.

Labor & Student Unrest

Teachers strike. Tens of thousands of Ecuadorean teachers struck from mid-May to mid-June to demand wage increases and other concessions from the military government.

The strike, which chiefly affected elementary schools, began on May 18, the day of a largely unsuccessful general strike called by Ecuador's three leading labor federations. The federations had demanded, among other things, a 50% salary hike, a freeze on food prices, abrogation of "anti-labor" decrees, enactment of a thorough agrarian reform and full nationalization of the oil industry.

While few workers joined the 24-hour general strike some 40,000 teachers began an indefinite stoppage affecting about 1.5 million students. The National Educators' Union (UNE) said the strike would continue until the government raised teachers' salaries, paid bonuses to teachers in isolated areas and consulted UNE on the proposed Education and Culture Law.

The government refused to negotiate with UNE, so the strikers took to the streets to press their demands. They were backed by student demonstrators from the universities.

Twenty demonstrating teachers and students were arrested in Guayaquil May 20, provoking larger student protests in the city May 24. Police dispersed the protesters with tear gas, and the government reiterated its refusal to negotiate until the teachers went back to work.

Police clashed with demonstrating teachers and students in Quito and Quevedo May 26, arresting about 20 protesters. Clashes continued in those cities and several others the following day. The rectors of eight Ecuadorean universities offered to mediate in the crisis, but the government ignored them.

The government revoked UNE's legal status May 30, provoking further protests. Two days later university students in Azuay went on strike and skirmished with police. In Cuenca, authorities dispersed a protest march by 1,000 teachers.

A worker was shot to death during a demonstration in Portoviejo June 2, and a student was killed in a protest in Guayaquil June 4. That day police dispersed another demonstration by teachers in Esmeraldas.

The government June 7 rejected offers of mediation from the rector of the Central University (Quito) and from parents who were meeting in a special congress in the capital. The regime threatened to end the school year and fire all striking teachers unless the stoppage ended by June 13. It said strike leaders would be prosecuted regardless of the outcome.

UNE pledged to fight "to the ultimate consequences," but the strike began to fall apart when the government carried out its threat to end the school year June 13. Most teachers were reported back at work June 16, although they claimed to be "on alert" to continue pressing the demands for which they had struck.

Despite the virtual end of the stoppage, about 200 arrested teachers remained in jail June 16.

Labor, church and political groups later asked the government to release persons who had been arrested in May for participating in the teachers' strike and the abortive general strike.

Msgr. Leonidas Proano, bishop of Riobamba, complained Oct. 5 that labor leaders had been "silenced and intimidated" since May. "These measures do not contribute to the formation of a free and sovereign people," he asserted.

Several political parties and labor unions had appealed Sept. 6 for an amnesty for arrested workers and teachers. The parties were the Democratic Left, the Unified Socialist Party, the Radical Liberals, the Social Progressive Front and the Progressive Conservatives. The unions included the Ecuadoran Union of Classist Organizations, whose leader had gone underground to try to organize a national labor front.

The groups' appeal was rejected Sept. 21 by Education Minister Fernando Dobronsky, who said the imprisoned strikers belonged to "an illegal organization"—the National Educators' Union (UNE)—and had engaged in "petty politics."

UNE's president and the president of the Ecuadoran Workers' Confederation had been sentenced to two years in jail for organizing the May strikes, it was reported July 8.

Sugar strikers die in police raid. At least 25 persons died Oct. 18 when police opened fire on striking workers who had occupied the government's sugar refinery in Canas Province.

The government claimed that one person was shot in the head and another 23 drowned when they stumbled into an irrigation canal that surrounded the refinery. But labor sources in Guayaquil charged that more than 100 persons had died, many from gunshot wounds.

The government's explanation infuriated Ecuador's political parties, 12 of which issued a letter Oct. 25 demanding the resignation of the officials they considered responsible—Government Minister Bolivar Jarrin, who controlled the police, and Labor Minister Jorge Chiriboga.

The sugar workers—who numbered 1,800 or 4,000, depending on the press report—seized the refinery early Oct. 18 to demand a wage increase in view of a rise in sugar prices decreed in August. The workers' collective contract provided for such an adjustment, but the government had refused to grant it.

About 300 policemen surrounded the refinery after dark and attacked when relatives of the strikers were giving them food for the night. The government said that in the ensuing melee, 23 strikers and/or relatives got lost in the dark and fell into the irrigation ditch.

The government later blamed their deaths on strike leaders, asserting that "agitators" had led the victims to the canal "in a suspicious manner."

Beside the deaths, there were dozens of arrests. The Canas police chief said Oct. 19 that he was holding 80 strikers, but Guayaquil labor leaders charged the next day that "hundreds" had been detained.

The French newspaper Le Monde Oct. 25 reported eyewitness accounts that contradicted the government's explanation of the Canar deaths. According to the official version, 24 of the 25 victims had drowned when they fell into a deep irrigation ditch that surrounded the refinery. But witnesses cited by Le Monde said that many of the corpses dredged out of the ditch bore gunshot wounds and signs of beating. The government refused to turn many of the bodies over to relatives, and it hastily cremated some of them, Le Monde reported.

Strike deaths protested—There were demonstrations in several parts of Ecuador following the deaths of the 25 sugar strikers.

Protesters occupied the village of Troncal near the refinery Oct. 26. Students rioted in Guayaquil and Milagro, and sugar workers demonstrated at the San Carlos and Valdez plantations near the refinery, it was reported Oct. 28.

Meanwhile, thousands of sugar workers in Canar and Guayas provinces continued the strike for raises. The strikers also demanded the dismissal of the Cabinet ministers responsible for the Canar raid; the release of union leaders arrested since the incident, and the awarding of indemnities to relatives of the raid's victims. The strike had cut Ecuador's sugar production by two-thirds, it was reported Nov. 4.

Other Developments

Government buys Gulf assets. The military government announced Jan. 1 that it had bought the local assets of Gulf Oil Corp. of the U.S., effective the previous day.

The purchase gave the government a 62.5% share in Ecuador's petroleum operations. The other 37.5% was held by Texaco Inc. of the U.S., which had begun a joint venture with Gulf in Ecuador in 1965. The two companies had developed the Oriente oilfields, which currently produced about 200,000 barrels per day, and had built the trans-Ecuadorean pipeline which carried the petroleum to the port city of Esmeraldas.

A spokesman for Gulf estimated the company's unamortized investment in Ecuador at $120 million. He said Ecuador had agreed to pay Gulf $82 million in cash immediately, and the balance on completion of an audit by an international firm.

Gulf had said in mid-1976 that it had "chosen to withdraw from Ecuador because of continued inability to achieve an understanding with the Ecuadorean government which would allow Gulf to receive a reasonable return on its invested capital along with being unable to reach acceptable solutions to other problems."

U.S. bars Israeli jet sale to Ecuador. The U.S. State Department disclosed Feb. 7 that the U.S. had rejected a request by Israel to sell Ecuador 24 fighter-bombers equipped with American jet engines. The monetary loss as a result of the rejection would reportedly be offset by a Carter Administration decision to ask Congress to add $285 million in economic aid to the 1977 assistance package for Israel proposed by Gerald Ford just prior to expiration of his presidential term. This would bring the total aid package for Israel to $1.78 billion for the fiscal year ending Sept. 30.

A State Department spokesman said it was decided to bar Israel from selling the planes to Ecuador because it "would run counter to our own policy against the transfer of advanced and sophisticated weapons to Latin America."

The proposed $150-million transaction involved Israeli-manufactured Kfir jets fitted with General Electric J-79 engines. Israel was required to seek U.S. permission for the deal because of the use of the American engine.

Israeli Defense Minister Shimon Peres had said before the State Department announcement that Israel "will never be reconciled" to U.S. refusal to permit the export of the Kfirs. If the U.S. blocked the sale, he warned, France, which also had been negotiating with Ecuador on warplanes, would benefit.

The U.S. decision to stop the sale underscored Washington's concern about Israel's emergence as an exporter of sophisticated military equipment, much of it derived from American technology.

Mrs. Carter on tour. Rosalynn Carter, wife of U.S. President Jimmy Carter, visited seven countries in the Caribbean and Latin America May 30–June 12 on a tour that combined goodwill gestures with substantive political and economc discussion.

Mrs. Carter visited Ecuador June 1–3. On her tour she was accompanied by Grace Vance, wife of U.S. Secretary of State Cyrus Vance, and by two of the Carter Administration's experts on Latin America—Terence Todman, assistant secretary of state for inter-American affairs, and Robert Pastor, senior staff member for inter-American affairs on the National Security Council.

Mrs. Carter's tour was marked by student protests during her visit to Quito city. An estimated 150 to 200 students demonstrated outside the Legislative Palace June 2, shouting "Rosalynn Carter, go home!" and throwing stones, bricks and at least two gasoline bombs at policemen and reporters. Mrs. Carter, who was inside the building conferring with members of Ecuador's military junta, apparently did not hear the disturbance. By the time she emerged from the palace the protesters had been dispersed or arrested.

Ecuador's leaders told Mrs. Carter of their concern over the military buildup in neighboring Peru and of their objections to President Carter's February veto of the proposed Israeli sale of Kfir fighter planes to Ecuador. Mrs. Carter replied that the veto was not directed against Ecuador but was part of her husband's "global policy" to reduce armaments.

Mrs. Carter also said that her husband was asking Congress to revoke 1974 legislation that denied preferential trade treatment to Ecuador because it belonged to the Organization of Petroleum Exporting Countries (OPEC).

(In Washington June 3, President Carter praised the Ecuadorean junta's program to return power to elected civilian officials.)

El Salvador

Political Violence & Repression

Political turmoil plagued El Salvador during much of 1977. After Gen. Carlos Humberto Romero won the February presidential election, charges of election fraud and political repression provoked violent clashes with security forces. Hundreds of the government's opponents were murdered or were reported to have disappeared. Jesuits and other Roman Catholic priests who supported peasants in land reform demands were attacked by right-wing terrorists and security forces.

Siege imposed after disputed election. The victory of the government's candidate in the Feb. 20 presidential election was denounced as fraudulent by the National Opposition Union (UNO). Riots and other protests by UNO supporters led to shootouts with security forces and the imposition of a 30-day state of siege Feb. 28. (The state of siege later was extended on through June.)

UNO had begun charging vote fraud before the election. The opposition group asserted Feb. 8 that the government had put 400,000 ineligible persons on the voting lists—including dead persons—and had placed an excessive number of voting tables in rural areas where the regime's support was strongest. In San Salvador, press reports noted, all voting was scheduled to take place in an industrial showground in the middle of wealthy suburbs, far from the working-class districts where most UNO supporters lived.

On election day, UNO charged that most of its poll-watchers were kept away from the voting tables; many were arrested, the opposition group asserted, and some were beaten by security officers. UNO member Jose Leonidas Crespin was shot to death early Feb. 20 as he pasted a campaign poster on a wall in the town of Santiago Monualco.

UNO protests grew Feb. 21 as the government candidate, retired Gen. Carlos Humberto Romero, denied the vote-fraud charges and claimed victory. An unofficial vote count was reported giving him a wide lead over the UNO candidate, retired Col. Ernesto Claramount. However, employes of the Central Electoral Council sent a letter to foreign correspondents in San Salvador saying they had been ordered to destroy UNO ballots in the counting. The order, the employes said, had come from Jose Vincente Vilanova, president of the council, and Ruben Alfonso Rodriguez, president of the Legislative Assembly (Congress).

UNO members charged Feb. 21 that they had intercepted government radio communications instructing members of the ruling National Conciliation Party (PCN) to put more "sugar" (PCN votes) than "coffee" (UNO votes) in the "tanks" (ballot boxes). The charge was later corroborated by a foreign journalist who heard the same message in a PCN office during the vote count, the London newsletter Latin America reported March 4.

Col. Claramount charged Feb. 21 that the government had closed "the electoral process" and "the paths of legality, preventing true democratic development in the country." Nothing could be expected from the electoral council, Claramount said, because it was a "puppet" of the regime.

Tens of thousands of persons had gathered in San Salvador's Freedom Plaza late Feb. 20 to protest the apparent vote fraud. Demonstrations continued Feb. 21 and 22, culminating in another huge rally in the plaza late Feb. 22 at which UNO called for a general strike to force annulment of the election. However, only isolated striking was reported in the capital Feb. 23.

The protests became more serious Feb. 25 when the electoral council issued a final count giving Gen. Romero 812,080 votes to 394,661 for Claramount. More than 40,000 UNO supporters occupied Freedom Plaza, building barbed-wire barricades and refusing to leave until the election results were annulled. Sympathy strikes were begun by students, teachers and construction, factory and public transport workers. President Arturo Molina made a radio broadcast appealing for calm and blaming the protests on "foreign Communists" who allegedly were trying to incite a revolution in El Salvador.

Three UNO demonstrators were killed Feb. 26 in a shootout with police in Santa Ana, the country's second-largest city. In San Salvador the number of demonstrators in Freedom Plaza decreased, but several thousand remained, including Claramount and his vice-presidential candidate, Antonio Morales Ehrlich.

Police cordoned off the plaza early Feb. 28 and, after the intercession of the U.S. ambassador and the auxiliary bishop of San Salvador, allowed the Red Cross to evacuate the protesters. Claramount, given the choice between prison and exile, took a private flight to San Jose, Costa Rica. Morales Ehrlich and two other UNO leaders took asylum in the Costa Rican Embassy in San Salvador.

After dawn demonstrators returned to the city's center, burned cars and tried to storm government and newspaper offices.

Police and soldiers opened fire on the rioters, killing at least three persons and wounding scores of others. In Santa Ana at least two persons were killed and 50 wounded in similar confrontations. The government declared a 30-day, nationwide state of siege, blaming the bloodshed on "Communist elements."

Heavily armed soldiers patrolled the streets of San Salvador March 1-2, and shops in the city's center remained closed. President Molina said that he hoped to lift the state of siege before 30 days were up, and the government released some of the 200 persons that were officially listed as arrested. Molina noted that there were many UNO members hiding in the Costa Rican Embassy, and he asserted all but three of them could leave the embassy without fear of arrest. The three were all army officers, Molina said.

The electoral council March 3 formally rejected a UNO petition to have the election results invalidated. But Molina admitted that day that there had been "minimal" vote fraud. "Only God is perfect," he said, according to Inter Press Service.

In Costa Rica, meanwhile, there were unconfirmed reports that at least 100 persons had been killed and more than 5,-000 arrested in the Salvadoran disturbances, Inter Press reported. However, Molina insisted that only five persons had died and 200 had been arrested.

(A sixth person, described officially as a "mental patient," was killed March 1 when police ordered him to stop and he refused.)

The San Salvador newspaper La Cronica del Pueblo was shut down indefinitely by police March 4 for allegedly exaggerating the number of anti-government demonstrators in its reports of the post-election riots. The paper's owner, Jose Napoleon Gonzalez, said police had ransacked his office and forced four of his employes to the floor, tying their thumbs behind their backs. Gonzalez expressed fear for his life, asserting: "They have trampled on my newspaper. There is no guarantee that they won't trample on me."

Meanwhile, the Financial Times (London) reported March 18 that 30-50 persons—not five as the Salvadoran government claimed—had been killed in popular disturbances that followed the elections. Two of the known victims were members of the extreme right-wing Nationalist Democratic Organization (Orden)—Salomon Salgado, shot in San Salvador Feb. 11, and Manuel Antonio Sanchez, killed in San Pedro Perulapan Feb. 17. Roberto Poma, president of the national tourism institute, reportedly died of wounds he suffered when he was kidnapped by guerrillas of the left-wing People's Revolutionary Army (ERP) Jan. 27. Three of Poma's bodyguards were killed trying to prevent the abduction. The bodies of Poma and two unidentified persons were found Feb. 25 in a shallow grave in a tourist center in San Salvador, according to press reports.

Romero had conducted an anti-Communist campaign, promising to "promote health, employment and complete freedom." The National Opposition Union candidate, Col. Ernesto Claramount, vowed to divide big estates among peasants, wipe out government corruption and remove the armed forces from politics. Claramount's coalition, UNO, was composed of the Christian Democratic Party, the Revolutionary National Movement and the National Democratic Union Party.

(Romero was the fourth military man elected president of El Salvador on the PCN ticket in the past 15 years. His predecessor, Molina, had been elected in 1972 under similar circumstances: extensive vote fraud was charged, there was an attempted military coup, a state of siege was imposed and the opposition candidate was exiled.)

Eight die in May Day violence. At least eight persons were killed and 16 wounded May 1 when security forces in San Salvador clashed with workers and peasants who defied a government ban on May Day demonstrations.

Witnesses said police and soldiers opened fire on a crowd of about 1,000 persons who were protesting government economic policies and political repression. However, a police spokesman said the security officers had fired only after being attacked by about 50 "terrorists" armed with "shotguns, pistols, Molotov cocktails and dynamite."

Police and soldiers patrolled the city May 2 to prevent any further protests. A Panamanian priest, Rev. Jorge Sarsanedas, was deported May 6 on charges of having participated in the May Day clashes. The Roman Catholic Church denied the allegations.

Later in the year two persons were killed Oct. 27 when police in San Salvador fired into a crowd of workers and peasants who had gathered in a park to demand higher wages for picking the current coffee crop. The police said they had fired in self-defense after they heard gunshots coming from the crowd.)

Church & opposition under attack. The church had made several charges of government repression, and many priests had suffered retaliation as a result. Church leaders issued a statement April 23 demanding that the military regime "stop torturing and threatening priests." Specifically, the church asked the government to break up two right-wing commando groups that were allegedly protected by officials.

(A rightist group calling itself the White Warriors' Union was presumed responsible for the murder of a teenager May 11 at a Catholic youth meeting in San Salvador. The young man was fatally wounded when terrorists shot at a priest, Rev. Alfonso Navarro Oviedo, whom the White Warriors' Union had accused of responsibility for the kidnap-murder of Foreign Minister Mauricio Borgonovo Pohl.)

Meanwhile, opponents of the government continued to disappear or to be arrested, tortured or murdered, according to religious, political and diplomatic sources cited by the Miami Herald April 8. The sources estimated that 300 persons had been arrested and another 130 had disappeared since the disputed presidential election and its bloody aftermath in February. The vanished included political leaders, union officials, teachers and university professors.

Christian Democratic leader Ruben Zamora was arrested April 22 outside the Catholic University in San Salvador, where he worked. His Nicaraguan wife and a university professor were arrested with him. Christian Democratic sources said almost the entire leadership of the party either had been arrested or had fled the country.

Archbishop boycotts inaugural—The heavily guarded presidential inaugural was boycotted by the archbishop of San Salvador, Oscar A. Romero, who charged the

Roman Catholic Church had been "badly treated" by the previous government, in which Gen. Romero was defense minister. "Security forces have tortured and ill-treated priests and other members of the church," the archbishop asserted.

Since the February election, dozens of priests had been arrested without charge, about 25 had been expelled from the country and others had disappeared. Two priests had been shot to death by right-wing commandos believed to be protected by the police. Most of the priests belonged to the Society of Jesus, which the government had accused of abetting "left-wing terrorism."

Archbishop Romero said July 3 that he was willing to talk with the new president to reconcile the church and the government, but he called first for the release of all political prisoners and the return to El Salvador of all priests and opposition politicians who had been forced to leave the country after the election.

President Romero in office. Gen. Carlos Humberto Romero began a five-year term as president of El Salvador July 1 with a pledge to "preserve, protect and maintain peace and harmony."

"My government does not want violent confrontations with anyone," said Romero. "However, [I] will exercise with vigor the right of legitimate defense of society," the new president asserted.

Terrorism

Guerrillas slay foreign minister. Left-wing guerrillas kidnapped Foreign Minister Mauricio Borgonovo Pohl April 19 and killed him May 10 after the government refused to negotiate with them.

Borgonovo, 38, was found shot to death beside a road outside San Salvador. In a communique to the press May 11, the Farabundo Marti Popular Liberation Forces (FPL) said they had "executed" him in a "revolutionary war to establish socialism."

Upon kidnapping Borgonova April 19,

the FPL had demanded that the government free 37 alleged political prisoners and fly them to Mexico, Venezuela, Costa Rica or Cuba. Costa Rica agreed to take the alleged prisoners, who included peasant leaders, Communist Party militants, members of the Revolutionary People's Bloc and captured FPL guerrillas. However, Arturo Molina, who then was president, said April 22 that the government held only three of the 37 and that these could not be freed until they were tried by the courts.

The FPL said it would execute Borgonovo if the demands were not met by April 27, but it let the deadline pass. Meanwhile, the outlawed Communist Party expressed full support for the guerrillas, and the archbishop of San Salvador offered to mediate in the crisis. The Roman Catholic Church asked April 27 that the government free the 37 alleged prisoners and that the FPL release Borgonovo.

Molina went on nationwide radio and television April 29 to say he would not negotiate with the insurgents. To do so, the president said, would be to "renounce the government's obligation to maintain social peace." He said most of the 37 alleged prisoners had been freed earlier, and that the ones held by the government must undergo "the judicial process."

United Nations Secretary General Kurt Waldheim May 1 urged the guerrillas to free Borgonovo. In a reply May 2, the FPL asked Waldheim why he sought freedom for a government official but not for "imprisoned workers, peasants, students, teachers and professors." Pope Paul VI appealed to the guerrillas May 8 to release the foreign minister, to no avail.

Kidnapping mars IDB meeting. The abduction of a Salvadoran official disrupted the 18th annual meeting of the board of governors of the Inter-American Development Bank (IDB), held in Guatemala City May 30–June 1.

El Salvador's ambassador to Guatemala, Col. Eduardo Casanova Sandoval, was kidnapped May 29 by members of the Guerrilla Army of the Poor, a small Guatemalan leftist group. Casanova was released unharmed June 1, after the IDB met his abductors' one demand—that a statement by the guerrillas be read aloud at the bank meeting.

The statement, read by an IDB official at the meeting's opening session, denounced the bank, Casanova and the military-dominated governments of El Salvador and Guatemala.

"The millions in credits from the [IDB]," the statement charged, "strengthen the exploiters of [the Latin American] people and support violence, repression and violation of human rights. As an instrument of international imperialism, the bank uses the mask of social welfare and foreign aid to disguise the domination of our countries by foreign countries."

Casanova, the statement asserted, was responsible for the murder of workers and peasants in El Salvador. The Salvadoran and Guatemalan governments consistently violated the human rights of their subjects, the statement added.

After the statement was read, Guatemalan President Gen. Kjell Laugerud entered the assembly hall under heavy armed guard and the meeting got under way.

Rightists threaten Jesuits. Right-wing terrorists threatened in June to kill all Jesuit priests who had not left El Salvador by July 21. The 33 Jesuits in the country defied the warning, and the deadline passed without incident after the government took special precautions to protect the priests.

The Salvadoran Catholic Church had become increasingly concerned with the plight of poor peasants over the past 10 years, working closely with two reformist groups, the Christian Peasant Federation and the Union of Agrarian Workers. Church support of the peasantry had intensified in 1976 after the government instituted a mild agrarian reform and then revoked it under pressure from landowners.

No other Latin American country had a land ownership system with such disparities as El Salvador's: 4% of the population owned about 60% of the land and employed itinerant laborers to tend coffee, sugar, cotton and banana crops at a maximum wage of 40¢ a day. The military governments that had ruled the country for 45 years unwaveringly supported the landowning families, crushing land-reform movements or condoning repression by the families' hired thugs.

The terrorists, who called themselves the White Warriors' Union, were believed to be retired soldiers and policemen hired by powerful landlords to stop the Jesuits and other Roman Catholic priests from working with poor peasants and promoting land reform.

In pamphlets they distributed June 21, the Warriors accused the Jesuits of "Communist subversion" and vowed to "execute" the priests systematically if they were not gone from the country within a month.

The Jesuits unanimously rejected the threat. Rev. Cesar Jerez, head of the Jesuit order in Central America, declared July 17: "We will stay until we are all either killed or expelled."

Catholic laymen came to the aid of the Jesuits, accompanying them in twos and threes in the streets of San Salvador in hopes of warding off attacks. The right-wing military government unexpectedly added its support, apparently because of the bad international publicity El Salvador was receiving as a result of the terrorists' threats.

President Carlos Humberto Romero July 18 denounced violence "from any source" and heatedly denied that the government had any connection with the White Warriors' Union. The next day the Defense Ministry increased police and military patrols throughout San Salvador and placed special guards near the Basilica of Guadalupe, the Church of San Francisco and the Jesuit seminary.

On July 21 the Jesuit priests were moved temporarily into heavily guarded church schools, and the government set up roadblocks outside San Salvador where police and national guardsmen searched all cars entering the city.

"So much attention has been drawn to the death threat that we don't expect anything to happen now," a Jesuit said July 22. "The government is very worried about its image abroad and will do anything to prevent new violence now."

The new Salvadoran government was particularly concerned about its image in the U.S., where the Carter Administration and the Congress had expressed displeasure over abuse of human rights in El Salvador.

The U.S. State Department said July 20 that it had voiced its concern several times to the Salvadoran government over the threats against the Jesuits. On July 21, the day of the terrorists' deadline, the

U.S. House of Representatives' International Relations subcommittee on international organizations began hearings on the human rights situation in El Salvador.

The first witness before the subcommittee was Ignacio Lozano, U.S. ambassador to El Salvador until June 1. Lozano said that during his tenure in El Salvador, the U.S. Embassy had received "little to none support from Washington" on human rights abuse until "we went public on it." He said the embassy had denounced Salvadoran rights violations "pretty much on our own," not because the Carter Administration was insincere in its defense of human rights but because El Salvador "is so small and the U.S. has no vital interest [there]."

A Salvadoran priest, the Rev. Jose Inocencio Alas, told the committee he had been kidnapped and tortured by right-wing terrorists in 1970 after he spoke out for land reform. He said he moved to the U.S. in 1976 following frequent death threats, hostile articles in the press, a bomb explosion at his home, an arson attack on his parish house and two arrests by security forces.

Priests and political observers in El Salvador agreed that it was because of their support of land reform that Salvadoran priests were being persecuted by terrorists and the security forces. Both the priests' activism and the attacks on churchmen had increased since March, when assassins cut down a Jesuit priest, the Rev. Rutilio Grande Garcia, who had been working with peasants in the town of Aguilares.

Grande, an outspokenly progressive priest, had been the target of threats from "powerful landlords" who opposed his work with Salvadoran peasants, according to the Mexican newspaper Excelsior March 14. In the previous month, five other priests had been expelled from El Salvador and one had been beaten badly for allegedly preaching "Marxism-Leninism" and "armed revolution." Among other things, the priests had urged workers to demand payment of the legal minimum wage.

The assassination had galvanized the archbishop of San Salvador, Msgr. Oscar A. Romero, who, like most Salvadoran priests, had been reluctant to oppose the military government openly. The archbishop March 17 publicly denounced the priest's murder and the torture, ha-

rassment and killing of opponents of the government since the allegedly fraudulent presidential election Feb. 20.

In subsequent months there were numerous attacks on Catholic priests, particularly Jesuits, who were considered the most militant Catholic supporters of land reform. A second priest was killed, several were tortured, dozens were arrested without charge, about 25 were expelled from the country and others simply disappeared. The Jesuit-run Catholic University was bombed six times, and then the Jesuits were threatened by the White Warriors' Union.

The Roman Catholic archdiocese of San Salvador charged Sept. 1 that members of the security forces had shot and killed three Catholic youths in the town of Tejutla Aug. 26. The archdiocese urged President Carlos Humberto Romero to "stop the persecution of the church and the repression of the Salvadoran people."

A Salvadoran bishop charged Oct. 4 that priests in his country were embracing Marxism as "the only means of fighting against oppression." Speaking before the Fifth Synod of Roman Catholic bishops at the Vatican, Msgr. Rene Revelo Contreras said it was a "tragedy" that Salvadoran priests were "making themselves Communists or Maoists." He was rebuked Oct. 8 by the Vatican radio station, which said he was ignoring the "genuine, brave and heroic ministry that many priests and catechists are developing in El Salvador."

Ex-official killed. Rene Guzman Alvergue, former secretary of the Central Electoral Council, was shot to death in Santa Ana late July 1. The police could not identify his killers but said they suspected members of the Farabundo Marti Popular Liberation Forces, who had killed Foreign Minister Mauricio Borgonovo Pohl in May.

Two bombs had exploded in Santa Ana June 30, one destroying local offices of the National Conciliation Party. Despite the blasts, the government had lifted the state of siege imposed in February amid post-election violence.

Former president slain. Unidentified gunmen murdered former President

Osmin Aguirre Salinas outside his home in San Salvador July 12.

Police said they had no leads in the case, but radio stations received letters from professed members of the Farabundo Marti Popular Liberation Forces (FPL) who claimed to have "executed" Aguirre for his role in crushing a land reform movement in 1932, when he was chief of the national police. Some 30,000 peasants were said to have been killed in the police action.

Aguirre, an 85-year-old retired army general, had been president of El Salvador for five months in 1944 45. He took power in a military coup against another army general and then yielded the presidency to yet another military dictator.

Other incidents. Among other incidents involving terrorism:

■ Twenty-seven bombs were exploded in various parts of the country Aug. 21, according to the Salvadoran police. One of the blasts slightly injured six persons in San Salvador. The left-wing People's Revolutionary Army issued a communique Aug. 22 claiming responsibility for the explosions and asserting it had planted another eight bombs that had not gone off.

Carlos Alvarez Geoffrey, a member of an elite Salvadoran family, was kidnapped Aug. 11 and freed Aug. 19 when newspapers printed an anti-government manifesto. Elena Lima de Chiorato, wife of a prominent American businessman in San Salvador, was kidnapped by armed men Sept. 6.

■ The rector of the National University, his driver and a bodyguard were shot to death by leftist guerrillas in San Salvador Sept. 16.

Members of the Farabundo Marti Popular Liberation Forces left behind leaflets claiming responsibility for the attack and calling the rector, Carlos Alfaro Castillo, a "black servant of the oligarchy and the military regime." Alfaro belonged to a wealthy family traditionally linked to right-wing organizations. He had had repeated trouble with leftist students since assuming his university post in 1974.

Police cordoned off San Salvador Sept. 17 to search for the guerrillas, who were also being sought in connection with the May kidnap-murder of Foreign Minister

Mauricio Borgonovo Pohl and the July assassination of former President Osmin Aguirre Salinas.

■ The FPL also carried out several attacks in different parts of El Salvador Sept. 21.

Some of the insurgents assaulted a police station in Concepcion de Oriente, leaving three persons dead. Other guerrillas occupied a high school in Zacatecoluca, lecturing the students on revolutionary politics. And still others occupied 15 radio stations in San Salvador and rural towns, forcing the stations to broadcast a half-hour tirade against the government.

All police and military units in the country were put on alert Sept. 22 to prevent further guerrilla attacks.

■ Two police officers and an unidentified man were shot to death Oct. 28 when shooting broke out between policemen and alleged leftists at a cemetery in San Salvador. The violence occurred during the burial of two persons killed by police the day before in a demonstration in the city. Police identified the leftist gunmen as members of the "Revolutionary People's Bloc," according to the news agency LATIN.

■ About 1,500 militant workers and peasants occupied the Labor Ministry building in San Salvador Nov. 10, taking at least 86 hostages and vowing not to leave until the government increased the wages of farm workers and striking textile workers. The hostages included Labor Minister Roberto Escobar Garcia, Economy Minister Roberto Ortiz Avalos and employes of the Labor Ministry. The occupation ended Nov. 13 after Escobar Garcia reportedly agreed to study the protesters' demands.

■ The government enacted a new law Dec. 6 that provided prison sentences of two to seven years, without public trial, for anti-government demonstrators who damaged property or endangered the peace.

■ Raul Molina Canas, a wealthy industrialist, was killed in San Salvador Nov. 12 when he resisted an attempt by several gunmen to kidnap him.

U.S. Relations

U.S. aid in rights-issue dispute. El Salvador March 16 became the fifth Latin American country to reject U.S. military assistance because the Carter Administration had linked the aid to observance of human rights.

The Salvadoran government issued a communique asserting that "national dignity cannot tolerate the very idea that the prestige of our country is being examined by an organization or a governmental dependency of another nation . . . in frank disregard of our sovereignty. . . ."

Two subcommittees of the U.S. House of Representatives' International Relations Committee had held a hearing in Washington March 9 to consider evidence of human rights abuse in El Salvador, particularly regarding vote fraud in the Feb. 20 presidential election.

Members of the subcommittees and many State Department employes who also attended the hearing heard a tape recording of broadcasts made Feb. 20 in which members of El Salvador's ruling National Conciliation Party (PCN) referred to "stuffing tamales in the tanks." This meant "stuffing fraudulent votes in the ballot boxes," according to William Brown of the Washington Office on Latin America, a coalition of church and human rights groups. The coalition presented the tape as evidence of what it called "massive fraud" in favor of the victorious PCN candidate, Gen. Carlos Humberto Romero.

Rep. Donald M. Fraser (D, Minn.), chairman of the House international orga-nizations subcommittee, asserted that "the right to vote and to have free and genuine elections is a basic human right," which "should play a role in determining U.S. foreign policy—and particularly U.S. assistance programs."

Deputy Assistant Secretary of State Charles W. Bray III testified that while human rights violations occurred in El Salvador, they had not formed a consistent pattern to justify cutting off U.S. aid, which he estimated at under $10 million. (El Salvador received about $2.5 million in U.S. military supplies and training assistance, according to the Associated Press March 17.)

Bray refused to testify in public on whether the Feb. 20 voting was fraudulent. He said it was impossible, in any event, to say if fair elections would have changed the result. Romero's official margin of victory had been almost 2–1.

U.S. ties deteriorate—Relations between the U.S. and El Salvador, already strained over the human rights issue, had been damaged further by the disappearance of a U.S. citizen in the Central American country, it was reported March 26.

U.S. Ambassador Ignacio Lozano said ties between the two countries would not improve until El Salvador adequately explained what had happened to Ronald James Richardson after he was arrested by Salvadoran immigration authorities in September 1976. The immigration department said Richardson, 35, had been deported. However, there were reports that he had been killed in custody.

Guatemala

Violence & Human Rights Abuses

Political violence spreads. Members of both the governing and opposition parties protested the spreading political violence that was claiming the lives of some 40 Guatemalans per month.

Following the assassination of a federal congressman in Escuintla Aug. 23, legislators from the ruling National Liberation Movement proposed the censure of Interior Minister Donaldo Alvarez Ruiz for his failure "to halt the violence and the bloodbath." The motion failed for lack of a quorum.

Alvarez Ruiz, a member of a party formerly allied with the government, had admitted Aug. 18 that political violence was spreading. However, he blamed this not on subversive groups—the government's usual target—but on "the poverty of large strata of the population and the lack of education among the majority sectors of the country."

The leading opposition party, the Guatemalan Christian Democracy Party, repeatedly denounced the violence and alleged abuse of human rights by the government. The party's general secretary, Vinicio Cerezo Arevalo, Aug. 12 said Guatemala was in a "virtual state of civil war." The Christian Democratic presidential candidate, Ricardo Peralta Mendez, charged July 14 that the government was "constantly violating human rights."

Following Peralta's statement, Christian Democratic leaders received death threats from a new right-wing terrorist group calling itself the "White Brotherhood," it was reported July 20. A similar new organization, the Secret Anti-Communist Army, simultaneously appeared making threats to "kill all Communists without mercy," it was reported July 21.

On the left, meanwhile, the most active violent group was the Guerrilla Army of the Poor (EGP), which had kidnapped El Salvador's ambassador, Col. Eduardo Casanova Sandoval, May 29 during a meeting of the Inter-American Development Bank in Guatemala City. The ambassador was freed after a guerrilla statement was read to the participants in the bank meeting.

The statement, read by an IDB official at the meeting's opening session, denounced the bank, Casanova and the military-dominated governments of El Salvador and Guatemala.

"The millions in credits from the [IDB]," the statement charged, "strengthen the exploiters of [the Latin American] people and support violence, repression and violation of human rights. As an instrument of international imperialism, the bank uses the mask of social welfare and foreign aid to disguise the domination of our countries by foreign countries."

Casanova, the statement asserted, was responsible for the murder of workers and peasants in El Salvador. The Salvadoran and Guatemalan governments consistently violated the human rights of their subjects, the statement added.

The EGP had been formed in 1974 from remnants of the Rebel Armed Forces (FAR), a guerrilla force of dissident army officers that was defeated by the government in the late 1960s. U.S. intelligence sources said the EGP's leader was Cesar Montes, a former FAR leader, the Miami Herald reported July 4. The EGP reportedly had four independent commands—rural groups in El Quiche, Escuintla and Zacapa, and an urban cell in Guatemala City. The most active command was in El Quiche, a mountainous region north of Guatemala City. Near Escuintla, on the Pacific coast, the guerrillas harassed large landowners, burning their sugar cane fields.

The guerrillas were believed to number about 300, recruited both in the countryside and in the universities, the Herald reported. They appeared to receive their arms from Mexican smugglers, although the government claimed the arms came from Cuba through the British colony of Belize. The government claimed the EGP depended heavily on Cuba for money, arms, training and even leadership in the field, but U.S. Embassy sources in Guatemala City said Cuban support for the guerrillas was more limited, the Herald noted.

Disappearances & executions cited—Amnesty International had reported Feb. 21 that about 20,000 persons had disappeared or been executed in Guatemala since 1966. Between July 1974 and April 1976 the first 22 months of President Kjell Laugerud's administration 379 persons reportedly had disappeared or been killed. All were presumed to have been executed for political reasons.

The Amnesty report was titled "Guatemala, a Country Without Prisoners, All Disappeared." The study said Guatemalan officials had justified summary executions as "a response to leftist violence and the violence of criminal delinquents."

"Paramilitary groups have operated with the knowledge and even, in many occasions, with the cooperation of the

government, and there is a death squad called White Hand in which civilians have been integrated systematically into the countersubversion apparatus in a semi-permanent fashion," Amnesty said.

However, the report conceded that Laugerud "has decided to take a much more energetic position against members of his own government who are responsible for paramilitary repression."

According to an Associated Press report Jan. 1, Amnesty International had estimated that there were 190 political prisoners being held in Guatemala.

Meanwhile, Guatemalan civilians continued to be kidnapped, tortured and murdered for apparently political reasons, the Mexican newspaper Excelsior reported Sept. 5. Peasants who were murdered in rural areas, presumably by right-wing commandos or plainclothed security officers, were often branded with hot irons before they were killed, Excelsior said.

◼ Several persons were killed before dawn Sept. 15 when police opened fire on rioters who had overturned an army truck and stoned the National Palace. Student leaders claimed Sept. 17 that at least 25 persons had died, many from bayonet wounds. But the Latin America Political Report said Sept. 23 that only four persons had been killed, although more than 50 had been wounded.

◼ The former minister of defense, Rafael Arriaga Bosque, was killed by gunmen in Guatemala City Sept. 29. He and his bodyguard were driving only three blocks from the National Palace when unidentified assailants intercepted their car and sprayed it with machinegun fire. The government said Sept. 30 that the murderers belonged to a "clandestine organization of the extreme left." A Guatemala City television station said it had received an anonymous telephone call attributing the slaying to the Communist-affiliated Guatemala Labor Party.

◼ A clandestine group calling itself the Secret Anti-Communist Army announced Oct. 10 that it would "execute" a dozen teachers and students for "communist activities" at San Carlos University in Guatemala City.

◼ Seven armed men invaded the university Oct. 14 and kidnapped a student. Other students captured two of the assailants, who turned out to be policemen. The students said they would hold the two as hostages until their kidnapped colleague was freed.

■ A study of 111 political murders that occurred in Guatemala in June, July and August indicated that 89 of the victims were peasants or workers, many of whom apparently had been involved in local grass-roots organizations, the New York Times reported Nov. 2.

Six of the victims were students or professionals and the remainder were landowners, businessmen, right-wing politicians, bodyguards and policemen, the Times said.

Guatemala rejects U.S. military aid. Guatemala became the fourth Latin American country to reject U.S. military assistance because the aid was linked to greater observance of human rights, it was reported March 16.

Guatemala's decision was disclosed to a subcommittee of the U.S. Senate Appropriations Committee by Lucy Wilson Benson, President Carter's designee for undersecretary of state for security assistance.

Guatemalan Foreign Minister Adolfo Molina Orantes had charged March 12 that the U.S. was interfering in "the internal affairs of Guatemala" by linking observance of human rights to proposed U.S. military assistance of $2.1 million in fiscal year 1978. "Human rights have been violated for a long time" in the U.S., Molina asserted.

U.S. resumes arms sales—The U.S. had resumed selling military equipment to Guatemala after a hiatus of several months caused by Guatemalan objections to President Carter's human rights policy, the Miami Herald reported Sept. 7.

In the past two months the Guatemalan army had purchased trucks, jeeps and automatic weapons from the U.S., the Herald said.

Other Developments

1978 vote set. The regime announced Oct. 16 that the 1978 elections would be held March 5. The four legally registered political parties all had chosen military men as presidential candidates. Col. Enrique Peralta Azurdia was nominated by the right-wing National Liberation Movement; Gen. Ricardo Peralta Mendez was supported by the center-left Christian Democrats, and Gen. Romeo Lucas Garcia was backed by a coalition of the center-right Democratic Institutional Party and the center-left Revolutionary Party, according to the Spanish news agency EFE.

Belize dispute; Panama ties cut. The Guatemalan government announced May 19 that it had broken diplomatic relations with Panama to protest Panama's support of independence for Belize. Belize was the British colony in Central America over which Guatemala claimed sovereignty.

Panama's military strongman, Brig. Gen. Omar Torrijos, had infuriated Guatemalan leaders by declaring the previous weekend: "Yes, I have my hands in Belize, and I'm not going to take them out. . . . I'm going to help those people because they need it, I'm going to help George Price because he's a mystic who needs it, and I don't care if it makes Laugerud mad." Price was prime minister of Belize; Gen. Kjell Laugerud Garcia was president of Guatemala.

In an angry reply May 20, Laugerud called Torrijos "a man who doesn't know the meaning of honor" and a "pseudoemulator" of Cuban President Fidel Castro and Ugandan President Idi Amin Dada. Laugerud warned Torrijos that if he "has his hands in Belize, he could get them burned."

Torrijos reiterated his support for an independent Belize May 20, on the first day of a visit to Panama by Price. Price said Guatemala's renunciation of ties with Panama was "an affront to the United Nations and to the countries of the Third World." (Both the U.N. General Assembly and the movement of nonaligned nations had passed resolutions in 1975 favoring Belizean independence.

Torrijos and others had argued that Belize's 150,000 inhabitants were not culturally, racially or historically related to Guatemala. The Belizean people, most of whom originally came from Jamaica, Trinidad and Tobago and other Caribbean islands, spoke English.

Guatemala's ambassador to Mexico, Gen. Doroteo Monterroso Miranda, subsequently charged that Torrijos was supporting Belizean independence because he had invested more than $9 million in hotels and condominiums in the British colony, and he feared losing the investment under Guatemalan rule, it was reported May 24. Torrijos denied the charge and recommended that it be investigated by an international tribunal.

A Panamanian television station reported May 27 that Torrijos had asked Mexico, Venezuela, Costa Rica and Colombia to intercede to help resolve his difficulties with Guatemala. (At least two of those countries—Mexico and Venezuela—had come out strongly for Belizean independence in the past year, seriously weakening Latin American support for Guatemala's claim to Belize.)

Alejandro Orfila, secretary general of the Organization of American States, had said March 1 that Latin American nations supported Guatemala's claim to full sovereignty over Belize.

Great Britain favored independence for Belize, but the colony did not want its freedom without a British commitment to defend it from attack by Guatemala. Price had given up trying to obtain an indefinite defense guarantee from London and was now aiming for a 10-year defense treaty, according to the Latin America Political Report May 20. Price reasoned that if Belize could survive the first 10 years of independence without attack from Guatemala, its diplomatic position in international forums would be established and its security thereafter assured, the Report said.

(Belize had announced in February that it would establish a defense force of regular and volunteer soldiers. British military officers would help set up the force, it was reported Feb. 13.)

Guatemala, meanwhile, opposed any unilateral action by Great Britain and asked for a continuation of talks between British and Guatemalan officials on the future of Belize. Laugerud had warned that Guatemala would "resort to arms" if Britain unilaterally made Belize independent, it was reported May 17.

In an earlier development, the Belize City Reporter had said Jan. 30 that Guatemalan nationals were crossing into Belize in droves. Border officials were capturing and deporting the illegal immigrants at a rate of 40 per day, the newspaper reported. It was unclear whether the migration was the result of hard times in Peten, Guatemala's border province, or was an invasion sponsored by the Guate-

malan government, the newspaper said.

Israel sells arms to Guatemala—Israel had sold Guatemala rifles and about 10 STOL (short takeoff and landing) fighter planes that were "ideal for the terrain in Belize," a British official said July 6.

Twenty-six tons of Israeli arms en route to Guatemala were seized from an Argentine plane June 25 by the government of Barbados, which opposed Guatemala's claim to Belize.

Belize talks continue—Representatives of Great Britain and Guatemala met in Guatemala City July 26–28 for another round of talks on the future of Belize.

At the end of the talks the two parties issued a joint communique pledging to ease tensions along the Belize-Guatemala border and to continue to negotiate on the future status of the Central American territory.

The chief British representative, Ted Rowlands, said July 28 Britain would not withdraw the troop reinforcements it had sent to Belize earlier in the month. Because the reinforcements were not mentioned in the July 28 communique, it was assumed Guatemala was no longer demanding their removal. However, after Rowlands' departure Guatemalan President Kjell Laugerud charged that the British military presence in Belize was "a physical aggression against Guatemalan territory," it was reported Aug. 5.

Laugerud was under intense pressure from the army and from extreme rightists to take a strong stand on the Belize issue, according to the Aug. 5 Latin America Political Report. These sectors had called repeatedly for the resignation of Foreign Minister Adolfo Molina Orantes, who was reported to feel that acquiring Belize would do nothing to solve Guatemala's economic and other problems, the Political Report said.

Guatemala was becoming increasingly isolated diplomatically as Latin American and Caribbean nations voiced support for Belizean independence. In a further blow to the Guatemalan position, Andrew Young, U.S. ambassador to the United Nations, told reporters in Costa Rica that the U.S. supported Belize's desire for independence, according to the Aug. 12 Latin America Political Report. The U.S. previously had been neutral on the issue.

Jamaica

Government & Politics

New Cabinet named. Prime Minister Michael Manley named a new Cabinet Jan. 4 and said that all ministers had agreed to a pay cut.

The most important change was Sen. Dudley Thompson's move from the Foreign Ministry to the Ministry of Mining and Natural Resources, where he succeeded Allen Isaacs, who had been expelled from the ruling People's National Party (PNP) in 1976. Percival Patterson, former minister of industry, tourism and foreign trade, was the new foreign minister.

Manley established two new portfolios—parliamentary affairs and national mobilization. The latter, meant to raise productivity, was assumed by D. K. Duncan, the PNP secretary.

The new Cabinet:

Defense—Michael Manley; finance and planning—David Coore; foreign affairs, foreign trade and tourism—Percival Patterson; housing—Anthony Spaulding; education—Eric Bell; public utilities and transport—Horace Clarke; mining and natural resources—Dudley Thompson; local government—Ralph Brown; youth development and sport—Hugh Small; labor—William Isaacs; health—Douglas Manley; agriculture—A. U. Belinfanti; social security—Winston Jones; national mobilization—D. K. Duncan; workers—Ernest Peart; justice and constitutional reform—Carl Rattray; national security—Keble Munn; public service—Howard Cooke; parliamentary affairs—Kenneth McNeil; industry and commerce—Vivian Blake.

PNP sweeps local elections. The ruling People's National Party (PNP) crushed the opposition Jamaica Labor Party (JLP) in local elections March 8, gaining control of all of the island's 13 parishes.

The PNP won 237 seats in town councils, to only 31 seats for the JLP. One election ended in a tie. The PNP increased its share of the vote by 12% from the December 1976 parliamentary elections, while the JLP's share fell accordingly. The vote results were considered a damaging personal defeat for JLP leader Edward Seaga, who was expected to be replaced as the party's head, according to the London newsletter Latin America March 25.

Mobilization minister quits. D. K. Duncan resigned Sept. 18 as minister of national mobilization and general secretary of the ruling People's National Party (PNP). Prime Minister Michael Manley took over the mobilization post and Local Government Minister Ralph Brown become PNP secretary.

Duncan charged that he had quit because of a "smear campaign" against him, including a charge by Jamaica's security force that he was plotting against Manley. His resignation came amid widespread reports of conflict within the PNP between a "radical" faction led by Duncan and a "moderate" one led by Manley.

The conflict apparently had come to a head at an acrimonious party meeting

Sept. 16 at which "moderates" won the party's four vice presidencies (Manley ran unopposed for the presidency) and Manley's wife, Beverly, denounced the party's youth for talking too much and working too little. Young members booed her and walked out of the meeting accompanied by Housing Minister Anthony Spaulding, a party "radical" and incumbent vice president. Following the meeting several other radicals resigned their party and government posts, although they remained within the PNP, according to the Miami Herald Sept. 30.

The radicals had been particularly critical of the deal through which the government had obtained a $74-million loan from the International Monetary Fund (IMF) in July, according to the Latin America Political Report Oct. 7.

Following the explosion of the party conflict, Manley appeared to be more in control than ever, the Political Report said. He took over the direction of the land reform program and promised to accelerate it, the report noted. And he told the PNP meeting Sept. 16 that he would delegate some of his government duties to other officials in order to assume personal responsibility for the "discipline and development" of the PNP.

Kingston violence flares. One man was killed and several others were wounded Feb. 2 in a new outburst of Jamaica's endemic political violence. The casualties occurred in a shootout that erupted in the Kingston slum of Trench Town when Housing Ministry agents tried to evict tenants who supported the opposition Jamaica Labor Party, according to the newsletter Latin America March 25.

Violence, spurred by an unemployment rate estimated between 33% and 40%, was a major cause in the sharp decline of tourism in Jamaica. During February, usually the busiest month for tourism, Jamaican hotels were half or less than half full, the Miami Herald reported Feb. 22.

In a highly publicized incident, armed robbers Jan. 6 raided the Montego Bay home of Lady Sarah Spencer-Churchill Roubanis, a cousin of the late Sir Winston Churchill. The intruders raped the British socialite, ransacked her home and wounded a houseguest. Police Jan. 10 said they had captured two suspects in the crime, whom they refused to identify.

The Economy

Emergency economic plan set. The government Jan. 19 announced a wideranging emergency plan to rebuild Jamaica's ailing economy.

The program, outlined to Parliament by Prime Minister Michael Manley, included import curbs, tighter foreign-exchange controls, a wage and price freeze, more taxes on higher-income residents, a cut in pay for top government officials and government acquisition of three commercial banks, a cement company and the British-owned Radio Jamaica.

Jamaica's import bill for 1977 would be restricted to $660 million (including repayment of the national debt), compared with $902 million in 1976. Jamaicans who emigrated would not be allowed to take any money out of the country, and those who vacationed abroad would be allowed to take only $55 per year in foreign exchange (compared with $550 previously). Jamaicans also would be prohibited from sending money to dependents abroad, and only on special humanitarian grounds would beneficiaries abroad be allowed to receive inheritances.

Commercial banks operating in Jamaica would no longer be allowed to buy or sell foreign exchange on their own but would have to act as agents of the Central Bank of Jamaica.

The tax rate on salaries and allowances above $11,000 would rise to 58% from the current 33%. Jamaicans making more than $22,000 would be taxed at a 70% rate (up from the current 60%), and those making more than $33,000 would pay an 80% rate. Wages and prices would be frozen for six months, after which the government would introduce a full price and incomes policy, including a ceiling on incomes. Prime Minister Manley said his salary would be cut to $17,600 from $24,200, while the salaries of Cabinet ministers would be reduced less drastically.

Manley did not reveal which three commercial banks would be nationalized but he said they would be one large bank and two small ones. The government later said it had agreed in principle to acquire an 80% interest in Barclays Bank of Jamaica Ltd., a subsidiary of the British-owned

Barclays Bank Ltd., it was reported March 23.

Manley also announced Jan. 19 that Jamaica would establish diplomatic relations with the Soviet Union and seek trade agreements with member nations of COMECON, the Soviet-bloc economic organization. Jamaican and COMECON officials had conferred in Cuba recently on potential markets in the Soviet bloc for Jamaican bauxite, bananas and coffee, among other products, it was reported Jan. 28.

Government buys Kaiser, Reynolds assets. The Jamaican government signed agreements to purchase controlling interests in two U.S.-owned bauxite mining firms, Kaiser Bauxite Co. and Reynolds Jamaica Mines Ltd.

Under the first deal, signed Feb. 2, Jamaica would pay about $11 million for a 51% interest in Kaiser Bauxite, a subsidiary of Kaiser Industries Corp. Kaiser would continue to manage the subsidiary's mining activities but policy decisions would be made by an executive committee in which the Jamaican government and Kaiser had equal representation. The new partnership would be called Kaiser Jamaica Bauxite Co.

Kaiser Bauxite would receive bauxite from the partnership at cost, and would pay the Jamaican government a return on its investment in the partnership, a spokesman for Kaiser said. In addition, Kaiser Bauxite would sell the government, for about $14.5 million, all 48,189 acres of its bauxite lands, resettlement lands and other property not required for plant operation.

Kaiser Bauxite also would receive a mining lease for a 40-year supply of bauxite that was sufficient to operate the parent company's two Louisiana plants at their current production rates. In return, Kaiser annually would pay the Jamaican government 7% of the government's purchase price for the land under the mining lease. This would be about $750,000 the first year, Kaiser said.

Kaiser would pay a tax on bauxite of 7.5% of the price per pound, with a provision for the levy to drop to 7% after production climbed to a certain level. The agreement apparently resolved Kaiser's dispute with Jamaica that arose in 1974 when the government increased its tax on bauxite by about 700%.

Prime Minister Michael Manley said the Kaiser deal would serve as a model for future arrangements with the four other U.S. bauxite producers operating in Jamaica, it was reported Feb. 10. The government's objective, Manley said, was "maximum local investment in the strategic resources."

A similar agreement was signed March 31 by the Jamaican government and Reynolds Jamaica Mines Ltd., a subsidiary of Reynolds Metals Co. Jamaica would acquire 51% of Reynolds' mining assets, full ownership of about 65,000 acres of land and all of Reynolds' agricultural operations in the country for an estimated $18 million plus interest, to be paid over 10 years. The resulting partnership would be called Jamaica Reynolds Bauxite Partners.

Jamaica would lower its tax on bauxite produced by Reynolds to 7.5% from 8% of the realized price of primary aluminum in the U.S. The 7.5% rate would extend through 1983, after which it could be renegotiated. The new rate also was retroactive to Jan. 1, 1974, a spokesman for Reynolds said.

Reynolds would receive a mining lease satisfying its bauxite requirements for 40 years. Reynolds would direct the partnership's mining operations under a seven-year "management contract" subject to "general policy direction" by an executive committee with four members each from the Jamaican government and Reynolds.

In return for the mining leases, Reynolds would pay Jamaica 7% of the purchase price paid by the government for reserve land covered by the leases. Reynolds also would pay the government a 12% annual return on the government's investment in the partnership's mining assets.

Prime Minister Manley hailed the Reynolds agreement as "setting the world an example of fair and successful partnership between poor Third World countries and giant multinational corporations." Reynolds also expressed satisfaction with the pact; its chairman, David P. Reynolds, said the partnership "means that we can rely on a long-range supply of our raw material."

Trade gap narrowed. Jamaica's trade deficit was cut sharply in the first six months of 1977 as exports rose and imports fell in comparison with the same period of 1976, it was reported Sept. 27.

Between January and June, exports totaled J$342.3 million (30% above the 1976 figure) and imports totaled J$345.9 million (16% below the 1976 amount). The resulting trade deficit of J$3.6 million was small compared with the January–June 1976 deficit of J$134 million. (US$1 = J$1.28)

Nevertheless, Jamaica was in serious economic trouble, with a 27% unemployment rate and poor performances in the sugar and tourism industries, which earned much of the island's foreign exchange. The Bank of Jamaica's foreign exchange figures for July (the latest available) showed a deficit of J$176 million in Jamaica's net reserves at the end of that month.

To help spur economic recovery, the Jamaican government had obtained a $74-million loan from the International Monetary Fund (IMF) July 12. However, the loan had been granted on condition that Jamaica "implement an economic program endorsed by the IMF," according to Finance Minister David Coore, who was quoted by the Miami Herald July 25. This program involved tight wage restrictions, budget reductions, a promise by the government to pay all outstanding foreign debts by June 1978, and an agreement to pay for imports in cash only, according to the Latin America Political Report Oct. 7.

In addition to the IMF loan, Jamaica obtained $20 million in credits from Venezuela and $8 million from Hungary, it was reported Sept. 27.

(Jamaica also contracted to sell Venezuela one million tons of aluminum over the next seven years, it was reported Sept. 2. The price for the aluminum was $200 million.)

Foreign Relations

Mrs. Carter visits. Rosalynn Carter, wife of U.S. President Jimmy Carter, visited seven countries in the Caribbean and Latin America May 30–June 12 on a tour that combined goodwill gestures with substantive political and economc discussion.

Mrs. Carter visited Jamaica May 30–31. On her tour she was accompanied by Grace Vance, wife of U.S. Secretary of State Cyrus Vance, and by two of the Carter Administration's experts on Latin America—Terence Todman, assistant secretary of state for inter-American affairs, and Robert Pastor, senior staff member for inter-American affairs on the National Security Council.

Mrs. Carter arrived in Kingston May 30. Prime Minister Manley and Mrs. Carter conferred for more than seven hours during the next day and a half. Their discussions apparently centered on Jamaica's economic problems and on U.S. relations with Cuba, whose government was on very friendly terms with Manley's.

Mrs. Carter said May 31 that she had told Manley the U.S. was "making some gestures and exploring to see if Cuba wanted normalization with the U.S., but that we had some very difficult problems to face with Cuba before we do reach any kind of normalization."

Mrs. Carter revealed later that she and Manley had discussed ways in which the U.S. might help Jamaica obtain loans from banks and international lending agencies. Jamaica was in a state of economic crisis, having suffered a $350-million trade deficit in 1976 because of declines in tourism and the international price of bauxite.

Manley was eager to improve Jamaica's relations with the U.S. following several years of strained relations with former Secretary of State Henry Kissinger, who was suspicious of Manley's friendship with Cuban President Fidel Castro. Manley told Mrs. Carter he would sign the 1969 American Convention on Human Rights, which President Carter was promoting.

Andrew Young on tour. Andrew Young, the U.S. ambassador to the United Nations, visited Jamaica Aug. 5–7 to stress the Carter Administration's interest in good relations with Jamaica.

Young, who had visited Jamaica 11 times before and said he considered himself "a Jamaican," was received warmly when he arrived in Kingston Aug. 5. He met with Prime Minister Michael Manley Aug. 6 and 7 and assured him that the U.S. respected his efforts to forge political and economic policies representing a "third way" between capitalism and communism.

U.S. officials accompanying Young said Aug. 7 that they would put together an economic package increasing U.S. aid to Jamaica from the current $10 million to a projected $50 million to $60 million. The program, which required approval by the U.S. Congress, would include a $12-million agreement covering surplus food sales; a $10-million commodity import loan that would allow Jamaica to purchase agricultural machinery and other badly needed equipment, and technical aid and development projects in agriculture and education.

U.S. resumes aid. The U.S. quietly resumed aid to Jamaica following the well-received visit to Kingston by Andrew Young, U.S. ambassador to the United Nations.

The U.S. State Department's Agency for International Development granted Jamaica a $2.1-million education loan, it was reported Sept. 12. The U.S. followed this up with a $63-million economic development credit, reported Nov. 9.

The U.S. had cut off aid to Jamaica in 1975 when the Jamaican government took over a U.S.-owned company, Revere Copper & Brass Inc.

Manley in U.S. Visiting Washington Dec. 16, Prime Minister Manley met with President Carter and Secretary of State Cyrus Vance. Speaking to reporters before the meeting, Manley defended Cuba's military involvement in Angola, urged the U.S. to restore normal relations with Cuba and warned that failure by the U.S. Senate to ratify the new Panama Canal treaties would be "catastrophic" for U.S. relations with Latin America and the Caribbean.

Castro visits. Cuban President Fidel Castro visited Jamaica Oct. 16–21 in an evidently successful effort to strengthen ties between Cuba and Jamaica and to bolster the political position of Prime Minister Michael Manley.

To the apparent approval of many Jamaicans, Castro projected a moderate image, denying that Cuba sought to interfere in the affairs of other countries, offering Jamaica extensive aid, giving advice on economic problems and warmly praising the socialist programs of Manley's government.

Nevertheless, Castro's visit was protested by the opposition Jamaica Labor Party (JLP) and other conservative sources. The JLP charged that Castro was a "Communist dictator" and urged Jamaicans to boycott all public functions at which he appeared.

The party's leader, Frank Phipps, said Oct. 16 that the visit was "ill-conceived and inopportune." He said Castro was "an individual with a history of interference in the internal affairs of Jamaica and other countries, who preaches subversion and revolution in the entire hemisphere."

The Kingston newspaper The Gleaner also criticized the visit, it was reported Oct. 23. Gleaner columnist Wilmot Perkins wrote that the visit was one of many "circuses" to which Jamaicans were being treated to cover up the "reality of worsening poverty, worsening unemployment [and] worsening crime."

Castro arrived in Kingston Oct. 16 to a warm greeting from Governor General Florizel Glasspole, Prime Minister Manley and members of the foreign diplomatic corps, including the U.S. ambassador to Jamaica. Manley praised Castro as a "hero to the peoples of the Third World" and "one of the great leaders of the 20th century." Manley also denounced "agents of imperialism" who had tried to prevent Cuba's friendship with Jamaica, and he called for an end to all international sanctions against Cuba, presumably including the U.S. trade embargo of the island. [See below]

Castro praised Manley's programs during a motorcade across Jamaica Oct. 18. He said that Manley was working to improve housing, employment and the general economic opportunities of Jamaicans, and that the Cuban people supported him.

Wherever he went in Jamaica, Castro stressed Cuba's eagerness to help the beleaguered island economically. He promised buses for a Cuban-built school, tractors for a sugar cooperative, prefabricated housing plants for construction workers and Cuban doctors, teachers and technicians wherever they were needed.

"We are willing to bring to Jamaica all our experience in agriculture, cattle-raising, public health, education, economic development, fishing, sports—in everything we can," Castro said at a rally in Montego Bay. "Our universities are open to you, our research centers, hospitals, technological institutes—we shall never keep a secret from you. Anything that might be useful for us, we are willing to offer to you."

Castro wept as he embraced Manley before his return to Cuba Oct. 21.

CIA plots vs. Manley reported, denied. An American magazine reported Nov. 2 that in 1976 the U.S. Central Intelligence Agency had tried to undermine the Jamaican government and to assassinate Prime Minister Michael Manley.

The CIA strenuously denied the story, calling it "absolutely ridiculous" and noting that U.S. government officials were forbidden to conspire in political murders.

The story appeared in the December issue of Penthouse magazine, which went on sale Nov. 2. In an article entitled "Murder as Usual," reporters Ernest Volkman and John Cummings said the CIA had embarked on its activities against Manley in December 1975 after Manley rejected an ultimatum from then-Secretary of State Henry Kissinger to cool his friendship with Cuban leader Fidel Castro and to stop interfering with U.S.-owned bauxite companies that operated in Jamaica.

At first, the reporters said, CIA agents in Jamaica fomented unrest, infiltrated the island's security force and supported the leader of the political opposition. When this failed to unseat Manley, the article continued, the CIA tried to have him assassinated.

The reporters alleged there were three plans to gun down Manley, all of which failed before shots were fired. The first plan was for July 14, 1976, when Manley's jeep was stopped at a roadblock; the second was for that September, when the premier was visiting Canada, and the third for Dec. 15, the night of the last Jamaican elections (which Manley's party won handily).

The story supported the Jamaican government's charge in 1976 that the U.S. was trying to "destabilize" Manley's administration. The CIA's denial was unusual, since the agency normally refused to comment on such reports.

Mexico

Civil Unrest & Strikes

Army occupies Oaxaca to quell civil strife. Following 10 days of bloody clashes between police and student and peasant protesters, the army March 3 occupied the city of Oaxaca and several towns in surrounding Oaxaca State, and state Gov. Manuel Zarate Aquino took a six-month leave of absence from his duties.

Zarate was replaced temporarily by Gen. Eliseo Jimenez Ruiz, a senator who belonged to the ruling Institutional Revolutionary Party. Under an agreement reached by protest leaders and the federal government, the leftist rector of the local university also resigned.

The rector, Felipe Martinez Soriano, had been at the center of controversy in Oaxaca since his election to the university post in January. Gov. Zarate had declared the election "irregular" and appointed a protege, Horacio Tenorio Sandoval, to be the new rector. When students at the university refused to accept Tenorio, Zarate sent in the police to enforce his decision. This touched off protests by students throughout the state, who claimed the university's autonomy had been violated.

The protests accelerated after police in the town of Juchitan arrested 38 students Feb. 22 for demonstrating against an increase in bus fares. Other students in Juchitan gathered to protest the arrests, and police fired into the crowd, killing at least two students (or as many as seven, according to varying reports) and wounding at least 15 more.

(The arrested students immediately were taken to a prison in Oaxaca. The corpses of three of the detainees were found outside the capital Feb. 24. A coalition of peasants and students said the bodies bore signs of extensive torture.)

Students in Oaxaca protested the Juchitan killings Feb. 23–25, burning and overturning vehicles and clashing with police. The state government appealed for federal military intervention to end the violence, but none was forthcoming. Businessmen in the capital agreed to stage a general lockout Feb. 28–March 1 to support the state government against the protesters.

The situation worsened March 1 when it was reported that police in the municipality of San Juan de Lalana had killed 29 peasants the day before. The peasants apparently had demanded land, and the police had opened fire on them at the behest of local landowners and *caciques* (political leaders).

A spokesman for the Oaxaca government admitted March 1 that there had been at least 10 deaths at San Juan de Lalana, but Gov. Zarate made matters worse by telling the press, "You can say that 80 or 100 peasants died....It doesn't matter. Look, for me it's like a soccer game, losing 5 0 is the same as losing 1 0." Zarate had just returned from a conference in Mexico City with President Jose Lopez Portillo, who presumably had advised him to resign.

Meanwhile, businessmen in the capital staged their lockout Feb. 28 March 1. Poor shopowners who did not close down those two days complained that they were beaten by gangs of thugs enforcing the lockout.

Several thousand students, workers and peasants demonstrated in the capital March 2, demanding the resignations of Zarate and his designee for university rector. The demonstrators insisted that peasants be given their own land. Police fired into the crowd and beat demonstrators with nightsticks, and the protesters threw bottles at the officers. One student leader was killed, another was mortally wounded (he died March 3) and at least 17 other persons were injured.

The federal government March 3 sent about 1,000 troops into the city of Oaxaca and a total of 500 into a few other towns. Order was quickly restored, and students gave up their protests under the agreement with federal authorities. In addition, a new rector of the university, Fernando Gomez Sandoval, a former Oaxaca state governor, was named.

Gov. Zarate was replaced not only because his intransigence had contributed to the student violence, but because his apparent indifference to the murder of peasants had helped forge closer links between students and peasants, two of the most dangerous sources of opposition to the federal government, according to the London newsletter Latin America March 11.

Nevertheless, a columnist for the Mexico City newspaper Excelsior asserted March 3 that the root cause of unrest in Oaxaca was not Zarate's behavior but the state's unusually high rate of illiteracy, unemployment and poverty, coupled with the violent rule of local landowners and *caciques.*

Police and soldiers occupied the local university in Oaxaca April 24 after rightwing and left-wing groups refused to honor the agreement they had reached in March to end earlier factional strife. One student was killed and several were wounded in the new occupation.

The feuding groups in Oaxaca, led by two men who both claimed the university's rectorship, reportedly reached a new agreement that entailed the naming of a third person to be the school's new dean. The rival rectors agreed to step aside.

Martinez Soriano was among 87 persons arrested during the occupation of the university April 24 and released shortly afterward. Martinez said he and his family had been beaten by police in custody.

At other universities, right-wing thugs hired by administrators were terrorizing the student bodies, according to press reports. The thugs, called *porros,* had killed 12 students at different universities in the previous two months, United Press International reported June 18. Another 100 students and teachers had been injured by the rightists, according to reports.

Authorities occupy Oaxaca university— Several thousand policemen and soldiers occupied Benito Juarez University in Oaxaca Dec. 14 after a recurrence of the campus violence.

The security officers evicted an estimated 3,000 students who had been occupying the university since Dec. 7, when the acting governor of Oaxaca dismissed the rector of the university in the wake of a shootout among students in which two youths were killed. The governor charged that student supporters of the rector, Felipe Martinez Soriano, were responsible for the gunfight.

It was the second time in 1977 that Martinez Soriano, a reputed leftist, had been removed from his post. Following repeated campus violence from February to April, a new election for rector was held and Martinez Soriano won again.

Acting Gov. Eliseo Jimenez Ruiz charged Dec. 14 that Martinez had allowed the university to become a center for subversive activities. Martinez heatedly denied this and asserted that the police and army occupation of the campus constituted "unprecedented repression." He charged that the culprits in the Dec. 7 campus shootout were "terrorists" hired by the government to attack left-wing students.

The rector charged that "dozens" of students had been arrested during the occupation, but the government denied it.

UNAM strike closes university. The Autonomous National University of Mexico in Mexico City (UNAM), the largest university in the country, was closed June 20 by an indefinite strike by non-academic employes and left-wing lecturers and professors. The strike, however, was settled July 10 after police raided the campus and arrested hundreds of strikers.

The strikers had demanded a new collective contract, a 20% wage increase for academic and non-academic employees and recognition of their union, STUNAM, as an official negotiating agent. The demands were rejected by the university's rector, Guillermo Soberon, who was backed by right-wing academics who had refused to join STUNAM.

Mexico's ruling Institutional Revolutionary Party (PRI) accused the Mexican Communist Party of organizing the strike, it was reported July 1. A PRI statement, which did not name the Communists, said: "What is being attempted is for a party to gain absolute control over the most important institution of higher learning in the country, displacing its inherent aims and turning it into an instrument to destabilize social normality."

Communist leader Arnoldo Martinez Verdugo denied the PRI's charge but said his party supported the strike. Press reports noted that STUNAM was linked closely with the Communists and that the strike's leader, Evaristo Perez Arreola, was a member of the party.

The UNAM strike was part of a general crisis in Mexico's universities, which were plagued by inadequate budgets, overcrowded classrooms and clashes between leftist and rightist factions, according to the New York Times April 13.

Several thousand policemen raided the university before dawn July 7, arresting 246 teachers and non-academic employes who had been sitting in at several buildings since June 20. Another 285 strikers were detained elsewhere in the capital.

All but six of the arrested strikers were released July 9, after unions of university employes across Mexico held a one-day strike to protest the UNAM detentions. The six, all leaders of STUNAM, the union that called the UNAM strike, were indicted on charges of robbing and vandalizing university buildings during the sit-ins.

The university administration and STUNAM reached the settlement July 10, and police left the campus two days later. Under the agreement, the university would recognize STUNAM as a bargaining agent and would negotiate new collective contracts for administrative personnel in November 1977 and for academic employes in February 1978.

Steel workers end strike. About 4,500 workers at the Fundidora de Monterrey steel complex returned to work after settling a 49-day strike, it was reported July 12.

The workers had struck after rejecting a one-year labor contract negotiated with the company by union leaders, but in the final settlement they accepted the 10% wage increase granted in the original contract. The government had asked workers to hold all wage demands to 10% to help control inflation.

Fundidora de Monterrey was Mexico's third largest steel producer.

Terrorism & Human Rights

Guerrillas kill eight. Guerrillas of the September 23rd Communist League killed eight persons in attacks in Mexico City Jan. 16 and 20.

A group of 14 insurgents invaded a government commodities store in the capital Jan. 16, stealing an estimated $15,000 and fatally shooting a cashier and three police officers. Four other persons were wounded in the attack. Police said later that they had identified all 14 guerrillas through descriptions provided by bystanders.

In two separate attacks Jan. 20, guerrillas killed two policemen at a stationery store and two businessmen at a construction site. One of the executives was an American, identified by the U.S. Embassy as Mitchell Andreski, president of the Duraflex Corp. of Hartford, Conn. Police said Andreski had been shot when he tried to stop the guerrillas from distributing political pamphlets.

In response to the attacks, the government announced an intensive police campaign to arrest leftist insurgents. Carlos

Hank Gonzalez, regent of the Federal District (Mexico City), said Jan. 21 the police had divided the capital into 22 patrol areas and had established a radio communications system linking police headquarters with such likely guerrilla targets as factories, business offices, stores and banks. In addition, police would radically alter their patrol methods and would acquire new equipment including long firearms, the regent said. Helicopters would be used to supplement automobile patrols.

Hank Gonzalez claimed police had identified 19 of the guerrillas involved in the recent attacks, whom he called "common criminals."

One result of these and previous guerrilla assaults was a sharp increase in the use of bodyguards by businessmen and government officials, the Washington Post reported Jan. 26. There were now thousands of personal guards in Mexico, many of whom used arms imported illegally from the U.S., according to the Post. Guerrillas also used U.S.-made guns, many of which were smuggled into Mexico by drug traffickers who obtained them in exchange for heroin. The army and the police were other sources of weapons sold on the Mexican black market, the Post reported. The Mexico City police chief said there might be as many as 30 million firearms in the country, or roughly one gun to every two inhabitants.

Nine guerrillas arrested. Mexico City police said they had arrested nine members of the September 23rd Communist League in raids and shootouts in the capital April 13 and 14.

Police said three of the captured guerrilas had confessed to four kidnappings and 19 slayings. The kidnappings reportedly included the 1976 abduction of Nadine Chaval, daughter of the Belgian ambassador to Mexico. The slayings reportedly included the January shooting of U.S. businessman Mitchell Andreski.

Police claimed to have confiscated arms, ammunition and $500,000 in ransom money hidden by the guerrillas in their main Mexico City "safehouse." One policeman and a female guerrilla were killed in the police raid on the safehouse April 14.

More than 10,000 security officials

reportedly were assigned to flush out members of the Communist League in Mexico City, Guadalajara, Veracruz, Culiacan, Ciudad Juarez and other cities. A woman who apparently belonged to the small guerrilla band was killed in a shootout with police in the capital June 12.

In another development, police in Guadalajara arrested 11 members of a violent anti-Communist group that appeared to be financed by wealthy Jalisco State industrialists, Inter Press Service reported Aug. 10. The police found arms, wiretapping equipment and a lie detector at the rightists' hideout. The anti-Communists operated mostly at the private Autonomous University of Guadalajara, where they had no-show academic positions and did paramilitary training exercises on the campus athletic field, Inter Press said.

Guerrilla bombings hit 3 cities. Left-wing guerrillas planted 40 bombs in Mexico City, Guadalajara and Oaxaca before dawn Sept. 14. Twenty-three of the devices exploded, injuring at least five persons and causing an estimated $20 million worth of property damage. The targets were mostly government offices, banks and American-owned businesses.

Credit for the blasts was claimed by a new insurgent group that called itself the People's Union. Leaflets left by the bombers protested hunger and unemployment in Mexico and called all other guerrillas "cowards of the left." Police in Guadalajara said they had arrested one member of the People's Union while he was planting a bomb inside Woolworth Mexicana.

More than 10,000 policemen and soldiers were put on alert Sept. 15 to prevent further attacks the next day, which was Mexico's independence day. The security officers set up roadblocks and made surprise raids on suspected guerrilla hideouts. The independence celebrations, including a fireworks display in Mexico City, were held without incident Sept. 16.

The People's Union bombings were the latest of a series of left-wing guerrilla operations in Mexico. In the most notable incident, at least eight persons were killed when a member of the People's Revolutionary Armed Forces

(FRAP) exploded a hand grenade on a hijacked bus.

Reports of the incident varied, but it was agreed that two FRAP members had boarded the bus in Mexico City Aug. 21 and commandeered it several hours later as it traveled in northwestern Mexico. The hijackers demanded that the government release an imprisoned comrade, Ramon Campana Lopez, and give them safe-conduct out of the country. But Mexican police intercepted the bus, and in the shootout that ensued a grenade held by one of the guerrillas went off. Some reports said one guerrilla and nine hostages died in the shooting and the explosion, while other reports said both guerrillas and six hostages died.

Two other FRAP members were reported killed in a shootout with police in Mexico City Aug. 17.

Other shootouts were reported between police and members of the September 23rd Communist League, Mexico's largest guerrilla group. One policeman and one guerrilla were killed Aug. 20 in a gun battle at the National Autonomous University of Mexico in Mexico City. Two police officers and an insurgent had been killed nine days earlier in a shootout in Hermosillo.

Political prisoners freed. The government announced April 11 that it had dropped political charges against 424 persons imprisoned on suspicion of aiding "subversive" movements. Authorities said 128 of the prisoners already had been freed, and others would be released soon. The rest would stay in jail to face criminal charges such as robbery, kidnapping and homicide.

"There are no more political prisoners in Mexico," Attorney General Oscar Flores said April 12. He noted that the prisoners who had been released had been accused of "political crimes, not of being guerrillas."

The government had promised March 14 to drop political charges against 76 prisoners, 46 of whom had been held without trial since 1971. Those favored by the amnesty included members of the Revolutionary Armed Movement, the Zapatist Urban Front and the September 23rd Communist League, according to the Latin America Political Report March 18.

The government appeared to be trying to forestall a major debate on human rights in Mexico in the light of U.S. President Jimmy Carter's vigorous promotion of the rights issue, the Miami Herald commented March 30. A U.S. State Department report on Mexico said that while the country had "a long tradition of civic freedom," human rights violations such as "cruel and degrading treatment" by security officers were common. "Arbitrary arrests and detentions occasionally occur of political oppositionists accused of illegal activities," the report added.

Lawyers of the state university of Guerrero had drawn up a list of 257 persons who had "disappeared" in the state in the past four years as the army scoured the mountains for leftist guerrillas, the Herald reported. The missing persons either were being held incommunicado by the army or police, or had died in detention, the lawyers said.

Former political prisoners added that relatives of suspected subversives were routinely arrested and held for long periods for questioning, the Herald noted. Seven relatives of the late guerrilla chief Lucio Cabanas had been detained and tortured, the newspaper reported. Cabanas' brother, Pablo, had been jailed for five years even though he had had no contact with his brother for several years before that, the Herald said.

Police raid rights group. Mexico City police July 7 seized the files and office equipment of the National Center for Social Communication, a church-related documentation office for the defense of human rights.

The files contained sensitive information about political prisoners and exiles, much of it provided by Amnesty International and the World Council of Churches. The files were not returned despite vigorous protests from the center and from other Mexican and international human rights groups.

Mexican law enforcement agencies all denied responsibility for the raid and denied knowing where the files were. The Mexico City police chief said the raid had been ordered by the Attorney General's office, but the Attorney General's office denied this. The Interior Ministry, which was in charge of the police, also denied ordering the raid.

The center's director, Jose Alvarez Icaza, believed the raid was part of a broad campaign against dissident groups associated with the Roman Catholic Church. "Serious things have been happening to progressive priests in Mexico," Alvarez told the New York Times Aug. 4. "Two priests have been murdered this year and the cases have not been solved. Another priest was wounded in an ambush and vicious attacks have been launched against the bishops of Cuernavaca and San Cristobal de las Casas." The two bishops were involved in the social problems of their dioceses. the Times noted.

Economic Developments

Economic aides replaced in austerity conflict. President Jose Lopez Portillo replaced his finance and planning ministers Nov. 17 after the two Cabinet officials were unable to reconcile their differences over economic policy.

For several months Finance Minister Julio Moctezuma Cid and Planning Minister Carlos Tello Macias had been quarreling over the stringent austerity measures adopted by the government at the behest of the International Monetary Fund (IMF). Moctezuma was the Cabinet's leading advocate of those measures, and Tello their major adversary.

The conflict apparently came to a head over the 1978 budget, which Moctezuma and Tello were preparing for submission to Congress by the end of 1977. Moctezuma reportedly insisted on keeping the budget increase to 15%. Tello, arguing that more government spending was needed because private investment was low, sought a larger increase that would be financed partly by printing more money.

Lopez Portillo instructed the two ministers to reach a compromise, but they were unable to. Tello resigned, giving the president a letter that advocated stimulation of production and employment to "correct the deflationary policy conducted by the Finance Ministry authorities and supported by the International Monetary Fund." Lopez Portillo accepted the resignation and, in a surprise move apparently designed to mollify supporters of Tello, he obtained Moctezuma's resignation as well.

The president replaced Tello with Ricardo Garcia Sainz, deputy minister of natural resources and industrial development, and he replaced Moctezuma with David Ibarra Munoz, director of Nacional Financiera S.A., the state investment bank.

Although Lopez Portillo tried to appear even-handed, he evidently resolved the Cabinet crisis in favor of Moctezuma's supporters. The new finance and planning ministers reputedly were middle-of-the-roaders, but they were closer philosophically to Moctezuma than to Tello, according to the New York Times Dec. 3. And the president himself told reporters that he saw "no alternative" to continuing the restrictive policies advocated by the IMF, it was reported Dec. 2.

Economic austerity program—An economic austerity program had been initiated at the end of 1976 in exchange for $1.2 billion worth of IMF credits. By the end of November 1977, the policies had succeeded in: reducing inflation to around 20% from a 1976 rate of more than 45%; reducing the trade deficit to below $1 billion from $2.73 billion; keeping the budget deficit within 6.5%, and stabilizing the Mexican peso at about 23 to the U.S. dollar, according to the Financial Times (London) Dec. 1.

While these results were considered impressive, they were obtained at the expense of poor workers and farmers who suffered the most from austerity measures. Unemployment and underemployment affected a record 53% of the Mexican work force, it was reported Nov. 18. Strikes and demonstrations against the 10% ceiling on wage increases were almost daily occurrences in the cities. Undernourishment was increasing in southern rural areas, and in the north increasing numbers of peasants were trying to enter the U.S. illegally to search for work. For the second year in a row the Mexican economy was expected to have grown only 2% while the population grew by 3.2%, the New York Times noted Nov. 17.

Private domestic investment was not

increasing, according to press reports, but foreign credits were. A group of 74 international banks, headed by Bank of America, Morgan Guaranty Trust Co., Deutsche Bank and Lloyds Bank International, had granted the Mexican government $1.2 billion worth of credits, it was reported Nov. 18. The Inter-American Development Bank said Nov. 22 that it would lend the government $1 billion over the next three years. The IMF had set a limit of $2 billion per year on Mexico's international borrowing, but it was expected to raise that ceiling in 1978 in view of the success of the government's austerity program, according to the Financial Times (London) Dec. 1.

The government needed international credits to develop its large petroleum reserves and to build a natural gas pipeline to the U.S. The state oil company, Pemex, had embarked on a $17-billion investment program that was expected to raise oil production to 2.26 million barrels per day and exports to 1.1 million barrels daily by 1982, the Financial Times noted. The program also would double Mexico's oil refining and triple its petrochemical capacity by the same date.

Eximbank grants two loans—The U.S. Export-Import Bank (Eximbank) Dec. 15 approved two loans worth a total of $590 million for a major gas-pipeline project and other ventures in Mexico.

The credits to the Mexican oil company Pemex would help it buy about $1 billion in goods and services from American suppliers.

'78 budget to ease austerity program. The government Dec. 15 announced its budget for 1978, which provided for a slight relaxation of the economic austerity policies adopted by President Jose Lopez Portillo.

The budget was an apparent compromise between supporters and opponents of the IMF policies in the Mexican Cabinet.

The finance minister, David Ibarra Munoz, said the '78 budget would allow the economy to grow about 5%—roughly double the 1977 growth rate—yet still limit inflation to 12%–15%. There would be an emphasis on creating jobs in agriculture and small and medium-sized indus-

tries, and on investing in the oil industry to strengthen Mexico's balance of payments.

The budget's $40 million in expenditures was 23.6% higher than 1977 spending levels, although after inflation was taken into account this figure was less than 10% in real terms.

Because of its emphasis on capital investment and control on current spending, the new budget was expected to be approved by the IMF, whose endorsement was all but necessary if Mexico were to obtain foreign credits.

Unemployment & other problems—The government still faced serious problems, including a high unemployment rate of 53% that must be alleviated by increasing domestic production, the Financial Times noted. Little new investment was currently taking place, but the private sector had promised to spend $10 billion to create new jobs before 1980, the newspaper said.

The Labor Ministry estimated Mexico's absolute unemployment at two million workers, or 11% of the total work force of 17.5 million, it was reported May 13. However, another five to seven million workers were reported to be underemployed.

The Mexican Workers' Confederation, the largest labor group in the country, said that between February and April 10,000 workers had been fired in the automobile industry and 2,500 in the textile industry, it was reported May 13. Layoffs in the construction industry totaled a staggering 400,000, according to the National Chamber of Construction Industries.

The government was offering fiscal and other incentives for the creation of 300,-000 jobs, more than one-third of them in border industries, it was reported May 13. The remaining jobs would be provided by expanding the industrial and service sectors, according to the Latin America Economic Report.

Industrial production in Mexico in the first quarter of 1977 was 2.9% below the level for the first three months of 1976, it was reported June 7. Industrial activity had fallen by 6.5% in January and February but had rallied in March. The steel, automobile and construction sectors were cited among industries suffering declines in the quarter.

The government steel firm Sicartsa had been forced to put off a $3-billion expansion of its plant in Las Truchas because of the economic crisis, it was reported April 1. The government later announced a plan to create a holding company comprising Sicartsa and other two leading steel producers, Altos Hornos de Mexico (AHMSA) and Fundidora de Monterrey, in an effort to increase production and cut capital needs, it was reported May 12. (The government owned all of AHMSA and 44% of Fundidora.)

Oil

Rise planned in oil production, export. The government had announced that in the next six years Mexican petroleum production would rise to 2.2 million barrels a day and exports of crude and refined oil would reach 1.1 million barrels daily, it was reported Jan. 14.

Mexican oil production for 1977 was estimated at 953,000 barrels a day, and exports were estimated at 153,000 barrels daily. The sharp increase planned by 1982 was dictated by the need to increase export revenues to pay back foreign creditors, according to the Financial Times (London) Jan. 25. At current prices, oil could bring Mexico $5 billion in annual export revenues by 1982, or 60% more than the value of the country's total visible exports in 1976.

The increased revenues would also help Mexico expand its petroleum refining installations and increase the proportion of refined exports to crude exports.

The rise in production and exports would be facilitated by the discovery of new oil deposits in four regions of the country: offshore near the port of Tampico, on the Gulf of Mexico; at Cotaxla near Veracruz, on the gulf further to the south; near Nuevo Laredo on the U.S. border and at Sebastian Vizcaino in Baja California Sur, it was reported Jan. 14.

Oil reserves above 60 billion barrels—The state oil company Pemex March 18 estimated Mexico's total petroleum reserves at more than 60 billion barrels.

Pemex Director General Jorge Diaz Serrano said the country's proven reserves were only 11.1 billion barrels. However, he said this figure did not include known reserves on the continental shelf off the state of Campeche, nor huge oilfields not yet in production.

The 60-billion figure, reported in the press in February, had been attributed to U.S. government officials and oil industry executives. The estimate made Mexico's petroleum reserves comparable to Iran's and Kuwait's and six times greater than the reserves in Alaska's North Slope.

Until Diaz Serrano's announcement, Mexican officials purposely had underestimated the country's oil reserves, apparently to minimize conflicting pressures from the U.S. and the Organization of Petroleum Exporting Countries. (Mexico heretofore had resisted joining OPEC because membership in the cartel would exclude Mexico from trade preferences available under the 1974 U.S. Trade Act and would add to the tensions in Mexico's relations with Washington, the Financial Times reported Jan. 25.) In addition, there had been considerable disagreement among Mexican officials over whether the oil should be exploited quickly for short-term economic advantage or should be saved "for future generations," according to the New York Times Feb. 18.

However, the president, Jose Lopez Portillo, had embarked on a program of accelerated exploitation and exports of crude oil, the Times reported. Lopez Portillo had acted not only because of Mexico's economic crisis and its desperate need for foreign exchange, but because of his confidence in the size of the reserves, the newspaper said.

Nevertheless, Mexico faced major financial and technological problems in extracting the oil. Pemex was particularly hampered by the enormous cost of extraction, delays in obtaining necessary equipment from abroad, and a shortage of skilled Mexican engineers and technicians, the Times reported.

In January Mexico had raised its crude sales price to $12.65 per barrel, 10% higher than OPEC's previous base of $11.50 per barrel but only 2.8% higher than the $12.30 per barrel Mexico had been charging, it was reported Jan. 14. Eleven OPEC nations had increased their oil prices by 10% effective Jan. 1.

$88 million worth of petrobonds issued—Mexico's first issue of petrobonds, which went on sale April 29, were heavily oversubscribed by April 18, the Journal of Commerce reported. The issue of $88 million worth of bonds was backed by the purchase of 7.2 million barrels of petroleum by the government development bank, Nacional Financiera, which was the issuing agency. The petrobonds would have a maturity value pegged to the world price of oil and were expected to stimulate domestic savings.

Tourism up. Earnings from tourism in the last quarter of 1976 and first quarter of 1977 totaled $409 million, up by 60% over earnings in the same period 12 months earlier, it was reported June 17.

Agrarian Problems

President backs '76 land seizures. President Jose Lopez Portillo told farmers in Sinaloa State May 4 that he could not return land that had been expropriated from them in November 1976 for distribution among peasants.

Lopez Portillo's predecessor, Luis Echeverria Alvarez, had seized a total of 253,000 acres in Sinaloa, comprising 94,-000 acres of irrigated wheat land and 159,-000 acres of scrubby grazing land. Nearly half of the wheat acreage had been expropriated illegally, Lopez Portillo admitted, but he warned that taking it back from its new owners could "set the country ablaze."

Instead, the president said, the government would offer the Sinaloa farmers compensation of about $500 to $1,700 per acre. He recognized that farmers might reject the offer and pursue court cases to regain their land, but he warned that the government would use all its power to prevent the land from being taken from the peasants who now owned it.

The Mexican government was plagued with agrarian problems, including the landlessness of at least four million peasants and the marked inefficiency of the *ejido,* the most common form of land ownership in the country.

More than 70% of Mexico's farmland was divided into about 30,000 *ejidos,* tracts of land that were owned by the government but subdivided into sections of up to 50 acres each for farming by individual peasants. The government was reluctant to alter the *ejido* system because it was a symbol of land reform undertaken in the 1910-17 Mexican Revolution and because *ejido* tenants provided essential support for the ruling Institutional Revolutionary Party.

Nevertheless, most *ejidos* were only subsistence plots, too small to use the modern technology available for large-scale farming. Most never had been provided with the credit, machinery and technical assistance necessary to make them work effectively, the Washington Post noted. Consequently, the 20% of Mexican exports that were agricultural were produced almost totally by the country's privately owned farms.

In Sinaloa, the Post reported, 77% of the farmland was controlled by *ejidos* and 23% by private owners. But the large mechanized private farms produced 66% of the total value of crops in the state and all of the $200-million worth of winter fruits and vegetables exported from Sinaloa to the U.S. in 1976.

Turning the *ejidos* into collective farms that emulated the large mechanized estates had been suggested to several earlier Mexican governments and promoted by ex-President Echeverria, but the idea had not taken root, the Post noted.

U.S. Relations

Lopez Portillo urges 'sensible' U.S. role. President Jose Lopez Portillo urged the U.S. Feb. 17 to establish "a sensible" policy toward Latin America. He said a backlash against the U.S. could occur if it allowed "private interests" to control its economic relations with Latin America. He made the remarks in an address to Congress during an official visit to Washington.

"If a new international economic order, based on rights and obligations, does not become effective, it is not surprising that weak countries should despair," Lopez Portillo told Congress. "Nor should it be surprising that we will seek to unite in order to save our weakness when faced with lack of understanding or abuse."

Lopez Portillo went on to say (as recorded in the Congressional Record Feb. 17):

"We are neighbors, and we shall go on being neighbors as long as the earth circles the sun....

"There are also questions pending between this great nation and developing countries: the Middle East conflict, currently in abeyance, with its implications for oil politics, and in Asia and Africa, problems of hegemonic influence, of poverty, oppression and racial discrimination, which forebode international turbulence in the near future.

"It would appear that for the United States, the basic problems with Latin America are limited to the negotiations on the Panama Canal and the evolution of relations with Cuba. The repression of human rights in Chile constitutes another though lesser irritant, due to the reaction of the American liberal sector.

"As far as Mexico is concerned, a special policy was established in 1933, when President Roosevelt stated: "In the field of world policy I would dedicate this nation to the policy of the good neighbor— the neighbor who resolutely respects himself and because he does so, respects the rights of others—the neighbor who respects his obligations and respects the sanctity of his agreements in and with a world of neighbors"....

"A whole series of factors has transformed the traditional relations between Mexico and the United States. Financing, trade, currency, foreign investment, tourism, migrant labor, drug traffic, prisoners, and relations with the Third World have all taken on new political dimensions.

"All these problems derive from the different levels of development on either side of the long border which is the busiest in the world. In order of importance, you are our first client and we are your fourth. The balance of trade is very unfavourable to us and, at times, restrictions are placed on imports that might eliminate the deficit, thus aggravating our economic problems by causing unemployment. It is understandable that many of our men want to work in your country in order to improve their standard of living, as has been the case in other times and places. Due to these and other well-known and reprehensible reasons, some of our people, together with some of yours, cultivate drug crops and deal in narcotics. Therefore many of the problems that bother you the most are closely related to our economic problems.

" Mexico must solve its own problems and you should examine those of your decisions which may adversely affect or undermine our development efforts and, above all, the spirit of the political ideal of international coexistence.

" Mexico has never been, nor is it now, the leader of any continent or group of countries. Our past major conflicts have taught us hard lessons. We fought alone, and alone won our independence and liberties. Neither do we proclaim isolation, because it is politically unattainable in the world in which we live. If we propose solutions to improve the living conditions of different peoples, we do so with deep respect for their national characters, as we are convinced that universality can only be attained through national solutions. It is not a matter of leadership, but of participation.

"I have come to contribute an awareness of reality and a conception of problems from our point of view, which we ask you to take into consideration. I have come to agree to continue reaching agreements, because neither dialogue nor analysis should cease.

"I am here to remind you that our common American continent continues south of the border, that it requires from your powerful nation the establishment of a sensible policy based on efficient mechanisms that will help to eliminate or reduce fundamental problems; a policy aimed at achieving a lasting equilibrium that only your government, as such, can establish, because the private interests that today almost exclusively rule our relationship are unable, or perhaps, unwilling to attain that balance.

"I have come to insist that unless a new international economic order, based on rights and obligations, is put into effect, it will not be surprising if weak countries despair in the absence of guarantees of fair treatment that often means survival itself and seek to unite, as the strong do, in order to overcome our weakness when faced with lack of understanding or abuse. This is not a crime, nor does it deserve punishment; it deserves a solution.

"In short, we, like you, want a better world for our children; we want to be freer and more respected; we want peace and justice. To a great extent, at least where my country is concerned, this depends mainly on the industrialized countries...."

Lopez Portillo focused on the same themes in an appearance before the National Press Club in Washington Feb. 15. He called for "a reasonable world order" and an international system based on "economic rights and duties" that would help spur development of poorer nations.

Lopez Portillo had conferred with President Carter at the White House Feb. 15. Their joint communique, issued Feb. 17, pledged close examination of mutual problems and regular consultation "on the search for worldwide peace, economic betterment and respect for the rights of man."

In welcoming his guest to the White House Feb. 14, Carter had pledged to work closely with Lopez Portillo on a personal and an official basis to tie the countries together in a "continual demonstration of common purpose, common hope, common confidence and common friendship."

In talking with reporters Feb. 15, Lopez Portillo said increased Mexican exports to the U.S. would create jobs at home and even solve the problem of Mexican migrant workers illegally crossing into the U.S. "To the extent that Mexico reestablishes its economic equilibrium," he said, "the problem [of illegal migrant workers] will be solved."

Lopez Portillo also offered his "good offices" Feb. 15 in helping normalize relations between the U.S. and Cuba.

U.S., Mexico sign commodity pact. The U.S. and Mexico signed a commodity agreement Dec. 2 that called for bilateral tariff reductions for Mexico's export of tropical fruits and vegetables and U.S. food shipments to Mexico.

The pact was the first negotiated between industrial and developing nations during the on-going Tokyo round of trade talks sponsored by the General Agreement on Tariffs and Trade. The pact was the first formal trade agreement concluded between Mexico and the U.S. since 1942.

Carter's program for illegal aliens. President Carter announced his proposals

Aug. 4 for dealing with the problem of illegal aliens in the U.S.

Appearing at a White House briefing, Carter urged Congress to act quickly on the proposals, which he said would "markedly reduce" the flow of such aliens into the country. The number of illegal aliens within the U.S. was estimated to range from four million to 12 million.

Basically, the President offered a permanent resident alien status to illegal aliens who entered the U.S. before Jan. 1, 1970 and had resided in the U.S. continuously since then.

Those who arrived between 1970 and Jan. 1, 1977 would be eligible for a temporary resident alien status for five years.

Federal social services, such as food stamps and welfare payments, would not be extended to those with the temporary status, only to permanent resident aliens. The latter, by law, also would be eligible for citizenship after five years of the permanent resident status.

Illegal aliens entering the country after Jan. 1 would be subject to deportation, as under current law applying to all illegal aliens. Application for the new status of permanent or temporary resident alien would have to be made within a year of enactment of the legislation.

Because a job was the major attraction for illegal entry of an alien, Carter proposed civil fines of up to $1,000 per illegal worker for employers who "knowingly" hired illegal aliens. Criminal penalties were proposed for those acting as brokers for employers hiring such aliens.

The President said enforcement would be limited to cases where a "pattern or practice" of hiring illegal aliens was detected.

Under the President's plan, Attorney General Griffin Bell was to determine a system of identification documents for the aliens. One of these would be the Social Security card, which would be accepted as proof of the legal status for a prospective worker.

The President also proposed to strengthen the U.S. Border Patrol with an additional 2,000 new agents along the U.S.-Mexico border, a major crossing for illegal aliens.

Andrew Young on tour—Andrew Young, the U.S. ambassador to the United Nations, visited Mexico Aug. 7 to stress the Carter Administration's interest in good relations with Mexico. He arrived in Mexico City Aug. 7 and conferred the next day with President Jose Lopez Portillo and Foreign Minister Santiago Roel. Their discussions apparently centered on President Carter's plan to resolve the problem of illegal Mexican immigration to the U.S.

Young called Carter's plan "one big step in the overall process of resolving the [illegal alien] problem," but he conceded that Mexico was not happy with it. Mexican officials wanted more trade concessions from the U.S. to help boost the Mexican economy, create more jobs and thereby relieve the pressure on Mexicans to emigrate. "Mexico will never be satisfied," Young noted, "until it exports commodities and goods to the United States and not people."

Despite tension in his talks with Mexican officials, Young described his Mexican visit as "very informative and very productive." He said he had covered "an amazing amount of material" in his talks with Lopez Portillo and Roel.

U.S. migrant plan scored—President Carter's plan to reduce illegal immigration into the U.S. was denounced by Mexico's leading expert on the problem, it was reported Aug. 28.

Jorge Bustamante, a teacher at the Colegio de Mexico and a consultant to President Jose Lopez Portillo's commission on migration, said Carter's proposals were "unilateral" and "unfriendly" measures that "imply a total lack of sensitivity to the economic situation of Mexico today."

The return of Mexican migrants from the U.S. would "bring social disruption to the border areas, where unemployment levels already are explosively high," Bustamante asserted. Migration to the U.S. had long been an escape valve for Mexico, whose economy was creating only about 150,000 of the 400,000 new jobs needed every year.

Bustamante's feelings reportedly were shared by most top Mexican officials, but the government was not making its dissatisfaction public because this might threaten its good relations with the U.S. In his nine months in office, Lopez Portillo had greatly reduced the tension in U.S.-

Mexican relations that existed under his predecessor, Luis Echeverria Alvarez.

Bustamante had proposed a plan in 1976 to attack the roots of the migrant problem. He suggested that labor-intensive units to process agricultural products be established in areas from which Mexican peasants were migrating. To discourage emigration to the U.S., the units could give preference in hiring to Mexicans who had no record of arrest by U.S. immigration authorities before the date the units were established.

The units would be privately owned, but they could be financed by the Mexican government or by international lending agencies. The U.S. could play an indirect role in the financing by agreeing to buy the units' products for its foreign aid program, Bustamante suggested.

The plan had not been implemented, apparently because of Mexico's acute shortage of capital resources. But the U.S. was considering an industrial-development aid program to help Mexico create jobs and thus reduce the flow of migrants northward, the Washington Post reported Sept. 23.

U.S. report on American prisoners in Mexico. Secretary of State Cyrus Vance submitted to Congress March 4 a report on progress toward achieving full respect for the human and legal rights of U.S. citizens detained in Mexico. The report details the continuing problems relating to the physical abuse of Americans at the time of arrest, failure to promptly notify the U.S. of an arrest and failure to respond to diplomatic notes protesting certain cases. According to the report, as published in the Congressional Record March 14:

During hearings before the House International Relations Committee from July, 1975 through January, 1976, the Department reported on its findings in some 475 cases of United States citizens who were detained in Mexico as of July 1, 1975. The Department indicated during those hearings that prisoners' allegations of physical abuse and denial of human and legal rights were substantiated in a disturbing number of cases in which U.S. citizens are not receiving the full rights guaranteed to them under Mexican law.

During the period from July 1, 1975 through January 15, 1977, over 1500 Americans were arrested in Mexico. A vast majority of that number were involved in minor offenses and the arrestees were released after only one or two days in jail and/or the payment of a fine. During this period, there were 58 cases of substantiated physical abuse at the time of arrest. In another 47 cases the evidence was not sufficient to reach a clear conclusion. There were also 17 cases wherein Americans were subjected to unscrupulous financial practices by attorneys who extracted large fees from the prisoner and/or his family for services which they then failed to provide and another 61 cases where the evidence of malpractice was not sufficient to reach a conclusion. In cases of substantiated abuse the Embassy at Mexico City and our consular posts throughout Mexico have made and continue to make protests to the Mexican authorities at both the local and federal levels. I should point out, however, that protests have not been made in those cases where the arrested American citizens specifically requested that no protest be made. The protests are normally made both orally and in writing to the appropriate local officials. In many instances, the cases are documented by constituent posts and forwarded to the Embassy at Mexico City so that protests can be lodged with the Mexican Foreign Ministry. In such cases, the Embassy sends a formal note of protest to the Ministry with a copy to the Mexican Attorney General. These notes include a description of the case, a sworn statement by both the prisoner and the consular officer where appropriate, and a request that a full investigation be made into the allegation of abuse. To date, the Embassy has not received satisfactory replies to the vast majority of such notes.

While it is true that the total number of cases of substantiated abuse represents a small percentage of the total number of arrests, we cannot be complacent. As was noted in our previous report, as long as one American citizen is not being accorded his human and legal rights under Mexican law, we will not be satisfied.

Timely notification to our consular officers of the arrest of an American in Mexico and subsequent early access to the arrestee continue to be major problems, which we have discussed repeatedly with officials of the Mexican Government at the highest levels. We have stressed in these discussions the importance the United States Government places on obtaining early notification of an arrest and subsequent prompt access to the detainee in accordance with the Vienna Convention on Consular Relations to which both of our countries are signatories. While we have succeeded in convincing the Mexican Federal Government of our position, practical results on the local level remain spotty and uneven. During the last eighteen months, there were some 269 cases where we did not consider notification of an arrest by police authorities as adequate.

In many cases the initial information on the arrest case came from outside sources such as friends or relatives rather than from local authorities. Once notification has been received, however, the gaining of con-

sular access to the arrested American is usually no longer a problem. Conditions of communication and or transportation, however, can be an obstacle, particularly in the many cases where the arrest takes place several hundred miles from the nearest consular office. In these instances initial contact with the arrested citizen is made by telephone and a consular officer visits as soon thereafter as practical. . . .

During the period covered by this report a new Mexican administration has assumed office and we have discussed the problem with newly installed officials. President Lopez Portillo is, of course, aware of the problem and, as you know, alluded to it in his address to the House of Representatives during his recent State Visit to Washington. We are hopeful that our continuing discussion of the plight of U.S. citizens arrested in Mexico with the new Mexican Government officials will lead to rapid improvement.

U.S. drug offenders released. Attorney General Oscar Flores announced April 16 that Mexico had freed 15 American drug offenders under a new policy to release persons arrested for possessing small amounts of marijuana, cocaine or heroin that were clearly intended for personal use.

Another 20 Americans were reported to have been released by May 11, when Flores announced that the new program would benefit 1,943 prisoners, including a total of 100 U.S. citizens. The U.S. Embassy in Mexico City said June 21 that "50 to 60" Americans were being freed, "including those who have already gone home or will be released in the next few days."

Flores said April 16 that the new program would benefit persons who had been arrested but not yet tried for possessing small amounts of drugs. Persons already convicted and sentenced would have to serve out their prison terms, which generally ranged from five to 14 years.

U.S.-Mexican prisoner exchange bill. President Carter Oct. 28 signed legislation that would allow U.S. citizens held in Mexican jails to be transferred, if the prisoners requested, to U.S. jails. Mexican prisoners in U.S. jails would have the same right to request transfer to their native country.

The treaty providing for the prisoner exchanges had been ratified by the U.S.

Senate July 21. The bill signed by Carter Oct. 28 was enabling legislation that allowed the treaty to be implemented.

Although other countries had prisoner exchange treaties, this agreement was the U.S.' first. Consequently, the treaty and enabling legislation had been fashioned with the idea of using it as a model for future agreements with other countries.

Under the agreement, a prisoner had to formally consent to all provisions of the transfer before he could be transferred. One of those provisions was that the country that convicted a prisoner retained jurisdiction over any appeal that prisoner might make of his conviction, even if the appeal were made after the transfer.

The provision attempted to forestall any possible diplomatic embarrassments that might occur if prisoners were able to win reversals of foreign convictions through appeals in their native courts. Specifically, it was feared that U.S. citizens convicted abroad might succeed, after being transferred to the U.S., in having their convictions overturned on the grounds that the foreign courts had not abided by U.S. conceptions of defendants' rights.

The enabling legislation had passed the Senate by voice vote Sept. 21. The House of Representatives cleared it Oct. 25, 400–15.

About 275 of the 568 American prisoners in Mexico would be eligible to serve out their terms in the U.S. More than half of the American prisoners had been jailed on charges of transporting cocaine from South America or dealing in Mexican marijuana or heroin to be sold in the U.S., the Washington Post reported April 17.

The transfer program, Flores had said April 16, was designed to reduce the chance that an American would be subjected to arbitrary arrest and to extortion by Mexican police and lawyers. U.S. consular officials said fewer Americans had complained of extortion, rough treatment and torture by Mexican police since the inauguration of President Jose Lopez Portillo in December 1976.

Prisoners exchanged—The U.S. and Mexico Dec. 9 made their first exchange of prisoners under the new treaty that took effect Nov. 30. Sixty-one U.S. citizens who had been held in Mexican jails were flown to San Diego, while 36 Mexican citizens who had been serving time in the U.S. were flown to Mexico City.

Accompanying the first group of Americans was an 18-month-old child born to one of the women convicts in prison in Mexico.

There were about 600 U.S. citizens held in Mexican prisons before the transfers began and about 1,200 Mexican citizens held in U.S. prisons. Not all prisoners were eligible for transfer under the treaty, and a prisoner, even if eligible, could choose not to be transferred.

(Mexican prisoners held in U.S. state prisons could not be transferred unless the state enacted enabling legislation. The Justice Department reported Nov. 30 that only Texas had so far passed such legislation.)

A federal prison official Dec. 12 said that 240 U.S. citizens had been already repatriated or would be within a few days. Forty-one of those prisoners were released Dec. 13 under U.S. penitentiary rules that mandated the release of prisoners who had served two-thirds of their sentences or were credited with time for good behavior.

Most of the other prisoners repatriated to the U.S. would be transferred to federal prisons after receiving parole hearings.

Many of the repatriated U.S. citizens were critical of the Mexican prisons. They charged that the Mexican prisons lacked adequate medical facilities, that prisoners were threatened with physical abuse to make them sign confessions, and that Mexican lawyers and prison authorities extorted money from prisoners and from people seeking to aid them.

At the same time, Mexican prisoners who chose to return to their native country had harsh things to say about U.S. prisons. Enrique Granados, one of the repatriated Mexicans, charged that the "treatment we got was savage and inhumane," the Mexican press reported Dec. 13. Granados said he had been "beaten savagely and a friend had several broken ribs." Granados added, "Homosexuality is rampant in that country—there are no conjugal visits like we have here."

Most of the U.S. citizens imprisoned in Mexico had been convicted on drug charges. Many of them complained that they were victims of a Nixon Administration attempt to crack down on drug traffic between Mexico and the U.S. They said that the Mexican government, under pressure from the Nixon Administration, had imposed harsh sentences for minor drug offenses, while major drug traffickers were often able to avoid convictions by bribes or other means.

Other Developments

Diaz Ordaz post stirs controversy. President Jose Lopez Portillo created a political controversy in April by appointing former President Gustavo Diaz Ordaz as Mexico's new ambassador to Spain.

Carlos Fuentes, Mexico's ambassador to France, resigned April 7 to protest the appointment. The renowned novelist charged that Diaz Ordaz, as president of Mexico, had been "the only man responsible for the bloody repression of students and workers at the Plaza of the Three Cultures in Mexico City in October 1968."

In the incident to which Fuentes referred, police and soldiers had opened fire on a crowd of demonstrating students and other Mexicans, killing more than 300 persons, according to unofficial estimates. The shootings had come to be known as the Tlatelolco massacre, after the area of the city in which they occurred.

Diaz Ordaz' appointment and Fuentes' resignation caused mixed reactions in Mexico. Some government officials accused Fuentes of being "impulsive and immature," while others remarked that "Tlatelolco cannot be forgotten so easily," the newspaper Excelsior reported. In Spain, meanwhile, the appointment was criticized by one of the most influential newspapers, the Madrid daily El Pais.

It seemed "paradoxical," El Pais said in an editorial April 12, that a country that had refused to recognize the fascist government of Generalissimo Francisco Franco "should now send as its ambassador the man who, from his repression of the railway strike in 1959, when he was interior minister, to the horrible killings at Tlatelolco in October of 1968, when he was president of the republic, has shown himself to be the most

repressive politician in Mexican history. . . ."

Diaz Ordaz defended himself April 12, asserting he was "a clean Mexican whose hands aren't covered with blood." He said he had "defended" and "preserved" Mexican institutions at great personal cost, and that only 30 to 40 "troublemakers" and "bystanders" had died at Tlatelolco.

Lopez Portillo added his defense of the former president April 22, asserting Diaz Ordaz was "the only president in the world who, in a personal manner, faced up to a nonconformist and disoriented youth."

The Mexican Communist Party and other leftist groups denounced Diaz Ordaz' appointment April 22, saying they would stage protests at his Senate confirmation hearings. However, the former president received congressional approval May 11 without any apparent difficulty.

Diaz Ordaz' appointment was a calculated risk by Lopez Portillo to win conservative support as he released some leftist political prisoners and introduced a few reforms to open up the political system, according to the Latin America Political Report May 6.

Tlatelolco was one of the most controversial and unresolved issues in recent Mexican history. There had been no government inquiry to establish what had happened, who was responsible or even how many people had died, according to the Latin America Political Report May 20. Documentary evidence had disappeared from hospitals, the Red Cross and government files. But while these details were unavailable, it was clear that the massacre had ended a student protest movement that had grown to include significant sectors of the urban middle class in the provinces as well as Mexico City, the Report noted.

Echeverria named UNESCO envoy. President Jose Lopez Portillo named his predecessor, Luis Echeverria Alvarez, to be Mexico's ambassador to the United Nations Educational, Scientific and Cultural Organization (UNESCO), it was reported July 8. Echeverria had been a roving ambassador to developing nations since May.

Nicaragua

Human Rights & U.S. Aid

Church & others score rights abuses.
The archbishop and six bishops of
Nicaragua's Roman Catholic Church accused government forces of resorting to
widespread torture, rape and summary
executions in their campaign to wipe out
leftist guerrillas.

"We are anguished by the suffering of
our people, be they urban or rural, rich or
poor, civilian or military, who cry out to
God for protection of the right to life and
the peaceful enjoyment of the product of
their labor," the church leaders said in a
pastoral letter issued in January and
quoted by the Costa Rican newspaper Excelsior Feb. 6.

The terror was centered in the northern
provinces of Zelaya, Matagalpa and
Segovia, the major operating area of the
insurgent Sandinista Liberation Front.
Documents prepared by the church listed
the names of hundreds of peasants in the
region who had been executed or had
simply disappeared since the National
Guard began its campaign against the
Sandinistas in early 1975, the New York
Times reported March 2.

Capuchin priests from the U.S. who had
visited the area said many peasants had
been shot for suspected collaboration with the guerrillas, according to the
Times. These priests and other sources
confirmed that some remote hamlets had

been bombed by light aircraft of the National Guard. Other Capuchins quoted
Feb. 25 by the London newsletter Latin
America said the use of helicopters to
maintain "free-fire" zones had driven 80%
of the rural population out of the region.

Capuchin missionaries sent an open letter to President Gen. Anastasio Somoza
Debayle in June 1976, citing examples of
rape, torture and executions by national
guardsmen, but the terror reportedly continued unabated. A spokesman for
Somoza told the New York Times that
many of the church's charges were false
and others were exaggerated.

Faced with government intransigence,
the normally conservative Nicaraguan
bishops issued the pastoral letter. Censorship kept the letter out of the Nicaraguan
press, but Nicaraguan priests read the letter to their parishioners at church services.
Church leaders and other opponents of
Somoza's harsh rule also appealed to the
U.S. to put pressure on Somoza to respect
human rights, the Times reported.

"The U.S. has always given moral and
material backing to dictatorships such as
Nicaragua's," said Pedro Joaquin Cha-
morro, editor of the frequently censored
Managua newspaper La Prensa. "It is now
time for President Carter to show that his
fine words [on respect for human rights]
can become a reality."

James D. Theberge, U.S. ambassador
to Nicaragua, told the Times that the U.S.

had "reason to believe that some of the allegations of human rights violations are accurate and our concern has been made clear to the Nicaraguan government on various occasions during the past year." A U.S. State Department spokesman said March 4, "We have information about violations of human rights in Nicaragua and we are making intensive efforts to gather more information on the basis of this data."

Eleven prominent Latin American intellectuals sent a letter to President Carter urging him to end all U.S. political and economic support for Gen. Somoza's government, it was reported March 25. The letter decried the "40 years of immoral and inhuman tyranny of the Somoza family" in Nicaragua and described the ways in which the Somozas had used their political power to become the country's dominant economic force. Signatories of the letter included Carlos Pellicer, a Mexican senator, and Miguel Otero Silva, publisher of Venezuela's leading newspaper, El Nacional.

Pastoral letter issued—The pastoral letter issued Jan. 8 by Nicaraguan bishops was entered by Rep. Edward I. Koch (D, N.Y.) in the Congressional Record May 4. Among excerpts:

We are distressed by the suffering of our people, be it urban dwellers, or campesinos, rich or poor, civilians or military personnel who beg to God in search for the protection of the right to life and the peaceful enjoyment of the product to their work.

Unfortunately many of the sufferings are caused and produced by many of our own Nicaraguan brothers.

With no partisan political motives we present and recall here some of the many facts with the only intention of obtaining the sincere involvement of each and all of us who are committed to the search for peace.

The state of terror force many of our campesinos to flee in desperation away from their own places and farmland, in the Mountains of Zelaya, Matagalpa, and Las Segovias.

The arbitrary accusations and subsequent detentions because of old quarrels and personal envy still continue to disturb the peace.

Inquiries of those under suspicion still continue utilizing methods which are humiliating and inhuman: from tortures and rapes to executions without a previous civil or military trial.

It has been verified that many villages have been practically abandoned: houses and personal property have been burned and the people, desperate and without help, have fled.

These action, far from bringing justice, rather inflame passions and disturb the public order. They even put the government officials beyond the jurisdiction of the institutional laws of the nation and of all sane principle of public order, and similarly to the so-called freedom movements that call themselves liberated but that actually favor the free burst of passions, lead to personal vendettas and end up in 'new lords' who take charge of the government with no regard for the right to enjoy the exercise of human liberties....

As an actual consequence of these events the confusion and ills of the nation are growing:

On the one hand the accumulation of land and wealth in the hands of a few is increasing.

On the other hand, the powerless campesinos are deprived of their farmlands through threats and are taken advantage of because of the state of emergency.

Many crimes are left aside without the corresponding legal sanctions, which damages the respect for the fundamental rights.

The number of prisoners who have not been presented for trial and who cannot have legal recourse is increasing.

Another violation that disturbs the practice of the fundamental liberties is the interference in the religious realm.

In some villages of the Segovias the commanders demand special permission for each religious meeting of Catholics.

In other locations in the mountains of Zelaya and Matagalpa, the patrols have occupied the Catholic chapels using them as barracks.

Some Catholic delegates of the Word of God have been forced to suspend their cooperation with the missionary priests.

There are cases in which delegates of the Word have been taken prisoners by members of the Army, have been tortured and others have disappeared.

Some committee leaders of grassroots communities have run the same fate....

National guardsmen charged with reign of terror. Nicaraguan bishops cited by the Washington Post June 13 said national guardsmen were conducting a "reign of terror and unjust extermination" in the northern province of Zelaya under the pretext of fighting left-wing guerrillas.

Priests, schoolteachers and peasants in Zelaya charged that the soldiers were working in league with large landowners who extended their holdings in the area by having small landowners and peasants executed. The soldiers not only killed local residents but stole their property and raped local women, the Zelayans charged.

The National Guard had occupied 26 rural chapels and turned them into barracks and torture centers, according to Capuchin friars from the U.S. who ran the Vicariate of Zelaya.

Contrary to the National Guard's assertions, few peasants aided the leftist guerrilla group operating in Zelaya, which called itself the Sandinista National Liberation Front, the Post reported. One farmer quoted by the newspaper said: "We are like the meat in the middle of the sandwich. If we don't give the guerrillas food, they threaten to kill us. If we give them food, then the military kills us. All we want is to be left alone."

The Post article said:

> According to informed sources, some 1,200 acres along the Iyas River in the Sofana district of western Zelaya were ceded to the local military chief, Col. Gonzalo Everts, last year, after the National Guard shot 40 Sofana peasants, including the family who owned the land.
> Everts' successor, Col. Gustavo Medina, recently authorized the takeover of lands south of the Dudu River by a large cattle rancher with adjacent holdings along the Matagalpa-Zelaya frontier, informed sources said. Of the 100 peasant families living on these lands, only 18 are left, the rest having fled or 'disappeared,' meaning they probably were shot by the military....

U.S. aid cutoff move defeated. The Carter Administration disclosed that it was withholding economic aid from Nicaragua and refusing to sign a new security assistance pact with its government because of alleged human rights abuses, it was reported April 7. The move, however, caused considerable debate in the House of Representatives, which finally defeated an amendment to cut off military aid to Nicaragua.

Charles W. Bray 3rd, deputy assistant secretary of state for inter-American affairs, told a congressional subcommittee that the economic and military assistance would be withheld "until it becomes clearer" that the human rights situation in Nicaragua has improved. The aid amounted to $20 million, Bray said.

Bray accused the National Guard, Nicaragua's only armed force, of resorting to "brutal and, at times, harshly repressive tactics in maintaining internal order." The National Guard was commanded by Nicaragua's president, Gen. Anastasio Somoza Debayle.

Despite Bray's testimony, the Carter Administration was asking Congress to appropriate several million dollars in aid to Nicaragua for fiscal 1978, presumably to be used as leverage to get the Nicaraguan government to show more respect for human rights.

However, the House Appropriations Committee June 14 passed an amendment to a military assistance bill that would cut off all military aid to Nicaragua. Rep. Edward I. Koch (D, N.Y.), one of the amendment's proponents, had cited allegations of human rights abuses made in January by Nicaraguan Roman Catholic bishops.

A House Appropriations subcommittee in late April investigated Nicaragua's human rights situation. The Nicaraguan government charged April 19, before the probe began, that the subcommittee had "no legal or moral right to pass judgment" on Nicaragua.

In a final move, the House June 22 overturned the Appropriations Committee amendment that would have removed $3.1 million slated for Nicaragua from the foreign military assistance bill. The vote was the result of an extensive lobbying effort by Nicaraguan representatives in Washington.

Among those who had lobbied against the amendment was the Washington law firm of Cramer, Haber and Becker, which represented the Nicaraguan government and was paid for its services by the Nicaraguan National Development Institute. A senior partner of the firm met many House members beginning in April to persuade them to vote against the amendment.

Another congressman, Rep. Clarence Long (D, Md.), apparently misrepresented the State Department's position on Nicaragua in an effort to defeat the amendment against military aid. According to Inter Press Service Aug. 6, rumors began to circulate in mid-June that the State Department was opposing the amendment. To squelch the rumors, Assistant Secretary of State Terence Todman wrote Long a letter June 21 in which he reiterated the State Department's support of the amendment. The next day, however, Long told Rep. Edward I. Koch (D, N.Y.), a strong opponent of military aid to Nicaragua, that Todman wanted the military aid to go through. Koch related this in a letter to President Carter July 1. Long refused to comment on the incident, according to Inter Press.

Nicaragua's strongest advocate in the House apparently was Rep. John M. Murphy (D, N.Y.), who declared June 21 that there were no political prisoners, executions, disappearances or torture in Nicaragua. Murphy reminded the House that Nicaragua had always complied when the U.S. asked it to speak up for Israel at the United Nations or to criticize the Soviet Union regarding disarmament.

Kennedy supports military aid cut. Sen. Edward Kennedy (D, Mass.) Aug. 5 announced his support for the amendment to cut military aid to Nicaragua. During Senate debate over foreign assistance, Kennedy said (according to the Congressional Record):

" We have been asked to appropriate $3.1 million in military assistance to Nicaragua—$600,000 for military training and $2.5 million for foreign military sales credits. This is in addition to $15 million in new economic assistance and over $58 million currently in the pipeline. The amendment I am now calling up would strike only the $3.1 million in military aid from the bill. It would therefore leave untouched the over $70 million in economic aid, but it would terminate our material support and implied moral condonement of that nation's brutal military establishment....

"The United States has a special historic responsibility to the people of Nicaragua. It was U.S. Marines who established and trained what the State Department has referred to as "the personal instrument" of the Somoza family for 40 years—the Nicaraguan National Guard and its auxiliary paramilitary formations. It has been the U.S. Agency for International Development that has provided the Somoza regime with almost 15 percent of its annual governmental expenditures. It has been U.S. Security assistance that has both trained and maintained the present national guard and its paramilitary auxiliaries, and it is our continuing military aid in particular that indicates to the Somoza regime and the world that we continue to condone prevailing conditions of arbitrary arrest, political suppression, murder, and atrocity....

"Current Amnesty International evidence, based on its latest mission to Nicaragua, has documented a policy of systematic torture and atrocities against detainees of the Nicaraguan National Guard. It has recorded continuing incidents of prolonged beatings with fists, rubber hoses, and rifle butts. Using cattle prods or wires connected to regular household current, severe electric shocks are applied to the most sensitive parts of the body.

"One particularly sadistic torture is referred to by national guard interrogators as 'el telephono', or 'the telephone', where prisoners' ears are struck so hard as to explode the eardrums, causing total or partial deafness.

Then, there are the detention camps—characterized by one religious source as little more than "corrals with the addition of armed guards"—where hundreds of campesinos have been imprisoned. Such allegations have been corroborated by a letter signed by 31 Capuchins missionaries—all American citizens—who cite the "disappearance" of over 200 campesinos over the past 2 years....

"The Somoza family has for 40 years relied on the American-trained national guard as its brutal means to power—State Department witnesses have referred to it as the "personal instrument" and the "principal power base" of the Somozas. The national guard depends on the United States for its military equipment, weapons and the training of its officer corps.

"All graduates of the Nicaraguan Military Academy receive postgraduate studies at the School of Americas—the American-run, staffed, and financed college of military science located in the Canal Zone. How can we possibly disclaim any responsibility for the national guard's role in the current state of affairs in Nicaragua, when 75 percent of its officer corps has received training from our own military?...

"The primary arguments for continuing American military support of Nicaragua are threefold: That such assistance enhances U.S. security and prevents a Cuban-inspired takeover in Nicaragua; that the Somoza government is one of our strongest supporters in Latin America; and that severing this link eliminates a key bargaining chip for future efforts to foster respect for human rights in Nicaragua. I remain completely unconvinced by each of these arguments.

"When asked on March 24, 1977, ' What would be lost to the United States and what security interests would be violated if the committee suspended all aid to Nicaragua in view of some of the gross violations of human rights in that country', Under Secretary of State Lucy Benson told the House Foreign Operations Subcommittte: 'I cannot thing, of a single thing.' The threat of Cuban intervention is minimal, according to all reasonably objective observers. Insurgent strength is estimated at only 50 men in Nicaragua—this is hardly a serious threat to a nation of 2.3 million with a military force of around 7,000. Surely the proponents of the Nicaraguan regime cannot be considering that Nicaragua might 'go Communist' ?

"The second argument is that Nicaragua under the Somoza family has been "our closest friend" in South America. It is true Nicaraguan foreign policy has been closely alined with our own, from support during the Korean war to providing bases for the Bay of Pigs invasion. But are we going to tell the world that American morality in foreign policy is for sale, that the closer you aline your foreign policy with ours the more guns we will give to oppress your peoples—and to better the bargain, we will even look the other way?

"This is not hyperbole. We have just learned that 5,000 M–16 rifles have been shipped to the 7,000-man Nigaraguan National Guard, financed by foreign military sales credits for fiscal year 1977. This is the result of an executive branch decision made during the transition period between the Ford and Carter administrations. The House did not have this information when it voted to appropriate military aid to Nicaragua. All it was told was that the administration would not approve further security assistance agreements until the Nicaraguan human rights situation improved. I submit that this shipment makes a mockery of those assurances.

"We should examine the friendship of our "closest ally in Latin America" in some detail. Following allegations of theft and corruption in the allocation of international disaster funding in the wake of last years' earthquake, the Agency for International Development commissioned a report by a reputable firm of Nicaraguan lawyers which revealed the 'direct participation of government employees in the land transactions, prior knowledge of land transfers and gain thereof by government officials,

inflated land values of up to 1,156 percent over a 3-month period, and lack of any ethics in transactions in which the public sector was involved.' What this represents in plain and simple language is a well-documented, and government sanctioned rip-off of millions of dollars of taxpayers' money by the "best friend" of the United States in Latin America.

"Nor can I accept the reasoning of the third proposition—that terminating military aid eliminates a key U.S. bargaining chip for human rights in Nicaragua. Over $70 million in economic aid remains unimpaired, including $185 million appropriated for fiscal year 1978. This surely is a legitimate source of diplomatic leverage.

"At the same time, termination of military assistance—the most intimately related to the Nicaraguan National Guard—will serve as an unequivocal signal that we disapprove of its repressive practices.

"The State Department has urged the Congress to give the administration this $3.1 million military appropriations as a blank check, stating that such assistance will be withdrawn if the human rights situation does not "improve". But what have past improvements really consisted of? Eleven times in the past 15 months we are told the State Department has made formal representations to the Somoza government—with no results. . . .

"Let there be no mistake about American identification with the repressive practices of Somoza's national guard—how could there be, when eyewitnesses have documented the Nicaraguan troops are purposefully dressed in American uniforms complete with American insignia, and drive American made vehicles emblazoned with U.S. Army markings. " Such links with the United States are fostered by President Somoza to promote an image of close personal ties with the powerful United States, not caring whether our name is tarnished by the atrocities of his regime. Is this a friend of the United States? Are these acts destined to win the support of the Nicaraguan people for the American ideals of democracy and friendship with Latin America? . . . "

State of siege lifted. Somoza lifted the 33-month-old state of siege Sept. 19. This apparently was the price exacted by the U.S. for signing a $2.5-million military sales agreement with Nicaragua.

President Anastasio Somoza Debayle, who announced the lifting out of the siege, had returned to Nicaragua Sept. 7 after convalescing in a U.S. hospital for more than a month following a heart attack.

'76 rights abuse detailed. Amnesty International Aug. 15 said the Nicaraguan National Guard systematically had kidnapped, tortured and killed peasants in rural areas of the country in 1976.

"The populations of entire peasant villages have been reported exterminated or taken away as prisoners of National Guard troops," the London-based organization said in a 75-page report. "The wholesale killing of *campesinos* (peasant farmers) and their 'disappearance' after detention is probably the most serious aspect of human rights violations in Nicaragua."

The report, based on testimony from former prisoners, other Nicaraguans and a two-man Amnesty commission that visited Nicaragua in May 1976, said the National Guard used a variety of torture methods, including rape, mutilation, near-drowning and simulated execution. It was "highly probable" that most Nicaraguan political prisoners had been tortured, the report said.

The Nicaraguan government denounced the report Aug. 16, calling it an "apology for terrorism" that was based on the testimony of alleged Communists and other opponents of the Nicaraguan president, Gen. Anastasio Somoza. Church and diplomatic sources said that while Amnesty's charges might be true, they believed human rights violations had decreased significantly in Nicaragua in 1977, the New York Times reported Aug. 16.

This improvement was attributed to pressure from the Carter Administration, which was stressing respect for human rights in formulating its foreign policy.

Guerrilla Activities

Guerrillas begin offensive. The Sandinista National Liberation Front, a leftist guerrilla group that was thought to have been virtually wiped out, began a major offensive against the government with attacks in at least four parts of Nicaragua.

The campaign began in the north Oct. 12 when Sandinistas attacked the National Guard barracks at Ocotal, near the Honduran border. Five soldiers and one civilian were reported killed in the action. The next day the guerrillas struck at the opposite end of the country, assaulting the San Carlos barracks near the Costa Rican border. Another six persons were reported killed, including the regional military commander and the San Carlos police chief.

The government rushed troops to the northern and southern frontiers, but the Sandinistas struck next in and near Managua. On Oct. 17 they attacked police headquarters in Masaya, 20 miles

Map: Joyce Sakala

Lower map shows Nicaraguan towns and border areas attacked in Sandinista guerrilla offensive Oct. 12-18.

southeast of the capital, and ambushed a convoy of troops sent in from Managua to repel the attack. At least eight persons were reported killed in the fighting, including a top Sandinista leader named Pedro Arauz. Meanwhile, other guerrillas invaded the town of Esquipulas, northeast of Masaya, and still others fired on National Guard headquarters in Managua.

All troops were placed on alert Oct. 18, and National Guardsmen in Managua set up barricades and searched automobiles. Still, there were two small incidents near the capital. In one, guerrillas attacked a concrete company in an apparently unsuccessful attempt to steal some dynamite.

The attacks constituted the first major action by the Sandinistas since December 1974, when they kidnapped and then ransomed several high government officials. The new offensive caught the country by surprise because the guerrillas were assumed to have been all but eliminated in the wave of repression that followed the 1974 incident.

The guerrillas made it clear that they felt the offensive would topple the government of Gen. Anastasio Somoza Debayle, whose family had ruled Nicaragua since the 1930s.

A guerrilla leader who was wounded in the San Carlos attack and hospitalized in Costa Rica told newsmen Oct. 16 that "this is the beginning of the decisive struggle to overthrow the bloody regime of the Somozas." He claimed that the Sandinistas had 500 guerrillas in Nicaragua, Costa Rica and Honduras, and collaborators in key Nicaraguan cities and towns.

A number of factors favored the guerrilla offensive. First, Gen. Somoza was recovering from a heart attack, and there were reports that his illness had touched off a power struggle within the National Guard. Second, Nicaragua was in disfavor with the U.S. for violating human rights. And third and perhaps most important, the Sandinistas were picking up support among virtually all political sectors.

Several self-described "radical Christians" were among the Sandinistas captured during the attacks. They said they were anti-Communists but had joined the guerrillas to fight for democracy, according to the New York Times Oct. 20. In addition, the Times noted, the Sandinistas had been praised publicly by 12 well-known conservatives. The 12, who included several wealthy businessmen and lawyers, issued a statement in Costa Rica noting the "political maturity" of the guerrillas and warning that the Sandinistas must participate in any solution to Nicaragua's problems.

Less direct support was given by the Democratic Union for Liberation, a broad-based opposition coalition. It declared that "the present violence is a result of the institutionalized violence in the country, particularly in the long years of dictatorship which have blocked all possible civil and democratic avenues toward resolving the acute economic and social problems suffered by Nicaragua."

The Democratic Union called for the restoration of political and press freedoms, amnesty for political prisoners and the replacement of Gen. Somoza as head of the National Guard, the Times reported.

The government appeared to take the guerrilla challenge seriously but it did not reimpose the state of siege it had lifted Sept. 19. The limited favor Somoza enjoyed in Washington apparently depended on the permanent removal of the siege's repressive measures, newspapers reported.

Nicaragua-Costa Rica border conflict— Following the guerrilla attack on San Carlos Oct. 13, Nicaragua and Costa Rica charged that each had violated the other's territory.

Three of the Sandinistas who assaulted San Carlos fled into Costa Rica, where they were arrested by Costa Rican authorities but not immediately handed over to Nicaragua. It was unclear whether the San Carlos attack was launched from Costa Rica, but the Nicaraguan government knew that some Sandinistas operated out of Costa Rica and it believed that the Costa Rican government turned a blind eye to their activities, according to press reports. Following the San Carlos attack the Nicaraguan regime accused Costa Rica of interfering in Nicaraguan affairs, and Costa Rica heatedly denied it.

Costa Rica closed its border Oct. 14 when Nicaragua rushed troops to the area. The tension increased later that day when Nicaraguan air force planes strafed a boat on the Frio River that was carrying Costa Rica's public security minister. The planes had mistakenly calculated that the boat had crossed into the Nicaraguan side of the river. Costa Rica protested the strafing and Nicaragua apologized.

Costa Rica rushed troops to its border Oct. 15 after it was reported that the Nicaraguan National Guard had been ordered to pursue Sandinistas into Costa Rica if necessary. In Washington, meanwhile, there was an exchange between the Nicaraguan and Costa Rican ambassadors to the Organization of American States. The Nicaraguan envoy asked Costa Rica to help Nicaragua contain the Sandinistas, and the Costa Rican representative replied that Nicaragua had deeper problems than the guerrilla movement.

The next day Costa Rica formally accused Nicaragua of violating its territory, and Nicaragua made the same charge against Costa Rica. Both countries apparently were referring to the strafing incident on the Frio River.

OAS mission visits—A three-member panel of the Organization of American States (OAS) arrived in Managua Oct. 26 to investigate the disagreement between Nicaragua and Costa Rica over alleged violations of each other's borders.

The head of the commission steadfastly maintained that he would investigate only the border dispute, which grew out of the Sandinista offensive. He said that he knew nothing of human rights violations in Nicaragua and was not interested in investigating allegations of such abuses.

Somoza, guerrillas reject 'dialogue.' In the lull following a week of guerrilla attacks against the government, representatives of Nicaragua's business community and the Roman Catholic Church proposed a "dialogue" between President Anastasio Somoza and all opposition forces. But the suggestion was rejected by both Somoza and the guerrilla organization, the Sandinista National Liberation Front.

The dialogue was proposed Oct. 26 at a meeting of priests and businessmen, the latter led by Alonso Roelo, head of the National Institute of Economic Development. They appointed a four-member committee to try to arrange the talks, which would have the goal of democratizing Nicaragua and restoring "social peace."

Gen. Somoza rejected their plan as soon as it was announced, saying he would not talk with anyone under pressure or threats of violence. He said negotiations could take place when political conditions were "right," but he did not say what that meant.

The Sandinistas rejected the proposal the next day, saying they would enter into talks only when Somoza and his wealthy family were out of the government. "Somoza must go," a guerrilla communique said. "There must not be a single Somoza in the ranks of the army or the government. The wretched apparatus of corruption and crimes represented by the dictatorship must be dismantled. Only then will the Sandinista Front be prepared to participate in the search for a national solution for all sectors of the country that are honest, patriotic and oppose Somoza."

Individual businessmen and Catholic leaders had been calling for political negotiations since Oct. 19, the day after the last Sandinista attack. Felipe Malpica Abaunza, former director of the Nicaraguan Chamber of Commerce, said that day that most Nicaraguan businessmen felt Somoza's rule posed a constant threat to peace. The dictator controlled too much of the Nicaraguan economy and authorized too much political repression, Malpica said.

The archbishop of Managua, Miguel Obando Bravo, Oct. 22 offered to mediate the proposed talks. The next day there was a preliminary meeting of priests and businessmen, at which business leaders threatened to hold a general strike if Somoza refused to agree to the talks. Three radio newsmen who reported the meeting were arrested, it was reported Oct. 24.

After rejecting the talks, Somoza charged Nov. 7 that there was an international communist conspiracy against Nicaragua. This plot, he said, received "the direct and open aid of the current communist government of Cuba, which not only has given asylum and protection to Nicaraguan and other foreign subversive elements, but has given them all manner of help, principally training and propaganda, in open violation of the fundamental principles of international law."

Sandinistas deny Cuban support—The Sandinistas denied receiving anything but moral support from Cuba. In an interview published by the New York Times Oct. 26, Sandinista leader Plutarco Hernandez insisted that the guerrillas received no money or arms from Cuba, and said none of them had been trained in Cuba since 1970.

"If we had received more effective support from Cuba or from any other country," Hernandez said, "we'd have been in power a long time ago. Our problem is that we've had to fight entirely alone. But it also means that when we achieve victory we will owe nothing to any outsiders."

Hernandez said the guerrillas lacked funds to buy modern weapons, but he claimed that there were about 1,000 armed Sandinistas in Nicaragua, with thousands providing logistical support. He said he felt the guerrillas could defeat the 7,500-member National Guard because it was weakened by infighting among leading generals.

The guerrillas' goal, Hernandez, said, was to overthrow Somoza and "hold the first free elections in Nicaragua's history." "Our basic program is not communist," he said. "It is a threat to no one who favors a just society."

Although the Sandinistas ultimately wanted a socialist Nicaragua, Hernandez said, they no longer favored the leftist dictatorship they had envisioned when they first organized in 1962. "We must pass through the stage of democracy because socialism cannot be built overnight," Hernandez said.

Once Somoza was overthrown, Hernandez said, the Sandinistas favored expropriation of his family's vast business empire, nationalization of the banking sector, broad land reform, emphasis on social welfare and education and establishment of diplomatic relations with "socialist" countries.

Hernandez said the U.S. could help restore democracy to Nicaragua by abandoning all aid to Somoza. "President Carter gives us hope that progressive American groups will help define American policy toward Nicaragua," he said. "Carter has spoken out against all dictatorships, including that of Somoza, but American arms continue to be supplied to the National Guard. The U.S. must understand that Nicaragua is a kidnapped country and that the National Guard is Somoza's private army."

Sandinistas get foreign asylum. Several Sandinistas or persons associated with the guerrilla movement took political asylum in Costa Rica and in foreign embassies in Managua.

The Costa Rican government announced that it had granted asylum to eight guerrillas who had crossed into Costa Rica after attacking the National Guard barracks in the Nicaraguan border town of San Carlos Oct. 13, it was reported Oct. 27. (The Costa Rican embassy in Managua also took in a national guardsman who said he had deserted to protest "the violations of human rights being committed by Nicaraguan government forces," it was reported Oct. 26.)

Four persons, however, had been arrested in Costa Rica Sept. 25 for plotting to smuggle arms into Nicaragua to aid the Sandinistas.

Three Nicaraguan students who had sought political asylum in the Mexican Embassy in Managua were flown to Mexico June 8 after receiving safe-conduct assurances from the Nicaraguan government. A fourth refugee remained in the embassy. He was a young lawyer who had been indicted for committing "irregularities" while defending prisoners accused of subversive activities.

Several Sandinistas took refuge in the Mexican Embassy in Managua during the guerrilla offensive Oct. 12-18. National guardsmen tried to enter the embassy Oct. 20 to arrest them, but they were rebuffed by embassy personnel. The Mexican ambassador said Oct. 21 that he would grant asylum to any Sandinista, no matter how much tension this caused in Mexican-Nicaraguan relations. Another guerrilla took refuge in the embassy Oct. 26.

Two Sandinistas took refuge in the French embassy, it was reported Oct. 20. The French ambassador said they would receive political asylum even though France had no asylum agreement with Nicaragua.

There also were two guerrillas in the Venezuelan Embassy, it was reported Oct. 28.

Government action taken against suspects. A military court sentenced 36 guerrillas to prison terms ranging from 18 months to 129 years and it tried 74 other persons in absentia for allegedly collaborating with the insurgents, it was reported March 2. Some 20 other Nicaraguans had reportedly sought asylum in Mexico.

The National Guard reported April 9 that its troops in northern Nicaragua had killed Carlos Aguero Echeverria, alleged to be a top leader of the Sandinista guerrillas. Five presumed guerrillas were killed later in a shootout with guardsmen in Managua, it was reported May 17.

Other Developments

Somoza hospitalized in U.S. President Anastasio Somoza was flown to the U.S. for medical treatment July 28, three days after he suffered a heart attack in Managua.

A special medical airplane provided by the U.S. Air Force took Somoza to Miami, where he was admitted to the Miami Heart Institute under the care of the institute's director.

The Nicaraguan Chamber of Deputies Aug. 18 rejected a proposal to name a temporary replacement for Somoza while he convalesced in the U.S. The leader of the Chamber said the country was functioning normally under the leadership of Government (Interior) Minister Antonio Mora, who was performing the president's administrative duties, and Brig. Jose Somoza, the president's brother, who was filling in for him as chief of the National Guard.

Congress president quits. Cornelio Hueck resigned as president of the National Congress and political secretary of the ruling Nationalist Liberal Party, it was reported Oct. 21.

Hueck apparently was forced out by President Somoza, who was recovering from a heart attack and trying to remove any potential rivals to his chosen successor in the event that he died or was incapacitated, according to the Latin America Political Report.

The report said Somoza's choice to succeed him was his brother-in-law and ambassador to Washington, Guillermo Sevilla Sacasa. However, the New York Times said Oct. 26 that Somoza was grooming his 27-year-old son, Anastasio Somoza Portocarrero, for the presidency.

Panama

Panama Canal Treaties Concluded

After long, bitter dispute, Panama and the U.S. in 1977 agreed on two treaties under which the U.S. would turn over control of the Panama Canal and the Canal Zone to Panama by the end of the century.

Latin leaders back Panama. Seven Latin American heads of state sent a letter to U.S. President-elect Jimmy Carter expressing support for Panamanian demands for sovereignty over the Canal Zone. The letter was delivered Jan. 18 to Carter's nominee for secretary of state, Cyrus Vance, by Gonzalo Facio, Costa Rica's foreign minister. It was signed by Gen. Juan Alberto Melgar Castro, Honduras' chief of state, and by Presidents Jose Lopez Portillo of Mexico, Arturo Armando Molina of El Salvador, Anastasio Somoza Debayle of Nicaragua, Daniel Oduber of Costa Rica, Alfonso Lopez Michelsen of Colombia and Carlos Andres Perez of Venezuela.

Facio told a Costa Rican newspaper that the Latin leaders did not seek immediate U.S. turnover of control over the canal, but only "recognition of Panamanian sovereignty as a starting point," the Miami Herald reported Jan. 9.

"We who are close to the picture recognize that effective Panamanian participation in either canal defense or administration is not something that can be worked out overnight," Facio said. "We may be thinking in terms of the year 2,000 for an ultimate solution, but we want something now as a concrete indicator that the U.S. takes Latin American aspirations seriously."

Schweppe study backs U.S.' rights—A historical study of the legal basis for U.S. possession of the Canal Zone and Canal was made by Prof. Alfred J. Schweppe, attorney and authority on constitutional law. His study was made at the request of Rep. Daniel J. Flood (D, Pa.) and inserted in the Congressional Record by Flood March 3. Flood said that in the past, there had been many "distortions and contrived confusions" over the 1903 Canal treaty. Among "errors" noted by Flood were:

"**First.** That sovereignty over the Canal Zone was not ceded to the United States but only certain rights;

"**Second.** That the Canal Zone is not U.S. territory but only leased Panamanian territory.

"**Third.** That the U.S. Supreme Court in 1948 referred to the Canal Zone as 'admittedly territory over which we do not have sovereignty.'

"**Fourth.** That the 1936 Treaty with Panama describes the Canal Zone as being 'Territory (of the Republic of Panama) under the jurisdiction of the United States.' "

According to Schweppe's analysis of the 1903 treaty:

In Article II, the Republic of Panama 'grants to the United States in perpetuity the use, occupation and control of a zone of land and land under water . . .' ten miles wide. This means "legal title" because in law, both domestic and international, the right to possession in perpetuity constitutes legal title.

Then comes Article III in which the Republic of Panama grants to the United States all of the 'rights, power and authority' described in Article II 'which the United States would possess and exercise if it were the sovereign of the territory' [the Zone], 'to the entire exclusion of the exercise by the Republic of Panama of any such sovereign rights.'

Simply stated, Panama, having initial sovereignty over the area constituting the Zone, by the treaty relinquishes in perpetuity to the United States title to the Canal Zone, and relinquishes in perpetuity all sovereign rights of Panama in the Zone.

Article VI of the 1903 treaty appropriately protected private property rights in 'any of the lands or waters *granted* to the United States' by the treaty. (Italics supplied.)

Such a treaty is the equivalent to a deed in fee simple by one country to another of all public property, saving private property rights which then become subject to the jurisdiction of the new owner.

The acquisition of Alaska, for example, was a ceding of all public property, saving private property rights. The same is true of the Louisiana Purchase and the Gadsden Purchase covering parts of Arizona and New Mexico.

Legal title is the right to possession in perpetuity good against all the world. Sovereignty is the supreme political power and dominion over an area. Panama in 1903 granted in perpetuity 'the use, occupation and control' of the Zone and 'all rights, power and authority within the Zone.' It thus granted title and sovereignty to the United States within the Zone and completely relinquished its own.

For this conveyance of title and relinquishment of sovereignty in perpetuity, the United States paid Panama $10,000,000 in gold and agreed to make an annual payment of $250,-000 in gold for the life of the treaty, beginning nine years from date, presumably an estimate of the completion date of the Canal. This annual payment, or annuity, was not rental but was part of the legal consideration for the grant. This annuity has since been negotiated upward and is now $2,300,000.

On March 3, 1936, some changes in the 1903 treaty were negotiated in the General Treaty of Friendship and Cooperation between the United States and the Republic of Panama. The principal ones were: (1) the elimination of Article I guaranteeing independence [it being, by reason of the 1922 treaty of the United States with Colombia hereafter referred to, no longer necessary],

(2) giving up the right of the United States to keep order in the Republic of Panama if Panama could not, in the judgment of the United States, maintain such order [it being no longer necessary], and (3) granting Panama a corridor over the Zone [which was legally necessary and desirable, although informally recognized from the beginning]. The corridor granted a legal easement over property of the United States, namely, the Canal Zone.

This 1936 treaty recognized the exclusive jurisdiction of the United States over the Zone, and the exclusive jurisdiction of Panama over all areas outside the Zone. 'Jurisdiction' was used in the sense of complete authority and dominion over territory, or the authority of a sovereign power to govern.

The 1936 treaty re-emphasized the United States' complete legal and political control of the Zone and its exclusive right to possession in perpetuity. . . .

Moreover, the Davis-Arias Boundary Agreement of June 15, 1904, refers to the Zone as territory 'ceded' to the United States by the 1903 treaty. The word 'ceded' appears four times in this provisional boundary agreement. The National Assembly of Panama, in Public Law No. 88 (1904) described the Zone as 'ceded.' The 1904 provisional boundary agreement was followed by the formal Boundary Convention of September 2, 1914, establishing 'permanently the boundary lines of the above-mentioned lands and waters as taken over by the United States.' The 1914 Convention confirmed the 1904 provisional Boundary Agreement as to areas covered.

This point was clinched by the United States Supreme Court in 1907 in *Wilson v. Shaw*, 204 U.S. 24, a suit to restrain the Secretary of the Treasury from paying out funds for the construction of the canal, on the ground that the United States did not have title. The unanimous court said:

'A treaty with it [Panama], ceding the Canal Zone was duly ratified. 33 Stat. 2234. Congress has passed several acts based upon the title of the United States . . .'

Quoting Articles II and III of the treaty granting in perpetuity 'use, occupation and control' and 'all rights, powers and authority' as if it were sovereign, the court concluded:

'It is hypercritical to contend that the title of the United States is imperfect, and that the territory described does not belong to this nation, because of the omission of some of the technical terms used in ordinary conveyances of real estate . . .'

This unanimous decision was written by Mr. Justice Brewer, one of the all-time great judges on the court, and concurred in by Chief Justice Fuller, and Justices Harlan, White, Peckham, McKenna, Holmes, Day and Moody.

In 1971, the United States Court of Appeals for the Fifth Circuit (*United States v. Husband R. Roach*, 453 F.2d 1054, certiorari denied 406 U.S. 935), in a case coming up for review from the Canal Zone, referring to both the 1903 and 1936 treaties, judicially declared:

"The Canal Zone is an unincorporated territory of the United States over which Congress exercises "complete and plenary authority." '

On January 25, 1955, another treaty was made with Panama which recognized the full force and effect of the 1903 and 1936 treaties and merely made some housekeeping adjustments, principally the status of Panamanian nationals in the Zone, some minor property transfers, and increased the annuity to 1,930,000 balboas. . . . ·

This 1903 treaty was a business transaction (money and a guarantee of independence) for title to, and exclusive control over, the Canal Zone, in perpetuity, made in the treaty of 1903 and confirmed in 1936 and 1955. These were carefully prepared bilateral agreements, for adequate legal consideration, voluntarily entered into, and repeatedly ratified.

The situation in no conceivable way partakes of colonialism.

Distinguished Secretaries of State, beginning with John Hay, Charles Evans Hughes, later Chief Justice, Attorneys General Bonaparte and McReynolds, later a Supreme Court Justice, have all vigorously maintained that title and sovereignty in the Canal Zone is in the United States. (John Hay, October 24, 1904; Attorney General Bonaparte September 7 ,1907; Attorney General McReynolds July 14, 1914; Charles Evans Hughes, July 21, 1921).

In 1923, Secretary of State Hughes declared (Foreign Relations, 1923, Vol. III, p. 64) that the United States could not, and would not, enter into any discussion affecting its full right to deal with the Canal Zone under Article III of the treaty of 1903 as if it were sovereign of the Canal Zone and to the exclusion of any sovereign rights or authority on the part of Panama. He added:

'It is an absolute futility for the Panamanian Government to expect any American administration, no matter what it was, any President or any Secretary of State, ever to surrender any part of these rights which the United States had acquired under the Treaty of 1903.'

But the State Department position in recent years has changed.

Secretary of State Henry Kissinger in 1974 signed an eight-point set of principles under which the United States would give up the American presence in the Zone at some future time and turn over to Panama all United States properties in the Zone. Current negotiators are said to be working on a new treaty intended to spell out the date when Panama will take over the operation and defense of the Canal.

The current position of the State Department is that the Zone was never ceded to the United States with the same effect as the cession of Louisiana and Alaska; and

that the United States did not acquire title or sovereignty, but only certain "rights" in perpetuity. It makes reference to Luckenbach S.S. Co. v. U.S., 280 U.S. 170 (1930), in which Chief Justice Taft remarked, without any decision on the point, that there were diverging opinions on the question of 'whether the 1903 treaty is so limited as to leave at least titular sovereignty in the Republic of Panama,' a position strongly rejected by Secretary Hay in 1904.

Reference is also made to Vermilja-Brown Co. v. Connell, 335 U.S. 377 (1948), a five-to-four decision, in which the majority of the Court, over the opposition of the Department of Justice, the State Department and the Wage and Hour Division, and over a vigorous dissent, stretched the Fair Labor Standards Act to cover a 99-year lease in Bermuda from Great Britain on the ground that it was a 'possession' of the United States under the Act. In the course of the decision the majority referred to the fact that the Wage and Hour Division had applied the Act to the Canal Zone, the court adding gratuitously: 'admittedly territory over which we do not have sovereignty.' The majority did not give effect to the obvious difference between a lease under which Great Britain retained sovereignty, and the grant of the lands and waters in the Canal Zone, in which the United States had title and a grant of sovereignty rights, with Panama renouncing all sovereign rights in the Zone. . . .

Where, in the face of all the precedents, the majority in 1948 got its idea of 'admitted' lack of sovereignty is not apparent, unless because of lack of U.S. sovereignty in Bermuda, the court felt it needed to create a parallel with the Canal Zone by predicating a lack of sovereignty there. At any rate, the majority concluded by necessary inference that the Canal Zone is a 'possession' of the United States over which the United States has 'sole power.' The decision in that context makes "sovereignty" largely a word of hollow meaning, because 'sole power' includes political as well as possessory control and is equivalent to sovereignty as the minority pointedly emphasizes, quoting the provisions of the 1903 treaty. . . .

The claim of some Panamanian officials that the original treaty of November 18, 1903, is somehow tainted because signed by a Frenchman who, though fully commissioned as official plenipotentiary, was not a Panamanian, is untenable, not only because of his official authorization, but by the subsequent ratification in Panama on December 2, 1903, by the new Panamanian government, and further ratification in 1936 and 1955.

In the face of the language of the 1903 treaty and the clear-cut pronouncements of prior Secretaries of State against the present State Department position, including even the 1948 'sole power' opinion of the Supreme Court, further comment would appear unnecessary as to the legal status of the United States in perpetuity in the Canal Zone, unless changed by treaty. . . .

Treaty talks renewed. U.S. and Panamanian negotiators met in Panama Feb. 14–23 and in Washington May 9–11 for talks on a new Panama Canal treaty. These were the opening talks under the new U.S. Administration of recently inaugurated President Jimmy Carter U.S.-Panamanian negotiations, however, had been in progress off and on for 12 years.

Before the Feb. 14–23 round of talks were held, several changes had been made in each delegation.

Romulo Escobar Betancourt had become leader of the Panamanian team Feb. 9 after Aquilino Boyd resigned as chief negotiator and foreign minister. Boyd quit to protest the decision of Brig. Gen. Omar Torrijos, Panama's military strongman, to reduce the authority as well as the role of the chief negotiator and to add new members to the delegation who had expertise on individual negotiating issues. Panama's ambassador to the U.S., Nicolas Gonzalez Revilla, was named foreign minister but left off the negotiating team.

Sol Linowitz, a Washington lawyer and former U.S. ambassador to the Organization of American States, joined the U.S. team Feb. 8 as President Carter's personal representative. The Panamanians seemed pleased with his appointment (Escobar Betancourt said approvingly March 3 that Linowitz "didn't avoid the issues"), but conservative U.S. legislators objected.

Sen. Jesse Helms (R, N.C.) charged Feb. 21 that Linowitz had business interests in Panama that raised the possibility of a conflict of interest. Helms, who opposed any new treaty giving Panama sovereignty over the canal, noted that Linowitz was a director of Marine Midland Bank of New York, which had a $4-million share of a $115-million loan made to Panama in 1973 by an international consortium. The first payment on the loan was due in 1977. Helms added that Linowitz was a director of Pan American World Airways, whose planes serviced Panama.

"Both [Marine Midland Bank and Pan American] have a direct financial interest in the support of the Torrijos regime because of their activities there and their need for the continued good will of the Panamanian government," Helms asserted. "It seems to me a grave error to

have a banker who is in bed with Torrijos negotiate the proposed treaty."

Two Idaho Republicans, Rep. George Hansen and Sen. James McClure, filed suit in U.S. District Court in Washington to remove Linowitz from the negotiating team for presumed violation of conflict-of-interest laws, it was reported March 16. The suit also alleged that the State Department improperly had appointed Linowitz to a term of less than six months to avoid having to submit his name for Senate confirmation. (Linowitz, a strong advocate of a new Panama Canal treaty, presumably would have had a hard time in the Senate, where there were vocal opponents of relinquishing U.S. sovereignty over the waterway.)

Linowitz subsequently resigned from the Marine Midland board, it was reported March 19. He remained on Pan American's board, however. "If we go into any aviation issues in our negotiations," a State Department spokesman said, "Linowitz said he would exclude himself from the negotiations."

The U.S. negotiating team received an important boost Feb. 2 when two senior U.S. senators, John J. Sparkman (D, Ala.) and Clifford Case (R, N.J.), declared it was "in our national interest" to "bring the negotiations to a successful conclusion at the earliest possible date." Sparkman was chairman of the Senate Foreign Relations Committee, which would first handle the canal treaty when it was submitted for Senate confirmation.

The May 9–11 session ended abruptly when Escobar Betancourt said he would return to Panama to discuss a new U.S. proposal with Torrijos.

The negotiations were near completion, according to the Financial Times (London) May 12. Perhaps the only substantive conflict remaining, the Financial Times said, was over the Pentagon's demand for a residual defense role in the waterway after it came under Panamanian control around the year 2000. Panama heretofore had asked that the United Nations guarantee the canal's neutrality.

The Washington Post reported May 17 that Torrijos was prepared to accept the extended U.S. defense role, but the general quickly denied it. In the Post story, correspondent Marlise Simons said Torrijos had told her: "Panama can accept the U.S. right to intervene against a third country to protect the neutrality of the canal. After all, this is what our Latin American neighbors and allies demand. To a great extent their economies depend on freedom of passage." Simons stuck by her story May 18.

According to the May 12 Financial Times report, the negotiating teams had agreed that the new treaty would give Panama immediate jurisdiction over the Canal Zone and full responsibility for running the waterway itself by the year 2000. During this period Panamanians gradually would be prepared to administer and defend the canal, while the U.S. would increase its annuity payments to more than $30 million from the current $2.1 million.

Both sides were eager to complete the negotiations in the summer, the Financial Times said. The Carter Administration wanted the canal issue out of the way well before the 1978 congressional elections, while Torrijos needed the treaty to reassure foreign and domestic investors that Panama's human and natural resources would be concentrated on rebuilding the country's sagging economy, the newspaper said.

The Panama Canal Co., a U.S. government agency that was the Canal Zone's largest employer, reported Feb. 1 that twice as many of its employes had quit in 1976 as in the previous year, apparently because they were worried about the terms of a new canal treaty. A company spokesman said 290 employes had resigned in 1976, compared with 148 in 1975. "Any further encouragement that there will be a new treaty will increase the present turnover rate," the spokesman said.

William Drummond, a leader of Canal Zone residents who opposed a new treaty, was detained by Panamanian national guardsmen twice—first for three hours Feb. 11 and then for 15 minutes the next day—as he prepared to board flights for Washington. Panamanian authorities said they merely had wanted to question Drummond about a bomb blast that had destroyed his car in the Canal Zone in October 1976. The U.S. Feb. 14 formally protested Drummond's two detentions.

Drummond, a Canal Zone policeman and labor leader, recently had filed a civil

suit in federal court in Washington asking for an injunction to stop the canal negotiations, it was reported Feb. 11. A similar suit filed by Drummond in the Canal Zone in 1976 had been thrown out of court.

The Panamanian government hired a New York firm, Public Affairs Analysts, to plan and execute a nationwide U.S. public relations drive to secure support for a new treaty, it was reported March 24. The firm's chief executive officer, Joseph Napolitan, said Public Affairs Analysts would charge Panama $150,000–$200,000 for its services over the first six months. He said the firm would send pro-treaty information to about 6,000 influential politicians, journalists, academics and business executives, and would monitor the activities of groups opposing a new treaty.

Carter sees negotiators. President Carter intervened personally in the Panama Canal treaty talks July 29, summoning the two negotiating teams to the White House.

Carter, flanked by Vice President Walter Mondale and their top foreign policy aides, expressed satisfaction with progress made in the talks and urged the negotiators to conclude a new treaty as soon as possible. The President alluded to the major issues that remained to be resolved, but his tone was essentially "upbeat," according to U.S. officials.

In a complementary move July 29, Carter sent a letter to Torrijos. In the letter the President said he was pleased that the treaty talks were "nearing completion," but he warned Torrijos not to expect any more major American concessions.

"Two most important issues remain to be resolved" in the talks, Carter wrote. These were "lands and waters"—that is, the schedule under which various segments of the Canal Zone would be transferred to Panamanian jurisdiction—and "economic arrangements," which included annuities the U.S. would pay Panama during the life of the treaty.

Carter said the U.S. had made "a number of major concessions in the land and water area during the past several months." He warned Torrijos that "any significant further adjustments" would "handicap us unacceptably in operating and defending the canal."

Carter said the U.S. Defense, State and Treasury departments were analyzing Panama's demands on annuities and economic aid, and the U.S. negotiating team would soon present its own proposals. These would "represent the most that we could undertake to do, based on our consultations with the Congress," the President said, alluding to the need to obtain Senate confirmation of a new canal treaty.

Panama's top negotiator said July 29 that Panama was demanding $3.91 billion in U.S. payments. Arriving in Panama City to deliver Carter's letter to Torrijos, Romulo Escobar Betancourt said Panama wanted $460 million in compensation when the treaty was signed and $150 million a year until the year 2000, when the pact would expire. The compensation was for revenues lost by Panama while the U.S. controlled the canal and for the cost of transforming the Canal Zone from a foreign military enclave to a domestic civilian sector. The annuities were rent payments for the canal and the remaining U.S. military installations in the Canal Zone.

The U.S., however, was willing to pay only $35 million to $50 million a year, according to sources close to the negotiations. The American team stressed that Washington would pay rent only for the canal—not for the military bases in the Canal Zone—and that the money must come from canal tolls. The Panama Canal Co., the U.S. government agency that ran the canal, collected $134 million in tolls in 1976, paying Panama only $2.3 million of the total.

Carter's intervention in the negotiations was considered an attempt to speed them up rather than to break a deadlock. The negotiators were said to have made steady progress in May and June, but the President was anxious to have a treaty for the Senate before its fall recess.

Carter had tried to put pressure on the Panamanian delegation July 21, saying at a "town meeting" in Yazoo City, Miss. that the U.S. was considering digging a second, sea-level canal through Panama to handle oil tankers, warships and other vessels that were too large for the existing waterway. The new canal could be used to carry natural gas from Alaska to the East Coast of the U.S., averting the need for construction of a more costly pipeline across the American mainland, Carter said.

The president of the Panama Canal Co., Harold R. Parfitt, said he wasn't aware that a new canal was being considered, and two experts on the matter said a new waterway was not economically feasible. Stephen R. Gibbs, an economist for the University of Washington's Institute for Marine Studies, told a House subcommittee July 25 that a new canal "would be a net economic loser for whomever undertook it." Leonard J. Kujawa, a consultant on financial and accounting matters for the Panama Canal Co., said a new waterway would be "poor from an investment standpoint."

Torrijos meets regional leaders. Gen. Torrijos met the leaders of five neighboring countries Aug. 5–6 to enlist their support for a new Panama Canal treaty.

At the weekend meeting in Bogota, Colombia, Torrijos said Panamanian and American negotiators were about to conclude a new agreement that would grant Panama sovereignty over the canal and the Canal Zone by the year 2000 but would allow the U.S. to defend the waterway indefinitely.

Torrijos and his fellow leaders—Prime Minister Michael Manley of Jamaica and Presidents Alfonso Lopez Michelsen of Colombia, Carlos Andres Perez of Venezuela, Daniel Oduber of Costa Rica and Jose Lopez Portillo of Mexico—issued a joint communique Aug. 6 commending the negotiating teams for their continued progress toward a new treaty and praising Torrijos and U.S. President Jimmy Carter for their general direction of the negotiations.

Perez told newsmen Aug. 6 that Latin Americans had "gained everything we wanted" in the canal negotiations. "Very soon we will celebrate the settlement of the canal problem," the Venezuelan president said.

All five of Torrijos' colleagues previously had supported Panama's demand for sovereignty over the canal. But Torrijos called the special Bogota meeting to obtain their approval of the draft treaty itself, particularly the clause granting the U.S. an extended defense role in the canal.

This support was important to Torrijos for two reasons, according to press reports: first, to help convince Panamanian nationalists that this was the best treaty that could be negotiated, and second, to present a united Latin American front that would discourage opposition to the new treaty in the U.S. Senate.

U.S. & Panama resume negotiations. The U.S. and Panamanian negotiating teams resumed their talks in Panama Aug. 8 predicting they would have a treaty within the week. The chief Panamanian negotiator, Romulo Escobar Betancourt, had said Aug. 5 that several small problems remained to be worked out. The last major problem—sharp disagreement over the amount of money the U.S. would pay Panama under the treaty—had been resolved by Torrijos and Carter in a long-distance telephone conversation, the New York Times reported Aug. 8.

Panamanian sources told the Times that the U.S. would not pay the $460 million Panama had demanded for signing the treaty, but it would give Panama a substantial sum through economic aid and a share of canal tolls.

'Agreement in principle' announced. Negotiators for the U.S. and Panama announced Aug. 10 that they had reached "agreement in principle" on "the basic elements" of a new accord to govern the Panama Canal and the Canal Zone.

The accord, comprising two treaties and a separate economic agreement, would give Panama complete control over the canal and zone by the year 2000, but would allow the U.S. to intervene indefinitely thereafter to protect the waterway's neutrality.

The settlement capped 13 years of sporadic negotiations for an agreement to replace the Hay-Bunau-Varilla treaty of 1903, which allowed the U.S. to build the canal and to control the waterway and the Canal Zone "in perpetuity." The 1903 arrangement, which many Panamanians considered humiliating, had caused recurring student unrest in Panama and persistent friction between the U.S. and Panamanian governments.

The new agreement was announced after three days of round-the-clock negotiations in the presidential suite of the Holiday Inn in Panama City. Delivering the news to the press, the top negotiators—Ellsworth Bunker and Sol Linowitz of the U.S. and Romulo Escobar and Aristides Royo of Panama—said the accord would improve U.S. relations not only with Panama but with all Latin American nations.

Bunker and Linowitz then flew to Washington where they briefed President Carter and the Joint Chiefs of Staff. Carter disclosed the key elements of the accord Aug. 12 in a statement that effectively opened his uphill campaign for Senate ratification of the new treaties.

Both pacts were still being drafted by legal specialists. But Carter said one treaty would govern the operation and defense of the canal before Dec. 31, 1999, while the other would guarantee the waterway's permanent neutrality. The latter, if ratified, would be deposited with the Organization of American States for possible signature by other nations in the Western Hemisphere.

Among the provisions of the treaties:

■ The U.S. would manage, operate and defend the Panama Canal until the end of the century, maintaining control over all lands, waters and installations—including military bases—needed for the task. The Panamanian government guaranteed the right of the U.S. to station troops in the Canal Zone for this purpose.

■ A new agency of the U.S. government would operate the canal until the year 2000, replacing the current operator, the Panama Canal Co. The canal would be open to all shipping on a non-discriminatory basis.

■ On the effective date of the treaty Panama would assume general territorial jurisdiction over the Canal Zone and would be entitled to use portions of the area not needed for the operation and defense of the canal. At the end of 1999 Panama would assume control of the canal's operation.

■ As of the year 2000 Panama would assume the primary responsibility to protect and defend the canal, but the U.S. would have the permanent right to intervene to defend the neutrality of the waterway if it were threatened.

■ U.S. warships would have the

permanent right to traverse the canal expeditiously and without conditions.

■ Until the year 2000, Panama would receive a share of canal tolls equivalent to 30¢ per ton of freight passing through the waterway (this would amount to $50 million a year, according to press reports). Panama also would get $10 million per year from toll revenues, and up to another $10 million a year if canal traffic and revenues permitted.

■ All U.S. civilians currently employed in the canal could continue in U.S. government jobs until they retired. They would enjoy the rights and guarantees of all U.S. government employes overseas.

In addition, Carter noted, the U.S. and Panama agreed jointly to study the possibility of building a new, sea-level canal in Panama, and the U.S. pledged its best efforts to arrange a five-year economic program of loans, loan guarantees and credits to Panama. The economic package, which did not require congressional approval, would include up to $200 million in Export-Import Bank credits; up to $75 million in Agency for International Development housing guarantees, and a $20 million Overseas Private Investment Corp. loan guarantee. The package would include standard "Buy American" provisions to benefit U.S. businesses that invested in and sold goods and services to Panama.

Carter gave a strong endorsement of the overall agreement. He said the Joint Chiefs of Staff and his principal advisers had been "involved in these talks at every stage," and all believed that "the implementation of the treaties ... are important to our long-term national interests."

The President claimed the treaties also would "help to usher in a new day in hemispheric relations." All Latin American countries, Carter said, "are joined with us in the conviction that a new treaty which properly responds to Panamanian aspirations and fully preserves our interests will give us an opportunity to work together more effectively toward our common objectives."

Carter & Torrijos sign Canal treaties.
President Carter and Brig. Gen. Torrijos signed the new Panama Canal treaties at a ceremony in Washington Sept. 7.

Presidents and prime ministers of 17 nations looked on as Carter and Torrijos signed two accords that would give Panama control over the canal at the end of 1999 and would guarantee the neutrality of the waterway thereafter.

A protocol attached to the second treaty invited all nations of the world to sign the pact and acknowledge the canal's permanent neutrality. The protocol was deposited at the headquarters of the Organization of American States, where the signing ceremony was held.

Carter and Torrijos each made a brief speech praising the treaties and urging the U.S. Senate to ratify them. Carter made his appeal indirectly, saying it was "extremely important for [the U.S.] to stay unified" on the canal issue. Torrijos addressed the senators directly, asking them to be "statesmen" according to Abraham Lincoln's definition ("A statesman thinks of future generations, while a politician thinks of the coming election").

Carter stressed the "fairness" of the treaties, their guarantees of the canal's neutrality and their importance to improving relations between the U.S. and Latin America. The new canal arrangement "opens a new chapter in our relations with all nations of this hemisphere," the President said. "This agreement is a symbol for the world of the mutual respect and cooperation among all our nations."

Carter said the initiative for a new canal agreement had been "bipartisan," having been supported by two Democratic presidents (Lyndon Johnson and Carter himself) and two Republicans (Richard Nixon 'and Gerald Ford). Carter noted that Ford, his former secretary of state, Henry Kissinger, Nixon's former secretary of state, William Rogers, and Johnson's widow, Lady Bird, were all present at the signing ceremony.

Torrijos said that while the new treaties were fairer than the 1903 accord they replaced, many Panamanians were still dissatisfied. The 23-year transition period from 1977 to 1999 "means 8,395 days during which the U.S. military bases will remain, turning [Panama] into a possible strategic target for reprisals," Torrijos said. The permanent neutrality treaty, he added, "places [Panama] under the Pentagon's defense umbrella," making it possible for the U.S. to intervene in Panama at any time in the future.

"Nevertheless," the Panamanian leader said, "what has been agreed upon is the result of an understanding between two leaders who believe in the peaceful togetherness of their people and who have the courage and the leadership to face their people with no weapon other than the truth and their deep conviction of what is fair."

The final drafts of the treaties, initialed by the chief negotiators and made public Sept. 6, differed little from the "agreement in principle" described by Carter Aug. 12. The U.S. would gradually relinquish control of the canal and the Canal Zone, completing the process at "noon, Panama time, Dec. 31, 1999." Until then, the U.S. officially would operate the canal and would station troops in the Canal Zone.

As soon as the treaties went into effect—six months after ratification—Panama would begin receiving the increased canal revenues previously announced.

More than half of the 648-square-mile Canal Zone would pass into Panamanian hands immediately, and the entire zone would be placed symbolically under the Panamanian flag. The U.S. flag could be displayed along with the Panamanian banner at canal headquarters and "at other places and on some occasions" approved by the Panamanian government.

The new Panama Canal Commission would replace the Panama Canal Co., a U.S. government agency, as the canal's operator. The commission would be supervised by a board of five Americans and four Panamanians, the latter proposed by the Panamanian government but appointed by the U.S. Until 1990, the canal's administrator would be an American and his deputy a Panamanian. After 1990 these positions would be reversed for the duration of the treaty.

The U.S. would increase the number of Panamanians employed by the canal and train them for their eventual assumption of control. (Panamanians currently composed about 75% of the 13,000-member canal work force.) U.S. citizens employed by the canal would be allowed to keep their jobs as long as they wanted or their jobs lasted. For those who resigned or whose jobs were eliminated, the treaties provided options such as early retirement or transfer to civil service posts in the U.S.

In addition, among other provisions, the treaties recognized the continued right of canal employes to bargain collectively and to belong to internationally affiliated trade unions.

Latin leaders back accords—The presence at the signing ceremony of representatives of 26 nations in the Western Hemisphere indicated widespread inter-American support for a new canal arrangement.

Seventeen of the foreign dignitaries were presidents or prime ministers. President Carter took advantage of their visits to Washington to hold individual meetings that he characterized collectively as a hemispheric "summit."

After conferring with Gen. Torrijos Sept. 6, Carter met with Vice President Adalberto Pereira dos Santos of Brazil and with Presidents Francisco Morales Bermudez of Peru, Alfredo Stroessner of Paraguay, Alfonso Lopez Michelsen of Colombia and Augusto Pinochet Ugarte of Chile. In his talks with each leader Carter apparently discussed trade and other issues besides the canal treaties.

(The arrival of several Latin American military dictators, particularly Pinochet, appeared to be one cause of a rash of demonstrations and bomb threats in Washington Sept. 6-7. Human rights activists criticized Carter for receiving rulers who, like Pinochet, were accused of condoning torture and political arrests. Administration officials replied that it was better to meet with dictators than to shun them, but they did not say whether Carter and the Latin Americans discussed human rights.)

Other heads of state or government who attended the signing of the canal treaties were Prime Ministers Lynden O. Pindling of the Bahamas, Pierre Elliott Trudeau of Canada and Eric M. Gairy of Grenada, and Presidents Jorge Rafael Videla of Argentina, Hugo Banzer Suarez of Bolivia, Daniel Oduber Quiros of Costa Rica, Joaquin Balaguer of the Dominican Republic, Alfredo Poveda Burbano of Ecuador, Carlos Humerto Romero of El Salvador, Kjell Laugerud Garcia of Guatemala, Juan Alberto Melgar Castro of Honduras, Aparicio Mendez of Uruguay and Carlos Andres Perez of Venezuela.

There had been reports before the signing that several Latin American nations were dissatisfied with the treaties, particularly the pact allowing the U.S. to intervene after 1999 to protect the canal's neutrality. Brazil and Mexico were cited by newspapers as opponents of the pacts, but their presidents assured Carter that they supported the new canal arrange-

ment, it was reported Sept. 3.

Despite official denials, it was apparent that Mexican President Jose Lopez Portillo's reasons for not attending the canal treaties ceremony in Washington Sept. 7 were that he felt the pacts were too generous to the U.S. and that he did not want to appear in public with the many Latin American military dictators who

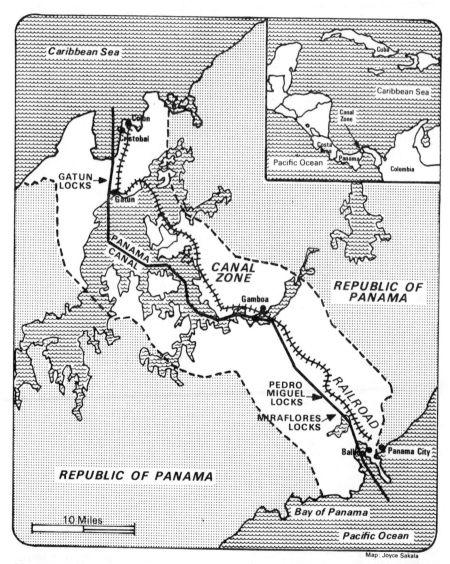

Map: Joyce Sakala

Map of the Panama Canal Zone at the time the new U.S.-Panama treaties were signed.

were in attendance, according to the Latin American Political Report Sept. 9. Lopez Portillo was said to object principally to the treaty allowing the U.S. to intervene to defend the canal's neutrality at any time in the future. He reportedly felt this violated Panamanian sovereignty.

—The Soviet news agency Tass said the canal accords had been negotiated too hurriedly, and consequently were progressive but not optimal for Panama, it was reported Sept. 10. The Chinese news agency Hsinhua called the treaties "a major victory for the Panamanian people's struggle to defend national independence and state sovereignty."

Texts of Treaties Signed by U.S. and Panama

Following are the texts of the Panama Canal Treaty, the treaty on the neutrality of the Panama Canal and a protocol to the neutrality treaty that were signed by President Carter and Gen. Torrijos in Washington Sept. 7.

Panama Canal Treaty

The United States of America and the Republic of Panama,

Acting in the spirit of the joint declaration of April 3, 1964, by the representatives of the governments of the United States of America and the Republic of Panama, and of the joint statement of principles of February 7, 1974, initialed by the secretary of state of the United States of America and the foreign minister of the Republic of Panama, and

Acknowledging the Republic of Panama's sovereignty over its territory,

Have decided to terminate the prior treaties pertaining to the Panama Canal and to conclude a new treaty to serve as the basis for a new relationship between them and, accordingly, have agreed upon the following:

Article I

Abrogation of Prior Treaties and Establishment of a New Relationship

[1]

Upon its entry into force, this treaty terminates and supersedes:

(a) The Isthmian Canal Convention between the United States of America and the Republic of Panama, signed at Washington, November 18, 1903;

(b) the Treaty of Friendship and Cooperation signed at Washington, March 2, 1936, and the Treaty of Mutual Understanding and Cooperation and the related memorandum of understanding reached, signed at Panama, January 25, 1955, between the United States of America and the Republic of Panama;

(c) all other treaties, conventions, agreements and exchanges of notes between the United States of America and the Republic of Panama, concerning the Panama Canal which were in force prior to the entry into force of this treaty; and

(d) provisions concerning the Panama Canal which appear in other treaties, conventions, agreements and exchanges of notes between the United States of America and the Republic of Panama which were in force prior to the entry into force of the treaty.

[2]

In accordance with the terms of this treaty and related agreements, the Republic of Panama, as territorial sovereign, grants to the United States of America, for the duration of this treaty, the rights necessary to regulate the transit of ships through the Panama Canal and to manage, operate, maintain, improve, protect and defend the canal. The Republic of Panama guarantees to the United States of America the peaceful use of the land and water areas which it has been granted the rights to use for such purposes pursuant to this treaty and related agreements.

[3]

The Republic of Panama shall participate increasingly in the management and protection and defense of the canal, as provided in this treaty.

[4]

In view of the special relationship established by this treaty, the United States of America and the Republic of Panama shall cooperate to assure the uninterrupted and efficient operation of the Panama Canal.

Article II

Ratification, Entry Into Force, and Termination

[1]

This treaty shall be subject to ratification in accordance with the constitutional procedures of the two parties. The instruments of ratification of the treaty shall be exchanged at Panama at the same time as the instruments of ratification of the Treaty Concerning the Permanent Neutrality and Operation of the Panama Canal, signed this date, are exchanged. This treaty shall enter into force, simultaneously with the Treaty Concerning the Permanent Neutrality and Operation of the Panama Canal, six calendar months from the date of the exchange of the instruments of ratification.

[2]

This treaty shall terminate at noon, Panama time, December 31, 1999.

Article III

Canal Operation and Management

[1]

The Republic of Panama, as territorial sovereign, grants to the United States of America the rights to manage, operate, and maintain the Panama Canal, its complementary works, installations and equipment and to provide for the orderly transit of vessels through the Panama Canal. The United States of America accepts the grant of such rights and undertakes to exercise them in accordance with this treaty and related agreements.

[2]

In carrying out the foregoing responsibilities, the United States of America may:

(a) use for the aforementioned purposes, without

cost except as provided in this treaty, the various in-stallations and areas (including the Panama Canal) and waters, described in the agreement in the imple-mentation of this article, signed this date, as well as such other areas and installations as are made avail-able to the United States of America under this treaty and related agreements, and take the measures necessary to ensure sanitation of such areas;

(b) make such improvements and alterations to the aforesaid installations and areas as it deems appro-priate, consistent with the terms of this treaty;

(c) make and enforce all rules pertaining to the passage of vessels through the canal and other rules with respect to navigation and maritime matters, in accordance with this treaty and related agreements. The Republic of Panama will lend its cooperation, when necessary, in the enforcement of such rules;

(d) establish, modify, collect and retain tolls for the use of the Panama Canal, and other charges, and es-tablish and modify methods of their assessment;

(e) regulate relations with employes of the United States government;

(f) provide supporting services to facilitate the performance of its responsibilities under this article;

(g) issue and enforce regulations for the effective exercise of the rights and responsibilities of the United States of America under this treaty and related agreements. The Republic of Panama will lend its cooperation, when necessary, in the enforcement of such rules; and

(h) Exercise any other right granted under this treaty, or otherwise agreed upon between the two parties.

[3]

Pursuant to the foregoing grant of rights, the United States of America shall, in accordance with the terms of this treaty and the provisions of United States law, carry out its responsibilities by means of a United States government agency called the Panama Canal Commission, which shall be constituted by and in conformity with the laws of the United States of America.

(a) The Panama Canal Commission shall be supervised by a board composed of nine members, five of whom shall be nationals of the United States of America and four of whom shall be Panamanian na-tionals proposed by the Republic of Panama for ap-pointment to such positions by the United States of America in a timely manner.

(b) Should the Republic of Panama request the United States of America to remove a Panamanian national from membership on the board, the United States of America shall agree to such a request. In that event, the Republic of Panama shall propose another Panamanian national for appointment by the United States of America to such position in a timely manner. In case of removal of a Panamanian member of the board at the initiative of the United States of America, both parties will consult in advance in order to reach agreement concerning such removal and the Republic of Panama shall propose another Pana-manian national for appointment by the United States of America in his stead.

(c) The United States of America shall employ a na-tional of the United States of America as administra-tor of the Panama Canal Commission, and a Pana-manian national as deputy administrator, through December 31, 1989. Beginning January 1, 1990, a Panamanian national shall be employed as the administrator and a national of the United States of America shall occupy the position of deputy adminis-trator. Such Panamanian nationals shall be proposed to the United States of America by the Republic of

Panama for appointment to such positions by the United States of America.

(d) Should the United States of America remove the Panamanian national from his position as deputy administrator, or administrator, the Republic of Panama shall propose another Panamanian national for appointment to such position by the United States of America.

[4]

An illustrative description of the activities the Panama Canal Commission will perform in carrying out the responsibilities and rights of the United States of America under this article is set forth at the Annex. Also set forth in the Annex are procedures for the dis-continuance or transfer of those activities performed prior to the entry into force of this treaty by the Panama Canal Company or the Canal Zone govern-ment which are not to be carried out by the Panama Canal Commission.

[5]

The Panama Canal Commission shall reimburse the Republic of Panama for the costs incurred by the Re-public of Panama in providing the following public services in the canal operating areas and in housing areas set forth in the agreement in implementation of Article III of this treaty and occupied by both United States and Panamanian citizen employes of the Panama Canal Commission: police, fire protection, street maintenance, street lighting, street cleaning, traffic management and garbage collection. The Panama Canal Commission shall pay the Republic of Panama the sum of ten million United States dollars ($10,000,000) per annum for the foregoing services. It is agreed that every three years from the date that this treaty enters into force, the costs involved in furnish-ing said services shall be re-examined to determine whether adjustment of the annual payment should be made because of inflation and other relevant factors affecting the cost of such services.

[6]

The Republic of Panama shall be responsible for providing, in all areas comprising the former Canal Zone, services of a general jurisdictional nature such as customs and immigration, postal services, courts and licensing, in accordance with this treaty and re-lated agreements.

[7]

The United States of America and the Republic of Panama shall establish a Panama Canal Consultative Committee, composed of an equal number of high-level representatives of the United States of America and the Republic of Panama, and which may appoint such subcommittees as it may deem appropriate. This committee shall advise the United States of America and the Republic of Panama on matters of policy affecting the canal's operation. In view of both parties' special interest in the continuity and efficiency of the canal operation in the future, the committee shall advise on matters such as general tolls policy, employ-ment and training policies to increase the participation of Panamanian nationals in the operation of the canal, and international policies on matters concerning the canal. The committee's recommendations shall be transmitted to the two governments, which shall give such recommendations full consideration in the formulation of such policy decisions.

[8]

In addition to the participation of Panamanian nationals at high management levels of the Panama Canal Commission, as provided for in paragraph 3 of this article, there shall be growing participation of Panamanian nationals at all other levels and areas of employment in the aforesaid commission, with the objective of preparing, in an orderly and efficient fashion, for the assumption by the Republic of Panama of full responsibility for the management, operation and maintenance of the canal upon the termination of this treaty.

[9]

The use of the areas, waters and installations with respect to which the United States of America is granted rights pursuant to this article, and the rights and legal status of United States government agencies and employes operating in the Republic of Panama pursuant to this article, shall be governed by the agreement in implementation of this article, signed this date.

[10]

Upon entry into force of this treaty, the United States government agencies known as the Panama Canal Company and the Canal Zone government shall cease to operate within the territory of the Republic of Panama that formerly constituted the Canal Zone.

Article IV

Protection and Defense

[1]

The United States of America and the Republic of Panama. Each party shall act, in accordance with its constitutional processes, to meet the danger resulting from an armed attack or other actions which threaten the security of the Panama Canal or of ships transiting it.

[2]

For the duration of this treaty, the United States of America shall have primary responsibility to protect and defend the canal. The rights of the United States of America to station, train and move military forces within the Republic of Panama are described in the agreement in implementation of this article, signed this date. The use of areas and installations and the legal status of the armed forces of the United States of America in the Republic of Panama shall be governed by the aforesaid agreement.

[3]

In order to facilitate the participation and cooperation and defense of the canal, the United States of America and the Republic of Panama shall establish a combined board comprised of an equal number of senior military representatives of each party. These representatives shall be charged by their respective governments with consulting and cooperating on all matters pertaining to the protection and defense of the canal, and with planning for actions to be taken in concert for that purpose. Such combined protection and defense arrangements shall not inhibit the identity or lines of authority of the armed forces of the United States of America or the Republic of Panama. The combined board shall provide for coordination and cooperation concerning such matters as:

(a) The preparation of contingency plans for the protection and defense of the canal based upon the cooperative efforts of the armed forces of both parties;

(b) the planning and conduct of combined military exercises; and

(c) the conduct of United States and Panamanian military operations with respect to the protection and defense of the canal.

[4]

The combined board shall, at five-year intervals throughout the duration of the treaty, review the resources being made available by the two parties for the protection and defense of the canal. Also, the combined board shall make appropriate recommendations to the two governments respecting projected requirements, the efficient utilization of available resources of the two parties, and other matters of mutual interest with respect to the protection and defense of the canal.

[5]

To the extent possible consistent with its primary responsibility for the protection and defense of the Panama Canal, the United States of America will endeavor to maintain its armed forces in the Republic of Panama in normal times at a level not in excess of that of the armed forces of the United States of America in the territory of the former Canal Zone immediately prior to the entry into force of this treaty.

Article V

Principle of Nonintervention

Employes of the Panama Canal Commission, their dependents and designated contractors of the Panama Canal Commission, who are nationals of the United States of America, shall respect the laws of the Republic of Panama and shall abstain from any activity incompatible with the spirit of the treaty. Accordingly, they shall abstain from any political activity in the Republic of Panama as well as from any intervention in the internal affairs of the Republic of Panama. The United States of America shall take all measures within its authority to ensure that the provisions of this article are fulfilled.

Article VI

Protection of the Environment

[1]

The United States of America and the Republic of Panama commit themselves to implement this treaty in a manner consistent with the protection of the natural environment of the Republic of Panama. To this end, they shall consult and cooperate with each other in all appropriate ways to ensure that they shall give due regard to the protection and conservation of the environment.

[2]

A Joint Commission on the Environment shall be established with equal representation from the United States of America and the Republic of Panama, which shall periodically review the implementation of this treaty and shall recommend as appropriate to the two governments ways to avoid or should this not be possible, to mitigate the adverse environmental impacts which might result from their respective actions pursuant to the treaty.

[3]

The United States of America and the Republic of Panama shall furnish the Joint Commission on the Environment complete information on any action taken in accordance with this treaty which, in the judgment of both, might have a significant effect on the environment. Such information shall be made available to the commission as far in advance of the contemplated action as possible to facilitate the study by the Commission of any potential environmental problems and to allow for consideration of the recommendation of the commission before the contemplated action is carried out.

Article VII

Flags

[1]

The entire territory of the Republic of Panama, including the areas the use of which the Republic of Panama makes available to the United States of America pursuant to this treaty and related agreements, shall be under the flag of the Republic of Panama, and consequently such flag always shall occupy the position of honor.

[2]

The flag of the United States of America may be displayed, together with the flag of the Republic of Panama, at the headquarters of the Panama Canal Commission, at the site of the combined board, and as provided in the agreement in implementation of Article IV of this treaty.

[3]

The flag of the United States of America also may be displayed at other places and on some occasions, as agreed by both parties.

Article VIII

Privileges and Immunities

[1]

The institutions owned or used by the agencies or instrumentalities of the United States of America operating in the Republic of Panama pursuant to this treaty and related agreements, and their official archives and documents shall be inviolable. The two parties shall agree on procedures to be followed in the conduct of any criminal investigation at such locations by the Republic of Panama.

[2]

Agencies and instrumentalities of the government of the United States of America operating in the Republic of Panama pursuant to this treaty and related agreements shall be immune from the jurisdiction of the Republic of Panama.

[3]

In addition to such other privileges and immunities as are afforded to employes of the United States government and their dependents pursuant to this treaty, the United States of America may designate up to twenty officials of the Panama Canal Commission who, along with their dependents, shall enjoy the privileges and immunities accorded to diplomatic agents and their dependents under international law and practice. The United States of America shall furnish to the Republic of Panama a list of the names of said officials and their dependents, identifying the positions they occupy in the government of the United States of America, and shall keep such list current at all times.

Article IX

Applicable Laws and Law Enforcement

[1]

In accordance with the provisions of this treaty and related agreements, the law of the Republic of Panama shall apply in the areas made available for the use of the United States of America pursuant to this treaty. The law of the Republic of Panama shall be applied to matters or events which occurred in the former Canal Zone prior to the entry into force of this treaty only to the extent specifically provided in prior treaties and agreements.

[2]

Natural or juridical persons who, on the date of entry into force of this treaty, are engaged in business or non-profit activities at locations in the former Canal Zone may continue such under the same terms and conditions prevailing prior to the entry into force of this treaty for a thirty-month transition period from its entry into force. The Republic of Panama shall maintain the same operating conditions as those applicable to the aforementioned enterprises prior to the entry into force of this treaty in order that they may receive licenses to do business in the Republic of Panama subject to their compliance with the requirements of its law. Thereafter, such persons shall receive the same treatment under the law of the Republic of Panama as similar enterprises already established in the rest of the territory of the Republic of Panama without discrimination.

[3]

The rights of ownership, as recognized by the United States of America, enjoyed by natural or juridical private persons in buildings and other improvements to real property located in the former Canal Zone shall be recognized by the Republic of Panama in conformity with its laws.

[4]

With respect to buildings and other improvements to real property located in the canal operating areas, housing areas or other areas subject to the licensing procedure established in Article IV of the agreement in implementation of Article III of this treaty, the owners shall be authorized to continue using the land upon which their property is located in accordance with the procedures established in that article.

[5]

With respect to buildings and other improvements to real property located in areas of the former Canal Zone to which the aforesaid licensing procedure is not applicable, or may cease to be applicable during the lifetime or upon termination of this treaty, the owners may continue to use the land upon which their property is located, subject to the payment of a reasonable charge to the Republic of Panama. Should the Republic of Panama decide to sell such land, the owners of the buildings or other improvements located thereon shall be offered a first option to purchase such land at a reasonable cost. In the case of nonprofit enterprises, such as churches and fraternal organizations, the cost of purchase shall be nominal in accordance with the prevailing practice in the rest of the territory of the Republic of Panama.

[6]

If any of the aforementioned persons are required by the Republic of Panama to discontinue their activities or vacate their property for public purposes, they shall be compensated at fair market value by the Republic of Panama.

[7]

The provisions of paragraphs 2-6 above shall apply to natural or juridical persons who have been engaged in business or nonprofit activities at locations in the former Canal Zone for at least six months prior to the date of signature of this treaty.

[8]

The Republic of Panama shall not issue, adopt or enforce any law, decree, regulation, or international agreement or take any other action which purports to regulate or would otherwise interfere with the exercise on the part of the United States of America of any right granted under this treaty or related agreements.

[9]

Vessels transiting the canal, and cargo, passengers and crews carried on such vessels shall be exempt from any taxes, fees, or other charges by the Republic of Panama. However, in the event such vessels call at a Panamanian port, they may be assessed charges incident thereto, such as charges for services provided to the vessel. The Republic of Panama may also require the passengers and crew disembarking from such vessels to pay such taxes, fees and charges as are established under Panamanian law for persons entering its territory. Such taxes, fees and charges shall be assessed on a nondiscriminatory basis.

[10]

The United States of America and the Republic of Panama will cooperate in taking such steps as may from time to time be necessary to guarantee the ·security of the Panama Canal Commission, its property, its employes and their dependents, and their property, the [armed] forces of the United States of America and the members thereof, the civilian component of the United States forces, the dependents of members of the forces and the civilian component, and their property, and the contractors of the Panama Canal Commission and of the United States forces, their dependents, and their property. The Republic of Panama will seek from its legislative branch such legislation as may be needed to carry out the foregoing purposes and to punish any offenders.

[11]

The parties shall conclude an agreement whereby nationals of either state, who are sentenced by the courts of the other state, and who are not domiciled therein, may elect to serve their sentences in their state of nationality.

Article X

Employment With the
Panama Canal Commission

[1]

In exercising its rights and fulfilling its responsibilities as the employer, the United States of America shall establish employment and labor regulations which shall contain the terms, conditions and prerequisites for all categories of employes of the Panama Canal Commission. These regulations shall be provided to the Republic of Panama prior to their entry into force.

[2]

(a) The regulations shall establish a system of preference when hiring employes, for Panamanian applicants possessing the skills and qualifications required for employment by the Panama Canal Commission. The United States of America shall endeavor to ensure that the number of Panamanian nationals employed by the Panama Canal Commission in relation to the total number of its employes will conform to the proportion established for foreign enterprises under the law of the Republic of Panama.

(b) The terms and conditions of employment to be established will in general be no less favorable to persons already employed by the Panama Canal Company or Canal Zone government prior to the entry into force of this treaty, than those in effect immediately prior to that date.

[3]

(a) The United States of America shall establish an employment policy for the Panama Canal Commission that shall generally limit the recruitment of personnel outside the Republic of Panama to persons possessing requisite skills and qualifications which are not available in the Republic of Panama.

(b) The United States of America will establish training programs for Panamanian employes and apprentices in order to increase the number of Panamanian nationals qualified to assume positions with the Panama Canal Commission, as positions become available.

(c) Within five years from the entry into force of this treaty, the number of United States nationals employed by the Panama Canal Commission who were previously employed by the Panama Canal Company shall be at least 20% less than the total number of United States nationals working for the Panama Canal Company immediately prior to the entry into force of this treaty.

(d) The United States of America shall periodically inform the Republic of Panama, through the Coordinating Committee, established pursuant to the agreement in implementation of Article III of this treaty, of available positions within the Panama Canal Commission. The Republic of Panama shall similarly provide the United States of America any information it may have as to the availability of Panamanian nationals claiming to have skills and qualifications that might be required by the Panama Canal Commission, in order that the United States of America may take this information into account.

[4]

The United States of America will establish qualification standards for skills, training and experience required by the Panama Canal Commission. In establishing such standards, to the extent they include a requirement for a professional license, the United States of America, without prejudice to its right to require additional professional skills and qualifications, shall recognize the professional licenses issued by the Republic of Panama.

[5]

The United States of America shall establish a policy for the periodic rotation, at a maximum of every five years, of United States citizen employes and other non-Panamanian employes, hired after the entry into force of this treaty. It is recognized that certain exceptions to the said policy of rotation may be made for sound administrative reasons, such as in the case of employes holding positions requiring certain nontransferable or non-recruitable skills.

[6]

With regard to wages and fringe benefits, there shall be no discrimination on the basis of nationality, sex or race. Payments by the Panama Canal Commission of additional remuneration, or the provision of other benefits, such as home leave benefits, to United States nationals employed prior to entry into force of this treaty, or to persons of any nationality, including Panamanian nationals who are thereafter recruited outside of the Republic of Panama and who change their place of residence, shall not be considered to be discrimination for the purpose of this paragraph.

[7]

Persons employed by the Panama Canal Company or Canal Zone government prior to the entry into force of this treaty, who are displaced from their employment as a result of the discontinuance by the United States of America of certain activities pursuant to this treaty, will be placed by the United States of America, to the maximum extent feasible, in other appropriate jobs with the government of the United States in accordance with United States Civil Service regulations. For such persons who are not United States nationals, placement efforts will be confined to United States government activities located within the Republic of Panama. Likewise, persons previously employed in activities for which the Republic of Panama assumes responsibility as a result of this treaty will be continued in their employment to the maximum extent feasible by the Republic of Panama. The Republic of Panama shall, to the maximum extent feasible, ensure that the terms and conditions of employment applicable to personnel employed in the activities for which it assumes responsibility are no less favorable than those in effect immediately prior to the entry into force of this treaty. Non-United States nationals employed by the Panama Canal Company or Canal Zone government prior to the entry into force of this treaty who are involuntarily separated from their positions because of the discontinuance of an activity by reason of this treaty, who are not entitled to an immediate annuity under the United States Civil Service Retirement System, and for whom continued employment in the Republic of Panama by the government of the United States of America is not practicable, will be provided special job placement assistance by the Republic of Panama for employment in positions for which they may be qualified by experience and training.

[8]

The parties agree to establish a system whereby the Panama Canal Commission may, if deemed mutually convenient or desirable by the two parties, assign certain employes of the Panama Canal Commission, for a limited period of time, to assist in the operation of activities transferred to the responsibility of the Republic of Panama as a result of this treaty or related agreements. The salaries and other costs of employment of any such persons assigned to provide such assistance shall be reimbursed to the United States of America by the Republic of Panama.

[9]

(a) The right of employes to negotiate collective contracts with the Panama Canal Commission is recognized. Labor relations with employes of the Panama Canal Commission shall be conducted in accordance with forms of collective bargaining established by the United States of America after consultation with employe unions.

(b) Employe unions shall have the right to affiliate with international labor organizations.

[10]

The United States of America will provide an appropriate early optional retirement program for all persons employed by the Panama Canal Company or Canal Zone government immediately prior to the entry into force of this treaty. In this regard, taking into account the unique circumstances created by the provisions of this treaty, including its duration, and their effect upon such employes, the United States of America shall, with respect to them:

(a) determine that conditions exist which invoke applicable United States law permitting early requirement annuities and apply such law for a substantial period of the duration of the treaty;

(b) seek special legislation to provide more liberal entitlement to, and calculation of, retirement annuities than is currently provided for by law.

Article XI

Provisions for the Transition Period

[1]

The Republic of Panama shall reassume plenary jurisdiction over the former Canal Zone upon entry into force of this treaty and in accordance with its terms. In order to provide for an orderly transition to the full application of the jurisdictional arrangements established by this treaty and related agreements, the provisions of this article shall become applicable upon the date this treaty enters into force, and shall remain in effect for thirty calendar months. The authority granted in this article to the United States of America for this transition period shall supplement, and is not intended to limit, the full application and effect of the rights and authority granted to the United States of America elsewhere in this treaty and in related agreements.

[2]

During this transition period, the criminal and civil laws of the United States of America shall apply concurrently with those of the Republic of Panama in certain of the areas and installations made available for the use of the United States of America pursuant to this treaty, in accordance with the following provisions:

(a) The Republic of Panama permits the authorities of the United States of America to have the primary right to exercise criminal jurisdiction over United States citizen employes of the Panama Canal Commission and their dependents, and members of the United States forces and civilian component and their dependents, in the following cases:

(i) for any offense committed during the transition period within such areas and installations, and

(ii) for any offense committed prior to that period in the former Canal Zone.

The Republic of Panama shall have the primary right to exercise jurisdiction over all other offenses committed by such persons, except as otherwise provided in this treaty and related agreements or as may be otherwise agreed.

(b) Either party may waive its primary right to exercise jurisdiction in a specific case or category of cases.

[3]

The United States of America shall retain the right to exercise jurisdiction in criminal cases relating to offenses committed prior to the entry into force of this treaty in violation of the laws applicable in the former Canal Zone.

[4]

For the transition period, the United States of America shall retain police authority and maintain a police force in the aforementioned areas and installations. In such areas, the police authorities of the United States of America may take into custody any person not subject to their primary applicable laws or regulations, and shall promptly transfer custody to the police authorities of the Republic of Panama. The United States of America and the Republic of Panama shall establish joint police patrols in agreed areas. Any arrests conducted by a joint patrol shall be the responsibility of the patrol member or members representing the party having primary jurisdiction over the person or persons arrested.

[5]

The courts of the United States of America and related personnel, functioning in the former Canal Zone immediately prior to the entry into force of this treaty, may continue to function during the transition period for the judicial enforcement of the jurisdiction to be exercised by the United States of America in accordance with this article.

[6]

In civil cases the civilian courts of the United States of America in the Republic of Panama shall have no jurisdiction over new cases of a private civil nature, but shall retain full jurisdiction during the transition period to dispose of any civil cases, including admiralty cases, already instituted and pending before the courts prior to the entry into force of this treaty.

[7]
The laws, regulations, and administrative authority of the United States of America applicable in the former Canal Zone immediately prior to the entry into force of this treaty shall, to the extent not inconsistent with this treaty, and related agreements, continue in force for the purpose of the exercise by the United States of America of law enforcement and judicial jurisdiction only during the transition period. The United States of America may amend, repeal or otherwise change such laws, regulations and administrative authority. The two parties shall consult concerning procedural and substantive matters relative to the implementation of this article, including the disposition of cases pending at the end of the transition period and, in this respect, may enter into appropriate agreements by an exchange of notes or other instruments.

[8]
During this transition period, the United States of America may continue to incarcerate individuals in the areas and installations made available for the use of the United States of America by the Republic of Panama pursuant to this treaty and related agreements, or to transfer them to penal facilities in the United States of America to serve their sentences.

Article XII
A Sea-Level Canal or a Third Lane of Locks

The United States of America and the Republic of Panama recognize that a sea-level canal may be important for international navigation in the future. Consequently, during the duration of this treaty, both parties commit themselves to study jointly the feasibility of a sea-level canal in the Republic of Panama, and in the event they determine that such a waterway is necessary, they shall negotiate terms, agreeable to both parties, for its construction.

[2]
The United States of America and the Republic of Panama agree on the following:

(a) No new interoceanic canal shall be constructed in the territory of the Republic of Panama during the duration of this treaty, except in accordance with the provisions of this treaty, or as the two parties may otherwise agree; and

(b) During the duration of this treaty, the United States of America shall not negotiate with third states for the right to construct an interoceanic canal on any other route in the Western Hemisphere, except as the two parties may otherwise agree.

[3]
The Republic of Panama grants to the United States of America the right to add a third lane of locks to the existing Panama Canal. This right may be exercised at any time during the duration of this treaty, provided that the United States of America has delivered to the Republic of Panama copies of the plans for such construction.

[4]
. In the event the United States of America exercises the right granted in paragraph 3 above, it may use for that purpose, in addition to the areas otherwise made available to the United States of America pursuant to this treaty, such other areas as the two parties may agree upon. The terms and conditions applicable to canal operating areas made available by the Republic of Panama for the use of the United States of America pursuant to Article III of this treaty shall apply in a similar manner to such additional areas.

[5]
In the construction of the aforesaid works, the United States of America shall not use nuclear exca-

vation techniques without the previous consent of the Republic of Panama.

Article XIII
Property Transfer and Economic Participation by the Republic of Panama

[1]
Upon termination of this treaty, the Republic of Panama shall assume total responsibility for the management, operation, and maintenance of the Panama Canal, which shall be turned over in operating condition and free of liens and debts, except as the two parties may otherwise agree.

[2]
The United States of America transfers, without charge, to the Republic of Panama all right, title and interest the United States of America may have with respect to all real property, including nonremovable improvements thereon, as set forth below:

(a) Upon the entry into force of this treaty, the Panama Railroad and such property that was located in the former Canal Zone but that is not within the land and water areas the use of which is made available to the United States of America pursuant to this treaty. However, it is agreed that the transfer on such date shall not include buildings and other facilities, except housing, the use of which is retained by the United States of America pursuant to this treaty and related agreements, outside such areas;

(b) Such property located in an area or a portion thereof at such time as the use by the United States of America of such area or portion thereof ceases pursuant to agreement between the two parties.

(c) Housing units made available for occupancy by members of the armed forces of the Republic of Panama in accordance with paragraph 5(b) of Annex B to the agreement in implementation of Article IV of this treaty at such time as such units are made available to the Republic of Panama.

(d) Upon termination of this treaty, all real property and nonremovable improvements that were used by the United States of America for the purposes of this treaty and related agreements, and equipment related to the management, operation and maintenance of the canal remaining in the Republic of Panama.

[3]
The Republic of Panama agrees to hold the United States of America harmless with respect to any claims which may be made by third parties relating to rights, title and interest in such property.

[4]
The Republic of Panama shall receive, in addition, from the Panama Canal Commission a just and equitable return on the national resources which it has dedicated to the efficient management, operation, maintenance, protection and defense of the Panama Canal, in accordance with the following:

(a) An annual amount to be paid out of canal operating revenues computed at a rate of thirty-hundredths of a United States dollar ($0.30) per Panama Canal net ton, or its equivalency, for each vessel transiting the canal, after the entry into force of this treaty, for which tolls are charged. The rate of thirty-hundredths of a United States dollar ($0.30) per Panama Canal net ton, or its equivalency, will be adjusted to reflect changes in the United States wholesale price index for total manufactured goods during biennial periods. The first adjustment shall take place five years after entry into force of this treaty, taking into account the changes that occurred in such price index during the preceding two years. Thereafter successive adjustments shall take place at the end of each biennial period. If the United States of America should decide that another indexing method is preferable, such method shall be proposed to the Republic of Panama and applied if mutually agreed.

(b) A fixed annuity of ten million United States dollars ($10,000,000) to be paid out of canal operating revenues. This amount shall constitute a fixed expense of the Panama Canal Commission.

(c) An annual amount of up to ten million United States dollars ($10,000,000) per year, to be paid out of canal operating revenues to the extent that such revenues exceed expenditures of the Panama Canal Commission including amounts paid pursuant to this treaty. In the event canal operating revenues in any year do not produce a surplus sufficient to cover this payment, the unpaid balance shall be paid from operating surpluses in future years in a manner to be mutually agreed.

Article XIV

Settlement of Disputes

In the event that any question should arise between the parties concerning the interpretation of this treaty or related agreements, they shall make every effort to resolve the matter through consultation in the appropriate committees established pursuant to this treaty and related agreements, or, if appropriate, through diplomatic channels. In the event the parties are unable to resolve a particular matter through such means, they may, in appropriate cases, agree to submit the matter to conciliation, mediation, arbitration, or such other procedure for the peaceful settlement of the dispute as they may mutually deem appropriate.

The United States of America and the Republic of Panama have agreed upon the following:

Article I

The Republic of Panama declares that the canal, as an international transit waterway, shall be permanently neutral in accordance with the regime established in this treaty. The same regime of neutrality shall apply to any other international waterway that may be built either partially or wholly in the territory of the Republic of Panama.

Article II

The Republic of Panama declares the neutrality of the canal in order that both in time of peace and in time of war it shall remain secure and open to peaceful transit by the vessels of all nations on terms of entire equality, so that there will be no discrimination against any nation, or its citizens or subjects, concerning the conditions or charges of transit, or for any other reason, and so that the canal, and therefore the Isthmus of Panama, shall not be the target of reprisals in any armed conflict between other nations of the world. The foregoing shall be subject to the following requirements:

(a) Payment of tolls and other charges for transit and ancillary services, provided they have been fixed in conformity with the provisions of Article III (c);

(b) Compliance with applicable rules and regulations, provided such rules and regulations are applied in conformity with the provisions of Article III;

(c) the requirement that transiting vessels commit no acts of hostility while in the canal, and

(d) such other conditions and restrictions as are established by this treaty.

Article III

[1]

For purposes of the security, efficiency and proper maintenance of the canal the following rules shall apply:

(a) the canal shall be operated efficiently in accordance with conditions of transit through the canal, and rules and regulations that shall be just, equitable and reasonable, and limited to those necessary for safe navigation and efficient, sanitary operation of the canal;

(b) ancillary services necessary for transit through the canal shall be provided;

(c) tolls and other charges for transit and ancillary services shall be just, reasonable, equitable and consistent with the principles of international law;

(d) as a precondition of transit, vessels may be required to establish clearly the financial responsibility and guarantees for payment of reasonable and adequate indemnification, consistent with international practice and standards, for damages resulting from acts or omissions of such vessels when passing through the canal. In the case of vessels owned or operated by a state or for which it has acknowledged responsibility, a certification by that state that it shall observe its obligations under international law to pay for damages resulting from the act or omission of such vessels when passing through the canal shall be deemed sufficient to establish such financial responsibility;

(e) vessels of war and auxiliary vessels of all nations shall at all times be entitled to transit the canal, irrespective of their internal operation, means of propulsion, origin, destination or armament, without being subjected, as a condition of transit, to inspection, search or surveillance. However, such vessels may be required to certify that they have complied with all applicable health, sanitation and quarantine regulations. In addition, such vessels shall be entitled to refuse to disclose their internal operation, origin, armament, cargo or destination. However, auxiliary vessels may be required to present written assurances, certified by an official at a high level of the government of the state requesting the exemption, that they are owned or operated by that government and in this case are being used only on government noncommercial service.

[2]

For the purposes of this treaty, the terms "canal," "vessel of war," "auxiliary vessel" "internal operation," "armament" and "inspection" shall have the meanings assigned them in Annex A to this treaty.

Article IV

The United States of America and the Republic of Panama agree to maintain the regime of neutrality established in this treaty, which shall be maintained in order that the canal shall remain permanently neutral, notwithstanding the termination of any other treaties entered into by the two contracting parties.

Article V

After the termination of the Panama Canal Treaty, only the Republic of Panama shall operate the canal and maintain military forces, defense sites and military installations within its national territory.

Article VI

[1]

In recognition of the important contributions of the United States of America and of the Republic of Panama to the construction, operation, maintenance, and protection and defense of the canal, vessels of war and auxiliary vessels of those nations shall, notwithstanding any other provisions of this treaty, be entitled to transit the canal irrespective of their internal operation, means of propulsion, origin, destination, armament or cargo carried. Such vessels of war and auxiliary vessels will be entitled to transit the canal expeditiously.

[2]

The United States of America, so long as it has responsibility for the operation of the canal, may continue to provide the Republic of Colombia toll-free transit through the canal for its troops, vessels and materials of war. Thereafter the Republic of Panama may provide the Republic of Colombia and the Republic of Costa Rica with the right of toll-free transit.

Article VII

[1]

The United States of America and the Republic of Panama shall jointly sponsor a resolution in the Organization of American States opening to accession by all states of the world the protocol to this treaty whereby all the signatories will adhere to the objectives of this treaty, agreeing to respect the regime of neutrality set forth herein.

[2]

The Organization of American States shall act as the depositary for the treaty and related instruments.

[3]

"Auxiliary vessel" means any ship, not a vessel of war, that is owned or operated by a state and used, for the time being, exclusively on government noncommercial service.

[4]

"Internal operation" encompasses all machinery and propulsion systems, as well as the management and control of the vessel, including its crew. It does not include the measures necessary to transit vessels under the control of pilots while such vessels are in the canal.

[5]

"Armament" means arms, ammunitions, implements of war and other equipment of a vessel which possesses characteristics appropriate for use for warlike purposes.

[6]

"Inspection" includes on-board examination of vessel structure, cargo, armament and internal operation. It does not include those measures strictly necessary for admeasurement, nor those measures strictly necessary to assure safe, sanitary transit and navigation, including examination of deck and visual navigation equipment, nor in the case of live cargoes, such as cattle or other livestock, that may carry communicable diseases, those measures necessary to assure that health and sanitation requirements are satisfied.

Article VIII

This treaty shall be subject to ratification in accordance with the constitutional procedures of the two parties. The instruments of ratification of this treaty shall be exchanged at Panama at the same time as the instruments of ratification of the Panama Canal Treaty, signed this date, are exchanged. This treaty shall enter into force, simultaneously with the Panama Canal Treaty, six calendar months from the date of the exchange of the instruments of ratification.

Done at Washington this 7th day of September, 1977, in duplicate, in the English and Spanish languages, both texts being equally authentic.

Annex

[1]

"Canal" includes the existing Panama Canal, the entrances thereto, and the territorial seas of the Republic of Panama adjacent thereto, as defined on the map annexed hereto (Annex B), and any other interoceanic waterway in which the United States of America is a participant or in which the United States of America has participated in connection with the construction or financing, that may be operated wholly or partially within the territory of the Republic of Panama, the entrances thereto and the territorial seas adjacent thereto.

[2]

"Vessel of war" means a ship belonging to the naval forces of a state, and bearing the external marks distinguishing warships of its nationality, under the command of an officer duly commissioned by the government and whose name appears in the navy list, and manned by a crew which is under regular naval discipline.

Protocol to Treaty Concerning the Permanent Neutrality and Operation of the Panama Canal

Article I

Whereas the maintenance of the neutrality of the Panama Canal is important not only to the commerce and security of the United States of America and the Republic of Panama, but to the peace and security of the Western Hemisphere and to the interests of world commerce as well;

Whereas the regime of neutrality which the United States of America and the Republic of Panama have agreed to maintain will ensure permanent access to the canal by vessels of all nations on the basis of entire equality;

Whereas the said regime of effective neutrality shall constitute the best protection for the canal and shall ensure the absence of any hostile act against it;

The contracting parties to this protocol have agreed upon the following:

The contracting parties hereby acknowledge the regime of permanent neutrality for the canal established in the Treaty Concerning the Permanent Neutrality and Operation of the Panama Canal and associate themselves with its objectives.

Article II

The contracting parties agree to observe and respect the regime of permanent neutrality of the canal in time of war as in time of peace, and to ensure that vessels of their registry strictly observe the applicable rules.

Article III

This protocol shall be open to accession by all states of the world, and shall enter into force for each state at the time of deposit of its instrument of accession with the secretary general of the Organization of American States.

Plebiscite set. Gen. Torrijos announced Sept. 9 that Panama would have a plebiscite on the new treaties.

Arriving in Panama City from Washington, where he and President Carter had signed the canal accords, Torrijos urged all Panamanians to participate in the plebiscite. "Not to vote that day means committing a crime against the country," he told a jubilant crowd of almost 200,000 persons who turned out to welcome him home.

"Never in the political history of this country could a leader have felt happier than I am," Torrijos declared. "Seventy years of dialogue with the deaf have ended. Panama was not heard . . . until the moral figure of President Carter emerged."

To applause and cheers from the audience, Torrijos read a message from Carter that said: "You, the people of Panama, have been very patient and understanding during this long process. We are fully conscious of what this has meant. We Americans look forward to coming here when we will be working together with you in understanding and friendship."

Torrijos closed by appealing for "consideration for the poor, ignorant residents of the [canal] zone who have really believed that this territory was theirs. The error they have committed does not justify a similar error by us."

Residents of the zone, whose southern end was adjacent to Panama City, had feared that the government-organized celebration would lead to a civilian invasion of the zone. American authorities had recommended that "zonians" not cross the line into Panama that day. But while the festivities lasted all night, with revelers dancing in the streets of the capital, there was no invasion.

A mistake in the drafting of the treaties' implementing agreements appeared to exempt American residents of the Canal Zone from future payment of income taxes, it was reported Sept. 14. As drafted, Article 15 of the implementing agreements said U.S. citizens and dependents employed by the canal authority "shall be exempt from any taxes, fees or other charges on income received as a result of their work." The article was supposed to have read, "any Panamanian

taxes, fees," etc., but the word "Panamanian" had been omitted accidentally. An employe of the canal company's information office said U.S. residents of the zone were "all jubilant" over the article, which apparently would stand because the treaties had been initialed and signed.

Panamanians demonstrate. Students and other Panamanians who opposed U.S. policies in general and the new Canal treaties in particular demonstrated in Panama before and after the treaties were announced.

At least 100 Panamanian students had invaded the Canal Zone Jan. 9 and burned two U.S. flags that had been painted with swastikas. The youths had broken away from a crowd of 3,000 students participating in a memorial service for 25 Panamanians and Americans who were killed in disturbances in the Canal Zone Jan. 9, 1964. These riots had led to negotiations for a new treaty. Police did not intervene to stop the flag-burning, according to press reports. However, U.S. Army troops in the zone had been on alert since Jan. 8 in anticipation of disturbances.

After the terms of the treaties became known, the Socialist Revolutionary League, a group of Trotskyist law students, denounced the provisions allowing American soldiers to remain in Panama until the year 2000. This was a "possible" treaty, not a "just" one, the students charged Aug. 9. The Independent Lawyers' Movement, which was politically to the right of center, charged that provisions allowing U.S. military intervention to protect the Canal after the year 2000 was nothing but "a new version—perhaps slightly less grotesque than before—of the hated American perpetuity on the canal issue," it was reported Aug. 11.

The Panamanian government conceded that the treaty was not the best imaginable, but it said the only alternative was an armed struggle that would "massacre . . . the best of our youth." The new canal accord was "good for us in some basic aspects, bad in others and ugly in others still," chief negotiator Escobar told a group of pro-government students Aug. 12.

The protesters wanted the U.S. to leave the Canal Zone immediately, not in 1999 as the treaties provided.

In the Canal Zone, meanwhile, residents who opposed the treaties staged a candlelight march of their own Sept. 7 to protest what they called "the death of democracy and human rights" in the zone. Many of the 35,000 Americans in the zone were afraid that once the area was under Panamanian jurisdiction they would lose the "due process of law" guaranteed by the zone's U.S. district court, according to John Williams, president of the 202-member Panama Canal Pilots Association.

While "zonians" expressed fear for their civil liberties and fear that the canal would not be run efficiently by the Panamanians, most were satisfied with the labor provisions of the new treaties, according to the president of the largest local union. However, the high rate of resignations among canal employes was expected to continue to rise as it had in the past year of negotiations for the new treaties, according to press reports.

Gun sales in the Canal Zone had risen sharply since the signing of the canal treaties Sept. 7, it was reported Sept. 18. U.S. residents were worried that the zone's crime rate—which had risen steadily in the past year as Panama's economic situation deteriorated—would increase even further as Panama assumed control of the area. Thieves preyed on the Canal Zone at least partly because zone security officers could not touch them after they crossed the border into Panama.

Panamanian students burned the U.S. ambassador's automobile in Panama City Oct. 4. The ambassador was out of the country at the time.

U.S. ratification battle looms. The Carter Administration admitted that it would have to work hard to obtain Senate ratification of the new treaties.

Sixty-seven Senate votes—a two-thirds majority—were needed for ratification, meaning that opponents of the new treaties needed to muster only 34 votes to defeat the accords. As recently as 1975, 37 senators had signed a resolution submitted by Sen. Strom Thurmond (R, S.C.) opposing any transfer of U.S.

"rights and jurisdiction" over the canal. Six of those senators were no longer in office, but Thurmond hoped to enlist the support of their successors and other senators in defeating the new treaties.

Joining Thurmond to lead the effort against the treaties were Sens. Jesse Helms (R, N.C.) and Orrin G. Hatch (R, Utah), it was reported Aug. 18. They would be aided by the American Conservative Union, which had budgeted $20,000 for newspaper advertisements against what conservatives called a canal "giveaway," according to a report Aug. 15. It was not known what role would be played by Ronald Reagan, the former Republican presidential candidate, who had staunchly opposed a new canal treaty during his 1976 presidential drive.

Preparing for an emotional national debate on the new treaty, the Administration had taken its case to editors and broadcasters around the country, it was reported Aug. 4. The White House Media Liaison Office had sent an 18-page "fact sheet" on the canal dispute to 3,600 grassroots outlets, according to the Washington Post. The document said, among other things, that "All Panamanian factions, no matter what their political ideology, want a new canal treaty and a more equitable relationship with the United States." Settlement of the canal dispute, the "fact sheet" added, would "remove the major issue which radical elements could exploit in Panama against the U.S."

The mention of "radical elements" was presumably a reference to leftist members of the Panamanian government and to Gen. Torrijos' well-publicized friendship with Cuban President Fidel Castro. Venezuelan President Carlos Andres Perez, one of Washington's closest allies in Latin America, had told Carter in June that the best way to reduce Cuban influence over Torrijos would be to negotiate a new canal treaty as quickly as possible, the Latin America Political Report said July 27.

To counter the Conservative onslaught in the Senate, the Administration planned a vigorous campaign under the leadership of Hamilton Jordan, the President's key political adviser. Bunker, Linowitz, Defense Secretary Harold Brown and the members of the Joint Chiefs of Staff were sent out to drum up support for the new treaties, and Carter himself pledged to campaign personally for Senate ratification.

The Administration almost immediately secured the support of former President Gerald Ford and his former secretary of state, Henry Kissinger, two figures considered essential to cracking Republican opposition to the new treaties.

Ford, who had been briefed on the canal negotiations since his departure from office, met Aug. 16 with Linowitz and Gen. George S. Brown, chairman of the Joint Chiefs, and declared afterward that the new treaties represented "an important step forward." He called for prompt Senate ratification of the accords and pledged to do what he could to convince conservative Republican senators to fall into line.

Kissinger met with Bunker Aug. 16 and said he intended to support the treaties. In a longer statement the next day, the former secretary of state expressed his "strong view that the new treaty is in the national interest of the United States" and that it "assures continuing, efficient, nondiscriminatory and secure access to the Panama Canal with the support of the countries of the Western Hemisphere instead of against their opposition and eventually their harassment."

(It was Kissinger who had given impetus to the canal negotiations in 1974 by signing an agreement on the negotiating principles with the Panamanian foreign minister. This agreement stipulated for the first time that one object of the negotiations was to remove the "in perpetuity" clause from the canal arrangement between the U.S. and Panama.

The Carter Administration scored another victory by convincing moderate Republican senators to withhold judgment on the treaties until they had seen the final drafts. Sen. Howard Baker (R, Tenn.), the Senate minority leader, and Sen. Ted Stevens (R, Alaska), the minority whip, acceded to the Administration's request Aug. 11.

While these senators remained quiet, opponents of the treaties in the House did not. Members of the House Merchant Marine and Fisheries Committee unleashed a barrage of criticism at hearings Aug. 17 to which they had summoned Bunker and Linowitz.

Rep. John M. Murphy (D, N.Y.), the committee's chairman, charged that the two negotiators had "caved in" to the demands of "the dictatorial regime" of Omar Torrijos. Murphy said that "many of our former military leaders are fearful of losing the only water passage between the Atlantic and Pacific Oceans." The "depth of feeling of the American people on this issue cannot be dismissed," the congressman added.

Linowitz acknowledged that "a very large percentage of the American people are opposed to the treaty," but he said this was because they "have not had the chance to learn the facts about what was involved." "The image that it is 'an immediate give-away' is entirely fallacious," Linowitz said. "We are going to be running the canal until the year 2000."

A Republican representative on the committee, Gene Snyder of Kentucky, charged that "The President and the Department of State have usurped the power of the Congress" in negotiating away U.S. rights over the Canal Zone. Rep. Robert K. Dornan (R, Calif.) called the new canal agreement "the worst foreign blackmail that I have seen since North Vietnam tweaked [Kissinger's] nose."

The "blackmail" was a reference to assertions by the Panamanian government—supported by Bunker and Linowitz—that the Senate's refusal to ratify the new treaties would lead to increased unrest in Panama.

Conservatives fight treaty ratification—Conservative senators and other opponents of the Panama Canal treaties were carrying out a concerted drive to prevent Senate ratification of the pacts, according to newspaper reports.

After the treaties were signed, Sen. Hatch said that he and like-minded senators would do whatever they could to defeat the treaties, including filibuster. Hatch and two allies, Sens. Thurmond and Helms, had carried their anti-ratification campaign to the Canal Zone Aug. 19–20, telling zone residents and Panamanian officials that the treaties were doomed in the Senate. Back in Washington Aug. 21 Thurmond repeated his contention that the canal was "American property" and should not be "given away."

The senators were counting on public opinion, which was reported running against the treaties, and on the influence of prominent opponents of the accords, such as the American Conservative Union (ACU), the Veterans of Foreign Wars (VFW) and Citizens for the Republic, the political organization of former California Gov. Ronald Reagan.

The ACU began a direct-mail and advertising campaign against the treaties Aug. 21. Its first newspaper advertisements appeared proclaiming, "There is no Panama Canal! There is an American canal at Panama. Don't let President Carter give it away!"

The VFW's national convention passed a resolution against the treaties Aug. 23, and the Sept. 1 issue of the newsletter of Citizens for the Republic warned against "surrendering" the canal. Citizens for the Republic was expected to contribute financially to the anti-ratification drive from the substantial store of funds left over from Reagan's unsuccessful bid for the Republican presidential nomination in 1976.

After meeting Aug. 25 with the treaties' American negotiators, Sol Linowitz and Ellsworth Bunker, Reagan said he would work personally to prevent ratification. He had called Aug. 23 for a national referendum on the treaties, arguing that polls showed the American people would reject the accords if allowed to vote on them.

The White House was conducting an intense campaign for ratification, reminding some observers of Carter's 1976 presidential drive. Administration officials warned that Carter's entire foreign policy might hinge on the canal treaties. If the pacts were rejected, the officials said, Carter's authority to negotiate in other areas might be impaired.

Prominent Americans continued to endorse the treaties. Three Republican senators announced their support of the pacts—Mark Hatfield (Ore.) and S.I. Hayakawa (Calif.) Aug. 20, and Lowell Weicker (Conn.) Aug. 29. AFL-CIO president George Meany also endorsed the treaties Aug. 29, saying "there is no particular reason for us holding onto territories 6,000 miles away just because we built the canal on somebody else's land back in 1904." The United Auto Workers added its endorsement Aug. 30.

In addition, the Carter Administration could count on the support of leaders of U.S.-based international banks and multi-national corporations, according to the Washington Post Aug. 22. These executives were worried about Latin American reaction to a rejection of the treaties, the Post reported. They noted that private U.S. investment in Latin America totaled about $24 billion—two-thirds of total American investment in developing nations—and that trade between the U.S. and Latin America totaled $34 billion in 1976.

In the U.S., meanwhile, the required Senate vote on the treaties was put off until early in 1978. Sen. Robert C. Byrd (D, W. Va.), Senate majority leader, Sept. 10 said he would not call up the accords until "January or February" because senators would need until then "to study the facts and to assess the merits."

Byrd said the treaties were of "such far-reaching importance" that "they ought not to be rushed." "The judgment should be based on the merits, not on jingoism or knee-jerk reactions," the senator declared. Byrd said he would not decide how to cast his own vote until after he heard "the evidence presented to the [Senate] Foreign Relations Committee" and discussed it with his constituents in West Virginia.

Byrd's support was considered essential to the treaties' success in the Senate. So was the backing of Senate Republican leader Howard H. Baker (Tenn.). Baker, who was under strong pressure from conservatives to oppose the pacts, Sept. 11 said he would make no decision "until I know what I am talking about."

Other legislators took strong stands, however. Sens. Barry Goldwater (R, Ariz.) and John Stennis (D, Miss.) came out against the treaties, it was reported Sept. 11. Sen. Paul Laxalt (R, Nev.) charged Sept. 9 that the Carter Administration had "completely misgauged sentiment on this issue" and announced that conservative "truth squads" would be sent across the country to oppose the canal accords.

Laxalt, who had managed Ronald Reagan's campaign for the Republican presidential nomination in 1976, said the "truth squads" would consist of senators and congressmen informed on all aspects of the treaties and canal history. They would concentrate on security considerations and the economic implications of the treaties, including the "extent of involvement of eastern banking establishments and big corporations," Laxalt said.

Noting that labor unions such as the AFL-CIO and the United Auto Workers were joining international banks and multinational companies in supporting the canal accords, Laxalt said the "truth squad" campaign would be directed as much against "big labor and big business" as against the Carter Administration. The canal issue was as "strong politically as anything that has come down the pike in a long, long time," Laxalt said.

Reagan delivered a long attack on the canal treaties in testimony before the Senate Judiciary subcommittee Sept. 8. The accords contained "some commendable ideas" but they had "a fatal flaw," the former California governor said. "They proceed from a false premise that we can expect reliable, impartial, trouble-free secure operations of the canal in the future by relinquishing the rights we acquired in the 1903 treaty."

Once U.S. "rights of sovereignty" over the Canal Zone were removed, Reagan asserted, "there is nothing to prevent a Panamanian regime from deciding one day to nationalize the canal and to demand that we leave immediately. That would present us with the very thing the treaty advocates say we want to avoid: confrontation, or its alternative, unceremonious withdrawal in the face of arbitrary demand."

Reagan added that enactment of the treaties might lead "influences hostile to hemisphere security" to "make their presence felt much greater than before in Panama." Chief among these "influences" was Cuban President Fidel Castro, "whose interest in exporting revolution is well known," Reagan said. Castro was a personal friend of Gen. Torrijos.

Human rights issue raised—Ronald Reagan Sept. 8 also questioned whether the Carter Administration—and not Congress—had the constitutional power to transfer U.S. property in the Canal Zone to Panama, and he criticized the President for promoting human rights at the same time that he was negotiating with Torrijos' dictatorial regime.

Charging that the U.S. was showing a "double standard" on human rights, Reagan said: "Human rights criticism has

been leveled at a number of nations in the Western Hemisphere which have always been friendly toward us, yet I cannot recall a single word of criticism by any representative of our government toward Panama in this regard." Reagan noted that Freedom House, a private organization concerned with repression around the world, had rated Panama as "one of 67 nations in the world that is 'not free.'"

Members of the House International Relations Committee also raised the human rights issue during testimony by the top U.S. negotiators of the canal treaties, Sol Linowitz and Ellsworth Bunker. Bunker said Panama's human rights record was "not perfect" but also not "horrible." He noted that in 1975 Amnesty International had not included Panama in a list of nations that engaged in torture, and that a State Department report said that while Torrijos' government had expelled political dissidents, it was not currently using brutality for political purposes.

Torrijos moved to defuse the human rights issue Sept. 13, inviting the Organization of American States (OAS) to come and "see firsthand the reality of our human rights policies." In a telegram to the chairman of the OAS' human rights committee, Torrijos said: "You are welcome to travel anywhere in Panama, to speak to anyone, and report to the world. I will give you the keys to our jails, and if you find any political prisoners, you can release them."

"Panama is not perfect," Torrijos declared, "but we do respect the human rights of all those people who live within our geography, and the new canal treaties are a symbol to the world of our desire to eliminate discrimination and injustice."

Torrijos also invited the United Nations to send observers to the October plebiscite and see "the freedom with which Panamanians [would exercise] their right to determine their destiny."

Torrijos' invitations were praised by officials of the Carter Administration, who feared the impact of the human rights issue on the Senate debate on the canal accords. "We're gratified by ... Gen. Torrijos' interest in dealing forthrightly with the allegations of human rights violations," Linowitz said Sept. 13.

In an attempt to defuse the human rights issue, Torrijos said he would allow the return to Panama of all political exiles on a list to be drawn up by a student organization, it was reported Sept. 17.

U.S. debate continues—Two former U.S. secretaries of state, Henry A. Kissinger and Dean Rusk, gave strong endorsements of the treaties Sept. 14 in testimony before the House International Relations Committee.

Kissinger said the agreements provided the chance "to modernize an outdated arrangement that has itself become a threat to the interests it was designed to protect." Senate rejection of the treaties, he warned, "would poison our relationship with all the countries of Latin America on all other issues and leave us for the first time in our history facing the unanimous hostility of all the nations to the south of us in our own hemisphere."

Rusk argued that under the new treaties, the U.S. was in a "far stronger" position to enforce the neutrality of the canal than it had been under the old 1903 agreement. Obliquely addressing the human rights issue, Rusk said the U.S. had obtained a better deal from Gen. Torrijos than it could have obtained from a democratic Panamanian government. A more representative Panamanian regime, Rusk asserted, would have demanded full control of the canal earlier than Torrijos accepted.

Leaders of two American veterans' associations argued the opposite position to the committee Sept. 16. Frank D. Ruggiero, national commander of the American Veterans (AMVETS), said the world would view the U.S. as "a 'pushover' " if the Senate approved the treaties. William J. Rogers, a past commander of the American Legion, charged that "human rights under Torrijos were not better than they were under Hitler during the 1930s and yet by supporting this treaty, our U.S. government is propping up a dictatorship."

In New York, the new treaties received the support of the National Council of Churches, which declared Sept. 14 that the agreements "symbolize the understanding that the true security of our nation rests on the power of a respect for justice rather than on the power of armed might."

Military chiefs reaffirm support—Under challenge from opponents of the Panama Canal treaties, top U.S. military leaders denied that their support for the pacts had been coerced by President Carter.

Rep. Samuel Stratton (D, N.Y.) charged Sept. 20 that the Joint Chiefs of Staff did not truly support the treaties. "The Joint Chiefs have been put on notice this year that they either express the party line or else," Stratton said. (He was presumably referring to President Carter's removal of Maj. Gen. John K. Singlaub from the command of U.S forces in South Korea because the general publicly had disagreed with Carter's stated Korea policy.

Stratton said the canal treaties contained no specific provision allowing the U.S. to intervene to defend the canal after 1999. "There is not a single word there that gives us any defense rights," he said. "We need it, and in words of one syllable, not an abstruse interpretation by some second-echelon flunky in the State Department."

Replying to Stratton and other critics Sept. 27, the chairman of the Joint Chiefs defended both his support of the treaties and their provisions to safeguard the canal's neutrality. Gen. George S. Brown told the Senate Foreign Relations Committee that he had "personally worked very diligently for four years to achieve these treaties." He and other military leaders supported the pacts "because we feel they are right," Brown said. He added that "the key point that finally found its expression in the treaty of neutrality was conceived within the Defense Department."

Brown's testimony was echoed by Lt. Gen. D. P. McAuliffe, commander of the U.S. Army's Southern Command in the Canal Zone, and by Adm. Robert L. J. Long, vice chief of naval operations.

McAuliffe said he had worked for two years with the Joint Chiefs and the U.S. canal negotiators to make sure that "our defense rights were taken care of" in the treaties. Long said it was his "view that the continued use of the Panama Canal for military purposes in our national defense plans is best assured through the provisions of the new treaties." Long assured the committee that "there has been absolutely no pressure made on the chief of naval operations" to support the canal pacts.

Defense Secretary Harold Brown appeared before the committee with the military leaders and testified emphatically that the new treaties would reduce the chance of internal attacks against the canal while allowing the U.S. to defend the waterway from outside threats.

Despite Gen. Brown's testimony, opponents of the treaties continued to doubt his sincerity. Sen. Strom Thurmond (R, S.C.) charged Oct. 4 that the Joint Chiefs were "under the gun" and were inclined to agree with the President, whatever their true feelings might be. Sen. Paul S. Sarbanes (D, Md.) scolded Thurmond for questioning Gen. Brown's integrity. Statements such as Thurmond's were "not a contribution to the debate" over the treaties, Sarbanes said.

Bugging & blackmail charges aired. There were allegations that the U.S. had wiretapped the Panama Canal treaty talks, and that after Panamanian officials discovered this, they used it to blackmail the U.S. into making concessions in the negotiations, CBS News reported Sept. 16.

U.S. and Panamanian officials publicly denied both the bugging and the blackmail, but sources in the Senate Intelligence Committee, which was investigating the allegations in closed session, said Panama's military ruler had been wiretapped.

According to the sources, which were cited by the Washington Post Sept. 20, U.S. officials told the committee that American agents in Panama had bugged the home and office of Brig. Gen. Omar Torrijos in 1974, after the canal negotiations began in earnest.

Torrijos discovered the surveillance when an American soldier gave him transcripts of his intercepted telephone conversations, according to the allegations before the committee. But, the Post's sources said, U.S. officials insisted to the committee that Torrijos had not made any issue of the wiretaps. The matter had been dropped by both sides and it had played no role in the negotiations, the U.S. officials claimed.

The sources did not name the U.S. officials they cited, but it was known that the committee heard testimony Sept. 16

from Ellsworth Bunker, the top U.S. canal negotiator. Bunker testified again Sept. 19, joined by his co-negotiator, Sol Linowitz, and the director of the Central Intelligence Agency, Stansfield Turner.

The intelligence committee's chairman, Sen. Daniel K. Inouye (D, Hawaii), said after the hearings Sept. 19 that the panel had found "no reason to believe or conclude that U.S. intelligence activities have in any way affected the final results" of the canal talks.

In Panama, meanwhile, the bugging and blackmail report seemed to cause consternation despite the fact that Gen. Torrijos had told a Washington Post reporter in May that he knew "the Americans" had wiretapped a telephone conversation between him and his negotiators.

The Panamanian government issued a statement Sept. 16 saying it was unaware of any electronic eavesdropping, any blackmail "or any other kind of threat against the U.S. negotiators." Panamanian negotiator Carlos Lopez Guevara called the CBS News report "baloney," and Foreign Minister Nicolas Gonzalez Revilla said it was "terrible, incredible, really wild." Gonzalez added: "I think it's part of the campaign against the treaty in the U.S., and we should expect more wild things like this in the future. These people are working hard to defeat ratification of the treaty in the Senate."

Following the intelligence committee's decision Sept. 19, the Senate Judiciary subcommittee on the separation of powers decided to investigate the matter. The subcommittee scheduled hearings for Sept. 30 and subpoenaed the directors of the Central Intelligence Agency, the Defense Intelligence Agency and the Federal Bureau of Investigation. But the hearings were postponed after Attorney General Griffin Bell complained that the subpoenas were too broad. The hearings presumably would be rescheduled since a majority of the subcommittee, including panel chairman James B. Allen (D, Ala.), opposed the canal treaties.

Poll shows U.S. public opposes pacts. A public opinion poll commissioned by the Associated Press showed that the American people were overwhelmingly opposed to the canal treaties, AP reported Sept. 21.

Of 1,548 adult Americans interviewed by pollsters over the telephone, only 29% favored the treaties. Fifty per cent opposed the pacts and about 21% expressed no opinion. When broken down along party lines, the poll results showed Democrats opposing the treaties by a margin of 44%–34%, and Republicans opposing them by 61%–26%. Independents rejected the pacts by 54%–25%.

Mail to U.S. senators was running even more heavily against the canal treaties, although this was at least partly the result of highly organized mail campaigns by conservative groups. Senate Majority Leader Robert Byrd (D, W.Va.) reported Sept. 24 that his mail was running "4,000 to 6" against the treaties, but he noted that the letters contained similar "verbiage" suggesting an organized effort.

The Republican National Committee rejected the treaties Sept. 30, but its statement referred to the pacts "in their present form."

U.S. Senate probes treaties. The U.S. Senate Foreign Relations Committee began hearings on the treaties Sept. 26.

The first witnesses before the panel were Secretary of State Cyrus Vance and his top canal negotiators, Ellsworth Bunker and Sol Linowitz. They spent much of their time trying to explain apparent discrepancies between American and Panamanian interpretations of the agreements.

Two committee members, Sen. Howard H. Baker (R, Tenn.) and Sen. Richard B. Stone (D, Fla.), noted that some statements by Panama's top negotiator appeared to contradict the Carter Administration's views on two major issues: the defense of the canal after 1999 and the right of U.S. warships to transit the waterway "expeditiously."

The Panamanian negotiator, Romulo Escobar Bethancourt, had told Panama's National Assembly Aug. 19 that the treaty on the permanent neutrality of the canal did not give the U.S. the right to intervene unilaterally after 1999 to defend the waterway.

Vance disputed this interpretation before the committee, insisting that the U.S. could determine on its own when the canal's neutrality was threatened and could intervene to meet the threat regardless of Panama's actions.

Linowitz added that he believed Escobar merely had been trying to win support for the treaties in Panama when he made the statement to the National Assembly. The U.S. negotiator said he had been assured by Panama's foreign minister and by its ambassador in Washington that Escobar would make no such statement again.

Escobar also had told the National Assembly that the right of "expeditious" passage for U.S. warships did not mean "privileged" passage. Vance disputed this too, saying that "in practical terms," "expeditious" passage meant that "our ships will go to the head of the line."

Baker and Stone urged the Carter Administration to get the Panamanian government to clarify its positions on these issues so they meshed with the President's. Vance, Bunker and Linowitz agreed to try, but Panamanian officials appeared to reaffirm Escobar's statements a few days later.

One of Escobar's assistants in the negotiations, Carlos Lopez Guevara, said on Panamanian television Sept. 30 that "nothing" in the canal treaties allowed the U.S. to intervene to defend the canal after 1999. "It is sad to see high officials of the United States" arguing otherwise, he said. He added that U.S. intervention would be legitimate only if there was an attempt to deny passage through the canal to an American ship.

Panamanian Vice President Gerardo Gonzalez agreed with Lopez in the same broadcast, asserting that "the principle of non-intervention" was established in a treaty article that forbade American military personnel or canal employes to participate in political activities in Panama.

The Carter Administration's position was further undermined Oct. 4 when Sen. Robert Dole (R, Kan.) released a confidential cablegram in which the U.S. Embassy in Panama informed the State Department of Lopez Guevara's views. The cable quoted Lopez as saying that American officials should stop using the term "intervention" because "intervention is simply forbidden by international law."

The Lopez cable also said that a statement made by Gen. Torrijos was being used inappropriately by U.S. officials. Torrijos had declared Sept. 7 that Panama was "under the Pentagon's defense umbrella," and Carter Administration officials had quoted this as evidence that Panama gave the U.S. the right to defend the canal after 1999. But Lopez Guevara argued that Torrijos was "stating a fact, not giving the U.S. the right to intervene," the cablegram said. According to Lopez, Panama had been under "the Pentagon's defense umbrella" since 1947, when the U.S. and many Latin American countries signed a hemispheric defense agreement.

Lopez also disagreed with the Carter Administration's interpretation of "expeditious transit" for U.S. warships, the cable said. Lopez said that at the beginning of the negotiations Panama tentatively had accepted the idea of preferential passage for U.S. warships, but later it had rejected this in favor of "expeditious" passage.

Trying to reconcile Lopez' views with its own, the State Department said Oct. 4 that Lopez had only been drawing a distinction between U.S. intervention in Panama's internal affairs and U.S. intervention to defend the canal, which was ostensibly a different matter. But Sen. Dole said the Senate must amend the treaties to make U.S. defense rights explicit.

The State Department denounced Dole Oct. 5 for releasing the cablegram. Department spokesman Hodding Carter 3rd said Dole had violated the confidentiality of the diplomatic process and had damaged the relationships of U.S. diplomats with their sources of information.

Acting Secretary of State Warren Christopher sent the Foreign Relations Committee a letter saying the State Department was "continuing contact with the Panamian government to clarify any points of interpretation regarding the treaties which may arise in either country." He reiterated the department's contention that Panama was ruling out U.S. intervention in Panamanian internal affairs, not U.S. action to protect the canal's neutrality.

But this was not enough for the committee's ranking Democrat, Sen. Frank Church (Ida.). "Let's be clear," Church said Oct. 5. "The Senate is not likely to ratify these treaties if crucial provisions are being interpreted differently by Panama and the U.S. This is a matter which must be clarified."

At the hearings' Oct. 10 session, three retired U.S. military leaders argued over the international consequences of a possible Senate rejection of the canal treaties.

Adm. Elmo Zumwalt, a former chief of naval operations, said "there will be a lot of cheers in Moscow and Havana" if the treaties were defeated. Gen. Maxwell Taylor, a former chairman of the Joint Chiefs of Staff, agreed. Rejection of the treaties would cause turbulence in Panama, he said, and this was "always good news in Moscow."

Adm. Thomas Moorer, also a former chairman of the Joint Chiefs, disagreed sharply. He said he believed the Soviet Union's support of Cuba was due principally to its interest in the Panama Canal. "We have in fact a Torrijos-Castro-Moscow axis," he said, referring to the Panamanian chief of government and to Cuban President Fidel Castro.

U.S. & Panama clarify treaty language. President Carter and Brig. Gen. Omar Torrijos issued a joint communique Oct. 14 that was intended to reconcile apparently conflicting U.S. and Panamanian interpretations of the Panama Canal treaties.

After meeting at the White House for an hour and 40 minutes, the two leaders released a "statement of understanding" on the two issues over which there seemed to be the most disagreement: the right of the U.S. to protect the canal's neutrality after the year 2000, and the right of U.S. warships to transit the waterway "expeditiously."

On the first issue, the statement denied that the U.S. would be allowed to intervene in the "internal affairs of Panama." Any U.S. military action, the statement asserted, "will be directed at insuring that the canal will remain open, secure and accessible, and shall never be directed against the territorial integrity or political independence of Panama."

As for the second issue, the statement said U.S. warships could go through the canal "as quickly as possible, without any impediment, with expedited treatment, and in case of need or emergency, [they can] go to the head of the line of vessels. . . ."

The statement confirmed what the U.S. State Department had been arguing for more than a week: that there was a difference between defending the canal's neutrality and intervening in Panamanian affairs, and that "expeditious" transit could simply mean preferential transit.

Panamanian officials, however, had agreed with only the first of those contentions before Torrijos met with Carter. Like the State Department, the Panamanian canal negotiators had argued that U.S. congressmen were wrong in using the term "intervention" to describe future U.S. military action to protect the canal's neutrality. But the Panamanians categorically had rejected American officials' assertions that "expeditious" passage meant "privileged" passage.

Gen. Torrijos further clarified the intervention issue as he departed for Panama after meeting Carter. "If a great power attacks the canal or puts the canal in danger," he said, "it is the right of the United States to go and defend the canal. But it does not have the right to intervene or interfere in the internal affairs of Panama."

The joint statement improved the outlook for Senate ratification of the canal agreements, although ratification was by no means certain. Before the statement was issued, even senators who supported the treaties had said ratification was impossible as long as U.S. and Panamanian officials disagreed about the meaning of the accords' vague language.

Senate Majority Leader Robert Byrd (D, W.Va.) said Oct. 15 that the joint statement was "a very important diplomatic achievement," in fact "more than I expected to be achieved." However, Byrd said he and "the great majority of senators" remained uncommitted regarding ratification.

Sen. Robert Dole, (R, Kan.), a vehement critic of the canal treaties, conceded that the joint statement was "a step in the right direction" and said the statement's language should be "incorporated into the treaty itself." But even if this were done, he said, he would oppose the accords until other changes were made. These included reducing the amount of money the U.S. would pay Panama under the treaties, and eliminating the clause that committed the U.S. to building any new isthmian canal in Panama.

Continuing his offensive against the treaties Oct. 13, Dole told the Senate he had received allegations that Gen. Tor-

rijos was involved in smuggling narcotics into the U.S. The Justice Department said Oct. 13 that Torrijos had never been the subject of a U.S. drug investigation, but the department conceded the next day that Torrijos' brother, Moises, had been indicted in New York five years ago on charges of drug smuggling. He was never arrested because he stayed out of the U.S. after the indictment was handed up.

Attorney General Griffin Bell had briefed President Carter, congressional leaders and members of the House and Senate intelligence committees on the allegations concerning the Torrijos family, it was reported Oct. 13. Sen. Byrd said Oct. 15 that Bell had assured him Gen. Torrijos had "no direct connection" to the international drug trade.

According to a statement by an aide to Sen. Dole Nov. 16, the U.S. Drug Enforcement Administration had agreed to give Dole its files on Moises Torrijos, brother of Panama's military leader. There was alleged to be a sealed indictment against Moises Torrijos in New York for heroin smuggling. The Panamanian government was growing increasingly bitter over unproved charges by opponents of the canal treaties that the Torrijos family was involved in the international narcotics traffic, the Washington Post reported Nov. 13.)

Other problems raised. Sen. James B. Allen (D, Ala.), another opponent of the canal treaties, charged Oct. 28 that the military and economic aid pledged by the U.S. to Panama in the treaty negotiations was unconstitutional. "These extrinsic financial arrangements appear to violate the doctrine of separation of powers inasmuch as they deny the Senate the right to give advice and consent to all aspects of the new proposed treaty arrangements with Panama," Allen said. The State Department said Nov. 15 that the aid was independent of the canal treaties, and would be provided to Panama even if the Senate failed to ratify the accords.

Raoul Berger, an authority on constitutional law, told a Senate subcommittee Nov. 3 that the treaties must be approved by the House of Representatives as well as the Senate. The former Harvard professor told the subcommittee on separation of powers that Article IV of the Constitution, which gave Congress the power to dispose of property, must take precedence over the President's authority to negotiate treaties with foreign nations. Conservative opponents of the canal treaties, including the subcommittee's chairman, Sen. Allen, had argued that the House must approve the transfer of U.S. property in the Canal Zone to the Panamanian government.

Torrijos seeks international support. Brig. Gen. Omar Torrijos embarked on a 10-nation tour Sept. 24 to seek international support for the Panama Canal treaties.

U.S. newspapers said these stops were designed to reassure major users of the Panama Canal that the waterway would run smoothly under Panamanian control. But Torrijos gave another reason:

"Pierre Trudeau [Canada's prime minister] gave me good advice," Torrijos said in Israel. "He said, 'Torrijos, you should go out into the world because some people believe you're a crazy loon.' "

Torrijos visited the U.S. Sept. 24–27 and Israel Sept. 27–30. In Israel he conferred with Premier Menahem Begin (a firm supporter of the canal pacts) and toured Jerusalem, the West Bank and the Golan Heights. The visit was widely interpreted as an attempt by Torrijos to win support for the canal treaties among American Jews.

Among the countries Torrijos visited after leaving Israel September 30 were Yugoslavia (Sept. 30–Oct. 1), Spain (Oct. 1–3), France (Oct. 3–4) and Italy (Oct. 4–6). He met the political leaders of each country and in Italy he had an audience with Pope Paul VI.

Torrijos said Oct. 6 that in Yugoslavia he had conferred with President Tito about the possibility the canal treaties would be rejected by the U.S. Senate. Torrijos said Tito had told him that if that happened, he should "exhaust all peaceful methods before resorting to force" to gain control of the canal.

Before leaving Panama Torrijos had responded to disparaging remarks made about him and his government by American conservative leaders who opposed the canal treaties. In an interview published in the Miami Herald Sept. 28,

Torrijos denied charges by Americans that he was "a dictator and a communist." He described himself politically as "conservative in some things, progressive in others." He was a "little less" communist than the late Franklin D. Roosevelt and a "lot less" communist than Abraham Lincoln, Torrijos said.

Torrijos invited his severest American critic, former California Gov. Ronald Reagan, to visit Panama and evaluate its government firsthand. "But please, tell [Reagan] to stop calling me a tinhorn dictator," Torrijos told the Herald. "At least wrap me in copper or something else."

Torrijos' willingness to leave Panama so soon before the Oct. 23 plebiscite on the canal treaties showed he was confident the Panamanian people would approve the agreements, press reports said. An increasing number of Panamanian organizations were coming out for the treaties, according to the New York Times Sept. 27. The economic benefits the treaties would bring Panama were apparently more important in the public's mind than the danger of American military intervention under the canal's neutrality treaty.

Panamanian nationalists on both the left and the right continued to criticize the canal agreements—particularly the neutrality treaty—but the government dismissed them as "traitors" and "bad Panamanians."

Panama plebiscite OKs treaties. In a nationwide plebiscite Oct. 23, the people of Panama approved the new Panama Canal treaties by a two-thirds majority.

With 90% of the ballots counted Oct. 24, it was unofficially reported that 468,-664 Panamanians had voted in favor of the agreements and 228,697 had voted against. Approximately 788,000 persons—about half the Panamanian population—were eligible to vote.

The two-thirds margin fell short of the 90% approval that the government had been predicting, but the regime was pleased nonetheless. Torrijos said the vote proved that "our people would not turn their backs on the country when the country demands their presence."

Torrijos said the U.S. Senate would be "irresponsible" if it ignored the plebiscite results in its debate on the treaties.

The Panamanian voting was orderly, with no report of unrest or government interference. The vote was supervised by a wide variety of Panamanians—including soldiers, firemen and schoolteachers—and by observers from the United Nations and from two dozen North and South American universities. Still, opponents of the treaties charged that there had been vote fraud.

Juan Carlos Voloj, an opposition schoolteacher, said he had voted "no" eight times under his own name to show that government registration practices were inadequate. Voloj had a camera crew film him voting twice at the same polling station. He was subsequently arrested, according to the Washington Post Oct. 24.

Under the balloting procedure, Panamanians over the age of 18 could vote if they showed their identity cards and dipped a finger in what was supposed to be indelible ink. However, opposition sources charged that identity cards could be forged and that the ink easily could be washed off. In response to such charges, election officials said the names of all voters would be fed into a computer to check for duplication.

The plebiscite was the first free vote to be held in Panama since 1968, when the country's last president was elected, only to be overthrown by the National Guard within a few days.

The plebiscite was preceded by a 40-day national debate in which opponents of the treaties were given access to the normally censored news media. However, the opposition's campaign proved so effective that the government, fearing defeat, censored criticism of the treaties in the last days before the plebiscite.

The most effective opposition group was the Independent Lawyers' Movement, a group of about 300 attorneys of varying political beliefs. The movement criticized not only the canal treaties but the lack of political freedom under Torrijos' government, it was reported Oct. 14.

Opponents of the agreements—who included students and intellectuals in addition to the lawyers—were most disturbed by the treaty on the permanent neutrality of the canal, which they feared would allow the U.S. to intervene in Panama in any way it saw fit to protect the waterway.

Opponents also charged that the treaties would legalize the presence of U.S. troops in the Canal Zone, and that they would help militarize Panama. The Panama Canal Treaty called for $50 million in U.S. military aid to Panama over the next 10 years, and Panamanians feared this would make the National Guard more powerful than it already was.

Opponents also feared that the large U.S. economic aid package foreseen in the treaties would only drive Panama further into debt. They preferred a direct U.S. payment for canal revenues "lost" by Panama during the years that the U.S. controlled the waterway.

Gen. Torrijos, who was out of the country during the first half of October, hammered home the government's arguments in the last days of the debate.

In a televised address Oct. 20, he made the surprising assertion that he was glad to be under the U.S. "defense umbrella." In case of a foreign attack, Torrijos said, "if we push the button here, the bell rings there, then they [the Americans] come to defend the Panama Canal." Presumably referring to the U.S. and the Soviet Union, he added: "I do not want to free myself from the threat of an alligator, only to be threatened by a shark."

Torrijos' statements amounted to a reversal of policy, for he had said previously that a U.S. military alliance was the price Panama would have to pay to gain control of the canal.

Responding to other criticism of the treaties, Torrijos said Oct. 21 that future U.S. aid would be used not to arm the National Guard but to buy tractors, build housing and finance public works. The canal agreements would give Panama control of its docks, allowing it to increase foreign trade, and would give Panamanians many high-paying jobs now held by Americans, putting an end to unemployment, Torrijos asserted.

The final vote count in the Oct. 23 plebiscite was 506,805 (66%) in favor, 245,-117 (32%) against and 14,310 (2%) void, it was reported Oct. 29.

The treaties were rejected in only one of Panama's 10 provinces. They did best in Veraguas, the native province of Brig. Gen. Omar Torrijos, Panama's chief of government. There the vote was 81% in favor and 18% against.

U.S. senators visit Panama. Seven Democratic senators visited Panama Nov. 9–12 to inspect the Panama Canal and find out how Panamanians felt about the new canal treaties signed by the U.S. and Panamanian governments.

The legislators, led by West Virginia's Robert C. Byrd, the Senate majority leader, all said at the beginning of the visit that they did not know how they would vote when the treaties came before the Senate for ratification in 1978. But by the end of the visit two of the senators said they supported the treaties without reservation, two offered qualified support and all were favorably impressed by Gen. Omar Torrijos.

The senators—Byrd, Howard Metzenbaum (Ohio), Spark Matsunaga (Hawaii), Donald Riegle (Mich.), Walter Huddleston (Ky.), Paul Sarbanes (Md.) and James Sasser (Tenn.)—arrived in Panama Nov. 9 and began traveling about the country with Torrijos the next day.

They first visited San Blas Province, an archipelago off Panama's Atlantic coast and the only province to vote against the canal treaties in the Panamanian plebiscite Oct. 23. The islands were populated mostly by Cuna Indians who depended on tourism for their livelihood and apparently feared that American tourists would stop coming to Panama once the treaties were enacted. The senators asked Indian representatives why the province had gone against the canal treaties, and the Indians replied that they were angry over the government's neglect of San Blas. Torrijos told them he would pay more attention to the province in the future.

The senators then visited Torrijos' summer home at Los Santos and returned to Panama City for talks with the Independent Lawyers' Movement, which strenuously opposed the canal treaties, and the Liberal Party, which reluctantly supported them. Both the lawyers' movement and the party felt the treaties compromised Panamanian sovereignty by giving the U.S. control over the canal and part of the Canal Zone until the year 2000.

The senators inspected the canal Nov. 11 and lunched with the top American officials in the Canal Zone—Maj. Gen. Harold R. Parfitt, the zone's governor, and Lt. Gen. Dennis McAuliff, commander of the Army's Southern Command in the zone.

Before returning to Washington the next day, the senators—minus Sen. Sasser, who departed early—conferred with representatives of the Panamanian Students' Federation, a leftist group that felt the canal treaties were injurious to Panamanian sovereignty but supported the pacts as a "patriotic duty." The students said that if the Senate rejected the accords, Panamanians might take up arms to gain control of the canal.

At a hastily organized press conference immediately before the senators' departure, Torrijos made a number of pledges intended to dispel American doubts about his government and the canal treaties.

The Panamanian strongman said he was prepared to resign from office if the Senate considered him an obstacle to passage of the treaties. (President Carter said Nov. 12 that he did not consider Torrijos an obstacle.) Torrijos also promised to lift press censorship and eliminate human rights abuse in Panama. To accomplish the latter, he said, he would abrogate the martial law provisions imposed in 1969, including one that allowed the government to jail suspects without trial for up to 15 years. Torrijos also pledged to allow the return of as many as 60 Panamanian political exiles (the Washington Post estimated Nov. 13 that there were 90 Panamanian exiles in Miami and elsewhere).

The pledges were directed at Americans who opposed the treaties or were undecided about them because of the Panamanian government's dictatorial image. Several of the senators who visited Panama admitted privately that the government was not nearly as repressive as they had imagined, according to the Washington Post Nov. 12. They saw on their tour of the Panamanian countryside that Torrijos was popular and that he exercised his nearly absolute powers with moderation, the Post reported.

Torrijos also had convinced the senators that he was not a communist, as conservatives in Panama and the U.S. charged. The senators said that despite Torrijos' radical rhetoric and his friendship with Cuban President Fidel Castro, he was not a communist and the Panamanian people would not accept him if he were one, the Post reported.

Sens. Metzenbaum and Matsunaga said Nov. 12 that they now supported the canal treaties without reservation, and Matsunaga said he would lobby for the pacts' ratification. Sens. Riegle and Huddleston said they would vote for the accords if Torrijos kept his promise to respect human rights. Byrd and Sarbanes reserved judgment on the treaties, although Byrd was known to be leaning toward ratification.

With his considerable power as Senate majority leader, Byrd was crucial to the Carter Administration's campaign for ratification. He had provided the Administration with a boost Nov. 8, the day before his departure for Panama, when he said he had detected a "shifting" of U.S. national opinion toward ratification of the accords. "What is required is a better education of the public and for all of us," Byrd said, echoing a recurrent Administration statement on the accords. "This will take some time."

A poll of the Senate by United Press International, reported by the Miami Herald Nov. 22, said 39 senators favored or were leaning toward the canal pacts, 29 opposed or were leaning against them, and 32 were undecided. This meant that to secure ratification, the Carter Administration would have to hold on to all 39 certain or probable "yes" votes and pick up 28 of the 32 uncommitted votes.

Republicans exploit Canal issue. The Republican Party was using the Panama Canal issue to raise money for future political campaigns, the Washington Post reported Oct. 30.

The Republican National Committee was sending out fund-raising letters signed by former California Gov. Ronald Reagan asking recipients to sign an enclosed petition against the canal treaties and to contribute toward "a minimum of two million dollars" for the Republican Party. "Unless these funds are raised," the letter said, "we won't defeat those Democrats who vote time and time again to support actions that weaken our national security . . . . Believe me, without your support, the canal is as good as gone."

Another group that opposed the canal accords, the American Conservative Union, began a television campaign against Senate ratification Oct. 29. A half-hour program broadcast in parts of Texas, Louisiana and Florida asked viewers to urge their senators to vote down the treaties and to contribute money to finance future broadcasts against ratification.

Four Republican senators—Jake Garn (Utah), Jesse Helms (N.C.), Strom Thurmond (S.C.) and Paul Laxalt (Nev.)—appeared on the program to denounce the treaties. So did a Republican congressman, Philip M. Crane of Illinois, and a former Canal Zone federal Judge, Guthrie F. Crowe. The dominant theme of the program was: "There is no Panama Canal. There is an American Canal at Panama." The program contended that the canal was vital to the U.S.' "economy, our national defense and our spirit," and should not be "given away" to Panama.

Meanwhile, other Republican senators worried that the canal issue was dangerously dividing the party. Senate Minority Leader Howard Baker (Tenn.) warned Nov. 13 that Republicans would "regret it for years" if they kept attacking each other over the treaties. "We really must not cannibalize our party," Baker said in a televised interview. "We're not big enough."

Eight Republican senators had written a letter to Republican National Chairman Bill Brock earlier in the week charging that Republican opponents of the treaties were trying to purge treaty supporters from Congress. One of the signers of the letter, Jacob K. Javits (N.Y.), said Nov. 13 that it was "extremely unwise" for a minority party such as the Republicans to foster bitter internal disputes.

Javits, a supporter of the canal pacts, said it would be "very unfortunate" if Baker assumed leadership of the anti-ratification forces in the Senate. Baker, meanwhile, remained uncommitted. "In a word," he said, "I've decided not to decide. I'm going to wait."

Economic & Foreign Developments

Economic package set. The government Jan. 3 introduced a series of economic measures apparently designed to restore business confidence in the economy.

The package included a 5% sales tax on all items but food, medicine and fuel; a reduction of income taxes for those in the lower brackets; a cut in government spending; a $300-million investment program to create jobs, and various modifications of the progressive 1972 labor code.

The labor code changes—including elimination of seniority rights, reduction of guarantees against dismissal, compulsory arbitration to avoid strikes, and a two-year freeze on labor contracts—were protested immediately by major unions.

The 14,000-member union of the Chiriqui Land Co., the Panamanian subsidiary of United Brands Co. of the U.S., declared an indefinite strike Jan. 4 to demand abrogation of the new measures. The same day, the 100,000-member National Workers' Council demanded the resignation of the government officials responsible for the labor code modifications.

Leaders of these unions subsequently met with Gen. Omar Torrijos, who assured them that the code changes would not increase unemployment. However, the labor leaders and others in Panama appeared convinced that as the economic situation worsened, the government was siding with business interests, the London newsletter Latin America reported Jan. 14.

"This is the hour of private enterprise," Labor Minister Adolfo Ahumada had said Jan. 5. The government's plan for economic recovery, according to the Latin America Economic Report Jan. 14, depended on a high level of public investment, which in turn depended on foreign loans. The public investment—expected to create 3,700 new jobs in 1977—was designed not only to make up for the sharp drop in private investment but to create new opportunities for private enterprise, according to the Report.

The government program did have some support on the Panamanian left, according to the newsletter Latin America. The Panamanian National Workers' Union backed the officials who drafted the program, and the communist People's Party and the pro-government students' federation described the economic package as "tactical readjustments in the revolutionary process." The government's supporters asserted opposition to the package was "counterrevolutionary."

Economy stagnated in '76. Panama's gross domestic product registered a zero growth rate in 1976, according to preliminary government statistics cited by the Latin America Economic Report April 22. It was the first time this had happened in 25 years.

Negative growth rates were registered in agriculture, manufacturing, construction, commerce and Canal Zone services. And the most dynamic sectors of the economy—public financial activities and services—expanded more slowly than in recent years.

Government and private economists agreed that the main causes of the country's economic stagnation were drops in export earnings and private investment, and the government's limits on expenditures and investments, according to the Latin America Economic Report. One major cause of the export slack was the low international price of sugar, one of Panama's leading exports.

Additional economic measures announced by Torrijos were wage and price controls and government pay cuts. The prices of beans, cooking oil, bread and other staples were rolled back (although this only partially compensated for rises in services, fuel, cigarettes and other goods at the beginning of January). All government salaries over $750 per month would be reduced by 1%–20%, and the government would disconnect 20% of its telephones and air conditioners to save costs and energy, Torrijos said.

Guatemala severs Panama ties. The Guatemalan government announced May 19 that it had broken diplomatic relations with Panama to protest Panama's support of independence for Belize. Belize was the British colony in Central America over which Guatemala claimed sovereignty.

Panama's military strongman, Brig. Gen. Omar Torrijos, had infuriated Guatemalan leaders by declaring the previous weekend: "Yes, I have my hands in Belize, and I'm not going to take them out. . . . I'm going to help those people because they need it, I'm going to help George Price because he's a mystic who needs it, and I don't care if it makes Laugerud mad." Price was prime minister of Belize; Gen. Kjell Laugerud Garcia was president of Guatemala.

In an angry reply May 20, Laugerud called Torrijos "a man who doesn't know the meaning of honor" and a "pseudo-emulator" of Cuban President Fidel Castro and Ugandan President Idi Amin Dada. Laugerud warned Torrijos that if he "has his hands in Belize, he could get them burned."

Torrijos reiterated his support for an independent Belize May 20, on the first day of a visit to Panama by Price. Price said Guatemala's renunciation of ties with Panama was "an affront to the United Nations and to the countries of the Third World." (Both the U.N. General Assembly and the movement of nonaligned nations had passed resolutions in 1975 favoring Belizean independence. [See 1975, pp. 1020C2, 840C3])

Torrijos and others had argued that Belize's 150,000 inhabitants were not culturally, racially or historically related to Guatemala. The Belizean people, most of whom originally came from Jamaica, Trinidad and Tobago and other Caribbean islands, spoke English.

Guatemala's ambassador to Mexico, Gen. Doroteo Monterroso Miranda, subsequently charged that Torrijos was supporting Belizean independence because he had invested more than $9 million in hotels and condominiums in the British colony, and he feared losing the investment under Guatemalan rule, it was reported May 24. Torrijos denied the charge and recommended that it be investigated by an international tribunal.

A Panamanian television station reported May 27 that Torrijos had asked Mexico, Venezuela, Costa Rica and Colombia to intercede to help resolve his difficulties with Guatemala. (At least two of those countries—Mexico and Venezuela—had come out strongly for Belizean independence in the past year, seriously weakening Latin American support for Guatemala's claim to Belize.)

Great Britain favored independence for Belize, but the colony did not want its freedom without a British commitment to defend it from attack by Guatemala. Price had given up trying to obtain an indefinite defense guarantee from London and was now aiming for a 10-year defense treaty, according to the Latin America Political Report May 20. Price reasoned that if Belize could survive the first 10 years of independence without attack from Guatemala, its diplomatic position in international forums would be established and its security thereafter assured, the Report said.

(Belize had announced in February that it would establish a defense force of regular and volunteer soldiers. British military officers would help set up the force, it was reported Feb. 13.)

Guatemala, meanwhile, opposed any unilateral action by Great Britain and asked for a continuation of talks between British and Guatemalan officials on the future of Belize. Laugerud had warned that Guatemala would "resort to arms" if Britain unilaterally made Belize independent, it was reported May 17.

In an earlier development, the Belize City Reporter had said Jan. 30 that Guatemalan nationals were crossing into Belize in droves. Border officials were capturing and deporting the illegal immigrants at a rate of 40 per day, the newspaper reported. It was unclear whether the migration was the result of hard times in Peten, Guatemala's border province, or was an invasion sponsored by the Guatemalan government, the newspaper said.

IDB loans. The Inter-American Development Bank (IDB) granted Panama a $98-million loan for the La Fortuna hydroelectric project, it was reported Sept. 2.

Peru

Politics & the Economy

The military government headed by Francisco Morales Bermudez suggested several times during 1977 that it was getting ready to turn control of Peru over to elected civilians. It was finally announced that the change would take place in 1980. In the meantime, however, political arrests and other curbs on free political action continued. As part of its plan for an eventual shift to civilian control, the regime promised to "institutionalize" the economic nationalizations and land reforms of the past 10 years, but it still appeared to be continuing efforts to strengthen the private sector of the economy. Rising prices and controversial austerity rules provoked wide protest.

Eventual civilian rule seen. President Gen. Francisco Morales Bermudez said Jan. 1 that the government might be handed back to civilians "within three to four years." This was Morales' first indication of when the armed forces intended to give up power, press reports said.

Political & economic reforms proposed. The government Feb. 6 published a political and economic plan for 1977–80 that contained a vague promise of democratic elections.

The program, called Plan Tupac Amaru after the 18th-century Inca revolutionary, replaced the more radical Plan Inca devised by ex-President Juan Velasco Alvarado, who was overthrown in 1975 by Francisco Morales Bermudez.

Plan Tupac Amaru retained some of the major reforms of the Velasco administration, including the restructuring of the agrarian sector, but it departed significantly from Plan Inca by stressing foreign investment, regional development, decentralization and administrative efficiency, and by scuttling the "social property enterprises" (EPS), one of Velasco's major innovations. The EPS were established in 1974 as decentralized, independent and profit-making companies controlled by their own workers.

It had been reported in November 1976 that the number of EPS described as "in formation" would be cut back from 63 to 23, and the number being planned would be reduced from 454 to 60, according to the Latin America Economic Report (LAER) Jan. 7.

President Morales in September had made clear his policy that EPS would not be allowed to compete with private companies. This policy conflicted with the 1974 Social Property Law. The government was seeking to encourage the recovery of private investment, on which its economic strategy was now based, LAER reported.

Another reason for the downgrading of EPS, according to LAER, was the government's desire to stem the growing popularity of Angel de las Casas Grieve, who had headed the National System of Social Property until July 1976, when he had been replaced by Gen. Cesar Rosas Cresto.

At the end of August 1976 there were three fully operational EPS employing a total of 2,480 workers, LAER reported. The 63 EPS "in formation" were controlled by committees dominated by government representatives. With the 454 projects still at various stages of preparation, the entire EPS sector involved planned investments of more than $1 billion and the creation of 200,000 new jobs, LAER said.

In the political sphere, Plan Tupac Amaru called vaguely for civilian participation in the government and said democratic elections would be scheduled within the plan's lifespan. The plan also called for a new constitution but did not say when or by whom the charter would be drawn up.

(Interior Minister Gen. Luis Cisneros Vizquerra said Feb. 12 that municipal elections would be held in 1978 and details of a presidential election would be worked out by 1980. He said he did not know whether the presidential vote would take place in 1980 or 1981.)

The government called for a "great national debate" on the new plan, but critics noted that such a debate was unlikely when the major newspapers were government-controlled, left-wing magazines were banned, individual liberties were suspended and opposition labor and political leaders were being arrested and/or deported.

To facilitate the debate, the government Feb. 18 set up suggestion boxes throughout the country in which individual citizens and groups were encouraged to place written comments on Plan Tupac Amaru. The deadline for comments was set for March 23 and later postponed to April 30.

The government said individual comments on the plan should be written on legal-size paper in an original and three copies, with the writer's address and his voter's-registration number attached. Legally authorized groups that submitted comments had to list the numbers of their tax booklets.

The major newspapers praised Plan Tupac Amaru, but individual journalists were less enthusiastic, noting that left-wing magazines remained banned under the plan and thus unable to contribute to the "national debate," the London newsletter Latin America reported Feb. 25. Other observers noted that the plan promised to "regulate the right to strike so that it does not affect the interests of the country and the workers," and to regulate the universities as well. "On the whole," Latin America said, "the plan depicts a closely controlled, regimented society, which it is difficult to reconcile with the stated aims of free expression, participation and electoral choice."

Nevertheless, political organizations soft-pedaled their criticism of the plan in hopes of improving relations with the government and ensuring that elections eventually took place. Victor Raul Haya de la Torre, the octogenarian head of the opposition APRA party, said Plan Tupac Amaru was an "honest rectification" of earlier government errors and a "new voice summoning the support of the whole country," Latin America reported. APRA stressed the "positive" aspects of the plan, noting that its emphasis on regional development, decentralization and foreign investment was consistent with the party's platforms since 1931. The opposition Popular Action party (AP) appeared split on the plan; AP's secretary general, Javier Alva Orlandini, dismissed the plan out of hand, but the party's leading political figure, Manuel Ulloa, was more eager to cooperate with the government, according to Latin America.

Development plan set. The government May 9 announced its national development plan for 1977–78, which envisioned a drop in foreign investment and foresaw considerable growth in the mining and petroleum sector.

Total investment under the plan was projected at $2.2 billion, 48% of which would come from the public sector and 52% from the private, cooperative and social property sectors. Non-public investments would rise by 9.7% over their 1976 level, while public-sector investments would decrease by 1.6%. Foreign investments were expected to decrease by 64.6% with the completion of the Cuajone copper mine.

The beginning of production at Cuajone and other mines and the completion of the trans-Andean oil pipeline were expected to help expand the mining and petroleum sector by 38%. The fishing sector was to grow by 10.9% (although an extremely poor fishing season in April called this into doubt). Agricultural growth was projected at 2.8% and that of manufacturing at 3%. With this expansion, imports were expected to fall by 5.7%.

Leftist military officers expelled. Four radical military officers were expelled from Peru Jan. 8 for allegedly trying to "convince public opinion, and particularly the armed forces, that the revolutionary process has been cut short."

The four, all retired from active duty, were army Gens. Leonidas Rodriguez Figueroa and Arturo Valdez Palacio, navy Capt. Manuel Benza Chacon and Rear Adm. Jorge Dellepiane Ocampo. All had signed the manifesto of the new Revolutionary Socialist Party in November 1976. Interior Minister Luis Cisneros Vizquerra had charged in December that the party sought to "distort" the "final aims" of the armed forces' "revolutionary" government.

More than a dozen leftist military officers and labor leaders had been expelled from Peru in recent months, according to press reports. "Deportations of union leaders and labor lawyers have become an almost weekly occurrence," the London newsletter Latin America reported Jan. 14. Julian Sierra, leader of the metalworkers' union, had been expelled Dec. 28, 1976; Camilo Valqui, lawyer of the Centromin miners' union, had been expelled the next day.

Sierra, Valqui, Rodriguez, Dellepiane and Benza all went to Panama, while Valdez chose exile in Mexico.

The most prominent of the new exiles was Rodriguez, who had headed the social mobilization agency, SINAMOS, under ex-President Juan Velasco Alvarado. Dellepiane had been Velasco's industry minister, and Valdez had chaired the commission that drew up the Social Property Law, now being reformed by President Francisco Morales Bermudez, who had overthrown Velasco.

Arrests continue under emergency rules. Arrests of leftists continued under the state of emergency, which suspended individual guarantees and established a nighttime curfew. (The curfew was reduced by one hour in Lima and Callao beginning Feb. 16, and was now in effect from 2 a.m. to 5 a.m.)

Police raided the Enrique Guzman teachers' college outside Lima before dawn Feb. 21, arresting about 650 students on charges of having turned the school into "a center for Marxist-Leninist indoctrination." All but 40 were reported released within the next five days, but one student died in custody. The Interior Ministry said the student had died of an "aneurism" after receiving proper medical care, but the Peruvian Students' Federation charged that he had died after being tortured and hit in the head with a rifle butt, it was reported Feb. 26.

Gustavo Espinoza, former secretary general of the Communist-backed General Confederation of Peruvian Workers, and Alfonso Barrantes Lingan, a leftist lawyer, were arrested in Lima early in March, it was reported March 11. Barrantes was linked with members of the teachers' college who were arrested Feb. 21, according to the newsletter Latin America. Another left-wing lawyer, Genaro Ledesma, was kidnapped by armed civilians Feb. 10, Latin America reported.

The curfew in Lima was lifted April 7, but the nationwide state of emergency and suspension of individual guarantees remained in effect. During the nine months of the curfew eight persons had been killed and daily arrests had averaged 1,000, according to government figures cited by the Mexican newspaper Excelsior April 8.

The government continued to limit political participation through its policy of selective repression, according to the Latin America Political Report April 1. Intellectuals were under particular pressure, the newsletter reported. Following the dismantling of the teachers college at La Cantuta, authorities had made over 50 arrests in the university town of Ayacucho, where students and staff at the Universidad San Cristobal de Huamanga had protested earlier detentions.

Velasco urges civilian regime—Ex-President Velasco gave his first interview for publication since his removal from office in 1975. In the interview, published by the Lima magazine Caretas Feb. 3, Velasco said that since the armed forces had abandoned his "revolution," they had lost their reason for governing and should hand power back to civilians.

Morales to stay on after army retirement. The commanders of Peru's armed forces announced April 22 that Gen. Francisco Morales Bermudez would stay on as president of the country after he retired from the army in January 1978.

The military chiefs said Morales would remain in office "to guarantee the stability of the revolutionary process and to attain the general objectives embodied in the Tupac Amaru government plan." They called for "national unity" behind Morales, who had been president since the ouster of Gen. Juan Velasco Alvarado in August 1975.

The Apra party, the largest political movement in Peru, said May 7 that it supported Morales' presidency but wanted an "open dialogue" with the military government to find solutions to the country's "grave problems." Apra and Peru's other civilian parties had rejected the government's earlier suggestion that they write down their criticisms of the Tupac Amaru plan and place them in special boxes set up in government buildings.

Apra also had protested when the government announced that it would take 18 months to register Peruvian voters properly, it was reported April 22. This presumably would force postponement of the 1978 municipal elections pledged by the government under the Tupac Amaru plan.

Ban on magazines lifted. The government Jan. 1 had lifted its ban on the publication of seven magazines, saying the conditions that led to the prohibition "have been overcome."

Six of the magazines had been closed in July 1976. They were: ABC, organ of the opposition APRA party; Unidad, organ of the Communist Party; Gente (rightist), El Tiempo (conservative), Oiga (center-left) and Equis-X (leftist).

The seventh, Caretas, had been banned in March 1975. Its co-publisher, Enrique Zileri Gibson, was subsequently expelled from Peru, but he was pardoned and allowed to return in May 1976.

The seven magazines had once been accused of promoting "campaigns to obstruct the enactment of measures for economic reactivation, to destroy the unity of the armed forces and to subvert order and public peace."

The magazines Equis-X and Oiga reappeared Jan. 14 under what Oiga called a "gentlemen's agreement." The agreement stipulated that extremist periodicals would remain banned, according to Oiga. The seven that were allowed to reappear were asked "not to threaten the unity of the armed forces, not to abet subversion, not to promote class warfare, to contribute to national unity and not to attack the dignity of the human person," Oiga reported.

Oiga criticized the continuing ban on allegedly extremist magazines, "which have needlessly benefited from gratuitous martyrdom." The ban, Oiga asserted, had harmed President Francisco Morales Bermudez' avowed effort to increase popular participation in the military government.

Equis-X urged the armed forces to "return to the barracks and not disgrace themselves." The Peruvian people, Equis-X asserted, wanted a "political plan" providing full freedom of expression, absolute respect for human rights, self-government on the municipal and regional levels, subordination of the armed forces to a democratically elected government, retention of the structural reforms enacted by the military government, and gradual establishment of democratic socialism "on the basis of economic pluralism, mixed management of companies and planning that is carried out through the mechanisms of the market."

The government decided Sept. 28 to lift the bans imposed on six other magazines since July 1976. The publications were the right-wing weekly Opinion Libre and the leftist magazines Marka, Momento, La Palabra del Pueblo, El Amauta del Mar and El Periodista. Most editors welcomed the government action, but some said Peru's press would not be free until the government lifted prior censorship on eight other magazines and reversed the "socialization" of Lima's daily news-papers. The newspapers had been expro-priated in 1974; the government had said then that it would put them under the con-trol of workers, peasants and other "na-tional sectors," but it had not yet done so.

Magazine censorship ends—The govern-ment lifted prior censorship of magazines Dec. 18, pledging to "re-establish full freedom of expression in Peru. "

The government, however, retained con-trol over the country's major newspapers.

Economy minister resigns in policy dispute. Economy Minister Luis Barua Castaneda resigned May 13 in a dispute with the special Cabinet commission on economic policy.

The commission, headed by the industry minister, Gen. Gaston Ibanez O'Brien, had rejected the economic program Barua had proposed to submit to the Interna-tional Monetary Fund (IMF). Peru was seeking IMF credits to alleviate its serious payments deficit.

Barua had suggested, among other measures, a reduction of the government's budget deficit; an increase in the price of gasoline and other petroleum products to overcome the deficit of the state oil com-pany, Petroperu, and a continuation of the Central Bank's program of "mini-devalua-tions" of the sol, the national currency. (The sol had been devalued once or twice a week since September 1976, when it was valued at 65 to the U.S. dollar. The most recent devaluation, announced May 26, put the currency at 77.82 to the dollar.)

The Cabinet commission had come up with its own proposals, which were quite different from Barua's. While the panel accepted Barua's call for reduced public spending—though not in arms acquisition programs—it opposed gasoline price increases, calling instead for price hikes of 150% for diesel fuel and lubricants. The commission also recommended easier credit and large wage raises to increase the amount of money in circulation, and it opposed devaluing the sol below 80 to the dollar in 1977.

Neither the commission's nor Barua's proposals conformed with the strict austerity measures expected by the IMF, although Barua's were closer. According to the Financial Times (London) April 13,

the IMF wanted Peru to increase taxes and gasoline prices; hold down inflation to 15% in 1977 (it was 40% in 1976); keep a low ceiling on government expenditures (including, implicitly, subsidies of essential goods), and devalue the sol to 100 to the dollar by the end of 1977.

The IMF's conditions were rejected by both the Cabinet commission and the Central Bank. The commission's alternate proposals were supported by leading Peruvian industrialists, while Barua's were backed by the Central Bank. The bank's management team, headed by Carlos Santisteban, resigned along with Barua May 13.

President Francisco Morales Bermudez rejected the Central Bank managers' resignations and, with their consent, re-placed Barua with Walter Piazza Tanguis, a prominent engineer and industrialist. The president agreed to maintain the Central Bank's approach to stabilizing the economy, according to the Latin America Political Report May 20.

Piazza Tanguis, who took office May 17, was left with the task of negotiating with the IMF. The job was considered extremely difficult because Peru's military leaders were implacably opposed to the IMF's stringent terms. But Peru desperately needed IMF financing in 1977, following a payments deficit between $500 million and $600 million in 1976. The IMF was offering Peru only $50 million in standby credits, but a consor-tium of U.S. banks was offering another $200 million on the condition that Peru ob-tain the IMF credits and accept IMF monitoring.

Austerity program—Piazza Tanguis June 10 announced an emergency austerity program to deal with what he called Peru's "desperate financial crisis."

Analysts said the program appeared to be a toned-down version of the austerity plan demanded by the IMF.

The new program's measures included:

■ A 50% increase in gasoline prices, with consequent rises in transportation fares.

■ An end to government subsidies of food prices.

■ A $200-million cut in imports in 1977, including imports of military equipment.

■ Substantial reductions in government spending—including bans on the hiring of new personnel and the purchase of new office equipment—with the aim of cutting the budget deficit by 56% in 1977.

■ An intensified effort to obtain $250 million in foreign financing to help meet 1977 payments of Peru's foreign debt.

■ A continuation of the Central Bank's program of "mini-devaluations" (a new devaluation June 11 set the exchange rate of the Peruvian sol at 78.84 to the U.S. dollar).

■ An unspecified series of measures to encourage production, particularly for export.

Piazza conceded that the plan would have "harsh effects" on the costs of food and transportation, but he said it was necessary to reduce Peru's "foreign indebtedness, which has reached the limit." Peru's debt-servicing requirements for 1977 were "alarming," the economy minister noted.

(The government decreed a wage increase June 11, but it fell far short of offsetting the price increases caused by the austerity program, according to analysts. The maximum wage hike was 15% for the lowest-paid workers.)

Piazza's program differed from the IMF's requirements only in certain details, according to the Latin America Economic Report June 17. The IMF, for example, would have preferred a larger reduction in the budget deficit and a big, immediate devaluation of the sol instead of continued mini-devaluations. However, the IMF was likely to accept Piazza's plan as adequate, the Report said.

The new program represented a defeat for Peru's industry minister, Gen. Gaston Ibanez O'Brien, who had pressed for measures to expand the economy. Piazza's unspecified provisions to encourage production were a concession to Ibanez, according to the Latin America Economic Report.

Newspaper scores program—La Prensa, one of the six government-controlled newspapers in Lima, charged June 13 that the economy minister's austerity measures would lead to "the complete destruction of the economic and social fabric of the country."

By causing "drastic" reductions in buying power and the demand for goods and services, the program would severely cut production and employment, the newspaper asserted. The June 11 wage increase was mystifying, the paper continued, since it did not even "create the illusion of compensating for the price rises."

Students, workers protest—Students and workers in several Peruvian cities staged demonstrations and clashed with police to protest the price increases that followed announcement of the new austerity program.

Police used tear gas and high-pressure water hoses to disperse student demonstrators in Lima June 13. The protesters retreated to university buildings and threw rocks and firebombs at policemen from the top floors. The same day bank clerks in the city staged a 1½-hour strike to protest the government's austerity measures.

The government imposed a curfew in Cuzco June 17 after three days of protests caused by large increases in bus and taxi fares. Students and some workers built barricades in the streets and threw rocks at security officers, while railway workers and bus and taxi drivers went on strike. The disturbances disrupted Cuzco's large tourism industry: tourists were forced to walk the two miles from the airport to their hotels, and were unable to reach the area's main attraction, the Inca ruins at Machu Picchu.

About 1,000 students clashed with police in Arequipa June 21 to protest a 50% increase in public transport fares. Protesters barricaded the city's main thoroughfare for two hours and then threw rocks at police after they cleared the street.

Disturbances also were reported June 21 in Sicuani, Ayacucho, Trujillo and Urubamba. In Sicuani about 3,000 students stoned the mayor's residence and sacked offices of the Agriculture Ministry, burning documents and causing an estimated $25,000 in damage.

General strike paralyzes Lima. A month-long series of protests against the government's economic austerity policies culminated in a bloody general strike that paralyzed Lima July 19.

At least six persons died as police and soldiers fired on rioting students and workers in various parts of the city. Unofficial reports said as many as 20 persons were killed in fighting in the shantytowns that surrounded the Peruvian capital.

Authorities arrested more than 300 persons in a dragnet of industrial areas and a raid on headquarters of the pro-Communist General Confederation of Peruvian Workers (CGTP). The CGTP had called the strike in defiance of government emergency measures that prohibited strikes and suspended individual guarantees.

Because long-distance telephone service was disrupted, it was not known whether the strike affected major cities in the interior, where there had been serious disturbances since the government announced its austerity program June 10.

The Lima strike was called to press a variety of demands, foremost a freeze on the prices of essential goods and an increase in wages to compensate for the rise in the cost of living. Other demands included resumption of annual bargaining for collective contracts, now suspended; abrogation of laws making it easier for employers to fire employes; reinstatement of employes dismissed under those laws; release of all political prisoners, and cancellation of the emergency measures that restricted freedom of the press, assembly and labor action.

A number of other unions joined the CGTP strike in an unusual display of Peruvian labor solidarity. Among these were the National Workers' Federation (CNT), a Christian Democratic union, and some groups affiliated with the Federation of Workers of the Peruvian Revolution (CTRP), which normally supported the government. The Confederation of Peruvian Workers (CTP), affiliated with the opposition Apra party, did not join the strike, nor did the national taxi and bus drivers' federation, which had benefited from a widely protested increase in public transport fares.

The government angrily denounced the strikers, reminding them that Peru was suffering a severe economic crisis and accusing them of trying to "destabilize" the "revolutionary" administration of President Francisco Morales Bermudez.

The government similarly had condemned students and workers who rioted against its economic policies earlier in July in the interior of Peru. The worst disturbances occurred July 11–12 in Huancayo, in the Andes mountains 187 miles east of Lima, and in Trujillo, on the Pacific coast 324 miles north of the capital.

Police putting down the protests apparently killed one person in Trujillo and at least five in Huancayo. A 5 p.m.–6 a.m. curfew was imposed in Huancayo, where demonstrators stoned shops, looted a supermarket, barricaded streets and sabotaged the local electric utility before being routed by security officers.

Five Roman Catholic bishops issued an angry statement July 13 denouncing what they called the excessive harshness of the government's response to the protests. The government had no right to use "violence and even torture" against "men who are fighting for the liberation of their people" and for "justice," the bishops asserted. Explaining the growing unrest, the bishops said: "The lack of liberties suffered by the people places them in a desperate situation that translates into rebellion and a state of violence."

The bishops called for radical change in Peru's "political, social and economic system," which, they said, "does not take into account the interests of the majority" and "allows a privileged minority to unload the entire weight of the economic crisis onto the shoulders of the popular sectors."

The government later charged July 21 that the general strike, called by the CGTP, had been political and subversive in nature. It authorized state and private companies to fire strikers and other "troublemakers," contravening labor legislation that had been a hallmark of the armed forces' nine-year rule. The authorization was extended July 24 to the state mining company, Centromin-Peru, which was struck the next day by some 9,000 workers demanding better pay and benefits.

The government's vindictiveness toward the strikers evoked new criticism from the Roman Catholic Church. The church privately expressed its concern to the government over the firings, and the archbishop of Lima said July 26 that "the state of economic crisis affecting our nation should be solved without hatred and violence through the cooperation of all."

(The top leaders of the July 19 general strike in Lima were released from prison

Aug. 24. They were Eduardo Castillo of the General Confederation of Peruvian Workers, Victor Sanchez Zapata of the National Workers' Federation and Sergio Aparicio of the Federation of Workers of the Peruvian Revolution. However, the labor unions' offices remained closed by the government, Agence France-Presse reported.)

Copper miners strike—More than 2,000 miners employed by the U.S.-owned Southern Peru Copper Corp. began an indefinite strike Aug. 2 to protest the dismissal of several of their union leaders for participating in the July 19 general strike.

The protest strike paralyzed the Toquepala copper mines in southern Peru, where 400 tons of ore were extracted in a normal day. The mines were losing $850,000 per day because of the stoppage, according to company officials.

The government, which had approved the dismissal of the union leaders, declared the protest strike illegal. The stoppage was "another move by politicized leaders to sabotage efforts to revive the economy," the regime charged.

Piazza Tanquis quits post. Economy Minister Walter Piazza Tanguis resigned July 6 after only 50 days in office. His departure, coupled with growing urban protests over the high cost of living, threw the government into one of its worst crises in recent years.

Piazza quit because the Cabinet would not approve a new austerity program he had worked out with the International Monetary Fund (IMF)

The new program reportedly was even harsher than the austerity measures announced by Piazza in June, touching off violent protests. Piazza apparently was able to win some concessions from the IMF in protracted negotiations, but not enough to satisfy the Cabinet and the president's council of military advisers.

The most important stumbling block appeared to be the monetary policy. Piazza had persuaded the IMF to accept a goal of 90 sols to the dollar, but the Cabinet had decided there would be no further devaluations, according to the Latin America Economic Report July 15.

The ban on future devaluations also caused the resignation July 11 of Central Bank president Carlos Santisteban and his top four aides. The bank executives, like Piazza, felt a compromise agreement with the IMF was necessary to keep Peru from defaulting on its massive foreign debt.

President Francisco Morales Bermudez agreed with them, according to the Latin America Economic Report, but he faced strong opposition from Cabinet ministers and military advisers grouped around the industry minister, Gen. Gaston Ibanez O'Brien. They wanted a policy that would pump money into the economy, fix the sol's exchange rate, reinstate food subsidies, cut the price of fuel and take other expansionist measures.

The appointment of Gen. Alcibiades Saenz Barsallo to succeed Piazza July 6 gave no indication of Morales' immediate intentions. Saenz, a former telephone company president and Economy Ministry aide, was known chiefly for his obedience to superiors, according to the Latin America Economic Report.

Civilian rule pledged for 1980. The military government promised July 28 to hand over power to an elected civilian administration in 1980.

President Francisco Morales Bermudez said in a televised address that a constituent assembly would be elected in 1978 to plan the transition. He said political parties, national organizations of peasants, workers and businessmen, and other civilian groups would be consulted "on each stage of the return to constitutionality."

"Without any question, there will be general elections in 1980," Morales declared. "[The armed forces] call on all sectors of the nation to create a climate of peace and mutual respect to make possible the transfer of power."

Although the government had pledged democratic elections in its political plan for 1977-80, observers saw Morales' speech as an attempt to defuse protests against his economic austerity program and to curry favor with foreign creditors, particularly the U.S. "That speech was aimed at President Carter as much as at our political parties," a Peruvian industrialist told the New York Times.

Constituent assembly vote scheduled— The military government announced Oct. 4 that nationwide elections for a constituent assembly would be held June 4, 1978.

The assembly would write a new constitution that would, among other things, prepare the country for general elections and a return to civilian rule in 1980. But the government made it clear that the assembly must follow guidelines laid down by the armed forces.

These guidelines were contained in the government's political plan for 1977–80, Plan Tupac Amaru, which was published Oct. 9 following a limited national debate on the armed forces' original draft.

The plan said the new constitution must "institutionalize the fundamental structural reforms of the revolutionary process" (that is, the reforms carried out by the military since it had seized power in 1968). These included the nationalization of many banks, the oil industry and other sectors of the economy; the seizure and redistribution to peasants of 25 million acres of land; the establishment of profit-sharing for industrial workers, and the "socialization" (expropriation) of Lima's daily newspapers.

The plan did not discuss the nature of either the 1978 or the 1980 elections. The transport and communications minister, Gen. Elivio Vannini, had said Oct. 3 that the elections would not be "like before," but he did not explain himself. The last congressional elections in Peru had taken place in 1966, and the last presidential election had been held in 1963.

Civilian response to the government's plans varied. The American Revolutionary Popular Alliance (APRA), Peru's largest party, Oct. 5 expressed "patriotic satisfaction" with the election schedule. But Popular Action (AP), the party of ex-President Fernando Belaunde Terry, said what Peru needed was not a constituent assembly but immediate general elections in which "the people can decide how to administer their present and invent their future."

The Revolutionary Socialist Party appeared to agree with AP, saying that "only a real democratic opening can guarantee the people's trust and belief" in the government.

Election law decreed—The government decreed a law Nov. 16 that would regulate the elections for a constituent assembly in June 1978.

The law would allow 18-year-olds to vote for the first time in Peruvian history. An estimated five million Peruvians would be eligible to cast ballots for the 100-member assembly. Illiterates would not be allowed to vote.

Molina picked to be prime minister. The man who was in charge of the transition to civilian rule, Gen. Oscar Molina Pallochia, would become prime minister in February 1978 upon the retirement of the current premier, Gen. Guillermo Arbulu Galliani. Until then Molina would continue as chairman of the joint chiefs of staff, it was announced Oct. 4.

State of emergency lifted. President Francisco Morales Bermudez Aug. 28 lifted the nationwide state of emergency, which had suspended individual liberties for nearly 14 months.

Gen. Morales said he was acting in response to "persistent objections [to the emergency] from the citizenry and the nation's labor organizations." But he warned that he would be "inflexibly severe" with anyone who used his restored freedoms to "create uncertainty, sow violence or provoke chaos."

The reestablishment of individual guarantees would facilitate national debate on Morales' plan to return the government to elected civilian officials by 1980. The president had said Aug. 7 that he wanted "political parties, mass organizations and social groups" openly to discuss his proposal for elections for a constituent assembly in 1978. "Anything said in this debate is acceptable and we respect it," Morales said.

The Popular Action party (AP) Aug. 7 called for immediate general elections, charging that the plan for a constituent assembly was a delaying tactic. Fernando Belaunde Terry, the AP's leader and Peru's last elected president, said Aug. 25 that a constituent assembly "cannot co-exist with a de facto [military] government." He said the 1933 Constitution, under which he was elected in the 1960s, was imperfect but adequate for the time being. What should be abrogated, he said, was the "Government Statute" under which the armed forces were ruling.

Another party, the National Odriista Union of former President Manuel Odria, said substantially the same thing as the AP, it was reported Aug. 7.

Scattered political arrests continued despite the lifting of the state of emergency Aug. 28. Antonio Meza Cuadra, secretary general of the Revolutionary Socialist Party, was held for questioning Aug. 30–31. Nicholas Asheshov, a British journalist, was questioned for 12 hours Sept. 6 about an article he had written in the Andean Report, an English-language monthly magazine that he edited in Lima.

Government & IMF reach agreement. The Peruvian government and the International Monetary Fund (IMF) had reached an agreement to avert a default by Peru on its massive foreign debt, it was reported Sept. 30.

The country was virtually out of foreign-exchange reserves, and it anticipated a trade deficit for 1977 due to the low prices of its chief exports—copper, sugar and fishmeal. U.S. and European banks had loaned Peru $360 million to pay off debts in 1976, but they had refused to make any new loans.

The accord, which would bring Peru loans from the IMF and other foreign creditors, was endorsed by the Peruvian Cabinet Sept. 20 but not immediately announced, according to the Latin America Economic Report.

The terms of the agreement were similar to those of an accord reached in July by IMF officials and Peru's former economy minister, Walter Piazza Tanguis. Piazza's successor, Gen. Alcibiades Saenz, had come to terms with the IMF after Peru's financial position became desperate and foreign creditors refused to grant the country any new loans until it accepted the IMF's recommendations on economic policy.

The new agreement, as described by the Latin America Economic Report, would require Peru to keep its 1977 budget deficit to 40 billion soles (there were about 80 soles to the U.S. dollar at current exchange rates). The sol would be devalued, and the prices of gasoline and other products in Peru would be increased. Despite this, Peru would try to reduce inflation to 20% in 1977, compared with 45% in 1976.

The agreement was expected to hit Peruvian wage-earners hard, according to the Economic Report. The limit on the budget deficit, for instance, would require wholesale dismissals of public employes, the report said. However, as most newspapers noted, Peru's only alternative to agreeing with the IMF was defaulting on its foreign debt.

While no official figures were available, Peruvian sources estimated that the government owed $4 billion abroad and the private sector owed $1.4 billion, according to the Financial Times (London) Aug. 31. Of those combined amounts, $1 billion was due to be paid between May 1977 and May 1978, and some $700 million were due in interest and amortization to foreign creditors in 1977. Meanwhile, the central bank's foreign exchange reserves had dropped to about $35 million in mid-August, according to the Financial Times.

Peru's export revenues were expected to reach only $1.6 billion in 1977, pushing the country's debt payments close to a staggering 50% of its export earnings (a figure of 20% was considered excessive). The government had targeted export earnings in 1977 at $2.8 billion, but the international prices of copper and sugar, Peru's leading exports, remained low. In addition, exports of fishmeal—another leading Peruvian commodity—were down because a mysterious current in the Pacific Ocean was keeping anchovies out of Peruvian waters.

Peru's bad luck with its exports was only one of many reasons for the country's desperate predicament, according to newspaper reports. At the root of the problem was the heavy borrowing in which the government indulged from 1974 to 1976 to finance its ambitious social and economic development projects.

According to the Wall Street Journal Sept. 1, commercial banks were eager to lend to Peru in those years, assuming that the country was on the verge of an oil boom and would soon earn enough money from petroleum exports to pay back the loans. The easy availability of credit led the government to devise a wide range of domestic projects including a $750-million oil pipeline, hydroelectric dams, irrigation networks, tourist hotels, a copper refinery and paper plants. In addition, the Peruvian armed forces bought new arms and equipment, much of it from the Soviet Union. In all, Peru took on some 400 creditors and increased its international debt fivefold, the Journal reported.

Then it was learned that there was little oil in Peru, and foreign oil companies all but abandoned exploration in the country's Amazon jungle. The world recession lowered the prices of Peru's other exports, and the country was left with little with which to repay its debts.

The fact that so many of Peru's loans were from commercial banks aggravated the situation because these banks extracted stiffer repayment terms than international lending agencies, such as the IMF and the World Bank. According to the Financial Times, Peru had been forced to turn to commercial banks in the early 1970s when the Nixon Administration blocked IMF and World Bank loans to Peru because of some of its left-wing programs and rhetoric.

The government admitted that it bore some blame for the financial crisis, but it also blamed the high prices of imported capital goods and food, and it accused the IMF of discriminating against Peru and other underdeveloped countries. President Francisco Morales Bermudez charged Sept. 8 that the IMF could not expect a Third World nation to be financially stable when international markets were so restricted. He also asserted that the IMF did not demand stringent austerity measures when it gave credits to Great Britain and other industrial nations.

Still, the IMF was all that stood between Peru and default. Apparently recognizing this, the government sent a number of missions to the U.S. to negotiate with the IMF and with private U.S. banks. Central Bank president German de la Melena headed a delegation that met with bankers in New York Aug. 19 and with IMF officials in Washington Aug. 22–23. President Morales, visiting Washington for the signing of the Panama Canal treaties, conferred with President Carter Sept. 7 and with Treasury Secretary W. Michael Blumenthal Sept. 8. Economy Minister Saenz also conferred with U.S. and IMF officials in Washington during the IMF-World Bank meetings Sept. 26–30.

The actual agreement between Peru and the IMF was negotiated by de la Melena and IMF economist Linda Koenig, it was reported Sept. 30.

Sol floated—The government relaxed exchange controls on the Peruvian sol Oct. 10, effectively floating it against the U.S. dollar. This action appeared to be a provision of Peru's agreement with the IMF.

Oil pipeline opened. The trans-Andean oil pipeline began operation May 25 with crude petroleum flowing from Peru's eastern Amazon jungle over the Andes mountains to the port of Bayovar on the Pacific Ocean.

Officials said the pipeline, which initially carried 30,000 barrels of oil per day, would enable Peru to reduce its daily oil imports to 10,000 barrels by July. Peru currently imported 50,000 barrels per day from Ecuador and Venezuela.

A feeder line to an oilfield operated by the U.S. firm Occidental Petroleum Corp. north of the pipeline was expected to be completed by the end of 1978. Officials said it would carry 80,000 barrels a day and make Peru self-sufficient in oil.

The state oil company, Petroperu, said it had spent about $997 million in the Amazon region for prospecting, exploration, exploitation and pumping operations, it was reported March 14. Of the total, $207 million went to exploration and production, $670 million to the pipeline and $120 million to the feeder line to the Occidental field.

The government March 3 had announced new terms for exploration and production contracts between Petroperu and foreign oil companies. It was an attempt to bring back to Peru many of the concerns that had left in recent years after claiming that operations in the country were unprofitable.

The new contracts would be more flexible, dropping provisions of the "Peruvian model" contracts, in effect since 1970, under which Petroperu took more than 50% of a company's production and paid it off with the rest. Under the new pacts Petroperu would continue to take a large share of production, but companies could choose to be paid in cash, and payments and terms would conform to changing world market conditions.

Other economic developments. The Peruvian government May 6 suspended anchovy fishing along most of Peru's coast because of a severe scarcity of suitably sized fish. The scarcity was attributed to warm sea currents that had reduced the amount of plankton on which the anchovies fed. The suspension, cutting short a fishing season that had begun only April 14, was expected to reduce Peru's income from fish-meal exports.

—The government March 17 declared a state of emergency in the sugar industry, taking over five sugar cooperatives and placing government supervisors in eight others. The regime banned all strikes and job actions in the cooperatives for one year; limited the cooperatives' social investments; restricted overtime pay and the hiring of new workers; increased the tax on sugar exports, and authorized a 15% raise in domestic sugar prices.

The measures followed a disagreement between the government and the sugar cooperatives' central authority, Cecoaap, on the causes of the economic and financial crisis in the sugar industry and on possible solutions to it, according to the Latin America Political Report March 25. Cecoaap felt the main problem was the low domestic price of sugar, added to the low international price, the Report said. The government argued that the causes of the crisis were inordinate wage increases for sugar workers, unwarranted overtime pay, unnecessary social expenditures and excessive long-term, interest-free loans granted to cooperative members.

—The government Feb. 2 published its modifications of the industrial community law, introduced in 1970 to give workers a share of control over the companies for which they worked.

The modifications, decreed in an effort to encourage private investment in Peruvian industry, annulled the workers' status as partners in their companies but granted them continued representation at board meetings. The maximum workers' share in a company's capital stock was reduced from 50% to 33%. It was stipulated that the workers' shares would be held by individual workers rather than by their "industrial community." The workers would be allowed to dispose of their shares as they wished after six years. Companies would continue to distribute 10% of their profits in cash among all their employes.

The modifications were denounced Feb. 17 by the Peruvian Communist Party, which normally supported the military government. The party said the modifications constituted a "dangerous step backward" from the "revolutionary process" begun by the armed forces in 1968. The industrial community law now "gives facilities for greater profits and absolute decision-making power to capitalists, including imperialist transnationals," the party charged.

—The Lima teachers' union, SUTELM, charged Feb. 9 that a general wage increase decreed by the government Jan. 26 should have been 10 times higher to offset the rise in the cost of living. The wage hike, amounting to $11.50 per month, followed a 40% increase in the cost of living in Lima from February 1976 through January 1977, according to government figures. Military officers were granted a $90 monthly housing allowance around the same time, it was reported Feb. 11.

—The government Aug. 17 authorized multinational banks to operate in Peru and carry out foreign currency transactions. The banks must have subscribed capital of $50 million, 80% of it in foreign currencies. The authorization, contravening earlier, more restrictive legislation on foreign banks, apparently was made to encourage the newly formed Arab-Latin American Bank to open a branch in Lima. Local bankers denounced the authorization, charging it gave foreign capital privileges not available to Peruvian interests, according to a report Sept. 16.

—The state mining company Minero Peru said Sept. 29 that it was seeking foreign capital to help double Peru's copper output to 400,000 metric tons in 1977.

—The government agreed to pay the U.S.-based Gulf Oil Corp. $1.54 million for the nationalization of its Peruvian subsidiary in 1975, it was reported Aug. 24.

U.S. Relations
& Human Rights Abuses

U.S. human rights reports. A U.S. State Department report released Jan. 1, charged Peru with human rights violations but nonetheless asked that military support for the country be continued for strategic and other reasons.

The report said that since the declaration of a state of emergency in July 1976 there had been an increased number of arrests and "unsubstantiated reports of missing persons." Most of those arrested were released after interrogation, according to the report, and human rights were generally respected. The State Department argued that elimination of the U.S. security assistance program "would deprive the United States of an important instrument of communication and cooperation with that country."

Another State Department report, released in Washington March 12, also said Peruvian rights generally were respected, although there had been some reports of police brutality.

A statement reaching similar conclusions was prepared by the progressive Peruvian Catholic organization, ONIS, and sent to Lima newspapers, it was reported March 18. Peru's premier, Gen. Guillermo Arbulu Galliani, prohibited publication of the statement and complained to the head of the Peruvian Catholic Church.

In 1976 the Peruvian government had granted a year-end amnesty to 197 persons and dropped prosecution of another 39 Several former government ministers were included in the pardon, AP reported Jan. 1.

Mrs. Carter's visit. Rosalynn Carter, wife of U.S. President Jimmy Carter, visited seven countries in the Caribbean and Latin America May 30–June 12 on a tour that combined goodwill gestures with substantive political and economc discussion.

Mrs. Carter was accompanied on tour by Grace Vance, wife of U.S. Secretary of State Cyrus Vance, and by two of the Carter Administration's experts on Latin America—Terence Todman, assistant secretary of state for inter-American affairs, and Robert Pastor, senior staff member for inter-American affairs on the National Security Council.

Throughout the tour Mrs. Carter emphasized her husband's desire for closer ties to Latin American nations and his commitment to promoting the observance of human rights.

Mrs. Carter visited Peru June 3–6. On her arrival in Lima June 3, her main topic of discussion was disarmament. She said there was a "need to control the growth of armaments throughout the world," and she reminded Peruvian leaders that they had not implemented an arms limitation agreement that Peru had signed with seven other Latin American countries in 1974.

Mrs. Carter conferred for several hours June 3 with President Francisco Morales Bermudez and his foreign minister, Jose de la Puente Radbill. Morales told her he would sign the American Convention on Human Rights, and de la Puente told her Peru was interested in signing an arms control agreement with the other four members of the Andean Group.

Morales said June 4 that his talks with Mrs. Carter had been characterized by "great understanding," and that the Peruvian and American people were working "hand in hand" on the human rights issue. De la Puente praised Mrs. Carter June 5, saying "she has won us all over with her charm, her sweetness, her simplicity and the way she has treated us."

Reporters accompanying Mrs. Carter said she hit her stride in Peru, conducting her talks with Morales with little help from her aides and handling her press conferences confidently. After being tense and unsure of herself on the first days of her tour, Mrs. Carter relaxed in Lima, and her Peruvian hosts responded warmly, according to the New York Times June 6.

U.S. rejects loan request. American sources in Lima said Dec. 15 that the U.S. government had turned down a request by the Peruvian government for $100 million in short-term credits.

The refusal was based in part on the probability that some of the money would be used to pay the Soviet Union $60 million that would come due in January

1978 for earlier arms purchases, according to the New York Times Dec. 16.

Peru had virtually no reserves with which to pay the $1 billion that would be due in 1978 in principal and interest on its massive foreign debt. A U.S. banker told the Times that Peru's financial crisis was now even worse than in June 1976, when a group of major U.S. banks lent the government $210 million to support a financial stabilization plan.

The banks were waiting for Peru to submit a new refinancing plan to avert what seemed to be an imminent default on its debts, the banker said. Previous Peruvian plans apparently had been unacceptable to the banks.

The U.S. Treasury Department said Dec. 17 that while it had rejected Peru's loan request, it was heartened by the agreement the Peruvian government had reached with the International Monetary Fund (IMF) to refinance some of the Peruvian debt. Following that agreement, the IMF had approved a standby arrangement allowing Peru to purchase up to 90 million special drawing rights until Dec. 31, 1979. The authorization, announced Nov. 18, was equivalent to a credit line of $76 million.

Chilean Border Dispute & Other Foreign Developments

Peru-Chile border buildup, arms sales detailed. Peru was building up defenses along the Peruvian-Chilean border, according to the Jan. 10 issue of Time magazine. Tensions were increasing over Peruvian claims to northern Chilean territory and over the two nations' inability to agree on how to grant Bolivia an outlet to the sea.

Peru had been moving tanks, troops and armored personnel carriers into military bases in its southern border provinces, Time reported. Chile had been mining the northern Atacama Desert, implanting tank traps and building fortifications to counter a possible invasion by Peru.

Peruvian leaders periodically had talked of regaining the Atacama, which was taken from Peru by Chile in the War of the Pacific in the late 19th Century. The desert had rich deposits of copper, silver and nitrates.

Peru continued to purchase large quantities of arms abroad, further compromising its financial position, according to the Financial Times Aug. 31. The government claimed, however, that the purchases did not aggravate the economic problem and that they were necessary to replace obsolete equipment and to protect Peru from a possible attack by Chile.

The government had signed arms contracts worth several hundred million dollars in 1976, including one agreement to buy 36 Soviet Su-22 assault jets, augmenting a stock of Soviet-made weaponry that included about 250 T-55 tanks and scores of SA-2 and SA-3 antiaircraft missiles. Added to the French jets, British patrol boats and U.S. transport planes that Lima had acquired since the late 1960s, the Soviet weapons made Peru the leading military power in South America's western coast, according to Time.

Chile, which had more men under arms than Peru, was comparatively underequipped because the U.S. and Great Britain had embargoed arms sales to the military government, Time said. The embargo included U.S.-made F-4 Phantom jets, which Chile eagerly sought and which could easily handle Peru's Su-22s, the magazine reported.

Peruvian President Gen. Francisco Morales Bermudez denied Jan. 1 that Peru was preparing for hostilities with Chile. "If we have bought air force equipment from the Soviet Union," Morales said, "it is, in the first place, because it meets the technical conditions for national defense. The purchase does not imply a plan of aggression against any neighbor. The economic conditions we were offered [by the Soviet Union] were superior to other offers from three or four countries."

Argentine A-plant accord signed. Peru and Argentina signed an agreement March 5 under which a research nuclear reactor would be built in Peru using Argentine technology and equipment.

The agreement was the highlight of a three-day visit to Lima by the Argentine president, Gen. Jorge Videla. He and his Peruvian counterpart, Gen. Francisco

Morales Bermudez, also signed an agreement to increase trade between Argentina and Peru and to promote Latin American economic integration.

The nuclear project, reportedly budgeted at $50 million, involved not only the experimental reactor—a 10-megawatt unit capable of producing radio-isotopes for medical and industrial uses—but the training of Peruvian scientists in all peaceful uses of nuclear technology. The project exemplified Argentina's promotion of regional cooperation in the use of atomic energy.

(Argentina led Latin America in nuclear technology, with one 300-megawatt nuclear power station in operation and a 600-megawatt station under construction. Since the 1950s the Argentine Atomic Energy Commission had trained several hundred nuclear scientists and engineers, the most advanced group in Latin America. The U.S. and other countries worried that Argentina, which had large reserves of uranium ore, would use its technology to build atomic bombs. Argentina refused to sign the Nuclear Nonproliferation Treaty.)

Gen. Videla visited Lima March 3–6. The Peruvian government took extraordinary security precautions for him, lodging him in the presidential palace (not the Argentine Embassy) and rounding up Argentine exiles who presumably opposed Videla's government. Videla held extensive talks with Gen. Morales Bermudez, with whom he exchanged national decorations—the Peruvian Order of the Sun for Videla and the Argentine Order of the Liberator San Martin for Morales.

Videla's visit was protested by major Peruvian labor and political groups, which denounced the widespread abuse of human rights in Argentina. A document condemning Videla for allegedly persecuting labor leaders and instituting an economic "policy of hunger" was issued March 3 by the pro-Communist General Confederation of Peruvian Workers, the pro-government Workers' Union of the Peruvian Revolution, the Christian Democratic National Workers' Confederation, the right-wing Single Union of Education Workers, the Christian Labor Movement and the Peruvian Peasants Confederation, among other groups.

The National Federation of Peruvian Bar Associations issued a statement demanding respect for human rights in Argentina. The Revolutionary Socialist Party, headed by exiled army generals, condemned repression in Argentina, and the Roman Catholic National Office of Social Information (ONIS) denounced the Argentine government for allegedly imprisoning, torturing and murdering its opponents.

Despite the protests, both the Peruvian and Argentine governments expressed satisfaction with the results of Videla's visit. Peruvian Foreign Minister Jose de la Puente noted March 8 that a number of the topics covered by the two presidents—including the nuclear reactor deal—had not even been on the agenda. The two leaders, de la Puente said, had shown "a high degree of mutual respect."

Peru & copper cartel cut production. Three major copper-producing countries—Zaire, Zambia and Peru—agreed Dec. 7 to reduce their production despite the refusal of Chile, the world's leading copper exporter, to join the cutback.

The four nations and Indonesia, which composed the Intergovernment Council of Copper Exporting Countries (CIPEC), had met in Jakarta to discuss ways to support sagging copper prices. Although CIPEC was regarded as one of the strongest producer cartels in existence, the meeting ended in a stalemate because of Chile's refusal to cut production. Chile contended that world demand would soon increase and cause prices to rise.

In London-based world trading Dec. 7, copper was selling at 56¢ a pound, its lowest level in 20 years and barely one-third the record $1.52 price reached in April 1974. World stocks of unsold copper were estimated at 2.5-million tons, more than double the usual inventory.

In 1975 CIPEC had tried and failed to support copper prices by reducing its copper output, which accounted for 40% of the total world production. CIPEC blamed the failure on Chile's refusal to comply fully with the cutback decision.

Uruguay

Political Repression & Human Rights Violations

The military-run government of Uruguay was accused throughout 1977 of political repression and abuses of human rights. The regime announced plans to hold controlled presidential elections in 1981 and 1986 as a step toward the restoration of democracy. Both civilian and military opposition intensified throughout 1977 in reaction to this plan, which, it was charged, would indefinitely extend military control of Uruguay. In an attempt to silence criticism of its political and economic policies, the government arrested many additional opponents or removed protesting officials from office.

Torture & other violations charged. Allegations of torture, political arrests and other rights violations continued in Uruguay in January and February. Amnesty International asserted Jan. 27 that there had been "large-scale arrests, mainly of doctors and teachers," in the departments of Artigas, Salto and Tacuarembo in December 1976. Two of the detainees had died in custody, Amnesty reported. One of them, a student, had been tortured to death, according to the Cuban newspaper Granma Feb. 6.

Granma reported Feb. 15 that several leftist leaders had been arrested and tortured recently, including Luis Iguini Ferreira, a union official, and Jaime Perez, a Communist leader.

Relatives of about 5,000 political prisoners had appealed in vain to the Supreme Court for release of the detainees, Inter Press reported Feb. 7. Court sources said there were about 7,000 political prisoners in military and civilian jails, but the government denied holding any political prisoners at all, Inter Press noted.

Meanwhile, Uruguayans who had taken political asylum in the Mexican Embassy to avoid arrest flew to Mexico City Jan. 16 after receiving safe-conducts from the Uruguayan government. More political refugees remained in the embassy.

U.S. protests rights abuses. The U.S. denied visas to two Uruguayan army officers in an apparent protest of alleged violations of human rights by the military-dominated government, it was reported Feb. 22.

The State Department refused to comment on the denial of visas to Maj. Nino Gavazzo and Col. Jose Fons, who had sought entry to the U.S. on official business. However, sources told the Associated Press that the two officers had been "implicated in the torture of political prisoners."

Earlier in February, a request for greater observance of human rights in Uruguay had been sent to the country's top military leaders by U.S. Secretary of State Cyrus R. Vance, according to the Latin America Political Report Feb. 25. The request was relayed by Alejandro Orfila, secretary general of the Organization of American States (OAS).

A few days later, Robert White, U.S. ambassador to the OAS, had told an inter-American cultural meeting in Montevideo that "culture cannot enrich the lives of our citizens unless the state protects certain rights. . . , the right of assembly, freedom of expression, protection against arbitrary arrest and punishment." Uruguayan officers had denounced the statement as a "veiled but direct attack on [Uruguay]" and a "subtle attack on military governments that fight against subversion," according to the Latin America Political Report.

While the Uruguayan government charged the U.S. with interfering in internal Uruguayan affairs, leaders of the Blanco and Colorado parties praised President Carter's defense of human rights, asserting it would force South American dictatorships "to become democratic governments," according to the news agency Inter Press April 1. A former Colorado senator said the U.S. could not be interfering in Uruguayan affairs since Uruguay was ruled by "an illegal and minority group."

U.S. aid cut—U.S. Secretary of State Vance disclosed Feb. 24 that the Carter Administration planned to reduce foreign aid to Uruguay because of rights abrogations.

The disclosure was made in testimony before the Senate Appropriations Committee's subcommittee on foreign operations.

State Department officials gave some details of the planned aid reductions. A $3-million request for military credits to Uruguay would be eliminated, and economic assistance would be cut to $25,000 from $220,000.

Congress had enacted legislation in 1976 opposing military aid for countries committing "gross violations" of human rights unless there were extraordinary circumstances warranting the aid. The Ford Administration generally had interpreted the restriction as counterproductive and had favored aid programs for continued U.S. influence in such countries.

A State Department report on human rights released March 12 found that Uruguay's long democratic tradition had been "altered substantially" in the campaign against urban guerrillas in the late 1960s and early 1970s. Now, the report said, the armed forces dominated the government and cases of terrorism, subversion and crimes against the nation were handled by military courts.

Uruguay rejects U.S. economic aid—Reacting to Vance's testimony, the government of Uruguay announced March 1 that it would refuse U.S. aid linked to observance of human rights.

Uruguayan Planning Minister Brig. Jose Cardozo said his government would reject "any type of economic aid from the U.S." Cardozo charged that the linking of U.S. assistance to respect for human rights "implies an inadmissible intrusion in the internal affairs of Uruguay . . . and total misinformation about Uruguayan reality."

Independent judiciary ended. The government decreed Institutional Act No. 6, which created a Justice Ministry and "intervened" the court that supervised Uruguayan elections, it was reported Jan. 27. Fernando Bayardo Bengoa was named justice minister. Five veteran members of the electoral court were dismissed, and only three persons were appointed to succeed them, it was reported Jan. 30.

Institutional Act No. 6 eliminated all pretense of an independent judiciary, according to the Latin America Political Report Feb. 4. The government would exercise greater control over the courts through the Justice Ministry, and it would control any future election through the new appointees to the electoral court. The dismissed electoral court members were associated with the Blanco and Colorado parties, which often were critical of the government.

Taking effect July 1 was Institutional Act No. 8, which abolished the independent powers of the judiciary.

The act, an amendment to the Uruguayan Constitution, placed the judiciary under the direct control of the executive branch. All judges, regardless of rank, were placed on a four-year trial period during which they could be dismissed without explanation. The Supreme Court's power to appoint lower court judges was transferred to the president and to the military-dominated Council of State.

The act was denounced by two Montevideo newspapers, El Dia and El Pais, which normally supported the government. "Judicial power is dead," El Dia said, killed by an act that "departs sharply and unalterably from a firm and peaceful tradition that . . . goes back to the very origins of our nation."

The controversy over Institutional Act No. 8 apparently emboldened Uruguay's suppressed political parties to speak out against the government. Jorge Batlle, a former presidential candidate and leader of the Colorado Party, July 16 called on the Colorados and their traditional rivals, the National (Blanco) Party, to "act together as of today" to restore political liberties in Uruguay. Blanco partisans welcomed Batlle's call July 17, but they told the Associated Press that they did not know how to act without risking arrest.

There had been at least 45 political arrests in Uruguay in late June and early July, according to the Latin America Political Report July 8. The detainees included the leaders of the telephone workers', municipal employes' and milkmen's unions.

Military officers reported seized. About 20 military officers were reported arrested in March for writing a document that criticized the government's political and economic performance.

It was unclear who the officers were, where they were being held or what their document actually said. However, it was reliably reported that the officers ranged in rank from captains to colonels and that they had called for constitutional reforms and a national referendum.

The arrests were first reported March 22 by relatives of the officers. According to sources cited by the Associated Press March 23, the officers were variously linked to the Blanco and Colorado parties—Uruguay's traditional political groups—and to the Broad Front, the outlawed leftist coalition. The sources said the officers were being held at police head-

quarters in Montevideo, where the Broad Front's leader, retired Gen. Liber Seregni, had been confined since January 1976. However, the Latin America Political Report April 8 said the officers had not been jailed but confined to barracks.

The armed forces command denied the arrests in separate statements March 23 and 26. The first statement called reports of the detentions "only a rumor," and the second called them "totally false and malicious." The arrests were not reported in the government-controlled Uruguayan press. An Argentine newspaper that reported them was seized in Montevideo March 24, and correspondents of AP and United Press International who cited the arrests were told they henceforth were barred from military installations.

The alleged arrests sparked off a political debate within the armed forces, according to the Latin America Political Report April 22. A group of colonels had met and asked that no reprisals be taken against the 20 officers. The colonels also were reported to have recommended the dismissal of the defense, economy, interior and foreign ministers.

The ruling Council of State, dominated by the military hierarchy, passed a resolution April 20 authorizing the dismissal of any military officer whose views were not "coherent" with those of the military command.

Controlled elections set, military opponents retired. A plan to allow controlled presidential elections in 1981 and 1986 was announced Aug. 9 by the military regime. The plan would keep Uruguay indefinitely under military tutelage.

Twenty-six colonels were then forced into retirement for demanding a restoration of democracy in Uruguay, according to the Latin America Political Report Sept. 23. They apparently opposed the controlled-election plan.

According to the plan, a new constitution would be drafted in 1980 on the basis of the "institutional acts" decreed by the government since the military assumed effective control in 1973. In 1981 there would be a presidential election with a single candidate chosen by the "traditional" political parties—the Colorados and the Blancos—and approved by the armed forces. In 1986 there would be a new election in which the Colorados and Blancos would be allowed to put up opposing candidates.

The plan appeared to institutionalize the governmental role of the armed forces by giving constitutional authority to their "institutional acts," and to ban future political activity by leftist parties and labor unions. In essence the plan was similar to the political program imposed in September 1976 when Aparicio Mendez became president of Uruguay. That program promised a presidential election in 1981 with a candidate selected by the Blancos and Colorados.

The new political plan, described by the armed forces as a step toward restoring democracy, apparently was announced to please Terence Todman, the U.S. assistant secretary of state for inter-American affairs, according to press reports. Todman visited Uruguay Aug. 17-19, conferring with government officials and with leaders of the Blancos and Colorados. The party leaders told him that they did not want elections without the abrogation of the armed forces' "institutional acts," according to the Latin American Political Report Sept. 16.

Todman's visit improved the strained relations that had developed between the U.S. and Uruguay since President Carter began promoting human rights throughout the world, according to United Press International Aug. 20.

Foreign correspondents arrested. The Uruguayan government arrested three foreign correspondents in July in an apparent attempt to stifle criticism of its policies in the foreign press.

Graziano Pascale, Uruguayan correspondent for the Mexican newspaper Excelsior, was arrested in Montevideo July 4. The government reportedly accused him of having "connections with subversives," but Excelsior attributed his arrest to a recent article in which Pascale assessed the last four years of military rule in Uruguay. The article alleged that during this period, all opposition leaders had been imprisoned, killed or exiled.

Excelsior denounced Pascale's arrest and mounted an international campaign in his behalf. The newpaper sent a telegram to Uruguayan President Aparicio Mendez July 6 demanding the correspondent's release; it reported July 15 that similar telegrams had been sent by Kurt Waldheim, secretary general of the United Nations, and by Alejandro Orfila, head of the Organization of American States. Pascale's release also was demanded by the Federation of Latin American Newspapermen and by journalists' organizations in Venezuela, Bolivia, Panama and other Latin American countries.

Uruguay finally released Pascale July 14. But within hours it arrested another correspondent for Excelsior, Flavio Tavares.

Tavares, a Brazilian citizen, was based in Buenos Aires, from where he reported Argentine news for Excelsior and the Brazilian newspaper O Estado de Sao Paulo. He had gone to Montevideo to help obtain Pascale's release. After Pascale was freed he went to the Montevideo airport to return to Buenos Aires, and suddenly disappeared.

The Uruguayan government did not admit until July 21 that it had arrested Tavares at the airport. Excelsior immediately mounted another international campaign, again enlisting the support of Waldheim and Orfila, but the Uruguayan government did not yield. It charged Tavares with possessing "incriminating documents" and held him for trial by a military court.

Excelsior denounced the charge as "coarse" and hired a Uruguayan law professor to defend Tavares. The attorney said July 30 that the correspondent was in "good physical condition," and that the charge against him was a "minor" one that did not require imprisonment upon conviction.

The third correspondent arrested by the Uruguayan government was Raul Garces of the Associated Press. He was held for 30 hours July 20-21, apparently for having reported a speech in which Jorge Batlle, a former Uruguayan presidential candidate, called for a restoration of political liberties in the country.

Later, Uruguayan President Aparicio Mendez was reported Sept. 6 to have called Tavares "just another delinquent" who was in jail for "the grave crime of espionage." Excelsior heatedly denied Mendez' charge and demanded Tavares' release.

Newspaper editor expelled. The editor-in-chief of an independent Montevideo newspaper was expelled from Uruguay Sept. 29, two days after the government closed the newspaper for 10 editions because it printed a disparaging reference to the armed forces.

Leonardo Guzman, editor of El Dia, was put on an airplane to Argentina. On arrival in Buenos Aires he charged that the insulting remark, which appeared in El Dia's Sept. 25 edition, had been inserted by a saboteur. He said it was contained in a classified advertisement over which he had no editorial control.

The government imposed economic sanctions on El Dia, including removal of its tax exemptions. As a result, when the newspaper reappeared Oct. 7 its price was increased. The government lifted the sanctions Oct. 29, allowing the regular price to be restored, but it did not permit Guzman to return to Uruguay.

Other press events. Among other press developments:

—The newspaper El Heraldo in the western town of Young was closed permanently Sept. 11 for printing "negative and insulting" reports about "public administration," according to the government's Official Daily. The offending reports apparently concerned the electric utility, UTE.

—Busqueda, a monthly magazine that covered economic and judicial affairs, was closed for two editions Aug. 30 for criticizing Institutional Act. No. 8, which effectively ended the independence of the Uruguayan judiciary. An article in Busqueda's July edition said the institutional act "does not help improve things" in the court system. The magazine reappeared Oct. 29.

—The joint military and police command issued an order Oct. 17 forbidding public libraries to allow anyone to read newspapers and other periodicals published in Uruguay between 1950 and 1974. The order characterized the 24-year period as a "political period" in which "most of the press was at the service of the Tupamaros [leftist guerrillas] and the Communists." The order also banned the works of many of Uruguay's most celebrated writers, including Juan Carlos Onetti and Mario Benedetti.

—The police disclosed Sept. 28 that Julio Castro, former assistant editor of the defunct magazine Marcha, had disappeared from Montevideo Aug. 1. Police officials said Oct. 3 that Castro was reported to be in hiding in Argentina, but friends suspected that he had been murdered by policemen or right-wing commandos. Marcha had been Uruguay's best-known political weekly before it was closed by the government in 1974 because of its leftist political orientation.

Economic Developments

Economic troubles deepen. Uruguay's economic situation continued to worsen in the first quarter of 1977 as prices rose, wages lagged and the government decreed regular devaluations of the peso, the national currency.

The cost of living increased by 11.45% in January and February, according to the Latin America Economic Report March 25. The price of food rose 12.7% during the period, following a 38.5% rise in 1976. The government Jan. 19 had increased prices of fuels, electricity, water and telephone service, with gasoline rising 11.6%.

The government granted a 10% wage hike effective at the beginning of March, it was reported Feb. 4. This increase did not make up for the rise in the cost of living, and it followed a 7.5% decline in real wages in 1976.

Agrarian crisis reported. Uruguayan agriculture and livestock-raising were in a state of crisis caused by the high cost of agricultural machinery and the low prices being obtained by agrarian exports, it was reported July 8.

Farming had become unprofitable and the entire agricultural sector was "losing capital fast," according to members of the Rural Association and the Rural Federation, which represented large and medium landowners.

Growers of sugar beets, grain and oil seeds were particularly hard-pressed, and stock-raising was "at a standstill," the representatives said. Dozens of stock ranches had fallen into a state of neglect, according to one cattleman, and the profits were being made only by exporting meatpackers who had ties to transnational companies.

The price of Uruguayan beef on the international market had fallen from $1,-342 a ton in 1974 to $747 a ton in 1976. At the same time, the cost of farm equipment had skyrocketed as the government repeatedly devalued the Uruguayan peso. Since 1971 the peso price of tractors had risen 1,242%, that of superphosphates 3,790% and fuel 9,900%.

The Rural Association and Rural Federation urged the government to declare a state of national emergency in the agrarian sector, and they asked specifically for a solution to the price situation, a tax extension to Dec. 31 and a three-year extension on payment of their debts. The government rejected all the demands. An official spokesman told the farmers: "If anyone goes under, gentlemen, that's their hard luck."

Other data. A local government survey indicated that only 10% of the 380,400 families in Montevideo earned a monthly income of more than $200, according to the Latin America Economic Report Nov. 18. Real wages had dropped by 5.43% since December 1976.

The government announced Dec. 6 that salaries would be raised by 7% across the board, retroactive to Dec. 1, and the minimum wage would be raised to $72 a month. The value-added tax on all sales would be reduced by 2% as of January 1978.

The government decreed three "mini-devaluations" of the peso in July. The devaluations—by 0.3% July 4, 0.2% July 8 and 0.1% July 28—dropped the exchange rate to 4.68 pesos to the U.S. dollar. There had been 12 "mini-devaluations" since the beginning of 1977.

Uruguay recorded a trade deficit of $30.2 million in 1976, with imports of $571.4 million and exports of $541.2 million, it was reported July 8. Oil accounted for 28% of the imports, and wool and meat for 47% of the exports.

The Uruguayan peso was devalued for the 23rd time in 1977, it was reported Nov. 25. The new rate was 5.36 pesos to the U.S. dollar for import dealings and 5.37 pesos to the dollar for export arrangements.

Venezuela

Government & Politics

Cabinet shuffled. President Carlos Andres Perez revised his Cabinet July 15, naming four new ministers and changing the portfolios of another three.

As a result of the shuffle:

Simon Alberto Consalvi, Venezuela's ambassador to the United Nations, became foreign minister, replacing Ramon Escovar Salom.

Luis Jose Silva Luongo, a lawyer and economist, became finance minister, supplanting Hector Hurtado. Hurtado was named minister of state and president of the Venezuelan Investment Fund, replacing Constantino Quero Morales.

Carmelo Lauria Lesseur, minister of state for basic industries, became secretary general of the presidency, replacing Jose Luis Salcedo Bastardo, who moved to the Ministry of Science, Technology and Culture.

Gustavo Pinto Cohen, an agronomist, became agriculture and livestock minister, replacing Carmelo Contreras.

Gen. Fernando Paredes Bello became defense minister, supplanting Gen. Francisco Alvarez Torres.

AD picks '78 presidential candidate. The ruling Democratic Action party (AD) chose its candidate for the 1978 presidential election in an unprecedented nationwide primary July 17.

The winner was the party's secretary general, Luis Pinerua Ordaz. He defeated the head of AD's congressional delegation, Jaime Lusinchi, by a margin of nearly two to one, according to unofficial returns reported by the Caracas newspaper El Nacional. About 65% of AD's 1.3 million registered members voted in the primary.

The nomination made Pinerua the favorite to win the 1978 election, according to press reports. The major opposition party, Copei (Social Christians), would choose its candidate later in 1977 at a party convention, not in a primary. Copei's leader, ex-President Rafael Caldera, ridiculed the AD primary as a carnival of political rhetoric.

The six-month primary campaign was heated despite the similarity of the candidates' views on most issues. Pinerua tried harder to distance himself from the government of President Carlos Andres Perez, which was unpopular because of growing economic problems (notably food shortages) and charges of administrative corruption. Perez remained neutral in the primary though he was thought to favor Lusinchi.

AD made a major effort to turn out the vote on primary day and was disappointed by the 35% abstention rate. The party's founder, former President Romulo Betancourt, urged the AD faithful early July 17 to "get out of bed, turn off the television set, jump off the hammock and walk down to vote. No one is born with a car under each foot."

241

Copei names presidential candidate. The opposition Social Christian Party (Copei) held its national convention in Caracas Aug. 18 and chose Sen. Luis Herrera Campins to be its candidate in the 1978 presidential election.

Herrera Campins, a lawyer whose politics were described as moderately left of center, was nominated by acclamation after his chief rival, Sen. Aristides Beaujon, unexpectedly withdrew from contention. Beaujon did not explain his action, but it was assumed he was admitting Herrera's insuperable lead among delegates to the convention.

Copei's platform accused the Democratic Action (AD) government of destroying the "exceptional economic prosperity" created by Rafael Caldera, Copei's only president (1969-74). The platform charged that under Caldera's successor, Carlos Andres Perez, prices had risen unacceptably, the gulf between the rich and the poor had deepened and Venezuela had become more dependent on foreign countries.

Copei pledged that its government would work more actively on behalf of the poor, "integrating" Venezuelan society and broadening democracy; fight inflation and promote consumers' organizations; streamline the federal administration, particularly the planning agencies; clearly define the boundaries between public and private enterprise, and generally improve the quality of life, paying particular attention to housing and education.

Other candidates—In addition to the AD and Copei nominees, there were three announced presidential candidates: Jose Vicente Rangel, nominated July 30 by the Movement to Socialism; Americo Martin, whose selection by the Revolutionary Left Movement was reported Aug. 20, and Renny Ottolina, whose independent candidacy was reported Aug. 26.

All three of the minor candidates were expected to hurt Herrera Campins by splitting the opposition vote. Rangel and Martin were leftists, while Ottolina was running a populist campaign with no discernible ideology. Ottolina, an extremely popular television personality, condemned both AD and Copei for their alleged inability to manage the Venezuelan government's affairs.

According to the Latin America Political Report Aug. 26, Ottolina's expensive media campaign was being financed by businessmen closely identified with former President Romulo Betancourt, who founded AD in the 1940s and now staunchly supported its candidate, Pinerua Ordaz.

PCV, MEP name presidential candidates. The Venezuelan Communist Party (PCV) and the People's Electoral Movement (MEP) each chose its candidate for the 1978 presidential election, bringing the total number of candidates to seven.

The PCV nominated Hector Mujica at its eighth national convention in Caracas Sept. 4. Mujica, 50, was president of the national journalists' association and professor of social communications at the Central University in Caracas. He said he offered an alternative to Venezuela's major parties.

MEP nominated Luis Beltran Prieto Figueroa, 75, at its fifth national assembly in the capital Sept. 25. Prieto, a three-time presidential candidate, said he would put Venezuela's oil wealth "at the service of all," emphasizing education and agrarian reform.

The MEP convention heard a taped message from Salom Meza Espinoza, a MEP member and former congressman who was in jail in connection with the still unsolved kidnapping of American business executive William Neihous.

MEP was formed in 1968 when Prieto and other leaders of AD broke away to create their own party. Prieto's candidacy in the 1968 presidential election split AD voters sufficiently to give a narrow victory to Copei's Rafael Caldera. In the 1973 election MEP and the PCV formed the short-lived New Force coalition and supported the losing candidacy of MEP's secretary general, Jesus Angel Paz Galarraga.

Auditor scores public administration. Venezuela's auditor general, Jose Andres Octavio, charged in his annual report for 1976 that the country's public administration was characterized by corruption, inadequate procedures and unsatisfactory provision of services and use of resources, according to the Latin America Economic Report May 27.

Octavio, whose predecessor was dismissed in 1976 for denouncing public corruption, reported that government ministries were guilty of inadequate planning, budgetary controls and information systems. The ministries of finance, defense and education were the worst offenders in terms of delaying fiscal registration and submission of accounts, Octavio reported.

Octavio also noted bad financial administration and overall planning in autonomous institutes and state companies. His report stressed a lack of accounting controls and inefficient disposal of funds by Venezuelan Guayana Corp., which was helping develop the eastern region of the country, and Venezuelan Development Corp. The latter had completed only 42% of the 1976 credit operations budgeted for it, Octavio reported.

Austerity measures set. President Carlos Andres Perez July 11 announced a series of austerity measures intended to control inflation, cut government spending and reduce the amount of money in circulation.

The measures included a freeze on the prices of clothing, shoes and cosmetics, among other products; obligatory monthly payment of credit-card financing; prohibition of increases in current expenditures in the 1978 budget; and curbs on speculation in real estate.

Perez announced the measures at the annual meeting of Venezuela's leading management organization, Fedecamaras, which immediately denounced the austerity program. Businesses, banks and finance companies unanimously rejected the program, noting that it would sharply reduce monetary liquidity and squeeze profits in the previously booming property market, according to the Latin America Economic Report July 15.

Foreign investment in real estate would be discouraged by a measure designed to encourage investment in "social interest housing" but prevent investment in office blocks and other commercial ventures, according to Latin America Economic Report. Another measure would limit to 15% the annual return allowed on leasing new buildings.

Curbs on speculation in the property market had been widely predicted following a recent tripling of land prices in some parts of Caracas. Some observers feared the curbs would adversely affect the construction industry, which had expanded at a 20% annual rate since 1975, according to the Latin America Economic Report.

To regulate the spiraling money supply, the Central Bank would raise to 75% the reserve requirement for official deposits in commercial banks. (The rate had been raised to 50% in April 1976 to counter the effects of a 47% rise in the money supply the previous year.) Another measure would impose a 50% reserve requirement on loans and deposits made by foreign financial institutions to Venezuelan borrowers.

January–June inflation of 8.2%. The Central Bank announced July 22 that the cost of living had risen 8.2% from January through June. This was 1.1 percentage points higher than the inflation rate for the first six months of 1976.

Government acts on food crisis. The government lifted restrictions on food imports for three months to alleviate severe shortages caused by a general crisis in the agrarian sector.

Massive imports from other Latin American countries, the U.S. and Europe were approved April 22 after angry housewives marched through the streets of Caracas banging on empty pots. Supermarkets in the capital and in other Venezuelan cities had been almost empty for a week, according to the Journal of Commerce April 28.

Shipments of meat, beans, salt, eggs and condensed milk were flown into Caracas at the beginning of May, easing the shortages but leaving the agrarian crisis unresolved, it was reported May 13.

A continuation of the nationwide food shortage forced the government July 11 to extend for another three months the suspension of tariffs on imports of poultry, eggs, cheese, beans, salt and other staples.

Agrarian crisis—Production of most Venezuelan agricultural crops had fallen in 1976, according to Agriculture Ministry statistics reported March 24. Production of coffee had fallen 23.3%, cocoa 13.9%, rice 23.7%, corn 18.5%, black beans 19.9%, milk 2.4% and eggs 5.3%.

The Agriculture Ministry blamed the sharp declines on heavy rains which destroyed crops in several states in May, June and July of 1976, and a shortage of rainfall that harmed the livestock industry in other areas. However, foreign and Venezuelan publications added other causes, including government corruption and mismanagement.

The newspaper El Universal of Caracas blamed the agrarian crisis not only on bad weather but also on the gap between costs and prices, lack of fertilizers and the alleged paralysis of government agencies in charge of channeling money and assistance to the agricultural sector, it was reported April 1.

The Latin America Economic Report June 3 said the fundamental problems of Venezuelan agriculture were corruption and organizational inefficiency. There were numerous reports of government money being diverted from agricultural development to more profitable ventures, the Economic Report noted. And even where agrarian production was sufficient to meet demand, shortages were caused by an inefficient distribution system, the newsletter reported.

In addition, farmers were angry over government-imposed price controls, which they characterized as vote-getting measures adopted at the expense of agrarian growth. Venezuela's antiquated system of land tenure also contributed to the crisis, leaving vast areas of agricultural land uncultivated, the Economic Report said.

The government did not expect many of its agrarian measures to bear fruit before five or six years, by which time Venezuela's rapidly growing population would have aggravated the problem, the Economic Report noted. The government's 1977 campaign to increase production of several foodstuffs was off to a bad start due to drought conditions in the states of Guarico and Anzoategui, the newsletter reported.

'77 budget approved. An $8.33-billion federal budget for 1977 had been voted through Congress by the ruling Democratic Action Party over the resistance of the opposition Copei party, it was reported Jan. 5. (The government later increased its estimate of the 1977 budget to $8.72 billion, it was reported April 14.)

Despite a total income of just over $10 billion, the government had a budget deficit of $332.8 million in 1976, with an overall balance-of-payments deficit of $286 million, it was reported April 4.

The government had spent $9.46 billion in 1976, far exceeding the year's approved budget of $7.71 billion. However, increased revenues from petroleum exports had provided a healthy surplus at the end of the year, according to the Financial Times of London. Since the Organization of Petroleum Exporting Countries (OPEC) raised crude oil prices in 1973, Venezuela's official spending had jumped from $4.04 billion to $10.11 billion in 1974 and $9.8 billion in 1975.

Oil. Petroleum output rose 17% in the first quarter of 1977, due chiefly to increased demand from the U.S., which suffered an unusually harsh winter, it was reported April 26. Production in the first three months of the year averaged 2.35 million barrels a day, up from an average of 2.29 million barrels per day in 1976. The Mines Ministry April 5 said it planned to cut oil production to keep it equal to 1976 levels.

The state-owned oil industry had had a total income of $9.9 billion in 1976, the Journal of Commerce reported Jan. 11.

Petroleos de Venezuela, the state monopoly, would spend $320 million in 1977 for new investment, with an emphasis on reactivating exploration, the Journal reported. Nearly $150 million would be spent to drill 55 wildcat wells and survey 7.7 million acres in traditional oil areas. Other surveys would be made in adjacent areas and off the northeastern coast near Trinidad, where foreign companies had made major commercial oil and gas strikes.

Venezuela currently was selling abroad 2 million barrels per day, with 1.1 million going to the U.S. The Exxon Corp. said Jan. 6 that although it would try to buy more low-priced Saudi Arabian oil, it would have to keep buying Venezuelan oil at current levels because demand for heating fuel in the U.S. was so high. Exxon said Venezuela had raised its oil prices by 6.1%–9.8% since Dec. 17, when OPEC approved price increases of 5% for Saudi Arabia and the United Arab Emirates, and 15% for its other member states, including Venezuela. Two-thirds of the 15% increase was effective Jan. 1 and the remainder July 1.

President Carlos Andres Perez said Jan. 1 that Venezuela would grant credits to Latin American nations to help them meet OPEC's new prices.

The entire board of directors of the Venezuelan Petrochemical Institute had resigned as a first step toward reorganizing the country's petrochemical industry, it was reported July 8. The industry had been plagued for years by operational failures, administrative inefficiency and construction delays, according to the Latin America Economic Report.

Occidental Petroleum Corp. of the U.S. filed suit in the Venezuelan Supreme Court May 27 demanding that the government pay it $42.3 million to compensate for the nationalization of Occidental's Venezuelan assets in January 1976. Venezuela had refused to compensate the U.S. company after it heard reports that Occidental had tried to bribe Venezuelan officials to obtain oil concessions.

Major bauxite discovery. The government announced the discovery of a major deposit of high-quality bauxite in a remote mountain range of the southeastern Guayana region, it was reported Aug. 22. The deposit comprised some 50-million tons of ore worth over $1 billion at current market prices, a government spokesman said. Exploitation of the reserves would make Venezuela self-sufficient in bauxite and its major derivative, aluminum.

Other economic developments. Among other economic developments:

Venezuela spent $6 billion on imports of goods and services in 1976, according to figures of the Venezuelan Foreign Trade Institute, cited by the Miami Herald Jan. 6.

Venezuelan imports rose by 22.8% over the year, with the U.S. taking $458.3 million of the $1.1-billion growth. The European Economic Community was next with $394.2 million.

Venezuelan exports, mainly crude and refined oil, fell to $10.3 billion in 1976 from $10.9 billion the previous year, the institute reported.

Venezuela's gross national product grew 11% in 1976, more than the GNP of any other Latin American country, it was reported March 11. Growth in the domestic sector was 10.2%, according to figures of the Banco Nacional de Descuento.

Representatives of Venezuela and 18 international banks March 28 signed an agreement arranging a $1.2-billion Eurocurrency loan to help finance Venezuela's $27.6-billion development program for 1976–80. The banks managing the loan included Bank of America, Chemical Bank, Citicorp International, Bankers Trust International and Chase Manhattan Bank.

President Carlos Andres Perez declared March 11 that he was prepared to force through Congress a tax reform law that would "allow a more just distribution of wealth." Perez denounced "national capitalism" and warned that without tax reorganization Venezuelans would have even less food, hospital care, water and sewage services in 1985 than they have now. The president said that by the beginning of the 1980s the contribution of the domestic private sector to the public treasury must be at least 14% of the gross domestic product. (GDP was the total output of goods and services—gross national product—minus net foreign investments and other income earned abroad.)

The head of the government's consumer protection agency, Col. Oscar Alvarez Beria, was dismissed without explanation June 15. He charged subsequently that the development minister and other government officials had sabotaged his efforts to enforce price controls. As the government's price watchdog Alvarez had incurred the enmity of leading businessmen and the publications and television stations they owned, according to the Latin America Political Report July 1.

Foreign reserves stood at $9.01 billion at the end of June, $1.24 billion higher than in June 1976, it was reported July 15. The country had a $400-million surplus in its balance on current account (the most widely used gauge of a nation's international payments position), compared with a $1.13-billion deficit at the end of June 1976. The change was due mainly to increased export earnings of $2.20

billion, which stemmed largely from a 42% increase in oil exports.

Foreign Relations

Perez charged with receiving CIA payments. President Perez was named in a Washington Post report Feb. 19 as one of a number of heads of various governments who allegedly had received secret payments from the U.S. Central Intelligence Agency.

Perez declared indignantly that the charge that he had received CIA payments while minister of the interior. was "vile and false." Venezuela recalled its ambassador to the U.S. and on Feb. 22 protested the charge at a Washington meeting of the Organization of American States. However, Venezuelan Foreign Minister Ramon Escovar Salom said Feb. 22 that the "very delicate" situation had been closed in a satisfactory fashion by a letter from Carter to Perez. Carter had dismissed the charge as "groundless and malicious," Escovar Salom said. The White House Feb. 23 acknowledged that Carter had sent Perez a letter but refused to release its contents because it was "a personal letter." A White House official quoted in the New York Times Feb. 24 said, "If it [Escovar Salmon's description of the letter's contents] wasn't correct we would tell you that."

Argentine leader visits. Argentine President Gen. Jorge Videla visited Caracas May 11-14 for consultations with President Carlos Andres Perez on a variety of political and economic issues.

Videla's visit was widely protested because of well-publicized violations of human rights in Argentina. Among the Venezuelan groups denouncing the Argentine leader were the national press association, the three labor union federations, high school and university students, left-wing political parties and leaders of the two major parties—Democratic Action (AD) and the Social Christians (Copei).

Students rioted May 11-12 to protest Videla's visit, burning at least 10 cars in the streets of Caracas. Nearly 100 students were placed under preventive detention by police, according to press reports.

(Students had been rioting in the city since May 5, when police raided the Central University to quell a protest over the school's large budget deficit. The university's public relations director charged May 5 that the police had damaged parked cars on the campus, used tear gas inside university buildings and beaten many students, professors and administrators.)

The Venezuelan press association issued a statement May 11 deploring the treatment of journalists in Argentina, which the statement described as "one of the most brutal repressions to have taken place in the Latin American subcontinent." The Venezuelan Committee for Solidarity with the Argentine People, headed by a Venezuelan Supreme Court justice, charged that under Videla's government 4,000 persons had died for political reasons, 20,000 had been arrested and 25,000 had disappeared.

The most prominent politician to protest Videla's visit was former President Romulo Betancourt, who had long opposed recognition of military governments, it was reported May 20. Also protesting the visit were members of the Venezuelan Senate, which had voted unanimously in March to condemn the Argentine government for abusing human rights.

Videla and Perez expressed satisfaction with the visit despite the protests. The two leaders exchanged praise and expressed confidence that the armed forces would restore constitutional democracy in Argentina. Videla and Perez signed a joint declaration May 13 supporting democratic forms of government; "universalism" in foreign policy; Panamanian sovereignty over the Panama Canal; economic cooperation and regional integration, and an end to all forms of colonialism.

Argentine officials were particularly pleased with the visit, expecting it to strengthen the hand of moderate military officers in Argentina and to help improve Argentine relations with the U.S., with which Venezuela enjoyed close ties, it was reported May 15.

Brazil relations deteriorate. Relations between Venezuela and Brazil had reached their lowest point in more than a decade because of President Perez' opposition to Brazil's atomic power policy, it was reported April 1.

In an address to Congress in March Perez had supported the U.S. policy on the spread of nuclear technology, calling for "supra-national control of atomic energy," warning against the spread of nuclear weaponry to Latin America and expressing "alarm that certain Western nations, who have identified themselves ethically and morally with the peace, dignity and liberty of mankind, are not living up to their fundamental responsibilities."

The last passage was considered a reference to West Germany's role in building Brazil's atomic energy industry. The U.S. vigorously had opposed Brazil's nuclear development, fearing it would lead to production of atomic weapons.

The Brazilian government took Perez' statement "as a premeditated insult," according to the Latin America Political Report. The Brazilian Foreign Ministry canceled a visit to Caracas by Foreign Minister Antonio Azeredo da Silveira that had been discussed but not formally scheduled.

Mrs. Carter's visit. Rosalynn Carter, wife of U.S. President Jimmy Carter, visited Venezuela June 10–12.

Mrs. Carter met with President Perez June 12. They discussed the U.S. law denying Venezuela preferential trade treatment because it belonged to OPEC; the upcoming OAS meeting in Grenada, and Perez' planned visit to Washington in July.

Mrs. Carter later said she had thanked Perez for "Venezuela's being a reliable source of petroleum" during the Arab oil embargo in 1973–74, but had told him she could not "promise" that Congress would repeal the restrictive trade legislation. Perez told her Venezuela had signed and ratified the American Convention on Human Rights.

Perez called Mrs. Carter "an extraordinary woman." "I was surprised, very pleasantly surprised, by her knowledge and her frankness," he said.

Perez sees Carter. President Carlos Andres Perez visited the U.S. June 27–July 2 for consultations with President Carter and with business leaders in New York and Chicago.

Perez appeared to establish a warm relationship with Carter, whom he had not met before. The two leaders praised each other generously and issued joint communiques detailing their agreement on a variety of issues, notably human rights.

After an overnight stay in Williamsburg, Va., Perez arrived in Washington June 28, where he was greeted at the White House by Carter, Vice President Walter Mondale, Secretary of State Cyrus Vance and Carter's national security adviser, Zbigniew Brzezinski.

At the reception ceremony Perez said that Carter's policies, "which are based not on economic or military predominance but on the defense of the great values of the human spirit, have reconciled Latin America with the U.S."

Carter expressed pleasure in welcoming "the leader of a sister nation dedicated to liberty, democracy and the representative form of government." He noted that Venezuela had "assumed leadership in the defense of human rights" at the recent general assembly of the Organization of American States (OAS), and was in the forefront of developing nations seeking a new economic relationship with the industrial world.

"Venezuela has acted responsibly on the world scene," Carter said, noting that during the Arab oil embargo of 1973 Venezuela had "followed its own policy and voluntarily increased" oil shipments to the U.S.

At a banquet hosted by Carter June 28, Perez defended the Organization of Petroleum Exporting Countries (OPEC), of which Venezuela was a founding member. "OPEC has generated awareness of world interdependence" and "has made it much more difficult for the developed world to continue exploiting the developing world," the Venezuelan leader said. He also called for "all countries in the international community to accept a code to regulate the actions of transnational corporations, which have weakened and violated the sovereignty of developing nations and have corrupted their morality with the generalized practice of bribery."

Perez flew to New York June 30, where he had breakfast with directors of Citibank and other banks and made an afternoon visit to Columbia University, where 70 Venezuelan youths were studying on a scholarship program that he initiated.

Perez flew to Chicago July 1, with a stopover in Philadelphia to dedicate a statue of Francisco de Miranda, a hero of Venezuela's revolutionary war and a fervent supporter of the American revolution. In Chicago he addressed a group of Midwestern businessmen after being received by Mayor Michael Bilandic.

While Perez was in Chicago, the White House released two joint communiques he had signed with Carter—one on general international themes and the other devoted exclusively to human rights. The two presidents defended "the ethical and political values of Western democratic society"; pledged continued support for the Inter-American Human Rights Commission of the OAS; vowed to fight terrorism and seek a more just international economic system, and expressed opposition to nuclear arms proliferation and the world arms race in general.

In one of the communiques Venezuela said that while it had nationalized its oil and steel industries, it welcomed foreign investment in all other areas and guaranteed investors against expropriation.

Perez returned to Venezuela July 2. He told reporters in Caracas he was certain his U.S. journey had been "significant" for "all Venezuelans."

Vance visits Venezuela. U.S. Secretary of State Vance visited Venezuela Nov. 23 to talk with President Perez and his foreign minister, Simon Alberto Consalvi. Vance urged Perez to oppose a new price increase by the Organization of Petroleum Exporting Countries (OPEC), but Perez already had said in Brazil that OPEC would raise prices by 5%-8% at its meeting in Caracas Dec 20. Perez said Nov. 23 that "an oil price increase is justified because the industrial countries have raised the prices for what we (the OPEC countries) import."

"If there were international efforts to stabilize steel, machinery and tractor prices, I would be the leader of an effort to freeze petroleum prices," Perez declared.

In any case, he said, Venezuela was not taking as "hard" a position on oil price increases as other OPEC nations.

Vance and Perez discussed human rights and other issues with more success. "We agreed on everything except oil prices," Vance noted before flying on to Washington.

Vance's visit to South America at a time of momentous developments in the Middle East emphasized the Carter Administration's interest in strong relations with Latin American countries, according to U.S. officials quoted in the Washington Post Nov. 24.

The trip also illustrated the Administration's country-by-country (rather than regional) approach to hemispheric relations. There were different priorities in Washington's relations with each Latin American nation, as shown in the varying topics discussed by Vance in Brazil and Venezuela.

Finally, the Post said, the Administration was treating Latin American nations not as special American allies but as members of the Third World, with problems, aspirations and alliances that were increasingly bound with other underdeveloped nations in Africa, the Middle East and Asia.

Perez urges OPEC price hike to aid poor countries. Venezuelan President Perez, in a speech Dec. 20 at the first session of the Organization of Petroleum Exporting Countries meeting, urged that the OPEC's prices be increased by 5% to 8% and that the additional revenue be contributed to non oil-exporting developing countries to help them meet their debt obligations. Perez conceded that his proposal was in conflict with what appeared to be the "present inclination" of the majority of OPEC members toward a price freeze.

In his speech, Perez claimed that the debts of the poorer countries had soared from $40 billion in 1973 to $180 billion at present. The price increase Perez suggested would have brought in from $7 billion to $11 billion in additional revenues.

Perez cited the failure of the Geneva talks—between industrialized and developing countries—aimed at the establishment of a reserve fund to stabilize world commodity prices. He said the sharp increase in the poorer countries' debt did not reflect OPEC oil price increases. The debt increase, Perez claimed, was caused instead by the decline in the prices the poorer countries received for their exports of raw material, coupled with price increases charged by industrialized countries for their exports.

Perez told the OPEC delegates that "we cannot accept, as raw material producers, that we be asked to continue subsidizing the world economy." He continued, "We reject the claim that oil prices are responsible for the ills of the industrial countries, or that we should sacrifice our well-being for the benefit of theirs."

Although Perez failed to get the price increase he asked for, his speech drew some expressions of approval. One of the oil ministers in favor of a price freeze was quoted in the Dec. 21 Wall Street Journal as saying, "I respect President Perez's proposal, and I admire his thoughts."

The OPEC meeting was held Dec. 20–21 at the beach resort outside Caracas.

Other Developments

Perez grants wide amnesty. President Perez granted Christmas pardons to about 100 common criminals. Government sources said a small number of persons were being held for trial for alleged guerrilla or subversive activities, AP reported. Amnesty International said there were 83 political prisoners in Venezuela.

Cuban exiles get military trial. Four Cuban exiles accused of bombing a Cuban airliner in October 1976 were being tried secretly by a Venezuelan military court, the Miami Herald reported Oct. 10.

Although the airplane crashed off the coast of Barbados, the trial was being held in Venezuela because two of the defendants were arrested in Caracas and the other two were seized in countries (Barbados and Trinidad and Tobago) that did not want the trial for fear it would hurt their tourist industries.

The trial had begun in a civilian court, but it was moved to a military court after Cuban exiles bombed a Venezuelan air force jet in Miami Aug. 14. Venezuelan

President Carlos Andres Perez requested the transfer to a military court on the grounds that the Miami bombing made the trial a matter of "national security."

The defendants' attorneys resigned to protest the transfer and the Venezuelan attorney general asked the Supreme Court to rule on its constitutionality. But the court was expected to endorse the transfer because most of the court's members belonged to Perez' Democratic Action Party, according to the Miami Herald.

Perez had filed a civil suit against one of the defendants, Orlando Bosch, for telling a Venezuelan newspaper July 4 that Perez had once authorized him to use Venezuela as a base for anti-Cuban operations. Bosch said Perez recently had betrayed the cause of Cuban exiles because he desired good relations with the government of Cuban President Fidel Castro. (Under Venezuela's penal code, disrespectful statements about the president were punishable with prison sentences.)

Besides Bosch, the other defendants on trial were Hernan Ricardo, Freddy Lugo and Luis Posada Carriles. Ricardo and Lugo had been employed as photographers in Venezuela before the October 1976 bombing, and Posada had been an important officer in the Venezuelan police.

Guerrillas seize rural towns. Guerrillas of the leftist Red Flag organization briefly occupied several small towns in the eastern state of Anzoategui in September and October.

About 35 guerrillas took over the town of Caigua on the evening of Sept. 4, subduing several policemen and herding residents into the town plaza for a lecture on the need for violent revolution. On Sept. 20 insurgents seized the town of Santa Ines for two hours, distributing propaganda to residents. And four days later guerrillas attacked the Altamira ranch of Urban Development Minister Roberto Padilla Fernandez, leaving behind a note in which they demanded that Padilla pay higher wages to his farmworkers.

The attacks caused a sensation in Caracas, where they were reported extensively in the press. But Interior Minister Octavio Lepage assured reporters Sept. 27 that the guerrillas were few in number, they lacked popular support and would soon be wiped out by security forces.

Newspapers in Caracas reported Oct. 13 that several guerrillas had been arrested in Anzoategui and the neighboring state of Monagas, among them Red Flag leader Argenis Betancourt. Betancourt reportedly had taken over the guerrilla movement temporarily during the recent illness of his brother, Carlos, who was known as Commander Geronimo.

Carlos Betancourt apparently recovered, for police said he was among several guerrillas who attacked the town of Orijuan about a week later. The raid, in which the guerrillas stole medicine from the local dispensary, was reported by the Caracas newspaper El Nacional Oct. 25.

Other Areas

ANGUILLA

New Anguillan chief minister named.
Emile Gumbs was appointed chief
minister of the Caribbean island of Anguilla Feb. 2 by the British Governor
General David Le Breton. The former
chief minister, Ronald Webster, had lost a
vote of confidence in the colonial assembly
the previous day after being accused of
corruption and the abuse of power.

Webster had asked the governor
general to dissolve the seven-member
assembly after the no-confidence vote but
Le Breton had refused. Le Breton had felt
that new elections so soon after the last
ones, which had been held less than a year
before, would contribute to the island's in-
stability.

Rioters supporting Webster were dispersed Feb. 9 by police using tear gas.
The British frigate H.M.S. Tartar entered
Anguilla harbor Feb. 11 to deter further
outbreaks of violence.

Webster had been chief minister of Anguilla for 10 years. He had led the
resistance in 1969 to constitutional links
between Anguilla and the nearby islands
of Nevis and St. Kitts.

Gumbs was Anguilla's former minister
of work and was regarded as a political
moderate. The economy of the 35-square-
mile island, with a population of about
5,000, was described as weak by observers.

BAHAMAS

Pindling returned to office. Prime
Minister Lynden O. Pindling and his
Progressive Liberal Party (PLP) soundly
defeated a divided opposition in the July 19
parliamentary elections.

The PLP won 30 seats in the House of
Assembly, to five for the Bahamian
Democratic Party (BDP) and two for the
Free National Movement (FNM). The
38th seat in the unicameral legislature was
being disputed in court following a one-
vote victory by the PLP candidate.

The solid PLP vote was considered an
endorsement of Pindling's plans for a
mixed economy and a rejection of opposition charges that the government was corrupt and incompetent. The PLP had been
hurt by the soaring unemployment rate
and a number of government scandals, but
the voters apparently believed Pindling's
contention that his party was best suited
to lead the Bahamas after 10 consecutive
years in office.

The opposition parties were hampered
by their identification with the white business community that once dominated the
islands—two of the winning BDP candidates were white—and by their inability to
unite against Pindling. Their persisting
rivalry was attributed to the same personality clashes that led the BDP to split
off from the FNM in December 1976.

Throughout the six-week campaign the two parties had charged that Pindling was abandoning the Bahamas' free-enterprise system in favor of Jamaican-style socialism. Big government spending programs, they said, had increased the nation's debt, discouraged private investment and contributed to the 20% unemployment rate. Servicing of the public debt had become the second-largest item in the Bahamian budget, the opposition noted.

The BDP and FNM also exploited a number of scandals involving the national airline Bahamasair, the Broadcasting Corporation, the National Insurance Board and the Ministry of Works, none of which the government was able to explain adequately. Pindling, whose previous efforts to curb bribery and corruption had been opposed by many PLP members, acknowledged during the campaign that the aura of corruption was one of his party's greatest liabilities.

The PLP also had been criticized by the labor unions, once the party's strongest supporters. But Pindling won the backing of the 15,000-member Trade Union Congress by accepting a number of labor candidates and granting the union federation a greater voice in national policy.

Pindling's new government faced serious social and economic problems, foremost the pressure for jobs, housing, education and health care from a rapidly growing population. The Bahamas had the second highest population growth rate in the Western Hemisphere, aggravated by thousands of illegal Haitian and Jamaican immigrants. In the past 20 years the Bahamian population had more than doubled to 200,000 and it was expected to double again by 1985. About 44% of the population was under 15 years of age.

The Bahamian government, meanwhile, was looking for foreign capital to spur domestic business expansion, it was reported Aug. 19. Hubert Ingraham, chairman of the ruling party, was planning measures to cut the bureaucratic red tape which he said had thwarted previous investment projects, and to market the Bahamas' industrial advantages as actively as its tourist attractions, the Journal of Commerce reported.

Clifford Cooper resigned Aug. 19 as secretary general of the Bahamian Democratic Party, which was defeated by the ruling Progressive Liberal Party in the July 19 parliamentary elections.

The newly elected Parliament was opened Oct. 20 by Queen Elizabeth II, who read the traditional Speech from the Throne to the legislature. The speech, prepared by the Bahamian government, outlined the government's plans to combat inflation and other local problems. The queen was in Nassau with her husband, Prince Philip, following a visit to Canada.

Pindling revises Cabinet—Prime Minister Pindling July 29 named a 13-man Cabinet consisting entirely of members of his Progressive Liberal Party (PLP). Ten of the ministers had been in the Cabinet before the July 19 parliamentary elections, which the PLP won decisively. The new members of the Cabinet were Phillip M. Bethel, transport minister; Perry G. Christie, health minister, and Kendall W. Nottage, who headed the new Ministry of Youth, Sports and Community Affairs.

Pindling remained economic affairs minister as well as prime minister, and Arthur Hanna stayed on as deputy prime minister and finance minister. Paul Adderley, another key Pindling aide, was reappointed external affairs minister and attorney general.

Pindling and the members of his revised Cabinet awarded themselves large pay increases and backdated them to July 20, it was reported Oct. 29. Pindling's annual salary rose 82% to $102,000; Deputy Prime Minister Arthur Hanna's rose 95% to $82,000, and all other Cabinet ministers' pay rose 67% to $57,000. Pindling's new salary was more than double the salary of the prime minister of Great Britain. (The Bahamas had been a British colony until 1973.)

Bahama tax evidence barred. U.S. District Court Judge John M. Manos April 28 ruled inadmissible evidence that had been gathered by the Internal Revenue Service in its probe of U.S. citizens' use of Bahamian bank accounts as secret tax havens. The ruling came in the case of Jack P. Payner, who had been charged with making a false statement in his 1972 tax return.

The evidence affected by the ruling was a list of about 300 persons holding secret accounts at a Bahamian bank, Castle Bank and Trust (Bahamas) Ltd. An executive of the bank had brought the list with him on a trip to Miami. There he was introduced to a woman by an IRS informer. The bank officer left the list in a briefcase in the woman's apartment while the two went out on a date; while they were out, IRS agents made a copy of the list.

The IRS probe into the Bahamian accounts, codenamed Project Haven, had been the subject of congressional hearings. Controversy had focused on two questions: whether the probe had infringed on the rights of the individuals under investigation, and whether former IRS Commissioner Donald C. Alexander had acted properly in suspending the probe.

Manos' decision to bar submission of the list as evidence was based on the method by which it was acquired—Manos termed the government an "active participant" in the criminal conduct through which the IRS informer gained a copy of the list.

Castle Bank closes—Castle Bank and Trust ceased operations in the Bahamas April 28. A bank spokesman said the bank would transfer its operations to Panama, where its parent bank—Castle Trust Co.—was headquartered. The Bahamian government, which had revoked the bank's license in March, said the parent bank had guaranteed full indemnity for any losses stemming from the Bahama bank's activities.

A spokesman for the bank said the closing was the result of bad publicity generated by the IRS probe. The probe, the spokesman said, had not produced "one shred of evidence" that the bank had violated the laws of any country, but it had made it virtually impossible for the bank to function.

The Bahama bank said it had given up its Bahamian license voluntarily.

BELIZE

Guatemala claim vs. independence. Alejandro Orfila, secretary general of the Organization of American States, said March 1 that Latin American nations supported Guatemala's claim to full sovereignty over Belize, the British colony formerly known as British Honduras.

Guatemala severs Panama ties—The Guatemalan government announced May 19 that it had broken diplomatic relations with Panama to protest Panama's support of independence for Belize.

Panama's military strongman, Brig. Gen. Omar Torrijos, had infuriated Guatemalan leaders by declaring the previous weekend: "Yes, I have my hands in Belize, and I'm not going to take them out. . . . I'm going to help those people because they need it, I'm going to help George Price because he's a mystic who needs it, and I don't care if it makes Laugerud mad." Price was prime minister of Belize; Gen. Kjell Laugerud Garcia was president of Guatemala.

In an angry reply May 20, Laugerud called Torrijos "a man who doesn't know the meaning of honor" and a "pseudo-emulator" of Cuban President Fidel Castro and Ugandan President Idi Amin Dada. Laugerud warned Torrijos that if he "has his hands in Belize, he could get them burned."

Torrijos reiterated his support for an independent Belize May 20, on the first day of a visit to Panama by Price. Price said Guatemala's renunciation of ties with Panama was "an affront to the United Nations and to the countries of the Third World." (Both the U.N. General Assembly and the movement of nonaligned nations had passed resolutions in 1975 favoring Belizean independence.

Torrijos and others had argued that Belize's 150,000 inhabitants were not culturally, racially or historically related to Guatemala. The Belizean people, most of whom originally came from Jamaica, Trinidad and Tobago and other Caribbean islands, spoke English.

Guatemala's ambassador to Mexico, Gen. Doroteo Monterroso Miranda, subsequently charged that Torrijos was supporting Belizean independence because he had invested more than $9 million in hotels and condominiums in the British colony, and he feared losing the investment under Guatemalan rule, it was reported May 24. Torrijos denied the charge and recommended that it be investigated by an international tribunal.

A Panamanian television station reported May 27 that Torrijos had asked

Mexico, Venezuela, Costa Rica and Colombia to intercede to help resolve his difficulties with Guatemala. (At least two of those countries—Mexico and Venezuela—had come out strongly for Belizean independence in the past year, seriously weakening Latin American support for Guatemala's claim to Belize.)

Great Britain favored independence for Belize, but the colony did not want its freedom without a British commitment to defend it from attack by Guatemala. Price had given up trying to obtain an indefinite defense guarantee from London and was now aiming for a 10-year defense treaty, according to the Latin America Political Report May 20. Price reasoned that if Belize could survive the first 10 years of independence without attack from Guatemala, its diplomatic position in international forums would be established and its security thereafter assured, the Report said.

(Belize had announced in February that it would establish a defense force of regular and volunteer soldiers. British military officers would help set up the force, it was reported Feb. 13.)

Guatemala, meanwhile, opposed any unilateral action by Great Britain and asked for a continuation of talks between British and Guatemalan officials on the future of Belize. Laugerud had warned that Guatemala would "resort to arms" if Britain unilaterally made Belize independent, it was reported May 17.

In an earlier development, the Belize City Reporter had said Jan. 30 that Guatemalan nationals were crossing into Belize in droves. Border officials were capturing and deporting the illegal immigrants at a rate of 40 per day, the newspaper reported. It was unclear whether the migration was the result of hard times in Peten, Guatemala's border province, or was an invasion sponsored by the Guatemalan government, the newspaper said.

Britain vs. Guatemalan claim—Great Britain strengthened its military presence in Belize July 7 to counter growing threats against the colony by neighboring Guatemala.

Britain sent several hundred soldiers and six Harrier jump jets to Belize in an all-night airlift that lasted into July 8. The troops were stationed as near as three kilometers from the Guatemalan border, where thousands of Guatemalan troops were said to have massed in recent weeks as the Guatemalan government threatened to invade the colony to prevent Britain from granting it independence.

Fears of a Guatemalan invasion subsided in Belize as the British troops arrived and newspapers reported conciliatory statements by British and Guatemalan negotiators. They had met in Washington July 6–7 in the latest round of their talks on Belize's future.

Both sides agreed to take "prompt steps to decrease tension" and to resume negotiations in Guatemala City before the end of July. However, it was unclear how the presence of the extra British troops would affect the talks. A Guatemalan spokesman said July 8 that the discussions could not resume until the British reinforcements were withdrawn; a British official replied July 12 that the additional soldiers would remain in Belize "as long as they are needed."

A spokesman for the British Foreign Office July 6 said Guatemala would drop its claim to sovereignty over Belize in exchange for substantial British economic aid. Other British officials said July 9 that they were working on an aid package. However, Guatemalan Foreign Minister Adolfo Molina Orantes July 8 said his government had "made it very clear we demand some territorial arrangements" in Belize, perhaps a Guatemalan corridor to the Caribbean Sea.

As a British dependent territory, Belize was self-governing except in foreign affairs, defense, internal security and the civil service, which were controlled by a colonial administration representing the British Crown.

Great Britain wanted to grant Belize full independence, but Belizeans—particularly members of the opposition United Democratic Party (UDP)—did not want freedom without a British commitment to help defend the territory against Guatemalan attack. The right-wing UDP repeatedly stressed that Belize's own defense force totaled only 350 men.

Both the UDP and Guatemala's rightist military government feared that once Belize was independent, Prime Minister George Price would ally himself with the leftist governments of Cuba and Jamaica, giving them a springboard to infiltrate Central America. UDP members called Price a Communist, a charge he heatedly denied.

The UDP held an anti-independence rally in Belize City July 11 in defiance of a government ban. Several hundred party members waved placards reading, "To Hell With George Price," "God Bless Our Queen" and "Referendum Before Independence."

Meanwhile, Ted Rowland, deputy foreign secretary in the British Foreign Office, visited several South American countries in August and September to discuss the Belize issue with their leaders. Leaving Peru Sept. 8, he reaffirmed Great Britain's full support for Belizean independence.

The statement was denounced by Guatemalan Foreign Minister Adolfo Molina Orantes, it was reported Sept. 23. Molina said negotiations between Britain and Guatemala over Belize's future could break down unless Britain removed its troops from Belize's Guatemalan border.

Costa Rica for independence—Costa Rican President Daniel Oduber asserted Sept. 30 that he was in favor of independence for Belize "following negotiations" between Britain, Guatemala and Belize.

The Costa Rican government had previously supported Guatemala's claim to Belize. President Oduber's statement added one more country to the majority of American and Caribbean nations that opposed the Guatemalan claim.

U.N. for independence—The United Nations General Assembly Nov. 28 adopted a resolution favoring "self-determination" and "independence" for Belize. The measure passed by a vote of 126–4 with 13 abstentions. Among the nations voting for it were Argentina and Peru, which had abstained on similar motions at the U.N. in 1976 and 1975.

A spokesman for the British Foreign Office said Dec. 9 that Britain had been having "confidential, exploratory discussions with the Guatemalans in an attempt to establish a basis for a further round of negotiations" on Belize's future.

BERMUDA

Internal party strife. Prime Minister Jack Sharpe announced the resignation of four Cabinet ministers Feb. 15 after members of his United Bermuda Party failed in an attempt to remove him from the party leadership. A no-confidence motion, sponsored by the former Cabinet members, had been defeated at a party meeting Feb. 11, by a 15-10 vote.

The conflict within Sharpe's party had begun the previous year when its majority in the House of Assembly was halved in the general election. Sharpe's party held 25 seats in the chamber after the election, while the opposition Progressive Labor Party held 15. The four resigned Cabinet ministers retained their assembly seats and their party membership.

As a result of this party strife, Sharpe resigned Aug. 26 as prime minister, a post he had held since 1975.

The United Bermuda Party Aug. 29 elected David Gibbons, 50, as prime minister.

Gibbons Aug. 31 named to the Cabinet four men who had participated in the successful revolt against Sharpe's leadership. Gibbons retained the position of finance minister, and he named his rival for party leadership, Jim Woolridge, as deputy prime minister and minister of tourism.

The racial make-up of the Cabinet remained the same—six whites and five blacks.

Executions spark Bermuda riots. The hangings of two black political activists who had been convicted of murder caused rioting and arson in Bermuda Dec. 1–3 by groups of militant black youths. Peter Ramsbotham, governor of the British colony, declared a state of emergency on the island Dec. 2—the day of the executions—and imposed a dusk-to-dawn curfew. On the advice of Prime Minister David Gibbons, the governor also asked for British troops to be sent to Bermuda to reinforce the island's security forces.

Great Britain sent 260 troops to the island Dec. 4, 80 from Belize and 180 from Britain. Most were confined to their camp after arrival to prevent local ill-feeling, although some were detailed to guard the island's power plant. Their major duty was to back up the regular police and the Bermuda Regiment (a militia unit), which were on alert under the emergency rules. It was the first state of emergency on the island since the 1968 race riots.

The two hanged men, Erskine Burrows, 33, and Larry Tacklyn, 26, had been convicted of several murders. Burrows had admitted to the 1973 murders of Gov. Richard Sharples and his aide, Capt. Hugh Sayers, and to the 1972 killing of Police Commissioner George Duckett. Burrows and Tacklyn both were convicted of killing two supermarket owners in 1974 during an attempted robbery.

(Acting Governor-General Peter Lloyd had said May 2 that he would not commute the death sentences.)

Burrows, a member of a disbanded black group called the Black Beret Cadres, had claimed throughout his trial that he wanted to make the people of Bermuda aware of the "evilness" and "wickedness" of colonial rule.

Allen Lister, chief police inspector, estimated that several thousand of the island's 33,000 blacks either were involved in the rioting or sympathized with the protests over the hangings. Lister said the riots were racial in nature and linked to the discontent of many black youths in the community.

Prime Minister Gibbons, on the other hand, blamed the riots on "about 400 or 500" young black men "who experience had shown over the last decade and a half are only too willing to take to the streets."

Over 25 fires were set in the course of the riots, causing an estimated $5 million in damage. Arsonists burned the island's largest liquor warehouse and several supermarkets, but most of the unrest was confined to poor black neighborhoods.

The worst of the fires occurred Dec. 2 when the Southhampton Princess Hotel burned, killing three tourists, including two U.S. citizens. Gibbons insisted that the fire was a tragic coincidence rather than arson and had been caused by an electrical failure. The police, who had at first said the fire was probably caused by arson, withdrew their judgment at the prime minister's request.

The riots began the night of Dec. 1 after the final appeals to stay the executions had failed. According to Dec. 5 news reports, the unrest had built up over the previous week, led mainly by the largely black, opposition Progressive Labor Party. A petition containing over 13,000 names calling for the abolition of the death penalty had been submitted to the government, and prayer vigils and marches had

been held. (Although Great Britain had abolished the death penalty, Bermuda had not.)

Mrs. Lois Brown-Evans, leader of the Progressive Labor Party, had served as Burrows' attorney and had been a key figure in the early protests. During the Dec. 1-3 riots she appealed for an end to the violence, but blamed the disturbances on racism in Bermuda's society. Gibbons criticized her statements on the situation, calling them "attempts to damage national unity."

The effect of the riots on the island's tourist industry, virtually its only source of income, was a cause of deep concern to Bermuda's leaders, according to Dec. 6 news reports. A convention of U.S. travel agents, which had been postponed earlier because of a hotel strike, was present on the island during the riots. Although there were some cancellations and early departures, no serious effects on tourism were noticed.

Some British troops leave island—Eighty of the 260 British troops sent to Bermuda to keep order, returned to their usual base in Belize Dec. 6. Their departure followed the second calm night in Bermuda after the Dec. 1-3 riots.

As calm returned to the island, the curfew was reduced Dec. 6 to the hours of midnight to dawn. The estimated value of the damage caused by the riots rose to $10 million. Except for the deaths at the Southhampton Princess Hotel, no serious injuries were reported.

Lois Brown-Evans, leader of the opposition Progressive Labor Party, Dec. 6 blamed the ruling United Bermuda Party for the riots. She said she would seek a motion of no-confidence against the United Bermuda Party in the island's parliament. The United Bermuda Party was biracial and relatively conservative in its policies.

COSTA RICA

Presidential campaign. Gonzalo Facio reassumed the post of foreign minister after abandoning his bid for the 1978 presidential nomination of the ruling National Liberation Party (PLN).

The PLN and the major opposition party, the Opposition Union, held primaries March 13 to select their presidential candidates.

The PLN chose its party secretary, Luis Alberto Monge, while the Opposition Union selected Rodrigo Carazo, a congressman and former PLN member.

Monge beat out the personal favorites of both President Oduber and ex-President Figueres. His victory was particularly resented by Figueres, and appeared to be one of the reasons why Figueres attacked the PLN in his April 23 interview with The New Republic, according to the Latin America Political Report June 3.

Figueres said in the interview that the U.S. Central Intelligence Agency had helped create and finance *Combate,* a social-democratic magazine once edited by Monge.

By early September, there were six declared candidates. Besides the major-party contenders, the candidates were: Jorge Gonzales Marteh (Independent National Party), Guillermo Villalobos Arce (National Unification Party), Rodrigo Cordero (Democratic Party) and Rodrigo Gutierrez (Popular Vanguard). The Popular Vanguard was a leftist coalition that included the Communist Party.

Vesco political financing scandal. A major scandal broke in May over allegations that Robert L. Vesco, the fugitive American financier, had given money to the political campaigns of President Daniel Oduber and members of his National Liberation Party (PLN).

The allegations were made by former President Jose Figueres in an interview published in the April 23 issue of the U.S. magazine, The New Republic. Figueres, a former PLN leader, said "many members of the Congress in [Costa Rica] as well as the current president were elected with Vesco's money." There was "a great deal of corruption" in Oduber's government, Figueres added. "For one thing, government contracts require the payment of a commission," he said.

The interview was translated into Spanish and published in Costa Rica early in May, provoking a denial from Oduber, calls for government investigations and

criminal prosecution and renewed demands for Vesco's expulsion.

Oduber May 11 released a letter he had written to The New Republic denying that he had used campaign contributions from Vesco. The president said his campaign had received a contribution from a company owned by Figueres, but said he had returned the money when he discovered it had come originally from Vesco. (Figueres and Vesco had been close business associates since Vesco's arrival in Costa Rica in 1972.)

The Costa Rican Congress voted May 18 to pursue a full investigation of Figueres' allegations, and all 27 congressmen from the PLN signed a petition asking Vesco to leave the country.

Rodrigo Carazo, who would be the leading opposition candidate in the 1978 presidential election, May 19 asked the attorney general to file criminal charges against Oduber and Vesco for violating the constitutional ban on interference by foreigners in Costa Rican politics. [See below]

The attorney general replied May 24 that it was not illegal for a Costa Rican politician to accept financial support from a foreign national. However, he said Figueres might be liable for prosecution on a charge of violating the electoral code prohibition against intervention by a president in political activities. Figueres had been president of Costa Rica when he obtained Vesco's financial support for Oduber in 1974.

Oduber June 9 said he had asked Vesco to leave the country, but not until "he puts his affairs in order" and "clears up his situation before the courts." Vesco could not leave San Jose until the courts settled a suit brought against him by a Costa Rican investor, Carlos Rechnitzer. Rechnitzer claimed that Vesco had defrauded him of $225,000 he had invested in Investors Overseas Services Ltd., a mutual-funds concern that Vesco was alleged to have looted.

Vesco said settlement of the suit, including a possible trial and appeal, "might take a few years," the Wall Street Journal reported June 13. "I'm not packing my bags," Vesco said.

The Supreme Court ordered that Vesco be tried on charges that he had defrauded Rechnitzer, it was reported Sept. 12. The trial was ordered by the First Supreme Criminal Tribunal in San Jose, which reversed a lower court's dismissal of the case.

Vesco won a libel suit against Rechnitzer for having used the word "mafia" in connection with Vesco and his business associates, it was reported Sept. 12.

Gerardo W. Villalobos, former presidential candidate of a small Costa Rican party, wrapped himself in a Costa Rican flag June 2 and fired several pistol shots at Vesco's home outside San Jose. Three of the shots entered a window of the residence, but neither Vesco, who was home, nor any member of his family was injured. Villalobos said in custody June 3 that he had acted to "fulfill my duty as a citizen" and "rid Costa Rica of a pernicious foreigner." Charges against Villalobos of attempted murder were later dropped.

Companies connected with Vesco were accused in the Costa Rican press of making more than $10 million from the nationalization of Costa Rica's gasoline distributors in 1975, the Washington Post reported June 11. The newspapers implicated Figueres and his son, Jose Marti Figueres, in the alleged schemes.

Mrs. Carter's visit. Rosalynn Carter visited Costa Rica May 31–June 12. She was cheered at the San Jose airport when she addressed Costa Ricans in Spanish. She conferred later with President Daniel Oduber and Foreign Minister Gonzalo Facio, apparently concentrating on trade issues.

Mrs. Carter said the next day that while she understood Costa Rica's desire to increase its beef exports to the U.S., she had told Oduber that "Jimmy could not promise him anything that we could not deliver." She said Robert Strauss, the U.S. special trade negotiator, was reviewing the quota system set by the U.S. Congress on beef imports.

Facio said June 1, after Mrs. Carter's departure, that it had been "an extraordinary visit . . . she is a great lady, studious, capable and very modest. She has absolutely no arrogance." Oduber said June 5 that Mrs. Carter's visit had been "of great value for Costa Rica because now it will be easier to overcome problems such as those we have sometimes encountered

with officials in Washington."

Oduber said Costa Rica "has been chosen by the Carter Administration as representative of Latin America in the defense of human rights." Costa Rican officials told Mrs. Carter they would bring up the human rights issue at the June meeting of the Organization of American States (OAS) in Grenada.

Young visits. Andrew Young, the U.S. ambassador to the United Nations, visited Costa Rica Aug. 8–9.

During Young's two-day visit, human rights dominated his talks with Costa Rican leaders. At a press conference the second day, Young defended Carter's emphasis on the rights issue, asserting national boundaries and sovereignty were less important "when human need cries out." "Nobody thought [the U.S.] was denying sovereignty when we gave earthquake assistance," he said, "and in many respects human rights assistance is like earthquake assistance." Young reiterated U.S. support for Costa Rica's initiative to have the United Nations appoint a human rights commissioner, or ombudsman.

DOMINICA

Independence. Premier Patrick John said independence negotiations with Britain had been completed and that his island would become an independent nation by January 1978, it was reported June 5. Dominica, a northern island in the Windward chain between the French islands of Martinique and Guadeloupe, had been a British Associated State since 1967. The Caribbean island has a population of 79,000.

Public meetings banned. The national police announced an indefinite ban on outdoor meetings and rallies between 6 p.m. and 6 a.m., it was reported Sept. 24. The ban was denounced by two opposition groups, the Dominican Revolutionary Party and the Social Christian Revolutionary Party, which accused the government of trying to limit their political activities before the 1978 presidential election.

DOMINICAN REPUBLIC

Communist Party legalized. On the initiative of President Joaquin Balaguer, Congress legalized the Dominican Communist Party Oct. 26. Other parties with communist aims remained banned.

Gen. Enrique Perez y Perez, who admired Chile's military dictatorship, was named commander of the army's key First Brigade Nov. 4. His appointment was widely interpreted as a move by President Joaquin Balaguer to placate conservatives following the legalization of the Dominican Communist Party.

Presidential campaign. Gen. Perez y Perez called Nov. 5 for Balaguer's reelection in 1978. He described Balaguer as "a father to us, a guide and example of virtue ... [a] holy male."

The Popular Democratic Party chose retired Rear Adm. Luis Homero Lajara Burgos as its candidate in the 1978 presidential election (reported Sept. 11).

Lajara said that if elected, he would nationalize the assets of transnational corporations operating in the Dominican Republic. The three million hectares of land controlled by one transnational, Gulf & Western Industries Inc., would be distributed to Dominican peasant families in 100-hectare lots, Lajara vowed. (100 hectares equals 247.1 acres.)

Former Gen. Elias Wessin y Wessin, leader of the Quisqueyan Democratic Party, also announced his candidacy for the 1978 presidential election (reported Sept. 30).

Wessin lived in exile in Spain, and it was unclear whether he would be allowed to return to the Dominican Republic to run in the election. President Joaquin Balaguer and his top military leaders opposed Wessin's return, according to the Miami Herald Oct. 2.

The Dominican Revolutionary Party (PRD), the largest opposition movement, chose Antonio Guzman, a wealthy rancher, as its presidential candidate for 1978. Guzman was considered one of the PRD's most conservative members, according to the Latin America Political Report Dec. 2.

General amnesty declared. As part of a general amnesty, President Joaquin Balaguer released Claudio Caamano and Toribio Pena Jaquez, who had infiltrated the Dominican Republic in 1975 to try to start a leftist guerilla movement, it was reported Sept. 2.

Court appeal. Gulf & Western was appealing a court decision ordering it to pay $6 million to several private sugar farmers for cane bought by the company but not paid for, it was reported Sept. 16. One of the farmers was Vice President Carlos Rafael Goico Morales.

FRENCH GUIANA

Government development plan fails. A two-year government program to settle and develop French Guiana was termed a failure by a French agency that reviewed government spending, it was reported Aug. 5. Cour des Comptes, the investigating agency, said in its report that the program had been started without proper study or funding.

The program was intended to settle about 30,000 colonists in the territory to develop its forestry and agricultural potential. The main project was to make the colony a paper supplier and save France about $500 million a year in foreign exchange.

Only about 30 new settlers finally emigrated to the colony, as most of those who applied failed to meet the health and training requirements. One forestry project was established, but it did not involve paper manufacture. Cour des Comptes charged that the plan's failure had caused bitterness in French Guiana and distrust of France in other nations because it appeared France had reverted to colonialism.

A spokesman for the Ministry of Overseas Territories refused to comment on the Cour des Comptes report. The spokesman noted, however, that Olivier Stirn, secretary of state for the ministry, had indicated in 1975 that the project would take years to accomplish.

French Guiana was located on the northeast coast of the South American mainland, between Brazil and Surinam. It was the last colony of the South American mainland and was best known for its diseases and the old penal colony of Devil's Island.

GRENADA

Political opposition leader Maurice Bishop charged that Grenada's growing links with Chile posed a "security threat" to the entire Caribbean region, it was reported Oct. 26.

Bishop, who was touring the region, said Grenada was opening the Caribbean to the extreme right-wing political ideas espoused by Chile's military government. He noted that Chile had offered Grenada arms and other assistance; that two members of the Grenada Defense Force had been trained in Chile, and that a Chilean military airplane recently had arrived in Grenada with two crates marked "medical supplies" of which the Grenadan Health Ministry had no knowledge. The Grenadan government called Bishop's statements "lies and propaganda."

GUYANA

Sugar strike. The National Assembly Sept. 1 passed a bill that gave the government powers of search and arrest and enabled the home affairs minister to impose a curfew. The government had sought the powers to put down a crippling strike in the sugar industry. The opposition-controlled Guyana Agricultural and General Workers Union had called the stoppage nine days earlier over a profit-sharing dispute. The government used its new emergency powers to arrest at least 10 leaders of a two-week sugar strike (reported Sept. 9).

The government had begun using members of the armed forces and "volunteer" laborers Aug. 30 to help out sugar workers who were ignoring the strike call.

However, under pressure from oil workers in Trinidad and Tobago who had halted all petroleum shipments to Guyana, the government of Guyana withdrew

300 strikebreaking troops it had been using to combat the stoppage in the sugar industry, it was reported Nov. 4.

The Anglican and Roman Catholic churches in Guyana charged that troops had seized food supplies collected by the churches for the 20,000 strikers, according to the Latin America Political Report.

Negotiations to end the strike had broken down over the issue of "scab" labor, according to the Latin America Economic Report Nov. 25. The state sugar company said it would absorb into its permanent labor force the 6,000 scab (strikebreaking) workers it was using during the stoppage. The strikers' union demanded that the strikebreakers be fired as a condition for further negotiations, and that any new sugar workers be hired according to traditional rules by which a worker participated in three consecutive harvests before becoming eligible for permanent employment.

Thugs claiming to be security officers were terrorizing sugar strikers and extorting money from them, according to the Economic Report.

People's Progressive Party coalition offer rejected. Prime Minister Forbes Burnham turned down a proposal by opposition leader Cheddi Jagan for a "national patriotic front government," it was reported Sept. 9. The front would have brought together "all progressive forces," presumably meaning Burnham's People's National Congress (PNC), Jagan's People's Progressive Party and other left-wing groups. Burnham said the PNC was "a vanguard party" that was not interested in a coalition.

Development aid. Textile experts sent by China were helping Guayana build a multimillion-dollar textile factory outside Georgetown, it was reported Sept. 2. The plant was expected make the country self-sufficient in everyday clothing.

Guyana also had signed technical cooperation agreements with the Soviet Union and East Germany. The Soviet pact called for the development of timber and mineral industries in Guyana, while the East German accord was for the development of Guyana's bauxite industry. Both agreements were reported July 11.

HAITI

U.S. returns refugees. The U.S. State Department announced Sept. 6 that it had returned to Haiti 97 of 101 refugees who had sailed into the U.S. naval base at Guantanamo Bay, Cuba, a month earlier.

A spokesman said State Department interviewers had determined that the 97 fled Haiti for economic reasons and thus did not qualify for asylum in the U.S. (Haiti, the poorest country in the Western Hemisphere, was beset by a drought that had crippled its weak agrarian economy.) The status of the other four Haitians at Guantanamo was not clear, although there was "a possibility" that they were political refugees, the spokesman said.

The Haitians arrived at Guantanamo Aug. 10 after a five-day journey through shark-infested waters from Haiti's southwestern coast, 200 miles away. They traveled in a small, leaking sailboat that was later determined to be beyond repair.

Spokesmen for the refugees said all 101 had left Haiti to escape political persecution and all would be beaten severely by Haitian authorities if forced to return home. However, State Department specialists sent to interview the Haitians found that almost all had left the island in hope of escaping poverty. After receiving assurances from the Haitian government that the refugees would not be punished, the U.S. flew the 97 to Port-au-Prince.

The incident posed a moral dilemma for the U.S. To have accepted the Haitians as political refugees would have created additional tensions with the Haitian government, which the U.S. was trying to pressure into respecting human rights. But to have accepted them as economic refugees might have encouraged other Haitians to flee to Guantanamo or the U.S. mainland, and might have encouraged the poor of other neighboring countries to do the same. "I think we have in a nutshell the whole humanitarian and refugee problem," a U.S. official said before the final decision was. reached. "What do you do with the world's poor?" another American official asked.

The U.S. Immigration & Naturalization Service later announced Nov. 8 that it would release about 120 Haitians who said they were political refugees and who were being held in detention in Florida. The service added that it would change its procedure for handling applicants for political asylum in the U.S. The applicants now would be able to argue their claim to asylum before an immigration judge. In the past, it had been U.S. policy to return Haitian refugees to Port-au-Prince without a hearing.

U.S. cites human rights violations. Haiti and five other nations receiving U.S. military aid had been charged with human rights violations in a State Department report released Jan. 1 by the House International Relations Committee.

The U.S. report observed that Haiti, lacking a democratic tradition, had a "basically authoritarian" government, and that prisoners were detained "for extended periods without regard to due process." Some improvement had occurred since 1971, the report said. U.S. military aid had been discontinued in 1963, partly because of human rights violations, but in 1975 a small training program had been started to help Haiti develop its air and sea rescue force. The report said that elimination of the program "would have no impact on Haitian government human rights practices."

Civilian political court set. The National Assembly voted to establish a state security court with civilian judges to try persons accused of political crimes, it was reported Aug. 23.

The action, ordered by the government of President Jean-Claude Duvalier, apparently was the result of prodding on the human rights issue by Andrew Young, U.S. ambassador to the United Nations, who had visited Haiti Aug. 14–16.

Young's visit—Young had denounced Haiti's human rights situation when he was in Port-au-Prince and in a private meeting with Duvalier. Young said after the meeting that Duvalier had agreed to review a list of 21 political prisoners submitted by the ambassador. After Young's departure, however, the Haitian government charged that many of the 21 were "common criminals" and it arrested the pastor of a Haitian church where Young had preached during his visit. One of the prisoners described by the regime as a "common criminal" was said to have been tortured to death after Young's departure, according to the Latin America Political Report Sept. 2

Amnesty granted to political prisoners. The government granted amnesty to 104 prisoners Sept. 21, calling them the last political prisoners held in Haiti. Eleven of them would be expelled from the country because they allegedly had been trained in subversive tactics by Cuba and the Soviet Union.

The amnesty was ordered by President Jean-Claude Duvalier to mark the 20th anniversary of his family's rule over Haiti. The president's late father, Francois (Papa Doc) Duvalier, was elected president in 1957. Like his father, young Duvalier was president for life.

Newspapers noted that the amnesty closely followed a visit to Haiti by Andrew Young.

Many of the Haitian exiles in the U.S., Mexico and France denied the government's contention that it had freed its last political prisoners, according the the Latin America Political Report Sept. 30

The exiles estimated that at least 300 political prisoners remained in the government's hands after 104 prisoners were freed Sept. 21. The unreleased prisoners included lawyer Hubert Legros and former Col. Kesner Blain, the exiles asserted.

But Terence Todman, U.S. assistant secretary of state for inter-American affairs, said the Haitian government had made "important progress" recently in the field of human rights, it was reported Oct. 21. He was apparently referring to the release of 104 Haitain political prisoners in September.

Amnesty International charged, however, that "many people" were still under arrest in Haiti and that recently freed Haitian prisoners said death and torture were still "daily occurrences" in Haitian jails.

Former Interior Minister Jean Julme had been released from prison and put on a plane to Martinique, it was reported Oct. 14.

Mehu slain. Haiti's ambassador to Brazil, Delorme Mehu, was shot to death by paid assassins July 3 in the northeastern Bra-

zilian city of Salvador.

The assassins, who were arrested soon after the slaying, said they had been hired by Louis-Robert Mackenzie, first secretary of the Haitian Embassy in Brasilia. Mackenzie heatedly denied the charge.

Police in Brasilia guarded Mackenzie at his home until a Haitian delegation arrived and escorted him to Port-au-Prince July 12 for questioning.

HONDURAS

Military staff changes. The military government Jan. 3 announced more than 20 military staff changes including the replacement of the chief of staff, Col. Cesar Elvir Sierra, by the defense minister, air force Gen. Mario Chinchilla Carcamo.

Press reports agreed the changes strengthened the hand of the chief of state, Gen. Juan Alberto Melgar Castro, but they disagreed over whether the military shuffle was designed to avert a coup by young officers.

The Tegucigalpa newspaper La Prensa, quoting "completely reliable sources," reported Jan. 6 that the shuffle had been ordered "to dismantle a coup d'etat being planned by young leftist officers" and by "several civilians." The paper noted that many of the lieutenant colonels removed from batallion commands Jan. 3 had not been at their posts for the three years stipulated by military law before a transfer could be ordered.

Other "reliable sources" insisted the military changes were "routine staff shifts that usually occur at the end of each year," the Miami Herald reported Jan. 8. These sources said there was "no evidence of a coup conspiracy."

Col. Elvir Sierra had been replaced as chief of staff so he could devote full time to his job as president of the government's advisory council, which was studying proposed legislation to allow democratic elections in 1979, the Herald's sources said.

Also reassigned Jan. 3 were two members of the ruling Superior Defense Council: Lt. Col. Gerardo Wildt Yates, commander of the 10th Infantry Battalion, was named military attache to the

Honduran embassy in Mexico, and Lt. Col. Mario Leonel Fonseca was named military attache in Venezuela.

Coup plot broken up. A government radio broadcast said Oct. 29 that security forces had broken up a plot by unnamed civilians to divide the armed forces and seize power. The broadcast said the civilians and some military allies had been arrested and turned over to the courts.

Amnesty—The government announced Dec. 6 that in a "magnanimous act," it had granted amnesty to 10 army sergeants and eight civilians who had plotted in October against President Juan Alberto Melgar Castro. The government said there was ample proof of the men's guilt, but they were being forgiven because of the "superlative degree of social harmony" in Honduras. The alleged plotters included Praxedes Martinez Silva, associate director of the newspaper La Prensa of San Pedro Sula.

NETHERLANDS ANTILLES

Strike caused blackout. Electric power was restored to the island of Aruba Aug. 17 after a two-day blackout caused by a strike of government employes and oil workers who sought Aruban independence. The manager of the island's main power plant said the blackout was the result of damage done by striking workers. They had walked off their jobs the previous week to protest the arrest of Hyacinto Geerman, the president of the oil-workers union, on charges stemming from protests against the refusal of the incoming premier of the Netherlands Antilles to include members of the Aruban independence party in his coalition. The People's Electoral Movement had won five of Aruba's eight seats in the 22-seat Parliament representing the islands of the Netherlands Antilles, but was excluded from the coalition because of its pro-independence platform. (Geerman was released Aug. 18.)

PARAGUAY

Political prisoners released. Paraguay released three Communist party leaders and 11 other political prisoners in apparent response to pressure from U.S. President Jimmy Carter, who had said respect for human rights would be a keystone of relations between the U.S. and other countries.

The three Communists, each of whom had been in jail for 19 years, were freed Jan. 27, according to Paraguayan exile sources in Argentina. Eleven women and their 17 children were released from a prison outside Asuncion early in February, the Associated Press reported Feb. 23.

Many observers credited Carter and Alejandro Orfila, secretary general of the Organization of American States (OAS), with obtaining the releases, the AP reported. Carmen de Lara Castro, president of the Paraguayan Human Rights Commission, said she had "a lot of hope regarding Carter. There seems to be an improvement in the situation here." The release of the the female prisoners and their children occurred during an official visit to Asuncion by Orfila. An associate of Orfila said the OAS leader had spoken with Paraguayan President Gen. Alfredo Stroessner, who said he felt Carter was "serious about human rights."

Paraguay still held 350 to 450 political prisoners, according to Amnesty International estimates, the AP reported Jan. 1. Local human rights activists said that the country was still under a state of siege imposed in 1954, when Stroessner seized power, and there were reports of continuing arrests and torture. Many children were imprisoned with their parents because there were no relatives outside of jail to care for them.

The three released Communists remained under close police watch, according to Communist sources cited by the Cuban news agency Prensa Latina Feb. 16. One source called the conditions of their release "virtual house arrest."

The party leaders were Antonio Maidana, 60, Julio Rojas, 64, and Alfredo Alcorta, 63. All had been arrested in 1958. Maidana had been seized for taking part in a general strike, and Rojas and Alcorta for allegedly violating the so-called law "for the defense of democracy." Rojas and Alcorta had later been acquitted in court but held on orders from Stroessner, according to Prensa Latina Feb. 1.

A.I. campaigns against political repression.

Amnesty International announced in Paris that it would mount an international campaign to denounce repression by the Paraguayan government, it was reported Oct. 28.

Amnesty said that underneath a "facade of legality," Paraguay was characterized by an absence of press freedom, restrictions on labor organizing, limits on a citizen's freedom of circulation, corruption and government domination of the judiciary. There were about 350 political prisoners in Paraguay, Amnesty said, and 10 inmates had "died under torture in 1976."

Indians face annihilation.

U.S. Sen. William Proxmire (D, Wis.) reported June 22 that the Indian societies in Paraguay faced virtual annihilation. According to a Washington Post article, Proxmire said that the Guarani and Guayaki Indian populations were being decimated. Proxmire's statement included these remarks:

"The Guarani Indians, a pre-Columbian society which numbered about 150,-000 in 1900, have been reduced to an estimated 30,000 individuals. The Guayaki population has been virtually destroyed. Only 1,000 Guayakis remain out of an estimated 10,000 a century ago.

' Accompanying the near extermination of the Indian population is a blatant racial hatred on the part of the whites and mestizos—mixed Indian-whites. The Post stated—

According to a survey by Paraguayan anthropologists. . . 77 per cent think (the Indians) are 'like animals' because they have not been baptized. On the ranches in the Chaco scrubland of western Paraguay, the name for Indian is 'pig.'

"They know the white man values them less than a horse or cow." said The Most Rev. Anibal Maricevich, bishop of Concepcion, on the Chaco frontier. . . .

"In Paraguay, according to the Post, 'Much of the country does not consider killing Indians a crime.'. . ."

Stroessner reelection facilitated.

A constituent assembly met in Asuncion March 7 11 and amended the 1967 constitution to allow the reelection of President Gen. Alfredo Stroessner.

The assembly, composed exclusively of members of Stroessner's Colorado party, removed from the constitution a clause that forbade the election of a president to more than two five-year terms. Stroessner, who had seized power in 1954, began his fifth term in 1973.

The assembly had been elected Feb. 6. The major opposition group, the United Liberal party, had boycotted the vote, calling it anti-republican and charging that Stroessner was trying to make himself president for life. Colorado candidates won 85% of the ballots, taking all 120 assembly seats. The other 15% of the votes were blank or spoiled ballots.

The United Liberal party had been formed Jan. 24, when the Liberal party and the Radical Liberal party reunited after a 15-year split. The two parties had been driven back together by "the generalized repression against all opposition groupings," according to the London newsletter Latin America Feb. 11.

In a manifesto reported Feb. 7, the United Liberals alleged violations of human rights in Paraguay, called the government a dictatorship and said Paraguayans were apathetic toward elections because the true results of the votes would never be known.

Stroessner to run for 6th term—

Gen. Alfredo Stroessner announced Sept. 11 that he would run for a sixth presidential term in the February 1978 election.

Stroessner, 65, accepted the presidential nomination of his Colorado Party, the only significant political organization in Paraguay. He was considered popular enough to win a fair election, but he had done several things recently to cripple the small opposition parties.

With Stroessner's approval, the courts had closed down the headquarters of the Radical Liberal Party, frozen its bank account and suspended publication of its weekly newspaper, it was reported July 8.

By banning the Radical Liberals, Stroessner effectively destroyed the United Liberal coalition. Later he allowed the old minority faction of the Radical Liberals to resume political activities and take control of the old party newspaper, it was reported Sept. 23. This group posed even less of a threat to the general's 23-year rule than the United Liberals had.

Since July the government also had been rounding up students and intellectuals who opposed the government's policy on the most important national issue, the construction with Brazil of a huge dam and hydroelectric station on the Parana River. The dissidents claimed that Brazil was gaining too much power over Paraguay through the project, according to press reports.

In arresting them, the government aimed not only at silencing opposition to its Parana policy but at eliminating the last vestiges of the dissident Independent Movement at Paraguay's universities, according to the Sept. 23 Latin America Political Report.

Despite this repression, Paraguay was persuading the U.S. that its observance of human rights was improving, the Political Report said. Stroessner favorably impressed President Carter and the State Department when he was in Washington for the signing of the Panama Canal treaties Sept. 7, the report said. U.S. Assistant Secretary of State Terence Todman had visited Paraguay Aug. 17–18 and conferred with both Stroessner and opposition leaders. Stroessner told him that there was "peace and tranquility" in Paraguay, but the opposition members said repression had increased in 1977.

Opposition candidate announced. German Acosta Caballero announced that he would be the candidate of the opposition Radical Liberal Party in the February 1978 presidential election, it was reported Oct. 21.

Paraguay stands firm on electric grid frequency. In a major reverse for Brazil's hydroelectric power plans, Paraguay refused to change the frequency of its electric grid from 50 cycles to Brazil's 60 cycles. As a result, Brazil and Paraguay announced Nov. 11 that their joint power station at Itaipu on the Parana River would have half its generators at 50 cycles and half at 60 cycles.

Brazil had wanted Paraguay to change to 60 cycles because Brazil would be using most of Itaipu's power and because the change would have made it more difficult for Paraguay to pursue joint power projects with Argentina, which had a 50-cycle grid, according to the Latin America Economic Report Nov. 8.

Under the Itaipu treaty, Brazil and Paraguay were to share the station's power equally. Since Paraguay would be able to absorb only 5%–10% of its share of the power, and since it was prevented by the treaty from selling any of its surplus to Argentina, Brazil would have to install expensive converters to purchase Paraguay's surplus of 50-cycle electricity.

Nazi war criminal reported in Paraguay. Nazi hunter Simon Wiesenthal reported Aug. 17 that Nazi war criminal Josef Mengele was living a life of luxury in Paraguay under the protection of Stroessner's government.

Wiesenthal, director of the Jewish Documentation Center in Vienna, said Mengele had obtained Paraguayan citizenship and occasionally traveled abroad under assumed names. The West German government repeatedly had asked Paraguay to extradite Mengele for trial on war-crimes charges, but Paraguay had replied that it could not locate him.

Mengele was a doctor at the Auschwitz extermination camp in German-occupied Poland during World War II. He was known to Auschwitz inmates as the "Angel of Death."

PUERTO RICO

Romero Barcelo takes office. Carlos Romero Barcelo was inaugurated Jan. 2 as the fifth elected governor of Puerto Rico. In a 15-minute address in front of the capitol in San Juan, Romero Barcelo made no reference to President Ford's proposal to make the commonwealth the 51st state, emphasizing instead the economic problems of the island.

In a statement read by Housing and Urban Development Secretary Carla Hills, Ford wished Romero Barcelo and Puerto Rico well but did not mention statehood. President-elect Jimmy Carter sent a message supporting Puerto Rico's "right to political self-determination, . . .

whatever ... your choice may be." Carter previously had said Puerto Rico, not Washington, should take the initiative in defining the commonwealth's future relationship with the U.S.

Meanwhile, former Gov. Rafael Hernandez Colon, the man succeeded by Romero Barcelo, said Jan. 5 that Ford's statehood proposal may have been instigated by the Interior Department in an effort to gain control of oil deposits thought to lie $2\frac{1}{2}$-10 miles off the island's north coast. Hernandez Colon said the department had been willing to grant Puerto Rico jurisdiction within three miles of the coast. Puerto Rico was demanding jurisdiction within the 200-mile limit proposed at the United Nations' Law of the Sea Conference, which the U.S., Hernandez Colon said, had not allowed Puerto Rico to join.

The three-mile limit requested by the Interior Department was the same as that accorded to all U.S. coastal states except Texas and Louisiana, which had jurisdiction up to 12 miles.

In one of his last actions as President, Gerald Ford sent to Congress Jan. 14 legislation to begin the process of granting statehood to Puerto Rico.

FALN bombs NYC office buildings. The Puerto Rican terrorist group FALN (a Spanish acronym for Armed Forces of Puerto Rican National Liberation) claimed responsibility for the bombings Aug. 3 of two New York City office buildings.

The first blast occurred at 9:30 a.m. in a 21st-floor office of the U.S. Defense Department, located in a Madison Avenue skyscraper. An hour later a bomb went off on the ground floor of Mobil Corp.'s headquarters on 42nd Street. That explosion killed one man and wounded seven other persons.

The incidents sparked a rash of telephoned bomb threats and forced the evacuation of more than 100,000 workers throughout the city.

A note discovered in Central Park stated that the bombings were a "warning" to the "multinational corporations" that "strangulate us with their colonial yoke" and demanded the release of five jailed Puerto Rican nationalists. The communique also repeated the group's determination to secure Puerto Rican independence.

An anonymous telephone call to police led to the arrest of two men on weapons possession charges, but they were not directly linked to the bombings.

Dud bomb found—An unexploded bomb was discovered Aug. 8 in the American Metal Climax Building, also in mid-Manhattan. An FALN spokesman who had telephoned a television news station prior to the fatal blast Aug. 3 had mentioned the Amax building as one of several locations where other bombs had been placed.

ST. KITTS-NEVIS

Nevis referendum supports breaking St. Kitts ties. A referendum on the Caribbean island of Nevis Aug. 18 demonstrated almost unanimous support for breaking the island's association with St. Kitts and returning to British colonial status. Election officials said 4,193 persons had voted out of an electorate of about 6,000. Fourteen voters opposed breaking ties with St. Kitts and 13 votes were nullified.

Robert Bradshaw, prime minister of St. Kitts-Nevis, Aug. 19 said the referendum was meaningless. He had indicated his disapproval of the planned vote before it had been held.

(Bradshaw refused to recognize the independence of Anguilla, formerly the third island of the British associated state of St. Kitts-Nevis-Anguilla. Anguilla had broken away in 1976 and had become a British colony. Bradshaw had hoped to make the island group completely independent from Great Britain during 1977. As a West Indies associated state, St. Kitts-Nevis was self-governing internally, but Great Britain was responsible for its foreign affairs and defense.

SURINAM

Arron & NPK win election. Premier Henck Arron and his National Party

Alliance (NPK) were returned to office Oct. 31 in the first national elections since Surinam gained independence from the Netherlands in 1975.

The final vote count gave the four-party NPK 22 seats in the Legislative Assembly to 17 for the opposition United Democratic Parties, the Washington Post reported Nov. 6.

Six other parties put up candidates in the elections without success.

The NPK had won 22 Assembly seats in the 1973 elections but had lost its majority following the impeachment of one legislator, the resignation of another and the defection of one of the coalition parties. The alliance's success Oct. 31 apparently was based on Arron's popularity among Surinamese Creoles (mulattos).

Surinam's population comprised diverse racial and ethnic groups, including Creoles (31%), East Indians (37%) and Indonesians (15%), according to a 1971 census.

Economic problems. The government confronted serious economic problems, including a 25% unemployment rate, an acute housing shortage and underproduction of food. The premier had said in a press interview that one of his goals would be "to do something about the one-sided character of our economy, which has primarily been based on the bauxite industry," the Post reported.

Surinam was the world's fourth leading exporter of bauxite. The ore accounted for 90% of the country's income and helped pay for its food imports.

Soemita jailed for corruption. Former Agriculture Minister Willy Soemita was sentenced to one year in jail for corruption (reported Sept. 9).

Former Agriculture Minister Willy Soemita was sentenced to one year in jail for corruption, it was reported Sept. 9.

TRINIDAD & TOBAGO

Loans & investments. The government received a $150-million Eurodollar industrial development loan from 20 banks in the U.S., Great Britain and other countries, it was reported Sept. 19.

Foreign investors were interested in Trinidad because of its increase in oil production and its prospects for natural gas development, according to the Aug. 22 issue of Business Week. The government-owned oil company had made after-tax profits of TT$28.8 million in 1976, according to official statistics reported July 27. (TT$2.40 = U.S. $1)

Index